W9-ABZ-395

Developments in Central and East European Politics 4

Developments in Central and East European Politics 4

Edited by

Stephen White
Judy Batt
and
Paul G. Lewis

Duke University Press
Durham 2007

JN
96
. A58
D48
2007

Selection and editorial matter © Stephen White, Judy Batt and Paul G. Lewis 2007

Individual chapters 1–16 (respectively and in order) © Judy Batt, Mark Pittaway, Frances Millard, Tim Haughton, Judy Batt, Andrew Wilson, Heather Grabbe, Ray Taras, Petr Kopecký, Sarah Birch, Paul G. Lewis, Krzysztof Jasiewicz, Cas Mudde, Kataryna Wolczuk, D. Mario Nuti, Dirk Berg-Schlosser 2007

All rights reserved

Published in the United States by
Duke University Press
Durham, NC 27708-0660
and in the United Kingdom by
PALGRAVE MACMILLAN
Houndmills, Basingstoke, Hampshire RG21 6XS and
175 Fifth Avenue, New York, N.Y. 10010
Companies and representatives throughout the world.

This book is printed on paper suitable for recycling and made from fully managed and sustained forest sources. Logging, pulping and manufacturing processes are expected to conform to the environmental regulations of the country of origin.

Library of Congress Cataloging-in-Publication Data
Developments in Central and East European politics / edited by Stephen White, Judy Batt and Paul G. Lewis—4th ed.
    p. cm.
  Includes bibliographical references and index.
  ISBN-13: 978–0–8223–3944–1 (cloth : alk. paper)
  ISBN-13: 978–0–8223–3949–6 (pbk. : alk. paper)
    1. Democracy—Europe, Eastern.   2. Europe, Eastern—Politics and government—1989–   I. White, Stephen, 1945–   II. Batt, Judy.
  III. Lewis, Paul G., 1945–
  JN96.A58D48 2003
  320.947—dc22   2007014060

Printed and bound in China

This new book is a direct replacement for *Developments in Central and East European Politics 3*, published in 2003, reprinted 5 times.

123232242

Contents

List of Tables and Figures

Tables

Figures

Preface

The dramatic changes of the late 1980s brought an end to the division of Europe and – at least, in its original form – to communist rule. The changes took a variety of forms, and governments changed more quickly than forms of ownership, still less the political culture that had developed over forty years of communist rule, and sometimes over a much longer period. But, by the early years of the new century, the Central and East European countries were facing a very similar set of challenges. Could they find a balance between effective leadership, often expressed in a presidency, and accountability, typically to an elected parliament? Could they reverse the economic decline of the late communist years? And how were changes of this kind affected by the enlargement of the European Union, which by 2007 had brought ten formerly communist nations into a new association that they themselves began to change?

These are just some of the issues that are addressed in this collection, which (as its three predecessors) brings together a group of leading specialists from both sides of the Atlantic. We begin with a chapter that seeks to define this elusive half-continent, and another that considers the dramatic changes that took place around 1989. We move on to consider the patterns of change that have taken place in individual groups of countries. The remaining chapters focus on the framework of politics across the region – constitutions, leaderships, parliaments, parties, and electoral systems – and the process of politics, including political participation, civil society, economic change, and the quality of democratic government within and beyond the region. There is a guide to further reading at the end of the book, and a bibliography of all the publications that are cited in earlier chapters.

The politics of Central and Eastern Europe have been changing, and so has this book. Nominally a fourth edition, it is, in fact, a substantially new book. The entire text has been rewritten, nearly half of the contributors are new to this or any previous edition, the chapter structure itself has been reconsidered, and every chapter takes account of developments up to the accession of Bulgaria and Romania to the European Union. But our objective has not changed, which is to provide a clear, well informed and sometimes challenging guide to the common patterns as well as individual variety of a group of states that were formerly modelled on the Soviet Union, but which are now a distinctive and varied presence within a continent that has been redefining its own boundaries and values. We hope not only our students, but also our colleagues and readers in other walks of life, will find something of value in the result.

STEPHEN WHITE
JUDY BATT
PAUL G. LEWIS

Notes on the Contributors

Judy Batt is Senior Research Fellow at the EU Institute for Security Studies, where she specializes in EU policy towards the Balkans, and Jean Monnet Chair and Professor of Central and South-East European Politics at the Centre for Russian and East European Studies/European Research Institute, University of Birmingham, UK. Her recent publications include *The Long-Term Implications of EU Enlargement: The Nature of the New Border* (with Giuliano Amato, 1999); *Region, State and Identity in Central and Eastern Europe* (co-edited with Kataryna Wolczuk, 2002); *The Western Balkans: Moving On* (editor, 2004), and *The Question of Serbia* (2005).

Dirk Berg-Schlosser is Professor of Political Science at Philipps University, Marburg, in Germany. He was Chair of the European Consortium for Political Research (ECPR) from 2003 to 2006, and is presently Vice-President of the International Political Science Association (IPSA). His recent publications include *Perspectives on Democratic Consolidation in Central and Eastern Europe* (co-editor with Raivo Vetik, 2001), *Authoritarianism and Democracy in Europe 1919–39* (co-editor with Jeremy Mitchell, 2002), and *Democratization: The State of the Art* (editor, 2004).

Sarah Birch is a Reader in Politics at the University of Essex, Colchester, UK. Her research interests include electoral systems and electoral conduct in democratizing and semi-democratic states, with a particular focus on Central and Eastern Europe. Her publications include *Elections and Democratization in Ukraine* (2000), *Embodying Democracy: Electoral System Design in Post-Communist Europe* (with others, 2002), and *Electoral Systems and Political Transformation in Post-Communist Europe* (2003). She is currently writing a monograph on electoral manipulation.

Heather Grabbe is Advisor to the European Union's Commissioner for Enlargement, Olli Rehn, Brussels, Belgium. This chapter represents her personal views, not necessarily those of the European Commission. She is also a visiting fellow at the European Institute of the London School of Economics, and a member of the Senior Common Room of St Antony's College, Oxford University. She is the author of *The*

Constellations of Europe: How Enlargement will Transform the EU (2004) and of *The EU's Transformative Power: Europeanisation through Conditionality in Central and Eastern Europe* (2006), among other publications on EU enlargement.

Tim Haughton is Senior Lecturer in the Politics of Central and Eastern Europe at Birmingham University, UK. He is the author of *Constraints and Opportunities of Leadership in Post-Communist Europe* (2005) and numerous articles and book chapters examining politics in Central and Eastern Europe (CEE). He is currently undertaking research on party politics in Slovakia, why countries take neo-liberal turns, the impact of EU membership on new member states and is embarking on a reassessment of the role played by EU conditionality in prompting change in CEE.

Krzysztof Jasiewicz is a Professor of Sociology at Washington and Lee University in Virginia, USA. In the early 1990s, he was the founder and first director of electoral studies at the Institute for Political Studies of the Polish Academy of Sciences in Warsaw. He has co-edited and contributed to *The 1991 and 1993 Elections to the Polish Sejm: Analyses, Documents, and Data* (2006); his other recent publications include articles in the *European Journal of Political Research, Communist and Post-Communist Studies*, and the *Journal of Democracy*, as well as chapters in edited volumes in English and Polish.

Petr Kopecký is a Research Fellow of the Netherlands Organization for Scientific Research and is based at Leiden University. He was Senior Lecturer at the University of Sheffield, and Visiting Fellow at the European University Institute in Florence and at the South African Institute of International Affairs in Johannesburg. His current research focuses on party patronage in new democracies. He is the author of *Parliaments in the Czech and Slovak Republics: Party Competition and Parliamentary Institutionalization* (2001), and co-editor of *Uncivil Society? Contentious Politics in Eastern Europe* (2003), and *Political Parties and the State in Post-Communist Europe* (2007).

Paul G. Lewis is Professor of European Politics at the Open University, Milton Keynes, UK. His books include *Central Europe since 1945* (1994), *Political Parties in Post-Communist Eastern Europe* (2000), and an edited work on *Party Development and Democratic Change in Post-Communist Europe* (2001). His main research interests concern the continuing development of political parties in Central and Eastern

Europe and currently focus on EU influence in this area. A book edited with Zdenka Mansfeldova on *The European Union and Party Politics in Central and Eastern Europe* appeared in 2006.

Frances Millard is Professor in the Department of Government at the University of Essex, Colchester, UK, where she specializes in post-communist politics. Her most recent books are *Embodying Democracy: Electoral System Design in Post-Communist Europe* (with others, 2002), and *Parties, Elections, and Representation in Post-Communist Europe* (2004). She has written widely on communist and post-communist political and social developments, particularly in Poland.

Cas Mudde is Senior Lecturer in the Department of Political Science at the University of Antwerp, Belgium. He is the founder and convener of the ECPR Standing Group on Extremism and Democracy and co-editor (with Roger Eatwell) of the *Routledge Studies in Extremism and Democracy* book series. His research focuses on extremism and democracy, parties and party families, (un)civil society, and democratization. Among his most recent publications are the edited volume *Racist Extremism in Central and Eastern Europe* (2005) and a research monograph on *Populist Radical Right Parties in Europe* (2007).

D. Mario Nuti is Professor of Comparative Economic Systems at the University of Rome 'La Sapienza', Italy. He studied in Warsaw with Oskar Lange and Michal Kalecki and with Nicholas Kaldor and Maurice Dobb at Cambridge, where he took his PhD in 1970. He has acted as economic advisor to the European Commission on relations with Eastern Europe (1990–93), and as consultant to the governments of Belarus, Poland and Uzbekistan. His many publications include *Post-Communist Transition to a Market Economy: Lessons and Challenges* (co-editor with Milica Uvalic, 2003), and focus generally on the economics of workers' participation and on economic reform and transition in Eastern Europe.

Ray Taras is Professor of Political Science at Tulane University in New Orleans, USA. He studied in Canada, England, and Poland, and has held visiting appointments at Harvard, Michigan, and Stanford Universities. He is the author of *Liberal and Illiberal Nationalisms* (2002) and of *Democracy in Poland* (with Marjorie Castle, 2002), and has also written a third edition of *Understanding Ethnic Conflict: The International Dimension* (co-editor with Rajat Ganguly, 2006), and *Old Europe and New: Nationalism, Transnationalism, and Belonging* (2007).

Stephen White is Professor of International Politics and a Senior Associate of the School of Central and Eastern Europe at the University of Glasgow, UK. He was President of the British Association for Slavonic and East European Studies in 1994–97, and is chief editor of the *Journal of Communist Studies and Transition Politics*. His recent publications include *Postcommunist Belarus* (co-editor, 2005), *Putin's Russia and the Enlarged Europe* (with Roy Allison and Margot Light, 2006), and *Party Politics in New Democracies* (co-editor with Paul Webb, 2007).

Andrew Wilson is Senior Lecturer in Ukrainian Studies at the School of Slavonic and East European Studies, University College London, UK. His recent publications include *The Ukrainians: Unexpected Nation* (2000), *Ukraine's Orange Revolution* (2005), and *Virtual Politics: Faking Democracy in the Post-Soviet World* (2005). He is currently working on a project examining how the techniques of 'managing democracy' have evolved since 2004. The assistance of Luke March (University of Edinburgh) in relation to Moldova is gratefully acknowledged.

Kataryna Wolczuk is Senior Lecturer in East European Politics, Centre for Russian and East European Studies at the European Research Institute, University of Birmingham, UK. Her research has focused on state-building in Eastern Europe and relations between the enlarging European Union and Ukraine. Her publications include *The Moulding of Ukraine: The Constitutional Politics of State Formation* (2002), *Poland and Ukraine: A Strategic Partnership in a Changing Europe?* (with Roman Wolczuk, 2002), and *Region, State and European Enlargement in Central and Eastern Europe* (co-editor with Judy Batt, 2002).

List of Abbreviations

ALDE	Association of Liberals and Democrats for Europe
AWS	Solidarity Electoral Action
BH	Bosnia-Herzegovina
BSP	Bulgarian Socialist Party
BTI	Bertelsmann Transformation Index
CDPP	Christian-Democratic People's Party
CDR	Democratic Convention of Romania
CEE	Central and Eastern Europe
CMEA/Comecon	Council for Mutual Economic Assistance
CPI	Corruption Perception Index
CSSD	Social Democrats
DANCEE	Danish Cooperation for Environment in Eastern Europe
EFA	European Greens–European Free Alliance
EP	European Parliament
EPP–ED	European People's Party–European Democrats
EU	European Union
EVS	European Values Survey
FDI	foreign direct investment
Fidesz	Young Democrats (Fidesz-MPSz from 2003)
FKGP	Independent Smallholders Party
FYROM	Former Yugoslav Republic of Macedonia
GDR	German Democratic Republic (GDR)
GUAM	Alliance of Georgia, Ukraine, Azerbaijan and Moldova
GUE-NGL	European United Left
HDI	Human Development Index
HZDS	Movement for a Democratic Slovakia
ICTY	International Criminal Tribunal for the former Yugoslavia
IDEA	International Institute for Democracy and Electoral Assistance
IMF	International Monetary Fund
IND/DEM	Independence and Democracy

KDU-CSL	Czech Christian Democrats
KSCM	Communist Party of Bohemia and Moravia
LPR	League of Polish Families
MDF	Hungarian Democratic Forum
MIEP	Justice and Life Party
MSzP	Hungarian Socialist Party
NATO	North Atlantic Treaty Organization
NDSV	National Movement Simeon II
NGO	non-governmental organization
NS/SL	New Union–Social Liberals
ODA	Civic Democratic Alliance
ODS	Civic Democratic Party
OECD	Organisation for Economic Co-operation and Development
OSI	Open Society Institute
PCA	Partnership and Cooperation Agreement
PCRM	Communist Party of the Republic of Moldova
PES	Group of European Socialists
PiS	Law and Justice Party
PO	Civic Platform
PPP	purchasing power parity
PR	proportional representation
PRM	Party of Great Romania
PSL	Polish Peasant Party
RMDS/UDMR	Democratic Alliance of Hungarians in Romania
SAA	Stabilization and Association Agreement
SdPl	Polish Social Democracy
SDS	Christian-Democratic Union of Democratic Forces
SEE	South-Eastern Europe
SFRY	Socialist Federal Republic of Yugoslavia
SLD	Democratic Left Alliance
SMD	single-member district
Smer-SD	Direction-Social Democracy
SNS	Slovak National Party
SO	Self-Defence
SSR	Soviet Socialist Republic
STV	single transferable vote
SzDSz	Free Democrats
UEN	Union for Europe of the Nations
UNDP	United Nations Development Programme
UP	Labour Union (Poland)

US	Freedom Union (Czech Republic)
UW	Freedom Union (Poland)
WSI	Military Intelligence Services
WVS	World Values Study

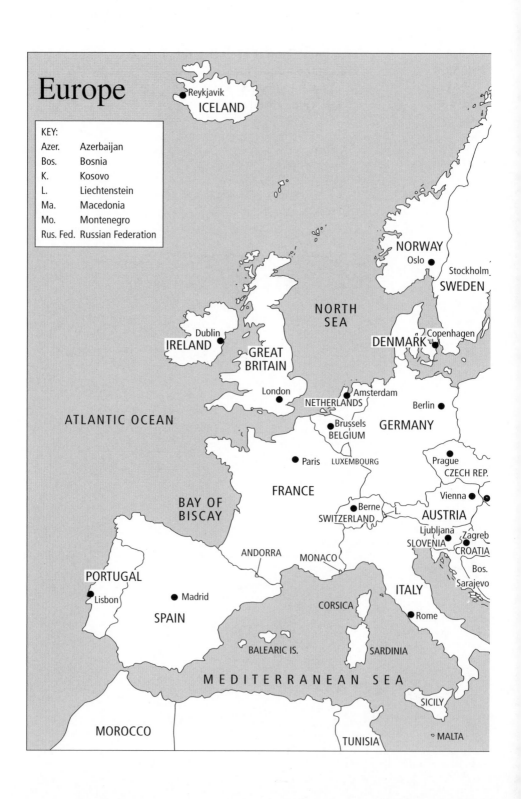

Europe

KEY:
Azer.   Azerbaijan
Bos.   Bosnia
K.   Kosovo
L.   Liechtenstein
Ma.   Macedonia
Mo.   Montenegro
Rus. Fed. Russian Federation

Reykjavik
ICELAND

NORWAY
Oslo
Stockholm
SWEDEN

NORTH SEA

DENMARK
Copenhagen

Dublin
IRELAND
GREAT BRITAIN

London
Amsterdam
NETHERLANDS
Berlin
GERMANY

Brussels
BELGIUM

ATLANTIC OCEAN

Paris
LUXEMBOURG

Prague
CZECH REP.

FRANCE

Vienna

BAY OF BISCAY

Berne
SWITZERLAND
L.
AUSTRIA

Ljubljana
SLOVENIA
Zagreb
CROATIA

ANDORRA

MONACO

Bos.
Sarajevo

PORTUGAL
Lisbon

Madrid

ITALY

CORSICA

Rome

SPAIN

BALEARIC IS.

SARDINIA

MEDITERRANEAN SEA

MOROCCO

SICILY

TUNISIA

MALTA

FINLAND

Helsinki
St Petersburg
Tallinn
ESTONIA

RUSSIAN

FEDERATION

Moscow

Riga LATVIA

LITHUANIA

KAZAKHSTAN

Rus. Fed.

Vilnius

POLAND

Minsk

BELARUS

Warsaw

Kiev

UKRAINE

CASPIAN
SEA

SLOVAKIA

Bratislava

Chisinau

Budapest

MOLDOVA

HUNGARY

ROMANIA

GEORGIA

Belgrade

Bucharest

AZERBAIJAN

SERBIA

BLACK SEA

ARMENIA

Mo.

BULGARIA

Azer.

K.

Sofia

Tirana

Ma.

Skopje

Istanbul

IRAN

ALBANIA

Ankara

GREECE

TURKEY

Athens

SYRIA

IRAQ

CRETE

Nicosia

CYPRUS

Chapter 1

Introduction: Defining Central and Eastern Europe

Judy Batt

This fourth edition of *Developments in Central and East European Politics* takes a fresh look at the countries that emerged from the collapse of communism in the years 1989 to 1991. From this common starting point they embarked, with varying degrees of commitment and success, on the 'transition to democracy'. Many of the countries covered in this book in fact first acquired or recovered independent statehood as part of this process. At the same time, democratic transition did not take place in a vacuum – the international context of the end of the Cold War and the East–West division of Europe, followed by the enlargement of the European Union and NATO into the region, have had a profound impact on the political trajectories of these states. The region has thus provided political scientists with an unprecedented rich testing ground for comparative theorizing on many questions of key importance for our understanding of the workings of democracy: what are the conditions for its establishment? How does the heritage of the communist past, or the existence of a strong and cohesive national identity, or geographical proximity to Western Europe affect the process? Where do new parties come from, and why do some succeed and others fail? To what extent can 'institutional engineering' – for example, the choice of electoral system, the formal definition of the political 'rules of the game' in the constitution – contribute to the stabilization of new democracies in an environment where the existence of a democratic political culture and a mature, independent civil society cannot be taken for granted, and a complete overhaul of the economic system is simultaneously reshaping the basic structure of social interests and social stratification?

The richness of this region as a testing ground for political science provides a basic justification for treating altogether in one book the politics of the Central and Eastern European states. Yet that very richness is due to its enormous complexity and diversity, which often chal-

1

lenge the very notion of Central and Eastern Europe as a distinctive and coherent region. As the Czech novelist Milan Kundera (1984) has put it, this is a 'condensed version of Europe in all its cultural variety', made up 'according to one rule: the greatest variety within the smallest space'. This amorphous region spans states as diverse as tiny Slovenia in the far south-west, a cohesive nation of just under 2 million, with a standard of living approaching that of the West European average and a lifestyle that has much in common with its Alpine neighbours Austria and Italy; and, in the east, vast Ukraine sprawling across the steppes, with a population of almost fifty million, a state that, having emerged almost by accident in 1991 on the collapse of the Soviet Union, has been struggling ever since with uncertainty as to its national identity and place in the world, with profound economic decline, mass impoverishment, and poor government by more or less corrupt, politically inept elites. The peoples of Central and Eastern Europe, their languages, religions and cultures, are extremely diverse (see Tables 1.1 and 1.2). Linguistic proximity, for example, among the largest, Slavonic language group, is cross-cut by the religious divide between the mainly Roman Catholic Poles, Czechs and Slovaks (the latter two also including Protestant minorities) and the Orthodox Russians, Belarusians and Ukrainians (the latter also including a significant minority of 'Greek' Catholics, combining Orthodox rites with recognition of the Pope in Rome as spiritual leader). Speakers of Serbo-Croat, once (but no longer) regarded as a single language within the South Slavonic sub-group, comprise four separate and mutually mistrustful nations – Serbs, Montenegrins, Croats, and Bosniaks – primarily identified by their respective Orthodox, Catholic and Muslim traditions. Romanians, who speak a Latin-based language, are by religion mainly Orthodox, with a sizeable Greek-Catholic minority; while Hungarians, whose language falls outside the Indo-European group, share with their Central European neighbours both the Western Catholic and protestant religious traditions.

The *diversity* that is the hallmark of Central and Eastern Europe – within countries as much as between them – has often been a source of political tension. Although the region's history has also been marked by long periods of peaceful inter-ethnic coexistence, the prevailing Western perception is one of chronic fragmentation and conflict between states and peoples. When we come to look for a common identity, as the commentator Timothy Garton Ash has written:

> we shall at once be lost in a forest of historical complexity – an endlessly intriguing forest to be sure, a territory where peoples, cultures, languages are fantastically intertwined, where every place has several

names and men change their citizenship as often as their shoes, an enchanted wood full of wizards and witches, but one which bears over its entrance the words: 'Abandon all hope, ye who enter here, of ever again seeing the wood for the trees' (1989: 197).

A first stop in the search for commonalities would be the fact that all the states covered in this book experienced several decades of communist rule until the dramatic changes of 1989–91. The communist system was a unique form of dictatorship that was characterized not only by the monopoly of political power in the hands of a single party, but also by far-reaching expropriation of private property and the direct subordination of the economy and society to political control. Communist ideology was universalist, in the sense that it predicted a common destiny for all mankind, a utopia of equality and justice transcending class and national divisions. The communist politico-economic system, pioneered by the Soviet Union, was justified as a universally valid 'model' that all peoples would follow on the path to this utopia. Communism was thus an experiment in enforcing conformity to this model upon the highly diverse region of Central and Eastern Europe. When it failed, all these countries faced broadly similar challenges in unscrambling its legacies and building anew: establishing new multi-party systems; holding competitive elections for the first time in decades; transforming parliaments from puppet theatres in which the communists pulled all the strings into working

Table 1.1 *Major languages spoken in Central and Eastern Europe*

INDO-EUROPEAN GROUP	NON-INDO-EUROPEAN GROUPS
Slavonic	*Uralic*
West: Polish, Czech, Slovak	Finnic: Estonian
East: Russian, Ukrainian, Rusyn, Byelorussian	Ugric: Hungarian
South: Serbo-Croat, Slovene, Bulgarian, Macedonian	*Altaic* Turkish Gagauz
Germanic German, Yiddish	
Baltic Latvian, Lithuanian	
Italic (Latin-based) Romanian (including Moldovan) Albanian	

Table 1.2   *Religious traditions in Central and Eastern Europe*

MAINLY ROMAN CATHOLIC	**MAINLY ORTHODOX**
Poles	Russians
Lithuanians	Bulgarians
Slovenes	Serbs
German 'Schwabs' in Hungary,	Montenegrins
Romania and former Yugoslavia	Macedonians
Croats	Moldovans
	Gagauzi
MAJORITY CATHOLIC WITH	
SIGNIFICANT PROTESTANT	**MUSLIMS**
MINORITY	Bosnian Muslims
Czechs	Turkish minorities
Slovaks	Sandzhak Muslims in Serbia
Hungarians	
	MAINLY MUSLIM WITH
MAINLY PROTESTANT	**CATHOLIC AND ORTHODOX**
Latvians	**MINORITIES**
Estonians	Albanians
German 'Saxons' in Romania	
(Transylvania)	JEWS: mainly urban dwellers
	throughout Central and Eastern
MAJORITY ORTHODOX WITH	Europe; much reduced by assimilation
SIGNIFICANT UNIATE	in the nineteenth century and the
(GREEK-CATHOLIC) MINORITY	Holocaust in the Second World War.
Ukrainians	
Rusyns	The ROMA throughout Central and
Romanians	Eastern Europe have tended to adopt
	the majority religion of the locality in
	which they live; but many recently
	have joined various Christian sects
	and the Seventh Day Adventists.

arenas for debate and legislation; dismantling the pervasive networks of the political police; as well as re-privatizing their economies and establishing functioning market economies virtually from scratch.

However, when we dig deeper into the communist past, we discover that communism took on markedly different forms across the states of Central and Eastern Europe. This started with Yugoslavia's breakaway in 1948 from the 'bloc' of countries under the control of the Soviet Union. The Yugoslav communists soon realized that in order to stabilize and consolidate their control without external help from the Soviet Union, they needed to develop their own 'road to socialism', more in conformity with their own conditions. They bolstered their independence by attacking the centralist form of communism imposed throughout the Soviet bloc as a 'bureaucratic deformation', and in its place they proposed a decentralized model of 'self-management'. The Yugoslav economic system was transformed into what became known as 'market socialism'. Central planning was abolished, enterprises were no longer controlled by the state but by their own employees, and market forces were allowed considerable latitude. The political system was federalized, and the six national republics and two autonomous provinces came to enjoy a large measure of political and economic autonomy. For many years the Yugoslav economy appeared to flourish, bolstered by growing ties with the West (including financial support), and by remittances sent home by large numbers of Yugoslavs allowed to work abroad in Western Europe.

Diversification also began among the countries remaining within the Soviet bloc after the death in 1953 of the Soviet leader Stalin, who had brought communism to the region at the end of the Second World War. Revolts and attempted revolutions in East Berlin in 1953, Hungary and Poland in 1956, Czechoslovakia in 1968, and Poland in 1980–81 demonstrated the fragility of the centralized Soviet model, its lack of genuine roots in the societies and cultures of the region, and its inability to provide the promised superior economy and standard of living to that provided by Western capitalism. Although these revolts were all put down by force and Soviet-style 'normalization' quickly re-imposed, it was clear that some leeway had to be granted to the different countries to respond more flexibly to national conditions. In the cases of Poland and Hungary, local communist leaders experimented with economic reforms, some aspects of which (particularly in Poland and Hungary) were similar to the Yugoslav experiment. The aim was to make the economy more flexible and dynamic, and so to buy popularity for the communist system, without weakening the communist party's monopoly of power. Nevertheless, reforms did lead to a significantly less oppressive political atmosphere in these countries than, for example, in the German Democratic Republic (GDR, or East Germany) and Czechoslovakia (after 1968), which stuck to a rigid form of barely modified Stalinist centralism, as did Romania. But in contrast to the GDR and Czechoslovakia, the Soviet Union's staunchest allies, Romania under Ceausescu pursued an independent foreign policy, cultivating ties with the Soviet Union's chief 'enemies', China, Israel and the West. This did not mean political relaxation at home: in fact, the Ceausescu regime was the most repressive of all, culminating in a personalized dictatorship that recalled inter-war fascist glorification of the Leader, drawing heavily on Romanian nationalist symbols to appeal to the masses, backed up by all-pervading secret police intimidation. However, by the end of the communist period, all of the countries of Central and Eastern Europe faced profound economic crisis. So when, in 1989, the then Soviet leader Gorbachev took the momentous decision to withdraw from Central and Eastern Europe, these communist regimes collapsed in rapid succession. This culminated in the Soviet Union in 1991 when the Baltic Republics, Ukraine and other former Soviet republics broke away to form new independent states.

Although all states faced challenges of post-communist political and economic transformation, they each did so in their own specific way. Precisely what had to be unscrambled when communism collapsed, and what material and human resources were available on which to build, varied widely. Hungary, Poland and Yugoslavia were all saddled with crippling debts and high inflation resulting from their failed reform experiments; but at least their elites contained political pragmatists and technocrats who had some understanding of the market economy, and their peoples had enjoyed an opportunity over the previous decades to engage in small-scale private entrepreneurship. Travel to the West, or at least access to information about it, was quite widespread. Yugoslavia, however, squandered these initial advantages when its crisis-ridden federation broke down in more than a decade of inter-ethnic war. One of the Yugoslav republics, Slovenia, did manage to escape unscathed, and having established its independence, joined the group of seven other Central European states that forged ahead in political and economic transformation and, in May 2004, acceded to membership of the European Union. Romania and Bulgaria lagged behind, their economic transformation burdened by impoverishment inherited from communist misrule, the ambiguities of their post-communist elites about change, and the political weaknesses and inexperience of alternative non-communist elites. But still, in January 2007, their reforms were deemed sufficiently advanced to allow them to enter the EU.

The end of communism reopened questions of statehood that had long been assumed settled in post-Second World War Europe. The GDR disappeared altogether after unification with the Federal Republic in 1991, which ensured its radical economic and political transformation by a unique process of absorption into another state (and also its exclusion from this volume). Czechoslovakia too disappeared by 1993, fractured into two independent states as a result of long-submerged national differences between Czechs and Slovaks that resurfaced after 1989. Nearly 70 years of common statehood and 40 years of communist centralism have not prevented the two new Czech and Slovak states from taking on quite different profiles. The same is even more obvious in the cases of former Soviet republics: the Baltic republics' experience of independent statehood in the inter-war period – albeit brief – seems to have given them a head-start over Ukraine and Moldova, both of which have been teetering on the brink of an economic and political abyss for most of the period since independence. In Belarus, on the other hand, independent statehood has seen the consolidation of an unreformed communist-style regime, heavily dependent on Russia.

Thus the diversity that was already becoming apparent in the communist period has further deepened since the end of communism, hence the question with which we started remains to be answered. What justifies treating together these highly disparate states? If we take a longer historical view, we can identify some broad, recurrent themes that have shaped – and continue to shape – the political development of the region and its interactions with the wider Europe.

The 'Lands in Between': a geopolitical predicament

Central and Eastern Europe often seems easier to define by what it is not, than by what it is. It is an area without clear geographical borders that stretches from the Baltic Sea in the north to the Adriatic in the south, and south-eastwards to the Black Sea. In the north, it comprises part of the Great European Plain that extends to the west across northern Germany and the Low Countries and to the east deep into Russia. In the centre is the upland plateau of the Czech lands and the Danubian Basin spreading out between the Alps and the Carpathian mountains. Further south still is the mountainous, often remote and inaccessible region of the Balkans, and to the south-east the land stretches away into the steppes of Ukraine. These are sometime called the 'Lands in Between', a broad frontier zone between Russia and Germany, Europe and Asia, East and West.

This indeterminate location has had a fundamental impact on the shaping of political identities throughout the region. The lack of natural borders exposed the region to successive waves of migration over the centuries, while inaccessibility and economic marginalization helped preserve distinctive local traditional cultures, languages and dialects – hence the region's ethnic diversity. An enormous variety of peoples came to settle here, not for the most part (until the twentieth century) in consolidated and clearly defined territories, but intermingled in a complex ethnic patchwork. As a result of its geopolitical exposure, the region has been chronically vulnerable to invasion by larger and stronger powers to the west, east and south. Between the fif-

teenth and seventeenth centuries, when in Western Europe the foundations of modern nation-states were being laid, Central and Eastern
Europe fell under the control of large multi-national empires. The
Balkans and most of Hungary were conquered by the Ottoman
Empire, and were thus isolated from the West in a formative period
when the cultural influences of the Renaissance and Reformation took
hold. The Ottomans were driven out of Hungary by the early eighteenth century by the forces of the Habsburg Empire, after which
Hungary fell under the rule of Vienna. Meanwhile, the Russian Empire
in the seventeenth and eighteenth centuries expanded its might south-
wards to the Black Sea and captured the southern shore of the Baltic in
the north from the Swedes. In the late eighteenth century, Poland was
partitioned between Russia, Prussia and Habsburg Austria.

The establishment of the various empires promoted (or forced)
further migrations of the peoples of the region as some groups fled
before one imperial army to seek protection under another, others
moved in to fill their place, and new ruling groups were brought from
far-away imperial capitals to run the local administration. Along with
ethnic diversity and intermingling, imperial rule promoted and
entrenched complex patterns of ethnic stratification. Typically, the
landowning nobility was of a different language and/or religion from
the peasants who worked their estates, and different again from the
administrative elites, commercial and professional classes in the towns.
Thus, for example, in Hungary, Magyar nobles lorded it over Slovak
or Romanian peasants; in Austrian Galicia, Polish nobles did the same
over Ukrainians and Rusyns; in the Baltic, it was Germans and Swedes
who dominated the Estonian and Latvian masses. Servicing the bureaucratic and military needs of empire brought fresh influxes of German-
speakers to the eastern towns of the Habsburg Empire, to join
long-settled communities of German craftsmen. Russians came to
govern the cities of Ukraine, Moldova and that part of Poland that had
fallen under Russian control at the end of the eighteenth century.
Greeks came from Constantinople in order to take on that role on
behalf of the Ottomans in much of the Balkans. Throughout the
region, Jews constituted a significant proportion of the urban population occupied in trade and commerce, petty crafts and the professions.
Ethnic stratification was exploited by imperial rule, which favoured
some ethnic groups over others, such as the Germans in imperial
Russia's Baltic provinces, or Slavic converts to Islam in parts of the
Balkans under Ottoman control. Challenges to the central imperial
authorities were thus fended off by a strategy of 'divide and rule'
whose consequences are still being felt in inter-ethnic relations in the
region today.

The lack of defensible territorial borders had led, by the late eighteenth century, to the whole of Central and Eastern Europe being swallowed up between rival multinational empires that, in the course of the nineteenth century, began to look increasingly ramshackle. Autocratic rule and socio-economic stagnation blocked the development of dynamic modern civil societies. The intermingling of peoples did not lead to a 'multicultural' paradise or the emergence of an integrated, coherent 'body politic' capable of calling the state to account. The very absence of clear territorial bases for the exercise of political power led rather to the accentuation of language and religion as key markers of social group formation.

'Catching up' with Europe

In the course of the nineteenth century, the challenge of cultural, political and economic modernization, posed by the example of more developed and dynamic nation-states in Western Europe, began to make itself felt among the peoples of the dynastic empires of Central and Eastern Europe. Defeat in war made the rulers of the region aware that the economic backwardness of their empires was a major source of military weakness. In the late nineteenth century, state-promoted industrialization drives were launched, but advanced unevenly, in fits and starts. 'Take-off' into self-sustained growth was held back by rigidly conservative political and social institutions, chief among which was the preservation of a feudal style of agricultural system in which peasants remained tied to the land as serfs. Despite, or rather, because of this social and economic backwardness, the ideas of individual liberty, social emancipation and national self-determination proclaimed by the French Revolution had an enormous impact on educated elites throughout the region, who came to see 'catching up' with the mainstream of Western Europe as the key goal for their societies. The ideal of the 'nation-state', a political order in which the state was held to be accountable to 'the People', provided would-be reformers with the intellectual ammunition with which to attack autocracy, feudal privilege, ossified conservative traditions and social injustice in the name of the European liberal ideals of individual freedom, equal rights, the rule of law, and constitutional government.

But problems arose with the redefinition of the state as representative of the 'nation'. In the French context, the 'nation' had been conceived as the whole 'People' inhabiting the existing state's well-established historical territory, a free association of individual citizens with equal rights. Transformation of the Central and East

European empires along the same lines was blocked not only by the entrenched resistance of the old regimes but also by lack of consensus on who precisely constituted 'the People' to whom the state was to be made accountable. By the early nineteenth century, under the influence of German Romanticism and especially of Johann von Herder, a native of the Baltic province of East Prussia, the idea of the 'nation' in the Central and East European context began to depart from the state-centred French concept, which defined 'citizens' in terms of residence on the state's territory, and moved towards a definition that drew political borders along cultural and linguistic lines. Thus, the demand for 'national self-determination' was raised on behalf of ethnic communities, and implied the creation of new states for the respective ethnic communities on whatever territory they claimed as their homeland. Effectively this meant that the multinational Central and East European empires could only be transformed into 'nation-states' by redrawing territorial borders and breaking them up. But further, because most of the empires' constituent territories contained more than one ethnic nation, and because of the extensive intermingling of peoples that had in the meanwhile taken place, competing claims were laid by the various ethnic nations to the various parts of the imperial territories.

The collapse of the Ottoman, Russian and Habsburg empires, culminating at the end of the First World War, left the victorious Western Powers with the task of implementing the principle of 'national self-determination' as promised by the American President Woodrow Wilson (see Macmillan, 2001). The way seemed open for the peoples of the region finally to acquire their own sovereign nation-states and so to reach political modernity on the pattern already laid down by their neighbours in the West. The disintegration of the Russian Empire into the chaos of revolution in 1917 and civil war in the following years allowed the Estonians, Latvians and Lithuanians to break free and form their own states. The simultaneous demise of the Habsburg Empire and the defeat of Germany paved the way for a united independent Poland to reappear on the map of Europe. The Czechs and Slovaks formed a new common state of Czechoslovakia, while the South Slavs of Austria-Hungary united with Serbia in the Kingdom of Serbs, Croats and Slovenes, later Yugoslavia. Romania, which like Serbia had wrested independence from Ottoman control in the late nineteenth century, acquired from Hungary to its west and Russia to its east extensive new territories where Romanians formed local majorities. Other nations were less successful, notably the Ukrainians, who remained divided between the Soviet Union in the east and Poland in the west; and the Hungarians, who gained independence from

Austria only to lose two thirds of their historic territory to Romania, Czechoslovakia and Yugoslavia.

The new nation-states of Central and Eastern Europe faced enormous internal and external challenges in the inter-war period. The heritage of history and the endemic problem of geopolitical vulnerability did not melt away overnight. First of all, the new states did not, for the most part, inherit ready-made administrations and integrated political communities of citizens. These had to be built almost from scratch on the territories inherited from various former rulers. So, for example, the Polish leader Pilsudski faced a huge task in 1918:

> Pilsudski had to weld together different economies, different laws and different bureaucracies. He had to rationalise nine separate legal systems. He had to reduce five currencies to one, and he did not even have the means to print banknotes. Railways were a nightmare, with 66 different kinds of rails, 165 types of locomotives and a patchwork of signalling systems (Macmillan, 2001: 220).

The new Czechoslovak Republic, comprised of Bohemia-Moravia, a province formerly ruled from Vienna, and Slovakia, which had been part of a semi-independent Hungary, had no rail link from its capital, Prague, in the west, to Kosice, the main city at its eastern end. Rail routes ran towards either Vienna or Budapest, which meant that in the early days of the republic one actually had to leave the country in order to get from one end of it to the other.

Most important of all, most states were not 'nation-states' in the sense in which their new rulers had expected – states of and for a single, united 'nation' in ethnic terms – but contained sizeable minorities, more or less aggrieved at the changes in borders that had taken place over their heads. Thus Poland, reborn in its pre-partition borders, contained large minorities of Ukrainians and other east Slavic, Orthodox peoples who identified more closely with kinsfolk over the border in the Soviet Union than with their Polish fellow-citizens; Germans, who found it hard to accept their diminished status in a state dominated by Poles whom they tended to disdain; and Jews, who were regarded as alien by their devoutly Catholic Polish neighbours. Both Czechoslovakia and Yugoslavia rested on unresolved questions of whether the aim was to construct a unified nation-state resting on a single composite political identity, or whether in fact they were multinational states that should give institutional recognition to their constituent national groups. The dismantling of historic Hungarian territory to the benefit of neighbouring Czechoslovakia, Romania and Yugoslavia transferred large minorities of Hungarians to rule by the peoples whom they had previously dominated, and who regarded them as 'foreigners' rather than fellow-citizens. Moreover, many individuals were of two (or more) minds as to their ethnic identity and how it related to the new political order, as the inter-war writer Odon von Horvath explained:

> If you ask me what is my native country, I answer: I was born in Fiume, I grew up in Belgrade, Budapest, Pressburg, Vienna and Munich, and I have a Hungarian passport: but I have no fatherland. I am a very typical mix of old Austria-Hungary: at once Magyar, Croatian, German and Czech; my country is Hungary, my mother tongue is German (quoted in Rupnik, 1990: 250).

The strategy adopted by state-builders across Central and Eastern Europe was to impose from above a centralized state apparatus in order to enforce maximum uniformity within tightly controlled borders. This accorded with their perception of the French republican model, and fitted well with their objectives of securing the sovereignty and hegemony of the majority nation in whose name the state had been founded. But it was to prove a recipe for internal instability and external conflict. Firstly, nationalistic policies of building up state strength by economic protectionism exacerbated the economic difficulties caused by the fragmentation of previously relatively open, large markets of the imperial territories, and made the whole region peculiarly vulnerable to the economic crisis of the late 1920s and 1930s. This was combined with the explosive fact that most states were multinational. On one side stood the 'nationalizing' elites, bent on entrenching the hegemony of the majority by means of centralized political and administrative structures, ostensibly in the name of modernization, efficiency and civic equality. On another side stood the national minorities, for whom this represented just another form of bureaucratic pressure for assimilation and subjection to the untrammelled 'tyranny of the majority'. Often too there was a third side, a neighbouring state aggrieved by the outcome of the peace settlement, which took upon itself the role of 'protector' of minorities abroad where these were ethnic kinsfolk, and aimed at eventual revision of the new borders (see Brubaker, 1996).

Bearing the brunt of European power politics

All of these tensions were exacerbated by the external threats posed in the inter-war period by the resurgence of Germany in the west and

Soviet Russia in the east. By the early 1930s, these rival powers were set upon expansion into the Central and East European territories they had 'lost' at the end of the First World War, and promoted their aims in the name of the radically opposed and profoundly illiberal ideologies of fascism and communism. Most of the new states in Central and Eastern Europe, by contrast, were small in size, economically weak, and deficient in military organization and capacities. Moreover, mutual mistrust among them obstructed any move toward common defence against the looming threats. The peace settlement had failed to provide an overarching security framework and structures to promote regional cooperation, without which 'national self-determination' was to be precarious and short-lived. This point was not lost on more perceptive individuals in the region, such as the Hungarian Oscar Jaszi, who quickly recognized the unsustainability of the situation:

> The only possible cure for Europe's ills is a democratic confederation of democratic peoples, the extirpation of rigid and selfish national sovereignty, peaceful and rational cooperation between all countries for the good of all. The fundamentals of this system are to be found in two basic institutions: one, free trade between all parties to the confederation; the other, a system of honest national and cultural autonomy for all national minorities living within the boundaries of the confederation. Under such conditions political frontiers would slowly become mere demarcations of administrative divisions (Jaszi, 1923: 280–1).

Voices such as Jaszi's were not heeded at the time. Instead, Central and East Europe fell prey to a new round of imperial conquest, more brutal and oppressive than anything experienced before. After 1939, Nazi Germany and the Soviet Union redrew the map of Europe by carving up the lands in between them. Poland once again disappeared, partitioned between the rival powers. Poles became forced labourers for the Nazi war machine, their military elite massacred by the Soviet army advancing from the east, and their country reduced to the site of the major death camps into which Jews from the whole of Europe were herded and exterminated. The Baltic republics were invaded first by Germany, and then forcibly incorporated into the Soviet Union. Divisions amongst the Central and East Europeans themselves were ruthlessly exploited: Czechoslovakia and Yugoslavia were dismembered, and Nazi-backed puppet states were formed in breakaway Slovakia and Croatia. Axis ally Italy seized the Dalmatian coast and ran an enlarged Albania, while Hungary seized the opportunity to regain lost lands in southern Slovakia, north-western Romania and northern Serbia. As Great Power rivalry was being fought out over their heads, bitter ethnic wars meanwhile broke out on the ground between Poles and Ukrainians, Hungarians and Romanians, Serbs, Croats and Bosnian Muslims; and Jews and gypsies suffered at the hands not only of the Nazi invaders but also of their own neighbours.

The peace that eventually came to the region at the end of the Second World War was bought at an exceptionally heavy price with the advance westward of the Soviet Army, by now in alliance with the Western powers. 'Liberation' from Nazi control by Soviet forces was rapidly followed by the installation of temporary governments stacked with local communist recruits and fellow travellers. For the Western Allies, preoccupied with the final defeat of Germany and Japan, keeping Stalin on side in the last months of the war was the priority. By the time they turned their attention to the situation in Central and Eastern Europe at the end of the war, the Western Allies' national capacities and will to intervene to avert the consolidating Soviet grip over the region were exhausted. The main result of belated efforts on the part of the new US administration under Truman to 'roll back' communism in Europe was to prompt Stalin to seal off the Central and East European states that his troops had occupied behind an 'Iron Curtain'. Thereafter, all remaining non-communist parties and politicians were ousted from government, and the local communist parties were tightly bound into a communist international system that enforced uniformity and subordination to the dictates of Moscow.

The states of Central and Eastern Europe thereafter found themselves set on a new course of 'socialist construction' following the Soviet model. This was a project of 'catching up' with the West, but one explicitly designed in opposition to the capitalist path relaunched in Western Europe with US support in the 'Marshall Plan'. The continent was divided into two opposing blocs, and Central and Eastern Europe became once again the front line of East–West superpower rivalry. Although the project of 'catching up and overtaking' the West presented by communist rule held some attractions for the peoples of the region insofar as it promised rapid social and economic modernization, communist rule was regarded as politically alien, a new form of imperialism that suppressed their political freedom, their religions, and above all their national identity. For centuries it had been Western Europe – not Russia – that they had regarded as the model to emulate and the centre of their cultural gravitational field. Although communist ideology was certainly a Western import into Russia, when it was forcibly imposed from the East onto Central and Eastern Europe, it was experienced as a form of 'Asiatic despotism' with which only a narrow minority could ever identify. The subsequent failure of communist regimes to deliver the promised economic and social progress only exposed the acute fragility of these regimes in the region, which explains why they all collapsed so quickly in 1989–91.

The 'return to Europe'

The slogan that best encapsulated popular understanding of the meaning of the revolutions of 1989–91 in Central and Eastern Europe was the 'return to Europe'. Of course, geographically they had never moved, but meanwhile Western Europe had surged ahead. Post-war recovery was followed by decades of economic growth and radical technological innovation; unprecedentedly prosperous societies enjoyed the additional security of extensive state welfare provision; and the problem of German power seemed to have been resolved by binding its larger western part, the Federal Republic, into political and economic integration within the European Community (later European Union) and military integration in NATO. Buoyed up by self-confidence and not a little complacency, the western side of the Iron Curtain had come to regard itself as 'Europe'. In 1989, it awoke to find long-forgotten neighbours clamouring to join in. For what the Central and East Europeans recognized in the 'Europe' represented by the EU and NATO was precisely that 'democratic confederation of democratic peoples' that Jaszi, among others, had envisaged: an overarching framework for the weak, small and divided peoples of the region to overcome their geopolitical predicament and achieve the security and prosperity without which the long-cherished goal of 'national self-determination' would remain unfulfilled. 'Returning to Europe' held the promise of a replicating a tried-and-tested formula that would allow them finally to 'catch up' with the West.

Western observers have often remarked on the apparent contradiction in the revolutions of 1989, seeking simultaneously to recover national independence and to join in West European processes of deepening political, economic and military integration that unquestionably affect key aspects of the traditional sovereignty of nation-states. The end of communist rule in Central and Eastern Europe saw an upsurge of nationalist rhetoric, leading not only to a revival of the sort of tensions between ethno-national majorities and minorities that had fatefully afflicted the stability of the region in the inter-war period, but also to the break-up of the three major multinational communist states – the Soviet Union, Yugoslavia and Czechoslovakia – to form a whole set of new nation-states. The temptation is to regard this as a symptom of some endemically recurrent Central and East Europe disease that sets apart this part of the continent from the West, which in turn raises questions about whether history has so shaped this region as to preclude its ever being fully integrated into the mainstream of modern Europe. Enlargement of the EU and NATO, from the Western perspective, could thus seem a profoundly risky undertaking. It threatened to overwhelm these elaborately constructed and highly valued European institutions with an influx of states whose fragile new political and administrative structures seemed unready to play by the established Western 'rules of the game', whose ruined economies would be heavily dependent on Western support for decades to come, and who seemed more likely to consume than to contribute to common security.

For Central and East Europeans, the contradiction between 'national self-determination' and joining the EU and NATO is much less obvious, for reasons that this chapter has sought to make clear. The notion of 'returning to Europe' usefully captures an essential fact of life in this region: the inseparability of the internal and external dimensions of politics. Establishing and consolidating democracy and the rule of law, overcoming inter-ethnic tensions, nationalistic rivalries and mistrust, creating flourishing and competitive economies all largely depend on a stable external environment, free of the threat of imperialist domination, in which borders can be freely crossed by people, products and capital. The EU, for all its shortcomings, has proved a markedly successful model in the West, where similar challenges were faced at the end of the Second World War. Integration into pan-European structures can now provide practical support for Central and East Europeans to stay the course of difficult, painful reforms and the wrenching social upheavals they may bring. Reciprocally, political stabilization and economic revival in Central and Eastern Europe offers Western Europe its best guarantee of security in a new era: 'Fortress Europe' ceased to be an option once the Iron Curtain came down and the balance-of-terror system of the Cold War collapsed. Security must be now rebuilt on the bases of intense cooperation with neighbours, and of explicit recognition that the benefits will be mutual and self-reinforcing. Arguments such as these in favour of EU and NATO enlargement eventually won out over Western scepticism. In 1993, the EU explicitly recognized enlargement into Central and Eastern Europe as a goal; eight states from the region acceded to EU membership in May 2004, and Romania and Bulgaria followed in January 2007. NATO took the first decision to expand into the region in 1996. Three new members (Poland, Hungary and the Czech Republic) were admitted 1999, and several more were invited to join in late 2002.

The process of EU and NATO enlargement, however, raises new questions for the definition of our region. Many states of Central and

Eastern Europe covered in this book will only join the EU after several more years, if at all. Although, in 2003, an EU summit confirmed the EU commitment to bringing all the states of the Western Balkans in, since the 2004 enlargement a mood of 'enlargement fatigue' has taken hold in several member states, notably in France and the Netherlands since their voters rejected the draft EU Constitutional Treaty in the summer of 2005. Germany and Austria are also showing signs of resistance to further enlargement. While this may have more to do with doubts about Turkish membership, it sends a signal to Western Balkan countries that their fate is not a priority concern for the EU. Meanwhile, the EU has steadily refused even to discuss the prospect of membership with the East Europeans, Ukraine and Moldova.

These distinctions have important consequences, because the new borders they set up between 'ins', 'pre-ins' and 'outs' cut across a region that is only just emerging from the damaging divisions imposed by communist rule to rediscover shared history and to identify strongly with the idea of a united Europe. The point was dramatically demonstrated in 1999, when, just three weeks after taking in the new Central and East European (CEE) members, NATO launched its bombardment of Serbia. For the Czechs, with strong historic sympathies for their fellow Slavs the Serbs, and for Hungary, with some 400,000 ethnic kin living over their southern border in Serbia, this proved an unexpected test of their loyalties. More generally, exclusion from enlargement has a demoralizing psychological impact. Because EU membership in particular has become equated with 'being European', and because in Central and Eastern Europe being 'European' has come to mean much the same as being 'civilized' and 'modern', exclusion from EU enlargement can be a national humiliation that may encourage a resentful backlash. Differentiation can also revive tensions and rivalries between states, as was the case in the 1990s, when Romania sometimes expressed the fear that if Hungary joined the EU before it, Hungary would exploit its position on the 'inside' to secure concessions from Romania as regards treatment of the still large and somewhat restive Hungarian minority in that country. In the event, this did not happen, and both states worked to rebuild a more constructive relationship. But similar tensions may arise and will need to be managed if, for example, Croatia joins the EU ahead of Serbia. Another point is that those states that join the EU first will benefit from full access to the single market and to substantial transfers from EU structural funds, far exceeding what is delivered in the various EU pre-accession funds to the Western Balkans and as 'neighbourhood' assistance programmes to the East Europeans. This could further accelerate the divergence in economic performance between states of the region.

Moreover, EU widening has taken place alongside accelerated deep-ening of integration in key fields. One result is that while nation-state borders are becoming less significant between member states, the EU's external border is becoming an ever more salient line demarcating the unified economic, monetary and trading space within from those on the outside. The EU's external border is also taking on the security and policing functions formerly exercised at national borders by member states. The EU now has a common visa regime, and is developing common policies on immigration and asylum, a common arrest warrant, and closer cooperation among member states' intelligence and security forces in the fight against terrorism. These have divisive impli-cations for the Central and East European region. For example, once the CEEs joined, they had to implement the EU common visa regime vis-à-vis the East Europeans and the Western Balkan states, which they did not previously need to do. It is hard to see how cultural and eco-nomic interchange between these states will not be severely affected as a result. Thus 'Europeanization' of the region, insofar as it takes place in stages, seems likely to become as much a factor for further diversifi-cation within the region as for its unification.

In the chapters that follow, we pursue the themes of convergence and divergence within the region, from the 'starting point' of transition in the decay and collapse of communist regimes, through chapters cov-ering groups of states – Chapters 3 and 4 on the eight 'new Europeans' that are now EU members, Chapter 5 on the Western Balkans, and Chapter 6 on the East Europeans, Ukraine, Belarus and Moldova. Variations in national patterns of democratization can be explained by reference to the histories of individual countries, to the specific legacies of communist rule, and to the external influences exerted by inclusion in or exclusion from the processes of EU and NATO enlargement. Even those furthest advanced in their 'return to Europe', such as Poland, Hungary, the Czech Republic and Slovakia, continue to face the challenges of underpinning their democratic institutions with popular confidence, efficient administrative practices and respect for the rule of law. Political developments in recent years in all four have raised questions about how far 'democratic consolidation' had actually proceeded, and deepened worries about whether Romania and Bulgaria were really ready for EU membership in 2007. Similarly, although much progress has been made since 2000 in postwar recon-struction and the stabilization of fragile states of the Western Balkans, with the exception of Croatia, one cannot yet say with confidence that this region has finally turned the corner and irreversibly embarked on the 'return to Europe'.

A credible perspective of eventual EU membership is now recognized as essential to support these states, and closer EU engagement is also seen as a vital factor in sustaining the motivation for reform in Ukraine and Moldova. But since the 2004 EU enlargement, and especially since the rejection of the EU Constitutional Treaty in the French and Dutch referendums in summer 2005, there is room for concern about whether the EU itself is ready to play its part. There is much talk of 'enlargement fatigue' and the EU's lack of capacity to 'absorb' further new members until its internal institutions are streamlined and made more readily intelligible for EU citizens. West European public opinion seems to have lost its enthusiasm for extending the benefits of integration further to the east and south-east, being more preoccupied with illegal immigration, the penetration of international organized crime, increased competition on labour markets from workers from new member states, and the generally more insecure global environment. Western democracies themselves are confronting challenges of political disaffection among citizens, social fragmentation and exposure to global economic pressures. The 'Europe' to which the CEEs are 'returning' is itself in a state of flux and uncertainty, and Western political leaders have not yet shown the capacity for collective leadership necessary to confront the increasingly complex internal problems of their societies and the rising demands on the EU as a major international actor with particular responsibility for the stability and prosperity of the continent as a whole.

Chapter 2

From Communist to Post-Communist Politics

Mark Pittaway

East-Central Europe's transition from Communist rule to pluralism is impossible to grasp adequately without an appreciation of the practices of communist rule in the region. The extension of Soviet power after its victory in the Second World War generated the political space for the creation of communist states across the region by 1948–49. The degree to which communist rule was the product of Soviet occupation and, thus, external imposition, and domestic radicalization brought about by the Second World War, varied from state to state. In Yugoslavia, the fact that communist rule rested principally on domestic political mobilization allowed it to break free of Soviet influence in 1948, after Stalin attempted to rein in the country's leadership. Albania was also an example of a state where communist rule was established through domestic mobilization – when Yugoslavia split with Moscow, it allied itself with the Soviet Union, in order to preserve its independence from Belgrade, though it would, in turn, split with Moscow in 1961. In the rest of the region communist rule was established under the hegemony of the Soviet Union; and policies of social transformation – rapid industrialization and the collectivization – were introduced across the region that copied the practice of Stalin's Soviet Union in the 1930s. Yet, it would be a mistake to overstate the degree to which Soviet practice was simply imposed – as communist rule matured it would become clear that it rested on a confluence of factors that were both external and internal. These constellations of external and internal factors determined the dynamic of communist politics, and the eventual pattern of transition at the end of the late 1980s.

The death of Stalin in 1953 sparked a major crisis of communist rule, though its roots lay in a lack of political legitimacy, reaction to the political repression of opponents, low standards of living that existed as a consequence of the regimes' industrialization drives, and opposition to other policies, especially the collectivization of agriculture across rural areas in the region. During the mid-1950s this crisis, created by the apparent bankruptcy of socialist governance, generated frequent explosions of popular discontent. Currency reform provoked waves of strikes in Czechoslovakia in May and June 1953; attempts to cut the industrial wage level and raise productivity sparked open revolt across East Germany in June of the same year; discontent combined with moves towards de-Stalinization to generate popular unrest in the Polish city of Poznan in June 1956, and outright political crisis in October. Most spectacular was the Hungarian Revolution of October–November 1956, in which the regime collapsed as a result of overwhelming pressure on the streets, and was only restored as a result of the intervention of Soviet troops.

The crisis of communist rule in the mid-1950s affected, to differing extents, all of the countries of the region. This crisis had two contradictory effects on the patterns of communist governance. On the one hand, it powerfully underlined the serious limits of support for, and the power of, Communist states over their populations, which left a heritage that in many states where the crisis had been most severe – especially Hungary – would set the stage for events at the end of the 1980s. On the other hand, in overcoming the crises communist rule was consolidated successfully, to varying degrees, across the region. This process of consolidation rested on a fundamental reconstitution of communist rule, a consolidation that represented a dictatorial, East–Central European variant of the postwar settlement. While communist governments in different nation-states differed widely in the terms of their governmental practices and strategies, this settlement had several common elements that, to a greater or lesser extent, were visible in all of the states of the region. First, the regimes aimed to integrate the industrial working class into the system. Communist parties claimed to rule in the name of the working class, yet at the same time many workers had taken to the streets. In order to bridge this gap, the regimes sought to placate them through labour and wage policies, and improving material rewards – this was done very successfully in states such as Czechoslovakia and Hungary, and less well in Poland, setting the stage for later political crises. Second, they tightened their grip over the countryside, completing the collectivization of agriculture in all states save Yugoslavia and Poland. Even outside these states collectivization went hand-in-hand with attempts at compromise with farmers that went furthest in Hungary. Third, communist regimes paid close attention to the standard of living, and to the material welfare of their populations, aware that anger at low living standards had played a decisive role in undermining their legitimacy. This also involved the modernization of the housing stock, and the development of a 'socialist consumerism' that went furthest in market-oriented Yugoslavia. Fourth, the communist regimes aimed to recast the bases of their legitimacy and their claim to govern; they became less openly revolutionary, and their use of repression more selective. Some, especially in Romania, deployed nationalism to legitimate their rule; others modified their practices, presenting themselves as advocates of a less repressive communism than had existed in the early 1950s (Pittaway, 2004: 65–85).

As early as the mid-1960s, this model of 'consolidated' communist rule confronted three obstacles. The first was economic: economies, managed through mechanisms of central planning that had been developed in the Soviet Union in the 1930s and transferred to East-Central Europe in the late 1940s, were simply incapable of delivering the increases in living standards necessary to provide the material foundations for East-Central Europe's variant of the postwar settlement. The second was social: industrialization, urbanization and the expansion of state-provided public services had created a large intelligentsia – a group of the highly qualified – who demanded greater cultural autonomy, and more opportunities to participate in an authoritarian political system that claimed it ruled on behalf of the working class. The third was political and external: the Soviet Union regarded the maintenance of communist rule across Central and Eastern Europe as a central foreign policy goal. This made many within the Soviet leadership deeply suspicious of reform, lest it lead to outright regime collapse. These obstacles were revealed clearly by the end of the 1960s. States sought to overcome the first of these problems through experimenting with economic reform that aimed to improve the productivity of industry through greater use of market-based incentives to correct the distortions in the planned economy. This process went the furthest in Yugoslavia and Hungary, and in both cases brought political tension. It threatened the state's settlement with the industrial working class, thus generating discontent that challenged the legitimacy of the regime. The second obstacle became visible with the emergence of popular demands for greater political liberalization that, by the late 1960s, had brought a wave of discontent in Czechoslovakia, Poland and Yugoslavia, and threatened it elsewhere. It culminated in Czechoslovakia's 'Prague Spring' in 1968, when the ruling party under its newly appointed secretary, Alexander Dubcek, launched a programme of parallel political and economic liberalization. Consequently it was Czechoslovakia that encountered the third obstacle – the Soviet leadership, concerned that Dubcek's political reform would destroy the established political order, intervened to bring the country's experiment of 'socialism with a human face' to an end.

The decay of communist rule

The Soviet Union's decision to end the Prague Spring, taken in concert with hard-liners in the Czechoslovak party in August 1968, represented a turning point. In the country itself Dubcek's successor, Gustav Husak, instituted a policy of 'normalization' in which the party was purged, large numbers of supporters of reform were removed from white-collar occupations and demoted to manual jobs as part of a policy of intimidation, while economic reform was reversed and social peace bought through privatized consumerism (Simecka, 1984; Williams, 1997). Within the Soviet Bloc, it demonstrated clearly the constraints that the Soviet Union placed on reform, showing that Moscow was inherently suspicious of substantial political reform. It generated a climate where, for example, Hungary's market-oriented economic reforms were mothballed during the early 1970s, and the party began to limit the freedom given to intellectuals during the relatively liberal 1960s. In East Germany, it played a role in the replacement of Walter Ulbricht by Erich Honecker, at the head of the regime, and Honecker's consequent avoidance of economic reform. The fear of many communist leaders that reform might escape their control further contributed to this reversal, leading the normalizing climate to spread even outside the Soviet Bloc to relatively liberal Yugoslavia, when Belgrade moved to restrain the party in the constituent republic of Croatia in December 1971 after they openly greater called for autonomy from the centre (Lampe, 1996: 313).

While the reversals of reform across the region did not lead to the restoration of repression on the scale of the early 1950s, they proved disastrous for three inter-related reasons. First, they alienated sections of East-Central Europe's intelligentsia from the communist regimes, shutting the door to their participation in decision making. Among a minority of them, this led to the emergence of open 'dissident' opposition during the decade, especially where normalizing tendencies had been at their strongest, and most prominently in 1977 in Czechoslovakia when 243 intellectuals signed a document – known as 'Charter 77' – demanding that the country's leaders guarantee basic human rights to its citizens. It also closed the door to their involvement in politics and the economy at a time when the region faced a hostile international economic climate. This, indeed, was the second reason: the region's economies all, to some extent, depended on cheap energy prices and on trade with countries outside the Soviet Bloc to maintain the living standards of their populations, and thus their internal social settlements. Increasing turbulence in the world economy had combined with the 1973 oil crisis to produce recession in the capitalist world economy, and thus falling demand for the goods that the states of East-Central Europe exported (Csaba, 1990). At the same time, it increased market prices for energy. These changes increased pressure on the economies of the region at a time when economic reform was suspended or reversed – the third reason why normalizing tendencies would prove so disastrous for communist regimes. At a time when measures to improve the efficiency and productivity of the economy were most necessary, the states, for political reasons, turned their backs on them.

The economic consequences were ones of mounting indebtedness, which culminated in the beginnings of outright economic crisis at the turn of the 1980s – Hungary was forced to shift to austerity and renewed reform by 1978, faced with the prospect of outright insolvency. Romania and Poland were forced to change policy as a result of insolvency in 1981, while Yugoslavia turned to the International Monetary Fund in order to escape a similar position in 1983. While in other states financial collapse was not as spectacular, governments across the whole of the region had to cope with deteriorating economic performance and a worsening fiscal situation, caused by mounting indebtedness, as a consequence of policy mistakes made since the early 1970s. Although for much of the decade the true gravity of the economic situation was hidden from their populations, by the late 1970s it was clearly apparent in the form of stagnant real wages, a huge semi-official economy, the deterioration of the quality of public services, and mounting corruption right across the region. Attempts by some regimes to paper over the cracks through limited austerity measures provoked open protest; in 1976, such measures sparked strikes in Poland, and in Romania in the following year miners in the Jiu Valley region struck as a consequence of cuts to pensions and sick pay.

It was in Poland, where the economic crisis had spun out of control, and where an intellectual-based 'dissident' opposition coalesced with working-class protest, that crisis erupted most spectacularly. A series of strikes in Poland's Baltic ports in August 1980, launched as a protest against attempts to force the population to pay more for meat as part of an austerity package designed to avert insolvency, acquired a momentum of their own after the government's attempts to settle them encouraged a nationwide strike wave. Aided by dissident intellectuals, the organizers of these strikes coalesced into a national organization, known as Solidarity (*Solidarnosc*). A mixture of a free trade union and a rallying point for political opposition to the communist state, Solidarity became a political movement that claimed to represent the whole of the Polish nation, ranged against the communist state during 1981. Though the movement fragmented and was driven underground after the state moved to smash Solidarity by introducing martial law in

December 1981, its defeat was only temporary; in many ways, it antic-ipated the outright collapse of communist states at the end of the decade (Laba, 1991).

Both the heyday of Solidarity and its eventual suppression coincided with the onset of the financial crisis generated by the outright insol-vency of many communist states in the region. This crisis generated a turn to austerity, in which the living standards of many East Europeans either stagnated or declined. The nature of the responses of the region's communist regimes differed, though all pursued policies of restriction. Poland, under its military ruler, General Wojciech Jaruzelski, used the advantages of martial law to push through massive price rises as part of a package to stabilize the economic situation. In Hungary, consumer prices were hiked in 1979, industrial prices were overhauled in 1980, limited privatization was introduced into the retail sector, major decen-tralization of the management of enterprises was planned for 1985 and the country joined both the IMF and World Bank in 1982. In Yugoslavia, an IMF-imposed stabilization package scrapped food sub-sidies, devalued the currency, and instructed enterprises to lay off workers in order to balance their books. While each of these states employed policies of marketization, which undermined the planned economy and resulted in increasingly visible inequalities that generated popular discontent, other states imposed austerity in the context of the unreformed structures of the planned economy. This was done in Czechoslovakia and East Germany, where the debt crisis was less severe than elsewhere in the region. This approach was pursued most wholeheartedly in Romania, whose leader, Nicolae Ceausescu, set full repayment as a central policy goal. Production was directed to export for hard currency, in order to finance it. While the debt was almost paid off by 1989, the social costs were enormous. Rationing of basic foodstuffs had to be introduced in 1981, as endemic shortages of basic goods spread; and energy use was subject to progressive restriction that culminated in crisis in the winter of 1984–5, when the homes of many urban Romanians went unheated.

Discontent in Romania, which exploded into violence when factory workers struck and rioted in Brasov in 1987, was met with repression. Elsewhere in the region, the discontent brought by stagnant or falling living standards, and the creeping dismantling of the communist regimes' social settlement, led to a decomposition of state authority, which most often was manifested in a climate of passivity towards political and social institutions. The scope of open opposition to the regime grew, especially in the westernmost states of the region, as the small 'dissident' oppositions of the 1970s, often restricted to a tiny number of intellectuals, was swelled with a diverse range of activists –

nationalists, the religious, environmentalists, pacifists, campaigners for gay and lesbian rights – who sought the ability to act independently of the state. Political demands that aimed at the creation of a 'civil society' created a space in which the various strands that made up the opposition could coalesce, while opposition discourses of 'Central Europe' that emphasized the links of many of the western states of the region to those beyond the cold war frontier contributed to the delegitimization of communist rule (Kenney, 2002). Often there were marked national differences between these oppositions; in Serbia, a sense of national resentment at the politics of compromise between Yugoslavia's constituent republics led to a prominence for nationalist demands not seen to the same extent elsewhere in the region (Magas, 1993). In Poland, on the other hand, the driving of Solidarity underground during martial law between 1981 and 1984 had created a diverse and large opposition that organized itself as almost a 'parallel society' to that promoted by the regime. In Bulgaria and Romania, meanwhile, opposition remained relatively weak – though in Bulgaria the regime's policies of active discrimination against the country's Turkish minority sparked protest. In Albania, isolated from the rest of the region as well as the outside world, it was non-existent: Slovenia, Hungary, East Germany, and Czechoslovakia, however, were all characterized by diverse opposition movements ready to press for greater democratization by the mid-1980s (Ramet, 1991).

The collapse of communist rule

In 1985, Mikhail Gorbachev was appointed to the position of General Secretary of the Communist Party of the Soviet Union. Over the following years, Gorbachev began to openly admit that the Soviet Union suffered from similar economic, social and political problems to those present in the Central and Eastern European states. Consequently, the Soviet leadership, previously suspicious of any innovation in the immediate East European neighbourhood, became progressively more open to far-reaching economic and political reform. Driven, too, by a foreign policy of rapprochement with the West following the years of renewed Cold War under his immediate predecessors, Gorbachev's policies of radical reform and a relaxation of political control over the Soviet Union's Central and Eastern European clients provided the backdrop to the collapse of communist rule in the region. Yet there was also a domestic backdrop, shared by states such as Yugoslavia that were outside of the direct Soviet sphere of influence – a backdrop of intractable economic crisis, crumbling authority and mounting opposition.

The way in which this crisis played out and how it led to the outright collapse of communism differed in each of the individual states; it was in those Central and Eastern European states most open to political reform, or where the strength of organized opposition was the greatest, that revolutionary transformation occurred first. In these states – Hungary, Poland, and Yugoslavia – what sparked outright collapse were the attempts of each of the communist regimes to recast the social bases of their rule; this then interacted with the social and political crisis of confidence in each of the countries to produce outright collapse. Perhaps the best managed of these transitions was the Hungarian, where, almost until the end of 1989, the local ruling party managed to control the process. Hungary's communists were aware of the growing crisis of authority; a younger, better-educated membership, frustrated at the hold of an older generation on leadership, looked to political change during the late 1980s. With persisting economic problems and Janos Kadar, the country's leader since 1956, showing increasing signs of age, groups within the party manoeuvred to secure the succession. Furthermore, reformers within the party leadership, most notably Imre Pozsgay, looked to recast the basis on which the party exercised its authority by seeking an alliance with political traditions outside the party – especially nationalism. With his encouragement, nationalist intellectuals founded the country's first non-communist political organization since 1956 – the Hungarian Democratic Forum – in September 1987. This led to the effective breaking of the party's monopoly over political organization, as a number of different groups – political liberals, farmers, the religious, students, and trade unionists – formed their own organizations during 1988. Kadar's own removal in May 1988 simply exacerbated the power struggle within the party, as hardliners were sidelined by both Pozsgay and the prime minister, Miklos Nemeth. By spring 1989, Hungary's communists were formally committed to a multi-party system and the introduction of a market economy to replace to the socialist economic system. At the same time, an increasingly organized opposition grew in strength – they brought 150,000 onto the streets of Budapest on 15 March 1989, the anniversary of the outbreak of the 1848 revolution. They were increasingly unified, forming an 'opposition round table' and demanding negotiations with the government over the nature and timing of democratic transition – negotiations that began in the summer and which had led, by September, to basic agreement over most of the details of Hungary's transition (Bozoki, 2002).

In Yugoslavia, opposition mobilization was shaped by the divisions between the constituent republics and the growing influence of nationalism, especially in Serbia. Communist responses to their decline in authority tended to reflect this, thus the parties in the individual republics became significant as political actors. The collapse in Yugoslavia began when the leaderships of the League of Communists in both Serbia and Slovenia addressed the different national mobilizations under way in each republic. Discontent over the issue of Kosovo, an autonomous province within the republic, provided the focus for an increasingly popular, nationalist mobilization in Serbia, which demanded an end to its autonomous status. One senior figure within the Serbian party, Slobodan Milosevic, began from 1987 to appropriate the slogans of nationalist mobilization for his own purposes – first extending his control over the Serbian Communist Party, and then sought to use it to reshape the nature of Yugoslav politics by seeking to create a Yugoslavia that was centred around Serbia and Serbian interests. Meanwhile, the Slovene party sought to appease its opposition by seeking autonomy and, later, independence, after the elevation of Milan Kucan to head the republic's communists in 1986. As relations with the centre deteriorated and fear of Milosevic's project to recast Yugoslavia grew within Slovenia, the party embraced democratization within the republic and turned to demand outright independence, especially after Milosevic had succeeded in ending Kosovo's autonomous status within Serbia in May 1989. Fear of Belgrade's intentions initiated a similar process in neighbouring Croatia, where political organization independent of the communist party emerged and grew during 1989 (Woodward, 1995).

The third case was that of Poland, where opposition was at its strongest, and where the economy remained crisis ridden throughout the 1980s. Jaruzelski and the communist party turned towards reform by granting a full amnesty to political prisoners in September 1986, and prepared a reform package to be put to the population in a two-question referendum in November 1987. As a result of low turnout, the two propositions – one on political, the other on economic reform – failed to gain the support of the required 50 per cent of the total electorate (not just of voters). Despite rejection at the ballot box, the government persevered with renewed austerity into 1988; workers responded with a strike wave in May and then a further outbreak of industrial disruption in August, as they demanded compensation. This unrest prompted the communist authorities to inch towards negotiations with the opposition, including Solidarity. These culminated in the beginning of round table negotiations between government and opposition in February 1989, which lasted until April and set the ground rules for Poland's transition. Solidarity was legalized, as part of a compromise between the party and the opposition. Jaruzelski remained president but all of the seats in Senate and 35 per cent of the seats in the *Sejm*, the lower house of parliament, would be elected on a competitive, democratic basis. In the June 1989 elections, which took place over two rounds, opposition candidates standing for Solidarity won a landslide with 65 per cent of the vote and 99 of the 100 Senate seats. In elections to the *Sejm*, they won all the 161 seats they contested. After protracted attempts to form a government, Solidarity demanded the position of prime minister. In August 1989, Tadeusz Mazowiecki, a Solidarity journalist, emerged as the first non-communist head of government in over forty years at the head of a coalition government that included communist ministers.

The developing revolutions in Hungary, Poland and Yugoslavia, and statements from Moscow that the Soviet Union would not stand in the way of radical political developments in the countries within the Soviet sphere of influence, sent shock waves throughout the rest of East-Central Europe. The crisis began to focus on East Germany. Hungary – a popular holiday destination for East Germans – dismantled its physical border with Austria in May 1989. Because of this and the developing political revolution in Hungary, many spent the summer in the country, in the hope of escaping to the West. As summer ended, many tourists refused to return home, demanding instead that they be allowed to leave Hungary for West Germany, through Austria – a request that was granted by the Hungarian government in the teeth of furious opposition from East Berlin in September 1989. The opening of the border led to a wave of mass migration. This stimulated popular protest, initially centred on the city of Leipzig, but which quickly spread across the country. The authority of the regime collapsed quickly, as Erich Honecker was forced to step down. The revolution culminated in the events of November 1989 when the East German state opened the country's western border in Berlin. The dramatic scenes in Berlin that accompanied this have not only come to symbolize the events of 1989: they represented a dramatic escalation of the revolutionary wave that gripped the region (Fulbrook, 1995: 241–65).

Within a day of the opening of East Germany's western borders, on 10 November 1989 reformers within the Bulgarian party organized by the foreign minister, Petur Mladenov, ousted long-standing party leader Todor Zhivkov, allowing Mladenov to become president, against a backdrop of growing opposition activism that centered both on the protection of the cultural autonomy of Bulgaria's Turkish minority and, more significantly, on the activism of the environmentalist opposition movement 'Eco-Glasnost'. As a result of what had been an effective coup within the party, opposition movements rallied, founding a Union of Democratic Forces that demanded a wholesale transformation of Bulgaria's political system. This culminated in the opening of roundtable talks with the opposition in January 1990. East Germany's revolution, however, had a direct and immediate effect on its neighbour, Czechoslovakia. Eight days after the breaching of the Berlin wall, 15,000 students gathered for a demonstration in Prague to mark the fiftieth anniversary of Hitler's suppression of student opposition to the German occupation and dismemberment of Czechoslovakia. The commemoration turned quickly into explicit political protest and then a violent confrontation with the police. The demonstrations ended in violence as the police broke up the protest; the popular anger that violence had ignited was exacerbated by rumours of the killing of one student by the police. Student protest quickly spread and was joined by Prague's actors, who began a strike in support of the students that in turn spread quickly beyond the capital. Major demonstrations on 20 November in Prague, Ostrava, Brno and Bratislava demanded political change, while the Czech opposition organized itself as Civic Forum, unifying an older generation, including Charter 77 signatories such as Vaclav Havel, with younger activists. In Slovakia, the opposition formed a parallel organization, Public Against Violence. Over the course of the following week, the communist regime lost control of the country as it was convulsed by ever larger non-violent protests, as the students and dissident intellectuals such as Havel were joined by veterans of the Prague Spring, most notably Dubcek, and by a large section of the population, including many from the industrial working class, frustrated at the stagnation and decay of the 1980s. The spread of insurgency to the factories, the collapse of party control of the media and the unwillingness and inability of the party to resort to military force, provoked the resignation of the party leadership at the end of the week. Negotiations over the composition of a new government were mired in disputes over its composition as the party attempted to cling to power before finally forming a coalition government with the opposition, which backed the election of Vaclav Havel, key mover behind Charter 77, to the presidency (Wheaton and Kavan, 1992).

The wave of change left only one socialist dictatorship still firmly in place within the Soviet bloc by mid-December 1989. Over the late 1980s, many within Romania's party and state leadership became increasingly frustrated with both the country's economic situation and Ceausescu's bizarre cult of personality. Widespread anger with the economic situation turned to popular revolt, which radiated from the city of Timisoara, after the security services moved in to arrest and remove a troublesome Hungarian Protestant minister, Laszlo Tokes, on 14 December 1989. In an unprecedented act of protest members of his congregation defended their minister, initially surrounding his house. Soon protests began outside the local headquarters of the communists, which were broken up by the army and security services, who fired on demonstrators. Events in Timisoara provoked two processes that together combined to produce revolution. Large sections of the army and the party laid plans to remove Ceausescu, while at the same time the news of events in Timisoara provoked widespread popular revulsion that paved the way for outright revolt. When Ceausescu was shouted down at a mass rally in Bucharest on 21 December, which he himself had called, revolution broke out. Representatives of the security services fired on demonstrators. The regime lost control of the country as the army sided with the demonstrators, as the revolution rapidly spread beyond Bucharest to major provincial population centres. The following day Ceausescu fled the capital, only to be captured by the army, while a new organization, the National Salvation Front, seized power. Heavy fighting followed between the army alongside demonstrators and the security services until the new government executed Nicolae and Elena Ceausescu on Christmas Day 1989 and broadcast the execution on television, thus ensuring the victory of Romania's violent revolution (Siani-Davies, 2005).

The events of the late months of 1989 had a radicalizing effect on the revolutions already underway elsewhere. In Hungary, they ended any chance that either the ruling party or Imre Pozsgay would emerge in real positions of power as a result of the revolutionary changes underway in the country. In September, against the background of the opening of Hungary's western border to East Germans, an increasingly impotent Communist Party voted to reconstitute itself as the Hungarian Socialist Party. In the same month, the national roundtable achieved partial agreement on arrangements for political transition, allowing Hungary to transform itself from a 'people's republic' to a democratic republic on 23 October – the thirty-third anniversary of the outbreak of the 1956 Revolution. However, the disputed clauses in the agreement, including provisions for a directly elected president, which were believed to be intended to assist Pozsgay to win the contest, were the subject of a referendum forced by a number of parties. Held in November on the weekend following Jakes's resignation in Czechoslovakia, the party was defeated, effectively winning the case that Hungary should be a parliamentary and not a presidential republic, thus blocking Pozsgay's attempts to win a key position for himself in the new political system. The November referendum and ensuing scandals over the bugging of opposition politicians' telephones by state security agencies effectively destroyed the chances of the Socialists in forthcoming elections set for spring 1990. These events thus ensured that Hungary's transition would mark a clean break with socialist rule.

The challenge of post-communism

At the beginning of 1990, outside of Albania, communist regimes had collapsed across Central and Eastern Europe. Albania's regime would collapse in 1992, in events that echoed those three years earlier in the rest of the region – a consequence of the small Adriatic state's isolation, and its extreme and isolationist version of communist rule. Elsewhere, with the exception of East Germany, which unified with West Germany in 1990 and thus no longer shared its fate with the other countries of the region, the difficulties faced by the new political elites that had taken over responsibility for government were formidable. The conflicts generated by a series of frequently interrelated challenges defined the nature of post-communism across the region. The first and most fundamental related to the role of nationalism in shaping the nature of post-communist statehood, which had especially tragic consequences in Yugoslavia but were by no means confined to it. The second challenge related to the creation of democratic institutions, and more problematically, the spread of democratic practices, among political elites and throughout populations. The third was the management of the economic crisis left by communist regimes, and the attempt to overcome it through the integration of the region into the capitalist world economy, as well as the social tensions this generated. Fourth, the legacy of the communist regimes themselves presented a major issue, which had polarizing effects on the politics of some states in the region.

Revolutionary change in 1989 reopened the possibility of changes in political borders between states. This made viable nationalist projects that had not had any realistic possibility of realizing their goals during the communist era. This was an especially serious issue in Yugoslavia, where the collapse of communist rule combined with the weakening of common Yugoslav institutions, and a dynamic that pointed to eventual independence for the state's constituent republics. What made the fragmentation of Yugoslavia especially violent was the determination of, first, the Yugoslav army, and then, increasingly as Yugoslavia dissolved, the Serbian communist leadership, to resist moves towards independence in other republics. This provoked open military conflict in states that sought independence from Belgrade where substantial Serb minorities lived. Thus, the political representatives of Serbian minorities in Croatia, the Yugoslav army supported by the Serbian leadership in Belgrade launched a war in summer 1991, provoked by Croatia's decision to seek independence. War broke out in similar circumstances, in multi-ethnic Bosnia-Herzegovina in 1992. This three-year war cost thousands of lives, brought tremendous material destruction, led to large-scale enforced movements of population as victorious armies sought the 'ethnic cleansing' of newly occupied territories of members of opposing ethnic groups. Ended as a result of the threat of Western military intervention and diplomacy in 1995, the war in Bosnia-Herzegovina revealed the tragic consequences of violent nationalism and state fragmentation.

The war in the former Yugoslavia, which rumbled throughout the 1990s, however, was exceptional, both in the way in which attempts to change political borders resulted in conflict, and in the failure to restrain nationalist radicals. Czechoslovakia split peacefully in January 1993, after the new political elites in the Czech and Slovak components of the federation failed to agree on economic reform. Furthermore, while Yugoslavia was the only state in the region where they resulted in a war, nationalist and ethnic tensions, often fuelled by those seeking political gain, were not unusual in the first years following post-communist transition. In Transylvania, for example, where Romanian nation building had been promoted by the Ceausescu regime, democratization produced mobilization around issues of nationality, both among the Hungarian minority as well as the Romanian majority. Political conflict promoted by this pattern of democratization spilled over into several days of riots in the city of Targu Mures in March 1990, when representatives of a Romanian nationalist group laid siege to the offices of the political party of the region's Magyars. Tension continued to exist throughout the decade, especially in Cluj, where the Romanian ultra-nationalist, Gheorge Funar, was elected mayor in 1992, and remained in office until 2004. Despite the persistence of considerable ethnic tension in Transylvania throughout the 1990s, the region remained largely peaceful.

While conflicts around nationality and ethnicity rumbled throughout the early post-communist period, all states created political systems that were based on multi-party systems, with representative bodies based upon free elections. In some states, the transition to fully-fledged democratic political systems was easier than in others. Hungary's negotiated transition brought about the creation of a parliamentary republic, and free elections held in March and April 1990. Poland's model of compromise between party and opposition broke down to be replaced by a wholly democratic system, following presidential and parliamentary elections in 1990 and 1991. Likewise, transition to a functioning parliamentary democracy in the Czech Republic and Slovenia was relatively trouble-free. It was in south-eastern Europe that the creation of democratic institutions was initially most problematic. In May 1990, in Romania, the National Salvation Front won elections which were widely regarded as flawed, and retained power until the Front split into two in 1992, after which new elections were held, in which sections of the Front around its leader Ion Iliescu held power through an alliance between the left and ultra-nationalist right. True alternation of power in the country only came as a result of the outcome of elections in 1996. In Bulgaria, the transition was pro-tracted; while the first elections in 1990 had allowed the country's former communists, renamed the Socialists, to win power, political instability forced new elections the following year that brought the opposition to power.

If the transition to democratic systems was problematic, yet achieved relatively quickly, then the spread of democratic practices was marred by signs of authoritarianism in many of the states of the region. In Slovakia, politics was dominated between 1993 and 1998 by the pow-erful personality of Vladimir Meciar. Meciar's regime, particularly during the period that followed the victory of his party in the October 1994 elections, was characterized by policies of authoritarian nation building and undemocratic behaviour directed at political opponents. Nation building was underlined by the decision to make Slovak the sole official language of state in 1995, and moves in the same year to make the teaching of Slovak compulsory in schools attended by the Magyar minority. Slovakia was not the only state in the region where the new political elite infringed democratic norms of behaviour. In the former Yugoslav states, both Serbia's Slobodan Milosevic and Croatia's Franjo Tudjman were noted for their authoritarian behaviour, while Albania's first post-communist president, Sali Berisha, elected after the communists were driven from power in 1992, was similarly criticized for muzzling the opposition and jailing political opponents (Kenney, 2006: 100–27).

As political authoritarianism cast a shadow over the uneven develop-ment of democratic systems in Central and Eastern Europe throughout the 1990s, then the transformation of the economies of the region con-tributed most markedly to social tension. All the countries of the region attempted to transform crisis-ridden socialist economies into capitalist market economies in the hope that this would eventually create economic prosperity. Oppositions and reformist groups had come to believe, by the end of the 1980s, that market 'reform' pro-vided a generalized solution to the 'failures' of socialism. Furthermore, Western Europe's relative prosperity seemed to add to the appeal of outright market transformation. These factors, the prestige of political liberalism, and the generalized anti-socialist mood of the first transi-tion years created a climate remarkably favourable to the import of neo-liberal economic prescriptions into the region. Western financial institutions, such as the International Monetary Fund and the World

Bank, applied pressure on governments in order that they implement packages of economic stabilization in the region. Poland's 1990 stabilization package, termed 'shock therapy' by many commentators, freed prices, slashed state subsidies, made the currency convertible, cut state spending, and held down wages. While most other new governments shied away from such radical measures, often wary of their social and political consequences, all were to attempt to build market economies on the ruins of what had been left by communism. All governments inherited crisis-ridden economies as a consequence of the economic decay of communist rule; and all sought Western financial assistance and some level of economic integration with Western Europe. Economic transformation was also driven forward by the nature of post-communist economic collapse.

Post-communist Central and Eastern Europe was affected by a severe recession that lasted into the mid-1990s in most countries. Behind this recession lay the collapse of established patterns of trade, triggered firstly by the insistence of Western financial bodies that new governments abandon the trading arrangements that they had inherited from the Soviet period. This was exacerbated by the collapse of the USSR itself at the end of 1991, thus destroying the markets of much of Central and Eastern European industry. Furthermore, Western Europe slipped into recession in 1991–92, making it considerably more difficult for the countries of the region to reorient their exports. These factors resulted in a severe recession. Economic transformation generated social tension, which increased demands on the state for social protection at a time when state revenues were falling, leading to persistent budget deficits. At the same time, as poverty and unemployment increased, greater demands were being placed on a shrinking safety net.

Policies that sought to stabilize economies through severe austerity were combined with measures that opened up the region's economies to multinational capital, largely through the massive privatization of state assets. While privatization and the opening of economies to foreign direct investment were often combined, post-communist governments had other motives for transferring state assets to private owners. Though they certainly believed that private ownership would transform bureaucratically run state enterprises into efficient profit making companies, privatization was also conceived as a tool of post-communist social engineering that would lead to the creation of a new capitalist class. With this intention, early post-communist governments pursued a wide range of privatization strategies from the sale of businesses to foreign multinationals to restitution to former owners. Some states, particularly Poland and Hungary, designed privatization policies to encourage foreign direct investment. Czechoslovakia, prior to its break-up, encouraged widespread share ownership by giving vouchers to the population, which could be exchanged for shares in newly privatized companies. The dismantling of the region's state sectors continued apace, driven by the mid-1990s as much by the need of many in government to alleviate chronic state indebtedness (Pittaway, 2004: 216–18).

The creation of market economies generated social tensions, as societies polarized. To this was added the political tensions that were generated by disputes about the extent to which the states of the region had made a clean break with their communist pasts. Many states in the period immediately following 1989 attempted, often under pressure from those who had suffered persecution for political reasons, to pursue policies that aimed 'to call to account' those who were perceived to have served the communist regimes. These measures went furthest in Czechoslovakia prior to its break-up. The so-called 'Lustration Act', passed in October 1991, gave the Interior Ministry the power to dismiss or demote those determined to have worked for the state security services of the previous regime. The measure was unevenly applied and partially reversed by Czechoslovakia's successor states, but nevertheless was far more radical than anything attempted elsewhere (Borneman, 1997: 152–3). Yet, the anti-communist moment that made such measures possible did not last long; by the mid-1990s, those parties that were legal successors to the ruling parties of the communist era had won considerable public support partly as consequence of social tension, generated by the difficult post-communist transition; they won power in election in 1993 in Poland, in 1994 in Hungary, and in 1995 in Bulgaria (we follow these developments in subsequent chapters). Such victories led many who had opposed the regimes to see the incomplete nature of the changes of 1989 as a factor that had underpinned a growing polarization during the 1990s (Pittaway, 2004: 226).

Chapter 3

The Czech Republic, Hungary and Poland

Frances Millard

From the outset, the Czech Republic, Hungary and Poland were among the front-runners in building democracy and capitalism in post-communist Europe. These countries made the task of democratization seem easy: peaceful regime change marked by free elections, the construction of new institutions, and a subsequent process of continuing democratic consolidation. They moved rapidly to reorient their economic and foreign policy away from the former Soviet Union, signalled by growing links with Western Europe, the break-up of the Warsaw Pact, and the withdrawal of Russian troops. The dissolution of the Czechoslovak federation was also both swift and peaceful: in January 1993, the decree absolute for the 'Velvet Divorce' added two new states, the Czech Republic and Slovakia, to the map of Europe. In 1997, Poland, Hungary, and the Czech Republic passed the European Union's 'democracy test'; in 1999, they became the first new members of NATO; and, in 2004, they became fully-fledged EU members.

Yet, along the way perturbations and crises punctuated the process of multi-faceted change. Turbulence and uncertainty did not disappear. Throughout 2006, Poland's governments were highly unstable; the Czech Republic entered a state of political paralysis following its June elections; and Hungary's polarized politics saw its first eruption of street violence later in the year. Though the achievements appeared indisputable and enduring, acute problems remained in many spheres of political and social life. Some spoke of a post-EU malaise following the period in which so much elite energy had been expended on the demands of membership. Certainly relations with Brussels were no longer the major focus of government concern. 'Transition issues' remained, particularly in Hungary and Poland. Along with the policy battles of 'normal politics' these dimensions continued to make Central Europe rather different from its West European neighbours.

Political institutions

Institutionally these three countries resembled stable West European democracies, with parliamentary systems of government based on the separation of powers. While Poland and the Czech Republic were bicameral, Hungary retained its single-chamber parliament. Poland had the strongest and the only directly elected president, though the new 1997 constitution shifted it from its earlier 'semi-presidential' model. In Hungary and Poland, prime ministers were strengthened by the 'constructive vote of no confidence', requiring agreement on an alternative candidate before the prime minister could be dismissed. Active constitutional courts played an important role in judging the compatibility of legislation with the constitution and in adjudicating disputes between other state institutions. All constitutions enumerated civil liberties and introduced mechanisms to safeguard individual rights. The Czech Republic (in 2000) was the last of the three to introduce the ombudsman, while Hungary had both a civil rights ombudsman and an ombudsman for the rights of national and ethnic minorities.

All three countries also moved from the communist model of extreme centralization to establish an enhanced role for local and regional government structures. Although the role of the EU in shaping Polish, Czech, and Hungarian democracy was largely indirect (see Chapter 7), the EU was a major force in promoting decentralization. Regional structures and functions developed in anticipation of extensive benefits from EU funds. Of the three, the Czech Republic proved the least enthusiastic about developing new administrative units and procedures (Baun, 2002: 268–70).

Constitutions were not set in stone, though as the 'supreme law' they were deliberately difficult to alter; and political parties continued to suggest various proposals for constitutional amendment. The direct election of the president had considerable support in the Czech Republic, and it was also mooted in Hungary. In Hungary there were proposals to reduce the size of parliament. In Poland, the 2005 election party manifestoes included a variety of proposals, including strengthening the presidency, abolishing the Senate, and changing the requirement for a proportional electoral system for the lower house, the *Sejm*.

Within this settled constitutional framework Hungary saw the greatest stability, with routine elections at four-year intervals and strong majority governments. The Czech Republic experienced recurring political deadlock, with minority or wafer-thin majority governments. In 2006, government formation was protracted because the 'left' and the 'right' each commanded 100 seats in parliament. Poland remained the most turbulent of the three, with more numerous elections (parliamentary and presidential), frequent changes of government, and the emergence of new political parties.

We can see these differences clearly in Table 3.1, which shows changes of prime minister and the status of their governments. Coalition government was the norm, but minority governments were frequent in Poland and the Czech Republic, where majority coalitions were often fractious. Zeman's single-party minority government in the Czech Republic survived because of a pact made with the leading opposition party. Marcinkiewicz's minority government in Poland lasted five months before finding new coalition partners, but he was removed and the coalition was twice disrupted. In some cases prime ministers changed but their coalitions remained intact; in other cases the prime minister remained to head a new governing coalition.

Elections were the major reason for changes of government. Of 29 governments, 11 changed because the government was defeated at the subsequent election. In Poland, no government saw successive re-election. Up until 2005, power oscillated between groups that had their origins in the Solidarity opposition movement and the social democrats in the Democratic Left Alliance (SLD), the transformed communist party. Governments became very unpopular during their terms of office, and in 2001 the two Solidarity parties that had governed after 1997 failed to enter the new parliament. Hungary saw similar shifts between former opposition parties and the successor party, the Hungarian Socialist Party, at each election. Only in 2006 did this change when the Socialists won a successive victory.

In the Czech Republic the position differed because the Communist Party (KSCM) remained 'unreformed' and it was not seen as a viable coalition partner for any other party. The historic Czech Social Democratic Party (CSSD) took over the political space occupied by the successor parties in Poland and Hungary. Power oscillated, but not at successive elections. Klaus's Civic Democratic Party (ODS) was returned to power in 1996. The CSSD were the largest party in 1998 and in 2002. They were overtaken again by ODS in 2006.

To the 11 governments replaced by elections we can add two more casualties related to electoral defeat. The first elections to the European Parliament in 2004 were a disaster for all three then-governing social democratic parties. In Poland, Miller resigned just before the elections, leaving a vacuum in government. Following their Euro-losses, Peter Medgyessy and Vladimir Spidla resigned in Hungary and the Czech Republic. Loss of their own parties' confidence and difficult coalition relations were the key to their departures.

Eight governments changed because of the resignation of the prime minister (including those of Medgyessy and Spidla). In the Czech

Republic, scandals brought the resignations of Vaclav Klaus and Stanislav Gross. Klaus departed after his coalition was rocked by party financing illegalities in his own ODS, and also in the smaller Civic Democratic Alliance (ODA). Gross was the only prime minister to resign because of allegations of personal wrongdoing (though he was never charged with an offence). Scandals also affected political leadership in Poland. The most bizarre case was that of Jozef Oleksy, forced out of office in 1995 after (never substantiated) allegations of spying for the Soviet Union and Russia. Oleksy's case was part of a wider conflict between President Walesa of Solidarity and the coalition of communist-successor parties. Later, Leszek Miller also came under huge pressure from persistent allegations of high-level corruption, leading to tensions within his own social democratic party and the government's plummeting popularity, with imminent Euro-elections.

As with Oleksy, Waldemar Pawlak's resignation was linked to Walesa's hostility to the government. The government finally acceded to Walesa's relentless pressure to remove Pawlak, bringing a change of prime minister through the constructive vote of no confidence. This negative experience of 'cohabitation' between a president of one political persuasion and a government of another was a major reason for reducing the president's powers in the 1997 constitution. The president's veto was made slightly easier to override, and the president lost his power to name three key government ministers. It was Walesa's outgoing man at the Ministry of the Interior who levelled spying charges against Oleksy after Walesa lost the presidential election. President Kwasniewski 'cohabited' uneasily with the Solidarity government from 1997–2001. After 2005, President Kaczynski openly served the interests of his brother's party, Law and Justice (PiS).

Kazimierz Marcinkiewicz briefly led a minority government in Poland after the two leading parties failed to form the coalition they had promised the electorate in the 2005 elections. Marcinkiewicz was the choice of the largest party, PiS, rather than its leader Jaroslaw Kaczynski. Kaczynski acknowledged that voters might feel uncomfortable with two Kaczynskis at the helm, and withdrew to assist his twin brother Lech's presidential campaign. Lech Kaczynski's victory strengthened PiS, and Jaroslaw negotiated the formation of a majority government with two hitherto marginalized parties. Andrzej Lepper's radical populist party Self-Defence (SO) and the religious-nationalist League of Polish Families (LPR) had previously been regarded as unacceptable coalition partners by all other parties. Bringing them into government (May 2006) marked the end of the Solidarity-successor divide in Polish politics. But Marcinkiewicz's personal popularity, his determination to avoid charges of being a Jaroslaw stooge, and his

Table 3.1 *Governments in Hungary, the Czech Republic, and Poland to 2006*

Prime minister	Period served	Nature of government	Leaning of government	Reason for change
Hungary				
Antall	1990–93	Majority coalition	Centre-right	Death of PM
Boross	1993–94	Majority coalition	Centre-right	Election
Horn	1994–98	Majority coalition	Centre-left	Election
Orban	1998–02	Majority coalition	Right	Election
Medgyessy	2002–04	Majority coalition	Centre-left	Resignation of PM
Gyurcsany	2004–06	Majority coalition	Centre-left	Election
Gyurcsany	2006–	Majority coalition	Centre-left	
Czech Republic				
Klaus	1992–96	Majority coalition	Centre-right	Election
Klaus	1996–97	Minority coalition	Centre-right	Resignation of PM
Tosovsky	1997–98	Caretaker	'Non-ideological'	Election
Zeman	1998–02	Single-party minority	Centre-left	Election
Spidla	2002–04	Majority coalition	Centre-left	Resignation of PM
Gross	2004–05	Majority coalition	Centre-left	Resignation of PM
Paroubek	2005–06	Majority coalition	Centre-left	Election
Topolanek	2006–	Majority coalition	Centre-right	
Poland				
Olszewski	1991–92	Minority coalition	Right	No confidence
Suchocka	1992–93	Minority coalition	Centre-right	No confidence
Pawlak	1993–95	Majority coalition	Centre-left	Resignation of PM
Oleksy	1995–96	Majority coalition	Centre-left	Resignation of PM
Cimoszewicz	1996–97	Majority coalition	Centre-left	Election
Buzek	1997–00	Majority coalition	Centre-right	Break-up of coalition
Buzek	2000–01	Minority coalition	Right	Election
Miller	2001–03	Majority coalition	Centre-left	Break-up of coalition
Miller	2003–04	Minority coalition	Centre-left	Resignation of PM
Belka	2004–05	Minority coalition	Centre-left	Election
Marcinkiewicz	2005–06	Single-party minority	Right	Formation of coalition
Marcinkiewicz	May–July 2006	Majority coalition	Right-populist-nationalist	Resignation of PM
J. Kaczynski	July–Sept. 2006	Majority coalition	Right-populist-nationalist	Break-up of coalition
J. Kaczynski	Sept.–Oct. 2006	Minority coalition	Right-populist-nationalist	Re-formation of coalition
J. Kaczynski	Oct. 2006	Majority coalition	Right-populist-nationalist	

Note: A government changes with (a) a new parliamentary term, (b) a change in the prime minister, or (c) a change in the composition of the governing coalition.

obvious dislike of the new arrangements proved his undoing. PiS withdrew its support and Jaroslaw Kaczynski assumed the post of prime minister, making Poland once again distinctive in its government-by-twins. Kaczynski ejected the troublesome Lepper from the coalition in September, only to restore him to government one month later.

The 1991 *Sejm* brought down two minority governments. These were the only cases where sitting governments were defeated on confidence votes. The introduction of the constructive vote of no confidence (1992) safeguarded the tenure even of vulnerable leaders of minority governments. Thus, Buzek and Miller lost their initial majorities because of the departure of parties from the coalition but remained in office because the opposition could not agree on an alternative candidate. In Hungary, though early governments saw their majorities erode, every government was a majority government. In the Czech Republic, relations within governing coalitions were difficult and their majorities (if any) were tiny, but governments could often rely on non-governing deputies. Social Democrat prime ministers often benefited from communist support while denying them a role in government.

Political parties and party systems

From this brief survey we can see why political parties are central to explanations of government formation and government stability. Parties are the main aggregators of policies into the manifestos offered to the electorate. They negotiate to form governments and their relations affect government stability. Generally, coalition partners have an interest in staying together to enjoy the fruits of office, though this is not always the case. Parties also structure parliaments into government and opposition. The importance of the role of parliamentary speaker was evident when the ODS agreed to support Zeman's minority government in the Czech Republic in exchange for gaining the speakership and certain other posts. The legacy of this unpopular pact made government formation even more difficult in the aftermath of the deadlocked 2006 elections. The role of speaker also became the object of controversy in Poland in 2005 when PiS reneged on its promise to support a candidate from PO, with whom it had agreed to form a government. Instead of the anticipated PiS–PO coalition, PiS negotiated with SO and LPR, gaining their support by promising deputy speakerships and other jobs.

Because of these party functions, much of the routinization of democratic politics in parliamentary systems depends on the nature of parties, including their cohesion and party discipline. The development of party systems – stable patterns of party interaction – proved variable in Poland, Hungary, and the Czech Republic. The extent to which party systems had stabilized by 2006 was still disputed. For example, Bakke and Sitter claimed that all three 'achieved a remarkable degree of party system stability' (2005: 245). We can see this stabilization in Hungary and the Czech Republic, but not in Poland.

In Hungary, the number of parliamentary parties gradually fell and a highly polarized two-bloc system emerged. The five new parties that entered the first parliament in 1990 had all gained visibility through their participation in the round-table negotiations of mid-1989. The clear victor was the Hungarian Democratic Forum (MDF), which won 42.5 per cent of the seats in parliament. In addition, the newly reconstituted successor party, now the Hungarian Socialist Party (MSzP), registered a small but loyal following. These six parties maintained their presence in 1994; but the MSzP's fortunes had risen (Agh, 1995). The Socialist Party dominated the centre-left, winning an absolute majority of seats (54.2 per cent), though choosing to govern with the small liberal party, the Free Democrats (SzDSz). Party splits and the unpopularity of its government drastically reduced the Forum's parliamentary strength (9.8 per cent) in 1994. The weakness of the Forum provided an opening effectively exploited by the Young Democrats (Fidesz, from 2003 Fidesz-MPSz), who began to recast their image. Abandoning its youthful radical liberalism, Fidesz moved steadily to appropriate the Hungarian centre-right space (Kiss, 2002; Fowler, 2004). When it emerged victorious in 1998, Fidesz had already effectively incorporated the Christian Democrats, as well as elements of the Forum and the Smallholders (FKGP). The FKGP became a junior partner in the coalition, but splits, scandals, and leadership ructions took their toll. In that parliament the extreme-right Justice and Life Party (MIEP), an offshoot of the Forum, also gained seats: neither entered parliament in 2002.

By 2002, the Hungarian party system had coalesced around two major actors, the Hungarian Socialist Party and Fidesz, along with two smaller parties, the SzDSz and the Forum. As much as 83 per cent of the vote went to the two largest electoral contenders, the Socialists and the Fidesz–Forum joint lists. Fidesz won the most seats in 2002, but Victor Orban's strategy of fielding joint lists with the Forum backfired because he had no partner with which to form a government. The SzDSz were Fidesz's implacable enemies, and they were available for coalition only with the MSzP. In 2006, the two-bloc line-up was identical: the giant Fidesz and the small Forum (which now stood separately) versus the giant Socialists and the small SzDSz. The 2002 campaign was closely fought and very bitter, with a clear divide between two camps offering different versions of 'identity politics' based on conservative nationalism and secular cosmopolitanism (Fowler, 2002). This was also the case in 2006, when the deep divisions reflected 'two irreconcilable visions of the world, with two moral orders, with two visions of right and wrong battling in a "cold civil war"' (Schopflin, 2006). Orban aimed to integrate all right-wing currents into a broad social movement that would appeal to a majority of voters, but Fidesz's campaign was misjudged. The Socialists gained ten seats more than in 2002 and, for the first time in Hungary, a sitting

Table 3.2   *Election results of major winning parties in Hungary, 1990–2006*

	1990		1994		1998		2002		2006	
Party	List vote %	Seats	List vote %	Seats	List vote %	Seats	List vote %	Seats	List vote %	Seats
Hungarian Socialist Party (MSzP)	10.9	33	33.0	209	32.9	134	42.1	178	43.2	186
Alliance of Free Democrats (SzDSz)	21.4	92	19.7	69	7.6	24	5.6	19	6.5	18
Fidesz	9.0	21	7.0	20	29.5	113	Joint with MDF	Joint with MDF	42.0	164
Fidesz-MDF joint candidates						50	41.1	188	–	–
Hungarian Democratic Forum (MDF)	24.7	164	11.7	38	2.8	2	Joint with Fidesz	Joint with Fidesz	5.0	11
Independent Smallholders (FKGP)	11.7	44	8.8	26	13.2	48	0.8	–	–	–
Christian Democratic People's Party (KDNP)	6.5	21	7.0	22	–	–	–	–	–	–
Justice and Life (MIEP)	–	–	–	–	5.5	14	–	–	–	–

Sources: www.essex.ac./elections; 2006 results from www.election.hu.
Independents and parties with single seats are excluded. In 2006 six candidates stood jointly for MSzP and SzDSz.

government returned to power. Table 3.2 shows this process of consolidation. The party system gradually acquired a measure of coherence
with a 'two and two halves' format. Deputies remained with their
parties, departing from the nomadic practices of 'party tourism' frequent in early parliaments, and party discipline was maintained.
Electoral volatility declined markedly in 2006, as voters cemented their
allegiance to the two major parties.

Political parties in the Czech Republic also showed a marked degree
of stabilization. Table 3.3 shows the election results, indicating the
reduction in the number of parliamentary parties, the changing relative
strengths of the four survivors, and the occasional arrival of new
parties (1998, 2006). As in Hungary, two large parties of right and left
came to dominate the political landscape. The Civic Democrats (ODS),
led by Vaclav Klaus until the launch (December 2002) of his successful
bid for the presidency (February 2003), were the largest party resulting
from the break-up of the umbrella opposition formation Civic Forum.
From 1992 to 1997, ODS was the major force in Czech politics and
the linchpin of its 1992–97 centre-right coalitions. Its main thrust was
economic liberalism, with Klaus himself the main architect of Czech
economic transformation. In 1997, ODS's party-financing scandals and
Klaus's personal style caused acute tensions within the minority coalition and a split in his party, resulting in the emergence of the Freedom
Union (US). ODS lost in 1998 to the Social Democrats (CSSD), who
had emerged as its major challenger in 1996. Although the former governing parties and the new US had a majority of parliamentary seats,
anti-Klaus sentiment in the US was too strong for the reconstruction of
the former coalition. Nor was the more nationalist, Euro-ambivalent
message of ODS's 2002 election campaign a success. The electorally
allied coalition of Christian Democrats and US (now tied to the small
Democratic Union) preferred a coalition with the CSSD. Unlike the
Free Democrats in Hungary, the Czech Christian Democrats (KDU-
CSL) were eager to play the pivotal role, capable of allying in coalition
with either ODS (1992–97) or the CSSD (2002–06). ODS emerged as
the largest party in 2006, when its new leader Miroslav Topolanek
steered it to its highest ever share of the vote. The Freedom Union disappeared from parliament, but the KDU-CSL was now amenable to a
coalition with ODS. ODS, the Christian Democrats, the CSSD, and the
Communists had proved enduring features of the political scene.

The 2006 campaign was particularly brutal (Plecita-Vlachova and
Stegmaier, 2007). Its outcome created complex problems for the political parties and highlighted some perennial problems of government
formation. Together the ODS, the KDU-CSL, and the new parliamentary party, the Greens (claiming to be 'neither left nor right'), held

exactly half the seats. The CSSD and the KSCM also held half. But the Communists, still unwilling to adopt an unambiguous reform agenda, had remained excluded from coalition calculations throughout the post-communist period. Despite effectively relying on communist support for its legislation when coalition partners proved uncooperative, the CSSD had since 1995 explicitly rejected the possibility of coalition with the communists. This reminds us again that, unlike Hungary and Poland, the left was not dominated by a successor party that assumed the mantle of European social democracy. Instead, the Czech Republic had a strong non-successor social democratic party, with historic roots in the inter-war period of Czechoslovak democracy. It also had a communist party that retained its radical edge (Grzymala-Busse, 2001; Hanley, 2001).

The problem of unacceptable coalition partners was also stark in 1996, when the communists and the Republicans occupied one fifth of parliament's seats. The communists on the left were matched by the extreme-right, xenophobic, and anti-democratic Republicans on the right, forcing a minority coalition as the only political solution. The Republicans split, and they failed to enter subsequent parliaments. And unlike Fidesz in Hungary, which bid for the votes of the extreme right MIEP, no mainstream party pandered so openly to the vicious sentiments of Czech extremists. Although elections still showed high levels of volatility, it was also the case that parties retained a core following of loyal voters (cf. Vlachova, 2001). Parties also became increasingly institutionalized and more stable; only two deputies left their parties in the 2002–06 parliament.

Poland offered a great contrast to this picture of growing stabilization. Not only did parties come and go with greater frequency, but the nature and relative strengths of parliamentary parties also changed more dramatically with each election. In Poland, neither 'left' nor 'right' settled into a stable configuration, though for a long period the communist-successor party, the SLD, dominated the centre-left. Three aspects are important here. First, until 2005 the oscillation of power noted in Hungary also characterized Poland. Power shifted from 'Solidarity' governments to 'successor' governments. Only in 2005 was this mould broken, when non-Solidarity parties with dubious democratic credentials formed a coalition with one strong Solidarity party and the main axis of competition was between parties of Solidarity provenance.

Second, in the first decade the SLD gained votes with each successive election. No contender seriously challenged the position of the SLD on the left of the political spectrum. At the same time, Solidarity's heirs remained fragmented and failed to consolidate a strong party. AWS

Table 3.3 *Results for parliamentary parties in Czech elections, 1992–2006*

Party	1992[1] Vote %	Seats	1996 Vote %	Seats	1998 Vote %	Seats	2002 Vote %	Seats	2006 Vote %	Seats
Civil Democratic Party (ODS)	29.7	76	29.6	68	27.7	63	24.5	58	35.9	81
Coalition (KDU-CSL + US-DEU)	–	–	–	–	–	–	14.3	31	–	–
Freedom Union (US)	–	–	–	–	8.6	19	Combined in Coalition	(9)	–	–
Christian Democratic Union-Czechoslovak People's Party (KDU-CSL)	6.3	15	8.1	18	9.0	20	Combined in Coalition	(22)	7.2	13
Civic Democratic Alliance (ODA)	5.9	14	6.4	13	–	–	–	–	–	–
Czech Social Democratic Party (CSSD)	6.5	16	26.4	61	32.3	74	30.2	70	32.3	74
Communist Party (KSCM)	14.1[2]	35	10.3	22	11.0	24	18.5	41	12.8	26
Republicans (SPR-RSC)	6.0	14	8.0	18	–	–	–	–	–	–
Society for Moravia & Silesia-Movement for Self-Governing Democracy (HSD-SMS)	5.9	14	–	–	–	–	–	–	–	–
Liberal Social Union (LSU)	6.5	16	–	–	–	–	–	–	–	–
Green Party (SZ)	–	–	–	–	–	–	–	–	6.3	6

Notes: [1] to Czech National Council (Czechoslovakia); [2] as part of Left Bloc.
Sources: www.essex.ac.uk/elections; www.volby.cz (2006).

owed its origins to the savage defeats of post-Solidarity parties in 1993, when most of them failed to cross the new electoral thresholds and a staggering 35 per cent of votes cast were wasted. AWS brought together an array of small Solidarity parties and groupings under the auspices of the Solidarity trade union. Although it aspired to create a unified party of the right, AWS imploded under the weight of internal dissensions among its constituent elements, the ineptitude of the AWS government, and the ignominious performance of the Solidarity trade union leader Marian Krzaklewski in the 2000 presidential election. In the 2001 election, neither the rump of the badly splintered AWS nor the (also riven) Freedom Union crossed electoral thresholds.

The disintegration of AWS brought three new self-styled right-wing parties into the *Sejm*, along with the SLD and PSL. PO was a liberal–conservative formation arising from the liberal wing of the UW and conservative elements of AWS. PiS, establishing itself essentially as a 'law and order' party, came largely from AWS and the personal following of the Kaczynski twins. The LPR was drawn from elements of AWS and small extra-parliamentary nationalist and clerical formations under the patronage of Radio Maryja, the powerful voice of Catholic fundamentalism. In addition, the radical maverick populist party, SO, known for its propensity for direct action, also entered parliament for the first time in 2001.

All these parties were also present in the 2005 *Sejm* (see Table 3.4). But the SLD was now a shadow of its former self. Beleaguered by corruption scandals, its fall in public opinion polls had been precipitous and the haemorrhage of its 2001 vote was massive, from over 40 per cent to just 11 per cent. In March 2004 the SLD had split, but its new offshoot, Polish Social Democracy (SdPl), failed in the 2005 elections. While the left splintered, the PO and PiS had prospered and the distance between them had eroded. PO retained its economic liberalism, and this divided the two parties; but its social conservatism closely mirrored that of PiS. However, PO and PiS failed to keep their electoral promise to form a coalition government. PiS unexpectedly emerged as the largest party in parliament (34 per cent of the seats) with PO a close second (29 per cent). Their relations had deteriorated badly during the overlapping election campaigns for parliament and president. PO and PiS provided the main presidential contenders, concentrating their fire on one another (Millard, 2006). PO leader Donald Tusk won the first round of the presidential contest, but Lech Kaczynski of PiS triumphed in the second, and PiS fully exploited its new advantage. PiS's determination to dominate key posts and the personal bitterness that spilled over from the campaign hampered negotiations, and PO chose the path of opposition.

Table 3.4   *Victorious parties in the Polish Sejm, 2001 and 2005*

Party/Grouping	2001			2005		
	Vote %	Seats	Seats %	Vote %	Seats	Seats %
Alliance of the Democratic Left (SLD)[1]	41.0	216	47.0	11.3	55	12.0
Civic Platform (PO)	12.7	65	14.1	24.1	133	28.9
Self-Defence (SO)	10.2	53	11.5	11.4	56	12.2
Law and Justice (PiS)	9.5	44	9.6	27.0	155	33.7
Polish Peasant Party (PSL)	9.0	42	9.1	7.0	25	5.4
League of Polish Families (LPR)	7.9	38	8.3	8.0	34	7.4
German Minority (MN)*	0.4	2	0.4	0.3	2	0.4

Notes: [1] in 2001 in alliance with the Labour Union (UP); [2] exempt from national threshold.
Source: www. pkw.gov.pl.

Thus, the 2005 parliament saw two strong antagonistic right-wing parties, both claiming to be heirs of Solidarity, facing a badly weakened SLD on the left, and no party of the centre ground. LPR, SO, and PSL voted for PiS's minority government. A stabilization agreement between PiS and SO and LPR included a list of laws these parties could support, and this accord was cemented by their coalition in May 2006 and by Jaroslaw Kaczynski's assumption of the premiership in July. The two junior partners in government were outside the old Solidarity–establishment divide. PiS held the key posts of the executive. The Kaczynski twins moved to reshape the political system and to consolidate their position by transforming PiS into an all-embracing hegemonic right-wing party comparable to Fidesz in Hungary. PiS sought to swallow the LPR, which was effectively moribund by the end of 2006, and also attracted local activists from SO.

Hungary thus developed predictable patterns of competition, while the Czech Republic remained rather more open, and Poland moved from a closed to an open mode with its new conservative-populist-nationalist alliance. In addition, the dividing lines between their parties were rather different. In Hungary, Fidesz was a party of the 'right' by virtue of its social conservatism and its national and religious orientation. By the late 1990s, its economic and social policies differed little from those of the Socialist Party and it was, in principle, just as amenable to state economic intervention. In Poland, too, the labels of 'left' and 'right' centred less on pro-market or pro-interventionist stances but more on historical, social, and moral issues. In the Czech Republic, economic divisions were salient, and moral/cultural issues played only a secondary role compared to issues of redistribution. Czech parties fell into the familiar left-right divisions and 'party families' of Western Europe.

How can we explain these divergent paths of party system development? The historical legacy, the institutional context, the character of new political elites, and social responses to the dislocations of transition interacted in different ways in these three countries. In Hungary, the fragmentation of the opposition in 1989 generated new political parties from the outset, while the reform oriented communist party was the first to position itself as a modern European democratic party. Parliamentary parties gained media visibility and political resources. The distinctive mixed Hungarian electoral system played a role because the complex interactions of its three tiers (see Chapter 10) stimulated party organization and favoured larger parties, while the 5 per cent constituency threshold also served as a bar to small parties and new entrants. The decline in the Forum was at least partly due to the impact of 'transition', permitting the Socialist Party to consolidate its position, while the charismatic Victor Orban shaped an effective organizational and electoral strategy that enabled Fidesz to displace the Forum.

In the Czech Republic, the apparent ease of economic transformation helps explain the dominance of ODS as the major beneficiary of the split in Civic Forum and its electoral victory in 1992. Its leader, Klaus, propagated an image as a tough reformer generating painless transition in the Czech lands (if not in Slovakia). It was only in the mid-1990s that the consequences of delayed enterprise restructuring led to a serious economic downturn, with a leftward shift of the electorate's attitudes already evident in 1996 (Mateju and Rehakova, 1997). The CSSD in turn benefited from the unreformed character of the KSCM, which maintained a small loyal electorate, buttressed by dissatisfied protest voters, especially in 2002. Though ODS increased its nationalist rhetoric, it did not attract the loyal confessional voters of the Christian Democrats. Electoral thresholds also played a role in excluding small parties (though the number of electoral challengers remained large, with 28 'parties' contesting the election in 2002 and 16 in 2006).

In Poland, Solidarity split into multifarious elements as the shock therapy of the first Solidarity government bit hard. Although the dislocations of the move to capitalism were apparent throughout the region, the initial impact – deep industrial recession, coupled with high inflation and emerging unemployment – was more savage than in either

Hungary or the Czech lands of Czechoslovakia. The timing of early party formation appears to be a major factor in party development, and in this respect Poland paid the price for holding its first democratic election during the worst economic upheavals. It is also the case that party elites squandered the opportunities offered by the creation of AWS in 1996. SLD leaders similarly wasted the advantages of their dominant position. They overestimated the solidity of their electoral support, and they failed to respond to growing concerns with corruption. In 2005, PiS captured right-wing voters with its social conservatism and demand for moral revolution and it attracted former left voters with promises of a massive welfare cushion. Party identification and voters' loyalty proved very tenuous as successive governments disappointed their voters.

The voters and the public

Indeed, nowhere did post-communist voters come to love their parties. Trust in political parties remained low in all new EU accession states (Rose, 2004: 6). In Poland in 2006 one survey found that 'despite a slight increase in levels of identification with a political party, Poles still do not like political parties and generally approach them with distaste' (CBOS, 2006). For a time this broad political alienation appeared to be reflected in steadily declining electoral turnout, but this was not maintained in 2006 in Hungary or the Czech Republic. Poland again remained an outlier, with persistent, exceptionally low turnout rates (sinking to 40.5 per cent in the parliamentary elections of 2006).

Mishler and Rose (2001) have linked levels of trust in political parties (and political institutions) to evaluations of their economic and political performance, mediated by individual values. Corruption played a significant role here, with the transfer of ownership from state to private hands providing wide opportunities for corrupt practices. Serious scandals linked to privatization plagued all three countries from 1990 onwards. After 1997, the EU's increasing concern with the impact of corruption on the rule of law and the quality of democracy increased the salience of this issue for the public at large. Indeed, the media's emphasis on corruption increased far more in East Central Europe than in other regions (Grigorescu, 2006: 528, 543).

Dubious practices brought down two prime ministers in the Czech Republic and contributed to Miller's resignation in Poland. Corruption was a theme in virtually every election campaign, including the most recent. In Poland in 2005 PiS promised a full-scale attack on the 'web of intrigue' and corruption that linked all post-communist elites after

1989. In government, as part of its moral revolution, it delivered a new Anti-Corruption Bureau with wide ranging police powers and abolished the Military Intelligence Services (WSI) – said to be implicated in numerous illegal affairs. But PiS lost moral credibility through its association with SO, whose leader (and some deputies) had been convicted of a variety of offences. In late 2006, television revelations of secretly filmed conversations showing the unsavoury practices used by PiS to recruit SO activists aroused a political storm. PO made great gains in the provincial and county elections of November 2006. Subsequent allegations of 'sex-for-jobs' in SO also shook the coalition.

Corruption allegations dominated the nasty Czech election of 2006 and may have affected its outcome. Police investigations were leaked to the media, including a report asserting links between Prime Minister Paroubek and the criminal underworld, as well as allegations of sexual misconduct. New allegations followed and in October – just before local and Senate elections – Paroubek was implicated in scandals surrounding the misuse of EU structural funds. Widely viewed as a 'referendum' on the indecisive parliamentary election result, the ODS scored a resounding victory in both local elections and the Senate.

In Hungary, the leaking of the text of a private speech by Prime Minister Gyurcsany to his parliamentary colleagues sparked several weeks of outraged, sometimes violent, protest in late 2006. Gyurcsany admitted to 'lying day and night' and using 'hundreds of little tricks', such as delaying the publication of official statistical data to hide the disastrous state of the Hungarian economy before the April elections; in October 2006, following the controversy, Fidesz achieved a comprehensive victory in the local government elections.

Current issues

A number of current issues were directly linked to economic circumstances. Economic pressures on the Czech and Polish governments eased somewhat with the boost given by EU membership. However, the position of the Hungarian economy remained extremely serious, as successive governments had failed to deal with underlying structural problems. Hungary had the largest relative budget deficit in the EU, rising inflation, and uncertain prospects for continuing growth. Following his re-election in April 2006, Gyurcsany promised the most intensive period of reform since Hungary had embarked on the road to a market economy. The government delayed implementation of the most painful elements of its 'New Balance' programme until after the local elections of late 2006. But early price rises led to a fall in the level of public support, as well as a legal challenge to elements of the pro-gramme by some unions and NGOs. The government's convergence plan suggested that Hungary would not be in a position to adopt the Euro before 2012. Gyurcsany maintained his position with the contin-uing support of his party and the SzDSz. Yet the autumn crisis severely depleted his stock of political capital, with the most painful austerity measures yet to come.

Poland's new prime minister, Kaczynski, displayed little interest in the economy or 'European' matters. The massive influx of funds from the European Union provided a buffer for the government, but despite progress under Marek Belka, no government had succeeded in reforming the public finances. Poland risked missing out on substantial EU funds if it failed to respond to EU requirements, but also because of internal bureaucratic ineptitude. The European Commission advised that Poland's current budget plans would not do enough to reduce its deficit to EU norms by 2007. Within the coalition, SO and Polish Families maintained pressure for more social expenditure. As Poland's young people headed in their thousands for the United Kingdom and Ireland, gaps began to open up in the labour market, with shortages in services, construction, and above all medicine and science.

The Czech Republic, on the other hand, had returned to the path of strong economic growth. Its main preoccupation, following the stale-mated 2006 election result, was the absence of a government; six attempts had failed by the end of November. Economic issues were important as the Czech election, as that in Poland the previous year, saw confrontation between the advocates of flat-rate taxes (PO in Poland and the Civic Democrats in the Czech Republic) and those endorsing the redistributive qualities of progressive taxation (PiS and the Social Democrats in Poland, CSSD and communists in the Czech Republic). Worried about the effectiveness of attacks on the regressive nature of the flat tax, the Civic Democrats also offered social pro-grammes to counter social democratic promises of increased family benefits.

Indeed, social policy issues were common to all three countries. Welfare benefits and pensions remained persistent sources of dispute, along with the health service. Most CEE countries moved to new insur-ance based, contract based health systems modelled on the perceived successes of the Bismarckian model of Germany and Austria. Not sur-prisingly, changing the health funding system did not prove the magic bullet that many had anticipated. Citizens remained deeply unhappy with access to and the quality of health care provision. Health workers often expressed their discontent over pay and working conditions with strikes and protest actions. Governments struggled to respond, but often their proposals resembled sticking plasters rather than major surgery. Czech reforms introduced in 2005 proved unpopular. In Hungary there were unpopular moves to increase patients' contributions, including the idea of a fee-per-visit adopted from Slovak health reforms (which the new 2006 Slovak government aimed to reverse).

Such issues are the normal stuff of politics. Yet wider systemic issues did not altogether disappear, and they were clearly manifest in the Hungarian crisis of late 2006. In Poland, the coalition government led by PiS aroused anxieties about the security of democracy itself, not only because of the presence in government of SO and the LPR, but also because of PiS's proclaimed revolutionary zeal. PiS's conflict with *Platforma* dominated politics after 2005, when PiS deemed *Platforma* complicit with the alleged conspiracy of ex-communists, liberals, and secret police agents. The interpretation of history again became an instrument of politics and old debates about decommunization gained fresh currency. Determined to root out vested interests, PiS introduced new measures to dilute the independence of the National Bank, to secure a more compliant judiciary, and to install party-loyal functionaries in public broadcasting and the civil service. Conflicts over the partisanship of the public media intensified after the 'tapes' incident. Kaczynski rejected the notion of an impartial, apolitical civil service in favour of a highly politicized public administration. Similar proposals were mooted in Hungary, where Gyurcsany was also accused of pursuing a centralizing agenda. In Poland and the Czech Republic governing politicians in 2006 continued previous practices of seeking to improve their own political fortunes by changing the electoral laws. However, Czech proposals to reduce the size of parliament from 200 deputies to 199 – thus preventing a future 50–50 split – were less contentious and seemed likely to succeed.

Although the ombudsman was viewed as a successful institution and the basic rights of free association, expression and conscience were secured, civil liberties issues were not absent. The Roma population experienced continuing social, economic, and political marginalization, especially in the Czech Republic and Hungary. Conservative attitudes to women were widespread, and women were underrepresented in the political sphere. The LPR resurrected ideas of a total ban on abortion. The concept of civil partnerships found favour only in the Czech Republic, and in Poland the LPR was openly homophobic.

Foreign policy matters remained the province of the executive, with little public engagement. None of the three countries rushed to meet EU requirements to join the Eurozone. The Czech president remained an outspoken Eurosceptic. In Hungary, Fidesz kept alive its central concern with Hungarians in neighbouring states (Waterbury, 2006).

Poland's inward turn and the lack of expertise of the new government saw a shift from constructive partner, particularly with regards to the Ukraine, to awkward assertiveness and a concomitant deterioration in relations with both Germany and Russia. The presence of troops in Iraq and Afghanistan was a source of contention within the coalition.

Conclusion

Following their 'exit from communism', Poland, Hungary, and the Czech Republic followed their own distinct trajectories of political, social, and economic change. Yet, we have identified similarities as well as differences in their development. Hungary had the most stable governments and the most stable party system. Poland was the most turbulent, with neither stable governments nor an enduring configuration of political parties. Both countries had strong social democratic successor parties throughout the 1990s; but in Hungary the Socialist Party retained its dominant position, while in Poland the SLD collapsed. The Czech Republic fell somewhere in between, with a degree of party system stabilization alongside continuing problems of government formation. They had not resolved their welfare systems, including health. Recurring problems of corruption and civic alienation continued to plague all three. In Poland and Hungary there was a worrying tendency for parties to question the legitimacy of their opponents, as Fidesz did with the Socialist-led government and PiS did with the PO and the CSSD. The intensity of this confrontational discourse went beyond mere campaigning hyperbole. Poland, Hungary, and the Czech Republic had completed their successful transition to democracy, but the democracy-building project could not be regarded as complete.

Chapter 4

The Other New Europeans

Tim Haughton

The magnitude of the changes accomplished by the states of Central and Eastern Europe (CEE) following the 1989 revolutions should not be underestimated. In addition to creating democracies, market economies and, in the case of many countries in the region, new states, these countries undertook the long, time consuming and occasionally rocky road of integration into the European Union and other Western clubs. For much of the decade and a half following the collapse of the communist regimes, politics was dominated by, or at least couched in the language of, these broad themes. In terms of Bulgaria and Romania, securing entry into the EU was still a salient theme in the early years of the new century, with much debate about whether the EU would delay entry beyond January 2007 by up to a year. But for the other countries covered in this chapter (Estonia, Latvia, Lithuania, Slovakia and Slovenia) the goal of EU membership had been achieved in 2004.

This chapter seeks to highlight the salient issues shaping contemporary politics in the seven countries under consideration. It argues that with the challenges of post-communism (democratization, marketization, state-building and integration) having been met, politics in the region entered a new era. Many of the themes of politics, such as how to flourish economically as an EU member state in an increasingly competitive world economy, were new. Other themes, however, such as corruption and policies towards ethnic minorities and former imperial masters, were variations on old, perennial themes. The politics of contemporary CEE highlight that although there are sufficient commonalities to justify treating these countries together, they cannot be considered in an undifferentiated way. As Batt argues earlier in this volume, thanks to different historical experiences, and linguistic, cultural and religious differences, diversity is the 'hallmark' of Central and Eastern Europe. Indeed, the themes of diversity and commonality in the region run not only through this chapter, but also the study of CEE as a whole.

Before embarking on an analysis of the salient themes of politics in the region, this chapter begins with a brief overview of recent political developments.

Meeting the challenges of post-communism

Following the end of communist rule in 1989–1991, the seven countries embarked on the process of marketization with varying degrees of enthusiasm. Whilst Estonia, for example, blazed a Thatcherite trail, introducing a radical liberalization package early in the 1990s, other states were reform laggards. Bulgaria and Romania, for instance, only began to undertake significant economic reform towards the end of the 1990s. Their initial reluctance has been ascribed to the success of the former communists in the first free elections (Fish, 1998), but the reasons go deeper. Not only were economic developments during the communist period viewed more favourably in those countries, but they also lacked ambitious reform-minded politicians along the lines of Poland's Leszek Balcerowicz or the Czech Republic's Vaclav Klaus. Moreover, Estonia's drive to a market economy was motivated, in part, by a desire to distance the country from its Soviet past and demonstrate its perceived rightful place among the European mainstream.

Equally, there were striking differences in the process of democratization in the region. Both Slovakia and Slovenia, for example, not only had to build new democracies, but they also faced the challenges of building the apparatus of a new state. Whereas the latter made a relatively easy transition to democracy, the former experienced a more troubled transition (Malova, 1998; Harris, 2002). In the mid-1990s, under Prime Minister Vladimir Meciar's government, Slovakia appeared to be veering away from democracy. Indeed, following strong diplomatic statements by the EU deploring developments in Slovakia, the European Commission's 1997 *avis* (opinion) highlighted concerns about the treatment of minorities, the behaviour of the government towards key institutions such as the Presidency and Constitutional Court and, more broadly the government's unwillingness to play by the rules and conventions of democratic politics (Henderson, 1999). Following the 1998 elections, however, a broad-based coalition under the leadership of Prime Minister Mikulas Dzurinda returned Slovakia to the path of liberalism and restored its image, which reaped international dividends.

The seven countries under consideration entered the new millennium at different stages along the road to EU membership – in part a product of their relative progress towards consolidated democracies and market economies. Estonia and Slovenia were ahead of the rest of the pack, having been invited to begin accession negotiations at the Luxembourg European Council in 1997, but the rest were given their much sought after present at the Helsinki summit just before Christmas 1999, beginning their negotiations early the following year.

EU accession played an important role in the politics of the region, especially from the mid-1990s onwards (see Chapter 7). Although the EU was not always the key driver of domestic change, the requirements of joining the club were significant in shaping the contours of politics. Much debate was couched in terms of meeting requirements. As EU membership was a widely shared goal advocated by the major parties in all the countries under consideration, the issue of EU membership became largely an issue of competence: that is, who was best placed to ensure entry. Although this tendency was noticeable in the politics of the 2004 entrants, especially Slovakia, it was more significant in recent times in the cases of Bulgaria and Romania. Indeed, for these two states securing EU entry became, as the Romanian journalist Adrian Lungu told the author of this chapter, 'a trophy'. Both Bulgaria and Romania completed accession negotiations in 2004 but, concerned about the lack of progress in specific areas such as judicial reform and stamping out corruption, the EU introduced postponement clauses that threatened a delay of up to a year if sufficient progress were not made (Phinnemore, 2006b). Keen to ensure a 2007 entry date, Bulgarian and Romanian politicians went on a charm offensive and, with a raft of new initiatives, sent out clear signals that they were doing their utmost to tackle these problems. In a largely symbolic act to demonstrate her country's commitment, the Romanian Minister of European Integration, Anca Boagiu, even restricted her civil servants' holiday entitlement in the summer of 2006.

The accession states were required to jump through a complex series of hoops including the laborious task of incorporating the body of EU law known as the *acquis communautaire* into domestic law. The process of integration, however, was not fully complete when the countries joined the EU. In addition to joining the Schengen zone, the states were also treaty-bound to join the single currency. Euro membership requires countries to fulfil the Maastricht criteria, specifying acceptable levels of debt, deficits, inflation and interest rates and requiring membership of the Exchange Rate Mechanism II for at least two years; goals that require tough fiscal and monetary policy.

Progress varied significantly across the region. Whilst Bulgaria and Romania concentrated on ensuring entry into the EU in the knowledge that the single currency was a goal for the following decade, Slovakia identified the end of the decade as its preferred target date. Estonia, Lithuania and Slovenia targeted entry in January 2007, but concerns emerged during the course of 2006 over a sudden burst of energy-related inflation in the two Baltic candidates, leaving Slovenia as the only country confident of joining the eurozone on 1 January 2007. Slovenia's position at the head of the pack was in no small measure a product of the widely held view amongst Slovene politicians that euro entry was both necessary and beneficial. No major politician sought to make political capital out of the necessary and restrictive policies adopted to secure entry in 2007.

The demands of EU entry, at times, were onerous, but it would be wrong to see the EU as the main driver of politics in the region. EU influence has been more significant at particular stages of the process, especially during the decision phase when the Union decided whether or not to open accession negotiations (Schimmelfennig and Sedelmeier, 2005; Haughton, 2007b). Moreover, in certain areas, such as policies towards ethnic minorities, EU influence may have helped change formal policy, but frequently there was a large gap between the declared policies and actual policy implemented on the ground.

A new challenge: achieving success as an EU member state

Membership as opposed to accession accords states much more room for manoeuvre. They are no longer merely objects of EU decision making, but rather have become political subjects with the ability to shape EU policy from the inside. Nonetheless, there are limits to any country's power in a union of more than two-dozen members, especially if the new member state is small and poor, and if their civil servants have relatively little experience of dealing with European institutions. Although the new member states' influence was limited in many areas, the only apparent exception was foreign policy. As member states, countries of CEE were accorded the opportunity to try to affect EU policy. The most striking attempt to do that was in the EU's policies towards its new neighbours, where the new member states from CEE, driven by their national priorities and trumpeting their intimate knowledge of the region, helped influence the focus of policy. Lithuanian politicians, alongside counterparts from Poland, were active during Ukraine's Orange Revolution (see Chapter 6). Indeed, officials in Brussels have noted that Lithuania's prioritization of its relations with two of its former federal partners, Ukraine and Belarus, helped Lithuanian politicians punch above their weight, pushing the issue of the EU's relations with the East higher up the Union's agenda.

As the case of Lithuania demonstrates, EU membership helped turned the focus of foreign policy in the new states. For much of the 1990s, Slovenia was desperate to distance itself from other former Yugoslav states, and keen to label itself an Alpine Republic. But with membership secured, the focus of Slovene foreign policy turned 180 degrees towards the Western Balkans. Slovene officials highlighted their expertise in the region, reminding their counterparts from other EU member states that, having been part of Yugoslavia, Slovenes are very well placed to understand the region and shape Balkan policy. The 2002–6 Slovak government also made enlargement towards the Western Balkans its foreign policy priority within the EU, pursuing the project with some gusto. In both cases, however, limited institutional capacity and expertise (not least due to the size of the states) reduced their impact (Bilcik, 2004; Haughton, 2007a).

Whereas membership of the EU and other international bodies encouraged the CEE states to pursue their foreign policy goals through these collective organs, membership of the EU also provided the new member states with more room for manoeuvre in domestic policy. Indeed, with the necessary reforms needed to secure EU membership undertaken, the CEE states could start to focus on facing up to the challenge of flourishing economically in an increasingly competitive world economy. Although it is arguably the most extreme example in the region, Slovakia demonstrates these changes with particular clarity.

Driven by an ideological belief in the free market and armed with a set of policy prescriptions inspired by the World Bank model, the 2002–06 Slovak government implemented a series of radical reforms in health care, pensions and fiscal policy, including the much vaunted 19 per cent flat-rate tax (Malova and Haughton, 2006). Despite dressing up these policies as solutions to the significant structural problems faced by all European countries and a means for all European states to achieve the Lisbon goals of making the EU the most dynamic, knowledge-based economy in the world, the reforms were designed primarily for domestic gain. The introduction of the neo-liberal policies was seen as a means of improving the efficiency of the economy, enticing in foreign investors and stimulating economic growth (O'Dwyer and Kovalcik, 2005).

The flat tax regime and general thrust of economic policy won plaudits from business gurus such as Steve Forbes, and helped transform Slovakia's image. The impact of the government's policies was in evidence in the inflows of large amounts of foreign investment, most notably in the automotive industry. Indeed, car manufactures such as Kia, Volkswagen and Peugeot all invested in the country. The success of the Slovak model encouraged other states in the region, such as

Table 4.1   *Parliamentary elections in Slovakia, 2006*

Party	Vote %	Seats	Change in vote % from 2002
Direction (*Smer*)-Social Democracy	29.14	50	+15.68
Slovak Democratic and Christian Union	18.35	31	+3.26
Slovak National Party	11.73	20	+4.76*
Party of the Hungarian Coalition	11.68	20	+0.52
People's Party – Movement for a Democratic Slovakia	8.79	15	-10.71
Christian Democratic Movement	8.31	14	+0.06
Communist Party of Slovakia	3.88	0	-2.44
Alliance of the New Citizen	1.42	0	-6.59
Others	6.7	0	-4.54
Totals	100.00	150	

Notes: turnout: 54.67%; *calculated using the combined total for Slovak National Party (95,633) and the Real Slovak National Party (105,084) in the 2002 elections.
Source: Statistical Office of the Slovak Republic.

Romania, to bring in low flat rates of tax. Ireland was also viewed as a model. Indeed, Latvia's First Party and Latvia's Way drew inspiration from the Celtic Tiger, proposing flat taxes in order to become a Baltic Tiger. Nonetheless, not all states, even with centre-right politicians at the helm, opted for flat taxes. Although some influential young economists in Slovenia had been encouraged and enthused by the Slovak model, Finance Minister Andrej Bajuk stopped short of introducing a flat tax in Slovenia in part due to effective mobilization by opposition groupings including trade unions (Fink-Hafner, 2006b). Moreover, despite the acclaim from international bodies Robert Fico's party Direction (Smer) capitalized on the unpopularity of the Slovak government's neo-liberal policies, helping his party win nearly a third of the vote in the 2006 elections (Haughton, 2006; Henderson, 2006). Indeed, even in Estonia, where a flat tax regime had been introduced in the 1990s, leading politicians from the Centre Party and the People's Union advocated a much more progressive fiscal regime.

New versions of old themes

The politics of the past

Although the countries entered a new era as EU member states, many of the salient themes of politics were new variations of old themes, intimately tied into the legacies of history. Indeed, the past, in both its communist and pre-communist variants, continued to play a role in the politics of the region. Central to debates surrounding the communist period in CEE as a whole was whether there had been sufficient reckoning with the past. Who did what to whom during communist times still animated some politicians but, beyond the occasional disclosure of a politician or high-ranking priest with links to the communist era security services in Slovakia and the debates surrounding the disclosure of Securitate (secret police) files in Romania (which provoked resignations and expulsions from political parties, such as Mona Musca from the Liberal Party), arguably the communist period was increasingly less significant in shaping the contemporary politics of the seven countries under consideration than others in CEE, such as Poland. Moreover, debates about the communist past became increasingly muddied by debates about who benefited politically and economically from the early post-communist years.

Nonetheless, the past continues to matter. The twentieth century saw two significant periods of redrawing of borders in CEE: in the aftermath of the First World War and after the collapse of the communist regimes. On both occasions, the three Baltic states became independent; the absorption into the Soviet Union, in the 1940s, was viewed by Baltic politicians as an illegal act, with knock-on implications for constitutional settlements and policies towards ethnic minorities in the post-1991 period (see below). But the history of incorporation into two Russian dominated empires, and the existence of a large ethnic Russian population in Latvia and Estonia who had moved during Soviet times, caused frictions, not least in the attitudes towards Russia. History had taught the titular ethnic groups in the Baltic states to view Russia with suspicion, whereas the ethnic Russians viewed their ethnic motherland in a far more favourable light. These different attitudes to Russia were well illustrated in the dispute provoked by the overwhelmingly Russian-speaking Estonian town of Narva's decision to erect a statue to Peter the Great in the late summer of 2006.

Both Slovenia and Slovakia became independent states in the early 1990s, but the legacies of being part of large multi-ethnic empires continued to play a role in contemporary politics. Despite generally good relations, tensions have flared up periodically between Slovenia and its former federal partner Croatia over fishing rights and the exact demarcation of land and sea border points. In a different vein, Slovakia's relations with Hungary have been shaped by imperial history and the injudicious remarks of some nationalist Hungarian politicians. These have helped Slovakia's nationalist politicians, most notably the Slovak National Party's Jan Slota, stoke up anti-Hungarian sentiment for electoral gain. At an election rally in his home town of Zilina in June 2006, for instance, Slota accused Hungary and the Party of the Hungarian Coalition in Slovakia of trying to turn the south of Slovakia (where the majority of ethnic Hungarians live) into another Kosovo. The inclusion of Slota's party in the government formed after the election soured relations between Bratislava and Budapest and was seen as partially responsible for some unprovoked physical attacks on ethnic Hungarians living in Slovakia.

Inglorious aspects of the history of the region continued to play a role in politics. Attitudes to the Second World War, for example, have long been a key dividing line of politics of the centre-right in Slovenia, but these were brought to the fore in 2005 when the new centre-right government proposed the so-called 'war bills'. These were seen by many on the left as an attempt to rehabilitate fascist collaborators. For many on the right, however, these moves, as well as the introduction of new national holidays in honour of national heroes, were part of an attempt to bolster pride in Slovene nationhood (Fink-Hafner, 2006b).

Policies towards minorities

Given historical experiences, especially imperial subjugation and the redrawing of borders, states' policies towards minorities have long been a salient feature of the politics of the region (Crampton, 1994). In more recent years, international bodies such as the EU have devoted much attention to the treatment of minorities in states such as Estonia and Latvia where such groups live in significant numbers. As mentioned above, the Baltic States were incorporated into the Soviet Union in the 1940s. For many from the titular ethnic groupings (that is, Estonians, Latvians and Lithuanians), these were viewed as illegal takeovers. The collapse of the Soviet Union and the emergence of independent states in the Baltics provoked questions of nationality, citizenship and loyalty to the state (Smith, 2003; Haughton, 2007a). In Estonia, for instance, the 'new' state was defined as the legal successor to the interwar republic and the postwar years were seen as an illegal Soviet occupation. In consequence, ethnic Russians who had moved to the then Soviet Republic of Estonia were now not automatically classified as citizens, resulting in them not being accorded the same rights as ethnic Estonians (Smith, 2003).

Discrimination against ethnic Russians in the Baltics provoked international bodies to criticize the governments in Tallinn and Riga. Pressure from the Council of Europe and the European Union was significant in ensuring some changes in the 1990s. A new Latvian state language law, for example, which required even private businesses and enterprises to conduct their activities in Latvian was proposed in 1998, but amended just days before the December 1999 European Council was due to take a decision on whether or not to open accession negotiations with Latvia. The eleventh-hour change highlighted both the pressure of the EU, but also the role of the newly elected Latvian president, Vaira Vike-Freiberga, whose refusal to approve the original bill forced other Latvian politicians into action (Schimmelfennig and Sedelmeier, 2005; Haughton, 2007b). With EU accession conditionality now at an end, however, the power of the EU to affect domestic policy in this area appeared to diminish. Indeed, during 2006 changes were proposed to the citizenship laws making the language requirement for Latvian citizenship even stricter.

In general, throughout the region relations between titular ethnic groups and ethnic minorities with a kin state, such as ethnic Hungarians, ethnic Russians and ethnic Turks, have neither significantly improved nor worsened in recent years. A number of parties representing ethnic minorities such as the Democratic Alliance of Hungarians in Romania (RMDS/UDMR), the Party of the Hungarian Coalition in Slovakia and the ethnic Turks' Movement for Rights and Freedom in Bulgaria have all participated in governments. Opinion is frequently split amongst the titular ethnic groups about these parties and their leading politicians. Such ethnically based parties tend to focus their attention on improving the position of their ethnic minority, but using their political muscle to achieve these aims can cause tensions with the titular ethnic groups. In Romania, for instance, RMDS/UDMR used discussions on a national security bill in 2006 to push for new statutes protecting the Hungarian minority. Although such tactics are understandable politically, they also provided ammunition for nationalists to question the parties' commitment to the state.

Ethnic Roma (known also as gypsies) constitute the most marginalized minority in the region (for example, Vermeersch, 2002; Rechel, 2005). Large numbers of ethnic Roma live in Bulgaria, Romania and Slovakia, constituting around 5 to 10 per cent of the population, although statistics vary significantly. Discrimination against the Roma is widespread. Most Roma are in the lowest socio-economic strata of society, frequently unemployed and living in dilapidated and overcrowded accommodation. Many Roma's life chances are limited by discrimination in education. Roma children are frequently either segregated into special schools or separate classes. Treatment of the Roma became a salient issue during EU accession, helping to change policy and ensuring the allocation of funds to tackle exclusion, but the results of the policies were limited. Lack of progress was blamed by the Roma on ill-conceived projects and a lack of genuine commitment on the part of the governments to tackle Roma exclusion, unemployment and discrimination. In contrast, titular ethnic groups laid the blame partly on the Roma's lack of organization and diligence. Treatment of the Roma was rarely a significant issue of domestic party politics, in part because strong Roma parties did not exist; nevertheless, the considerably higher birth rate of Roma raised concerns about the future implications of current demographic trends for domestic politics.

Values and lifestyle

In CEE as a whole, much of the most fervent criticism of the EU has come from the conservative right. Although most prominent in Poland – where the League of Polish Families have attacked the secular, liberal EU, imploring Europe to return to more traditional Christian values – there is a discernible streak of political opinion across the seven states which laments what is seen as the lack of moral values in post-communist societies. Despite being a member of the radical reforming 2002–06 Slovak government, the Christian Democratic Movement pushed a strongly Catholic message during its time in power. Indeed, the party left the government in February 2006 over the issue of a conscience clause in a treaty with the Vatican, which would, for example, have allowed doctors to refuse to perform abortions or prescribe contraceptives on the basis of religious belief. Moreover, the long-running dispute over abortion rights with one of its coalition partners, the liberal Alliance of the New Citizen, reinforced the party's adherence to Catholic dogma.

Tensions between social liberals and conservatives also came to the fore in the debates provoked by gay pride marches in Tallinn and Riga. In the latter case, the 2005 parade provoked a large-scale counter-demonstration and violence. Moreover, Amnesty International criticized Latvia's political leadership for helping to create a climate of hysteria. The events tarnished Latvia's international image and almost brought down the government. Twelve months later, another gay pride celebration provoked protests and condemnation from European politicians of intolerance in Latvia. Elsewhere, the social liberal agenda proved much less controversial. In 2005, for example, a law was passed in Slovenia permitting same sex unions, although gay rights groups were quick to complain that the measures did not go far enough.

Moral issues may become increasingly important, not just in terms of rallying support to a party's cause, but also in identifying a party's values. Nonetheless, the salience of such issues in the politics of CEE is unlikely to reach the levels witnessed in the USA, because only a small majority of voters appear to consider issues such as abortion to be decisive at election time.

Corruption, disillusionment with politicians and the fluidity of party politics

Corruption remained one of the most prominent themes of politics across the region, playing a significant role in the removal from office of dominant political parties such as Liberal Democracy in Slovenia in 2004, which had been in power for almost the entire previous decade and a half (Fink-Hafner, 2005). Moreover, the need to stamp out corruption was a central message of the European Commission's regular reports monitoring the progress (or lack thereof) in Bulgaria and Romania in the run-up to accession.

Allegations and investigations acted as a corrosive on once powerful political entities. By 2006, the Lithuanian Labour Party, for instance, was disintegrating as prosecutors continue to probe alleged misappropriation of funds and influence peddling. Such allegations often went to the heart of the politics, with accusatory fingers pointed at leading politicians. In summer 2006, for example, a criminal case was opened in Latvia against the Ventspils mayor Aivars Lembergs for bribery, money laundering and abuse of office on the very same day that the Greens and Farmers Union nominated him as the party's possible candidate for prime minister. Moreover, former Romanian Prime Minister Adrian Nastase was accused of buying land at massively discounted prices, and question marks were raised over his claims that he had inherited a large sum of money and three apartments from an apparently impoverished aunt who had died in 2005. Both Lembergs and Nastase were quick to blame their opponents for orchestrating campaigns against them, primarily for political gain. Allegations of corruption were, indeed, easy to make and found a receptive audience among ordinary citizens. Even in countries not widely seen by the outside world as corrupt, such as Slovenia, were viewed by their own citizens as suffering from widespread corruption.

Accession to the EU and the flow of EU funds not only provide opportunities to assist in economic and regional development, they have also opened up another source of potential income for corrupt officials. Although the states of CEE received less money than they had hoped for in the EU's 2007–13 financial perspective, unprecedented amounts of cash were earmarked to help agriculture, regional development and infrastructure projects. Being in power, or proximity to those in power, therefore, had its pecuniary advantages, helping to explain, for example, why some shady businessmen and left-leaning politicians made such happy bedfellows.

Widespread feelings that politicians frequently put their own (material) interests and those of their associates, before the interests of their countries, combined with the perceived lack of competence of incumbent politicians, proved to be fertile ground for the emergence of 'new' parties. Two examples from the region, the National Movement Simeon II (NDSV) in Bulgaria and Res Publica in Estonia, help to illustrate the phenomenon well. The former garnered no fewer than 42.7 per cent of the vote in its first parliamentary elections in 2001. The party's identity and appeal cannot be divorced from the man whose name forms part of the party's name. Expelled by the communist authorities in 1946 at the age of nine, the former monarch only revealed his political ambitions in 2001 and quickly set about forming a party for the impending elections. Bulgarian politics had been dominated for much of the 1990s by the communist-successor Bulgarian Socialist Party (BSP) and the Union of Democratic Forces (SDS), albeit often as part of broader coalitions. The latter had come to power in 1997 in the midst of an economic crisis caused largely by the policies of the former. The SDS's tough economic measures plus accusations of corruption and clientelism which dogged the party throughout its time in office, allied to BSP unwillingness to change, created space for a new party (Peeva, 2001; Harper, 2003). The NDSV carefully positioned itself as an attractive alternative to both BSP and SDS, and built on Simeon's reputation as a noble and honest man unsullied by the dirty deals of the 1990s.

Following on from the success of New Era in neighbouring Latvia the year before, Res Publica won 24.6 per cent of the vote in the 2003 Estonian parliamentary elections. The ingredients for Res Publica's success were similar to those of the NDSV in Bulgaria, although there were key differences, not the least of which was the absence of a figurehead with the appeal of Simeon. In a similar vein to New Era, created by the former Governor of Latvia's Central Bank, Einars Repse, the thrust of Res Publica's appeal was not ideological but was, rather, clean hands and relevant policies. Even though its radical economic agenda won plaudits abroad, the main centre-right party of the 1990s, ProPatria, was punished at the ballot box by its performance in

Table 4.2   *Support for selected Bulgarian parties in the 1997, 2001 and 2005 elections*

Party	1997		2001		2005	
	%	Seats	%	Seats	%	Seats
United Democratic Forces	52.3	137	18.2	51	8.3	20
Democratic Left/Coalition for Bulgaria (largely based on the Bulgarian Socialist Party)	22.1	58	17.2	48	34.2	82
Movement for Rights and Freedom	*	*	7.5	21	14.2	34
National Movement Simeon II	–	–	42.7	120	22.1	53

Notes: * part of the Alliance for National Salvation in 1997.
Sources: Central Electoral Commission, Harper (2003); Rechel (2005); Savkova (2005).

government, (Sikk, 2004). Instead Estonian voters were attracted by Res Publica's promise of open, ethical and accountable politics and its stress on fighting corruption. Nonetheless, the 2003 election also demonstrated the apparent solidity of support for two long-standing parties in the country, the Centre Party and Reform.

Such claims of competence and clean hands are easy to invoke, but harder to sustain. Although the NDSV's economic package promised to transform Bulgaria in 800 days, many ordinary citizens failed to feel any significant benefits. Moreover, dodgy deals associated with the Bulgarian telephone company, a tobacco enterprise and a highways concession scheme all led to a drop in support for the party in the 2005 parliamentary elections (Savkova, 2005). Equally, Res Publica found it hard to live up to the socio-economic expectations raised during their campaign. The experience of these new parties highlights that 'newness as a project' can be a very advantageous strategy for a new party, but it is a one-shot appeal (Sikk, 2005b). Once a party has entered government it cannot hang on to the novelty label. Unless it develops a detailed programme and/or delivers on its promises, it is unlikely to be able to repeat its success at subsequent elections, providing space on the political scene for a fresh set of new parties. Even those parties, such as Robert Fico's Direction (Smer), which stressed its novelty, but did not enter government following its first election, could not cling on to a vague newness appeal indefinitely. Ideological rooting was required (Haughton, 2006).

Will we see a continuation of the prevalence of this newness appeal for the remainder of the decade? On the one hand, it is worth stressing that the democracies of CEE are still relatively young. Although citizens have had a decade and a half of democratic rule, politicians and the electorate are still undergoing a process of democratic learning, so there may always be a market for 'newness' but yet, thanks to the frequent failure of politicians to deliver on promises, voters' expectations of what parties and politicians are able to deliver has been significantly altered.

Global and regional challenges: energy security and terrorism

Although politics in the seven states focused mostly on domestic issues, broader regional and global factors played their part. The ongoing conflict in Iraq and the deployment of troops from the region provoked much discussion and was used for political gain. During the 2006 Slovak election campaign, for example, the leading opposition politician Robert Fico announced his plans to bring the boys home: such measures highlighted that the pro-American stance taken by many CEE governments in the post-1989 period was not universally shared by the party politicians of the region. Indeed, although in the aftermath of 9/11 most states in CEE had stood shoulder to shoulder with the USA, as the Iraq conflict dragged on and the consequences of US-led invasions of Iraq and Afghanistan became clearer, support for President Bush's policy in the Middle East dropped markedly.

The conflict in Iraq, plus Russia's decision to charge Ukraine market rates for oil in January 2006 (see Chapter 6), highlighted one of the most significant developments affecting the continent as a whole: energy security. Concerns about reliable sources to meet energy needs were also fuelled in the Baltic states by the scheduled closedown of the last nuclear reactor in Lithuania. In addition, the planned German–Russian pipeline (which bypassed the Baltic States and Poland) not only provoked concerns about energy supply, but also highlighted a disturbing lack of solidarity amongst EU member states.

Even in states where imperial history was not mixed into the energy debate, acutely aware of the importance of energy security, politicians took the lead in trying to develop regional cooperation. Slovenia, for instance, was instrumental in initiatives such as the Caspian outlook conference in pushing for funds and energy to be directed at developing good connections with the southern Caucasus. Moreover, the need to ensure that energy demands were met in the future and a desire to ensure the country was not bypassed, for example, provoked Bulgaria in September 2006 to agree to cut its stake in a proposed Russian–Greek–Bulgarian pipeline and thereby increase the likelihood that the project would be realized.

Conclusion

The seven states covered in this chapter have entered a new era. For much of the 1990s and the early part of the new century, politics was dominated by the tasks of post-communism: democratization, marketization, state building and integration. As new EU member states, the countries of CEE have been accorded much more room for manoeuvre domestically and are feeding into the debates surrounding key European issues such as changes to the EU's institutional framework, reform of the European social model and the future of EU enlargement.

Socio-economic themes were at the heart of politics in the region in the first decade and a half after the collapse of the communist regimes and look set to remain central to political debate. But now the challenge is not to create a market economy or conform to the demands of EU conditionality, the states of CEE are faced with the need to prepare themselves for the demands of competing in the twenty-first century global market place. To meet those challenges, some governments in the region opted for radical measures drawn from neo-liberal theory, but the social consequences of these policy packages in countries such as Slovakia had ramifications at election time.

The 2006 elections in Slovakia brought back to power two parties, the Slovak National Party (SNS) and the Movement for a Democratic Slovakia (HZDS), whose previous spell in government had been characterized by illiberalism and a marked lack of willingness to engage in the usual give and take of democratic politics (Malova, 1998; Henderson, 1999; Haughton, 2005). Allied to developments elsewhere in Central Europe, such as the election of the Kaczynski twins in Poland (see the previous chapter), such events prompted some analysts to suggest the region was becoming 'unhinged' (Sobel, 2006). It is too early to draw definitive conclusions, but despite some unsavoury rhetoric from SNS leader Jan Slota, the first few months of the new government was striking for the lack of change. What changes there were fell within the boundaries of democratic politics. Indeed, the election of such governments highlight not the unresolved weaknesses in democratic consolidation, but the additional room for manoeuvre as an EU member state and the persistence of perennial themes of Central European politics.

Many of the major themes of politics in the region, such as corruption, are new versions of old themes. But it is worth stressing that CEE does not have exclusive ownership on corruption as the careers of political heavyweights such as Helmut Kohl and Silvio Berlusconi have demonstrated. CEE is still living with the consequences of its troubled and complicated history, especially the drawing and redrawing of borders in the twentieth century. The legacies of the past will not disappear overnight, but it is worth pausing to remember the nightmare scenarios sketched by many journalists in the immediate post-communist period in which the region was going to be embroiled in conflict driven by ancient hatreds and nationalist ideologies. With the tragic exception of Yugoslavia, the doom merchants of the early 1990s were proved wrong. Indeed, the past two decades suggest that the states of CEE are capable of rising to tough and complicated challenges. Success in politics is about dealing with the challenges of today and tomorrow, not fighting the battles of yesterday. The states of CEE are just as well placed, if not perhaps in some cases a little better prepared than others in the EU, to meet the challenges ahead.

Chapter 5

The Western Balkans

Judy Batt

The 'Western Balkans' is a term invented in 1999 by the EU to cover the heterogeneous group of countries that it had decided to draw together into a 'Stabilization and Association Process', designed to overcome the legacies of a decade of war in the former Yugoslavia. The group included all the states that had emerged from the defunct Socialist Federal Republic of Yugoslavia (SFRY), except for Slovenia, but also included Albania (which was not part of SFRY). Exactly how many states it comprises today is still not wholly clear: the political fragmentation of the former Yugoslav space is not yet over. At the time of writing, the group comprised: Croatia (population: 4.4 mn); Serbia (7.5 mn) and the internationally administered province Kosovo (est. 2.5 mn); Bosnia-Herzegovina (BH, est. 4 mn); Montenegro (620,000); Macedonia (internationally known as the Former Yugoslav Republic of Macedonia, FYROM, population: 2.05 mn); and Albania (3.2 mn).

In launching the Stabilization and Association Process, the EU recognized that these states had to be offered a 'perspective' of EU membership (something that is not yet on offer to the East European 'neighbours', considered in Chapter 6) in order to kick-start long delayed political and economic reform in this region (see the chapter by Lehne in Batt, 2004). The expectation is that now the wars are over, this region can be induced to move on and follow the Central European trajectory of reform leading to eventual EU membership (see Chapters 3 and 4). The EU subsequently firmed up its vague promise of a 'European perspective' for the Western Balkans, and at the Thessaloniki European Council in June 2003 made an unambiguous commitment: 'The future of the Balkans is within the European Union'. Progress towards this end has, however, been uneven, and the West Balkans group of countries, always very diverse, has become more so as time goes on.

Since 2000, some states have shown determination to follow the example of Slovenia, which, having extricated itself early in the 1990s from the Yugoslav quagmire and rebranded itself as an 'Alpine

Republic', joined the EU in May 2004. Croatia, never happy with the 'Balkans' label with its negative associations, made strenuous efforts to distance itself from the region and, after 2000, accelerated domestic reforms so that by 2006 it was judged ready to begin accession negotiations with the EU. Croatia now hopes to join in about 2009–10. Macedonia (internationally known as the Former Yugoslav Republic of Macedonia, FYROM) also made surprising progress after 2001, and was promoted to official EU 'candidate' status in late 2005. Nevertheless, the EU does not regard Macedonia as yet ready to join Croatia on the accession track. The other states have been less successful. Albania has at least got to the starting post, concluding a Stabilization and Association Agreement (SAA) – the first step on the road to EU integration – in early 2006 after protracted negotiations. But Bosnia-Herzegovina, Serbia and Montenegro have not even got that far (although Montenegro may catch up fast, as we shall see below).

Thus, it is really only Croatia that so far shows convincing evidence of having moved onto the self-sustaining trajectory of reform and EU integration pursued by the Central Europeans in the 1990s. The promise of EU membership is now on offer to the Western Balkans – but is it working? Many – both inside and outside the region – are frustrated by the slow pace of change, the continuing fragility of many states, and the lingering sense of precariousness that hovers over the region's stability. What is often loosely called 'political will' – the capacity to generate strong *internal* drivers of reform – seems to be lacking here. Why is this?

In this chapter, we approach the question not so much by case-by-case analysis of political institutions, party systems, electoral dynamics – which are still respectively weakly established and unstable in most of this region – as by drawing broad comparisons with the Central European experience. How far are the challenges of transition that these countries face really comparable to those surmounted by the Central Europeans after 1989? Is it a question merely of delayed transition, starting ten years late after the wars of the 1990s were brought to an end? Are we being too impatient, forgetting just how uncertain things looked in Central Europe in the mid-1990s, at a comparable point in their transitions? Or are the circumstances of transition in the countries of the Western Balkans 'special', burdened by some peculiar historical and structural inheritance? Three main possible factors that could explain divergence from Central European patterns can be identified: political culture; problems of statehood; and the impact of war on transition.

The impact of political culture

The Western Balkans region – with the exception of Croatia – is wholly comprised of territory that, historically, was shaped by the Ottoman Empire. This invites one to ask whether the legacies of that historical experience set the region apart from Central Europe, and account for Croatia's 'exceptionalism' within the region. Croatia's southern border was once the southern border of the Habsburg Empire, and today this border marks it off from the rest of the Western Balkans group. This border does indeed more or less coincide with one of Samuel Huntington's 'civilizational dividing lines' – between the Habsburg world of Western Christendom and the 'Eastern' former Ottoman domain (Huntington, 1996). Westerners have traditionally identified 'the Balkans' with a peculiarly intractable mix of characteristics including political fragmentation and bitter 'tribal' feuding, archaic social structures, chronic economic backwardness and sloppy, corrupt administrative habits (see Todorova, 1997; Jezermik, 2004). The question of whether this region is 'really part of Europe' is not new, and many would therefore ask whether it could ever be successfully assimilated into the Europe of the EU.

However, we have to avoid the trap of historical determinism. Why should the heritage of empires that collapsed a century ago still be decisive? Radical change has been as salient a feature of this region as continuity. One Balkan country – Greece – is an established, and increasingly successful, member state of the EU. Two others, Romania and, particularly, Bulgaria, have made remarkable progress and joined the EU in 2007. We should not forget that many in Western Europe were equally sceptical of the capacity of post-communist 'Eastern' Europe (as Poland, Hungary, Czechoslovakia and others were known in 1989) to 'return to Europe' – and yet these countries proved able to execute a radical break with the past, firmly detaching themselves from the former Soviet space, establishing functioning democracies, and implementing radical reforms. In principle, change is an option for any society if its leaders can mobilize national consensus and the necessary political will.

The political weaknesses conventionally attributed to the 'Balkans' as a region are by no means immutable; nor are such defects unique to this region. Benign 'Habsburg legacies' have often been invoked in recent years to explain the superior performance of the 2004 accession countries by comparison with the 'laggards', Romania and Bulgaria – and are regularly hinted at by Croats to emphasize their superior 'European' credentials. Such legacies may be part of the explanation for these countries' relatively higher level of socio-economic development and better-developed administrative and institutional structures, but they are not the whole story. Moreover, some 'Habsburg legacies' that one could cite are far from benign: one has only to recall the exposure of Habsburg social, political and bureaucratic pathologies in the nightmarish works of the Austrian novelists Franz Kafka and Robert Musil. Moreover, one could well argue that ethno-linguistic 'tribal' nationalism was quintessentially a 'Habsburg' product, subsequently exported to the Ottoman world – whose own record in cultural coexistence was for much of its history somewhat better than that of most of Europe (see Mazower, 2002).

What was characteristic of Central European states and societies after 1989 was – for all their political fractiousness – a basic national consensus that they rightfully belonged to the 'European family': this generated a strong will for change and reform in order to prove that. Underpinning their determination was the deeply felt strategic imperative of escaping forever from the external domination of the then Soviet Union. Today, opinion polls in the Western Balkans show high levels of popular support for European integration, fluctuating between 60 and 85 per cent, comparable to that in Central Europe (at least, before the sobering experience of preparing for EU accession tempered enthusiasm). What people in the Western Balkans region appear to want from the EU is no different from what the Central Europeans wanted in the 1990s: first, an overarching security framework to guarantee their newly-won independence; second, a decisive stimulus of social and economic modernization; and third, a powerful anchor for democratic governance and the rule of law to constrain corrupt and rapacious political elites.

What is striking about the political culture of the Western Balkans today is the ambivalence and lack of self-confidence in their 'European vocation'. While clearly wanting EU integration, people have absorbed the negative Western stereotypes of 'the Balkans' and worry that the special 'Balkan' character of their states and societies means they may not be up to the challenge. As one Bosnian journalist lamented as the war broke out, 'Thus, instead of being an integral part of Europe, we are again becoming the Balkans, we are sinking into it equally in Ljubljana as well as in Zagreb, in Belgrade, Stara Pazova and Foca, in Velika Kladusa, Pristina and Skopje' (quoted in Todorova, 1997: 53). One recent poll in Serbia is typical: asked what were the reasons for Serbia's lagging economic performance, a clear majority placed political instability and lack of consensus among the parties, corruption and poor quality legislation at the top of the list, followed (at some distance) by the 'mentality' of the people – laziness, disorganization, bad habits (Marten Board International, 2004). People from the region often ruefully confess, 'If I were the EU, I wouldn't let us in.'

An important factor underlying the Western Balkans' cultural diffi-
dence as to their 'European' prospects is a certain lack of strategic
clarity about their reasons for wanting to 'become European'. First,
they do not have that sense of an overwhelming external threat – such
as the Soviet Union posed for Central Europe – from which they must
at all costs escape through integration into the EU. Perceptions of threat
in the Western Balkans focus almost wholly on immediate neighbours
within the region, and on rival ethnic groups within states. These tensions in fact weaken and divert efforts at political and economic reform,
rather than strengthening and focusing consensus on EU integration.
Second, political discourse in former Yugoslav republics often betrays
the legacy of 'Yugoslav exceptionalism' – proud memories of the post-
Second World War period when this country went its own way independently of the Soviet bloc and developed a distinctively different model
of communism. And they were rewarded for this with privileged treatment from Western powers. Thus, some people today are resentful that
the EU has already admitted countries such as Romania and Bulgaria,
which former Yugoslavs have been used to regarding as somehow more
'backward' and 'Balkan' than they themselves. Yugoslav traditions of
'doing it our own way', as well as certain nostalgia for a Yugoslav era
that was certainly much more comfortable than the post-Yugoslav era,
still have an impact today in the form of a prickly reluctance to comply
with the EU's often burdensome and intrusive conditionality. The idea
that it might be *in their own interests* to implement the reforms
demanded by the EU is thus not always self-evident to political elites
and societies, and the EU itself can easily be construed in the familiar
image of an unfriendly, even 'imperialistic' actor.

And third, there is widespread scepticism in the region about
whether 'Europe' really wants them at all. From the perspective of the
region, the EU failed them in the 1990s by its feeble and incoherent
efforts to stop the outbreak of war. Initial EU reluctance to 'take sides'
in what was perceived as a civil war in Yugoslavia explains its hesi-
tancy to intervene but, as a result, the EU is still seen as a weak and
unreliable guarantor of security by Croats, Bosniaks (Slavic Muslims)
and Albanians. When, finally, more forceful measures were taken to
end the conflict, the 'international community' (led by NATO but also
including the EU) inescapably found itself taking sides. Economic sanctions were imposed on Serbia, which also had severe knock-on effects
on the whole region. Then NATO bombed Serbian positions in Bosnia
in 1995, and Serbia itself in 1999, in an intervention designed to
prevent 'ethnic cleansing' of the Albanian population of Kosovo, but
eventually paved the way for Kosovo's permanent severance from

Serbia; hence the particular ambivalence of Serbs towards 'Europe'. Moreover, during the wars, the EU reimposed a visa regime on the whole region to stem the outflow of refugees. Hitherto, Yugoslav citizens, unlike their Central European counterparts, had been able to travel freely to, work and reside in EU countries. This restrictive policy remains in force for all countries of the region apart from Croatia, and is a major source of popular grievance: with considerable justification they ask how they are supposed to effect the 'return to Europe' when they cannot even go there?

Many people in the region fear the EU could fail them again. Despite the EU verbal 'Thessaloniki commitment', people in the region are acutely sensitive to talk about 'enlargement fatigue' in the EU after the 2004 enlargement, which reached a crescendo in 2005 in the wake of the failure of the EU Constitutional Treaty in the French and Dutch referendums (although how far enlargement, and enlargement to the Western Balkans in particular, was a major factor is debatable). It is worth pointing out, however, that even after the sorry debacle of the referendums, in 2005 the EU proceeded to open accession negotiations with Croatia (and with Turkey too), promoted Macedonia to 'candidate' status, concluded the SAA with Albania and opened SAA negotiations with BH and Serbia and Montenegro. Not so bad, one might think, but there remains within the Western Balkans a lingering uncertainty as to whether the EU itself is really as deeply committed to their region at a strategic level as it was to Central Europe in the 1990s.

'Enlargement fatigue', however, is not a new phenomenon. Aspirant member states in their approaches to the EU have always encountered ambivalence, lack of interest and indecision on the part of certain member states when confronted with enlargement, and this was certainly apparent to the Central Europeans in the early 1990s. But the Central Europeans did not waver in their resolve; they simply got on with reform and thus presented EU enlargement sceptics with a new reality – a 'New Europe' – that simply could not be rejected. In the Western Balkans, on the other hand, people frequently ask, 'Why should we do all these painful reforms if the EU isn't going to let us in anyway?' The question itself is symptomatic of the weakness of the internal drivers of reform in the region. Significant sections of both elites and societies have not yet fully 'bought into' reform as a strategic imperative, necessary in its own right. They need constant reassurance and encouragement, and, too often, more than that – namely, a direct EU/international security presence on the ground to keep them on track. This brings us to the second point.

Problematic statehood

The Bulgarian sociologist Ivan Krastev boldly asserts: 'one clear thread is visible in the post-communist puzzle of success and failure: only nation-states have succeeded in the European integration project' (Krastev, 2003). By that he meant not 'ethno-national' states, but unitary states founded on basic national consensus, with functional institutions and unchallenged jurisdiction within secure borders. It was only with the consolidation of Croatia's independent statehood in the late 1990s, after the dismantling of ethnic Serbian separatist 'autonomous republics' (which resulted in the physical expulsion of the vast majority of Croatia's minority Serbian population), and after the death of the wartime nationalist leader Franjo Tudjman in 1999, that the country felt able to redefine its national identity in terms compatible with 'European' values, and to direct its energies fully towards reform, which was then rapidly rewarded by the EU (see the chapter by Vlahutin in Batt, 2004). All other states of the region remain, to various degrees, problematic – new, weak, some very small, most suffering deep internal political and/or ethnic divisions, mired in the unresolved conflicts of the past – 'unfinished' as states in vital respects.

Even the states that avoided direct involvement in the wars of the 1990s have proved weak and vulnerable to sudden breakdown. For example, Albania virtually imploded as a state in 1997, as a result of the collapse of several pyramid investment scams into which a large proportion of the population had deposited all their savings in the desperate hope of a quick exit from dire poverty. The government collapsed and anarchic social disorder followed, including raids on the army and police stores of weapons (many of which then found their way into Kosovo, where they helped transform the Kosovo Albanian nationalist movement into a national liberation army). There followed an explosion of organized crime in Albania, involving smuggling of drugs, weapons, illegal migrants, and trafficking in women for prostitution. With close international support and monitoring, the Albanian state has since been cobbled together again, but still functions weakly, with deeply polarized politics and endemic corruption.

Another case is that of Macedonia, whose population is deeply divided between an ethnic Macedonian (Orthodox Slav) majority and a large (about 25 per cent) Albanian minority, concentrated in the west, bordering Albania. Despite this internal weakness, Macedonia held together through the 1990s, carefully avoiding involvement in the wars (although it was hard hit by the economic shocks delivered by the break-up of Yugoslavia and the imposition of international sanctions on Serbia, its main market). But in 2001, Macedonia came close to ethnic civil war between the Macedonians and the Albanian minority; timely international (EU and US) diplomatic engagement led to a peace agreement (the Ohrid Accords), followed up by NATO (subsequently EU led) military and civilian police missions. Only constant close support and pressure from the EU has secured implementation of the agreement and the start of a still unfinished process of consolidating the state. Macedonia remains acutely vulnerable to developments beyond its borders, in particular to the political instability of its neighbours Albania and Kosovo, each of which host shadowy extremist nationalist movements intent on redrawing borders to create a 'Greater Albania'. Consolidation has not been helped by the dispute with Greece over the name: Greece still refuses to accept the title 'Republic of Macedonia', on the grounds that this represents an implicit territorial claim on northern Greece, a major part of historical Macedonia. Moreover, relations with Bulgaria, Macedonia's most sympathetic neighbour, have more recently been upset by Bulgaria's withdrawal of visa-free travel for Macedonian citizens, because Bulgaria has had to comply with EU visa policy as part of the obligations of EU membership.

It is now well over a decade since the signature of the Dayton Peace Agreement of 1995, which ended the fighting in Bosnia-Herzegovina (BH) and secured recognition of the new state by its neighbours. But the international protectorate then established to oversee implementation of the agreement and postwar reconstruction is still in place. Although democratically elected parliaments and governments exist, they function under the supervision of an internationally mandated High Representative with powers to overrule parliamentary decisions and even to sack elected officials. The High Representative's role is backed by a substantial international security presence (now under EU command, comprising the 7,000-strong EUFOR 'Althea' military mission, and the 370-strong EU Police Mission). Thus, today, BH is still not in practice a fully sovereign state, and serious question marks hover over its viability and sustainability.

The price of compromise at Dayton was a constitution that unfortunately entrenched the ethnic divisions between Bosniaks (South Slav Muslims), Croats and Serbs by recognizing the two powerful 'entities' that emerged in BH during the war: Republika Srpska, a 'quasi-state' that Bosnian Serbs had envisaged (and some still envisage) eventually uniting with Serbia; and the Federation of BH, arising from a wartime alliance formed under international pressure between Bosniaks and Croats (who, at times, had been fighting each other). The return of refugees to their former homes, particularly of minority communities driven out by 'ethnic cleansing' by forces of the ethnic majority in the given area, has only been partially successful. The complex and unwieldy structure of multi-level and highly decentralized government, set up to pacify the demands of the respective ethnic communities, has proved predictably dysfunctional in fostering consensus and implementing reform, the pace of which is slow and erratic.

Constitutional reforms, in particular, the strengthening of common state institutions at the expense of the ethnic entities and cantons, are required if BH is going to be capable of concluding and implementing the SAA. But reaching agreement between the three ethnic groups on constitutional reform is proving a bitterly contentious business. The Serbs vehemently resist the diminution of Republika Srpska's powers. The Croats contest the dismantling of the ten ethnic cantons into which the Federation itself is sub-divided – unless the two cantons in which they form the majority are allowed to break away and form a third, ethnic Croat entity (which some of them hankered after as the first step to uniting with Croatia). And the Bosniaks cherish the dream of centralized, unitary statehood for BH.

Although they often deploy the language of civic republican idealism to promote this option, the argument is nevertheless hardly ethnically neutral, and certain Bosniaks see it as a means of more effectively asserting their interests as the largest ethnic group. The October 2006 elections revealed once again the overwhelming appeal of ethnic nationalism to BH voters, and the intractability of the basic conflict over statehood: although the losers were the ethnic parties that had their origins in the war, the winners are new parties that still feature wartime leaders in prominent positions, who in the election campaign showed themselves ready to exploit ethnic insecurities as egregiously as ever. Whether the international community will, as planned, withdraw from direct political tutelage over BH in mid-2007, and whether the 'carrots' of EU conditionality alone will induce political elites to reform the state (a condition of concluding the SAA) and work together on the shared project of EU integration, is open to doubt.

Unresolved statehood issues have also bedevilled the progress of Serbia and Montenegro. These two republics remained hitched together in the rump Federal Republic of Yugoslavia, formed in 1992 after the other republics seceded. But by 1997, Montenegro found the alliance with belligerent Serbia under Slobodan Milosevic too costly. It began to go its own way, cultivating Western support, building up its separate institutions, and even adopting the euro as its currency. After Milosevic was ousted from power in Serbia in October 2000, Montenegro launched a campaign for outright independence. At the time, this was not welcomed by the EU, which wanted to avoid further destabilizing fragmentation in the region. Instead, Javier Solana, the EU's High Representative for the common foreign and security policy, brokered agreement on a reconstituted State Union of Serbia and Montenegro. However, the price of Montenegro's consent to this was that a referendum on independence would be allowed after the elapse of three years. As a result, neither republic had much interest in committing itself to the State Union as a long-term proposition. It finally became clear to the EU, and the majority of Montenegrin voters, that both republics were more likely to move faster to EU integration as separate states.

In May 2006, Montenegro held a referendum at which a majority (55 per cent) voted in favour of independence. Montenegro now hopes to make up for lost time. The rapid conclusion of the SAA is a spur to much-needed reforms. The country is poor, and, as most other states in the region, riddled with corruption and weak in administrative capacity; however, with EU support, its prospects are quite good. The various minorities (mainly Albanians and Bosniaks/Muslims) are quite well integrated, but the new state has to overcome the political alienation of the significant minority of voters who opposed independence. Many of these identify as Serbs by nationality (32 per cent of the total population), and regard Montenegrin identity merely as a variety of the larger Serbian identity. Reconciling this group to the new reality of independent Montenegrin statehood could be eased by accelerated EU integration, which all groups say they want. But – as is the case with the other communities of Serbs in the region – reconciliation also depends on how far Serb leaders, not least the leaders in Serbia's capital, Belgrade, continue to toy with traditional ethno-nationalist aspirations to unite 'all Serbs in one State'.

Serbia itself is a deeply troubled country (see Batt, 2005). It launched three wars in the 1990s in the name of Serbian national unity, and lost all of them. It is still smarting at its recent rejection by Montenegro, the one neighbour it took for granted as a loyal ally. And now it is facing the challenge of how to come to terms with the impending settlement of the 'final status' of Kosovo. This country, an estimated 95 per cent of whose population is Albanian, remains formally a province of Serbia but it has been governed independently since the 1999 NATO intervention under a UN mandated interim international administration. Albanians were treated dreadfully by the Serbian regime under Milosevic. By 1998, an armed Albanian rebellion had begun. The response of Serbian security forces in 1998–99 was brutal in the extreme, culminating in a deliberate large-scale campaign to expel the entire Albanian population from the province – at which point, NATO intervened.

After that, the Kosovo Albanians will settle for nothing less than independence, and the international settlement is likely to go a long way towards meeting that aspiration. But a continued international (NATO and EU) security presence will be maintained. Kosovo is politically unstable, with deep divisions among the Albanian parties; and economically impoverished, with very high levels of unemployment and large numbers of 'angry young men', ready to vent their anger and frustration on the Serbian minority population. The Serbs are almost wholly alienated from public life, and, now a dwindling population of about 120,000, they live in fear and insecurity in the face of regular attacks from vengeful Albanian neighbours and organized gangs. In March 2004, the Serbs faced a concerted series of mass pogrom-type assaults in which over 50,000 Albanians took part. Since 2004, when the international military and police forces lamentably failed to offer protection, minority security has risen to the top of the agenda set for Kosovo by its UN administration and the EU. But the local Serbs have no confidence in their future in Kosovo; the majority of them have already left, and many of the remainder are likely to leave soon too.

In Serbia, the permanent severance of Kosovo from its territory will be widely regarded as a national catastrophe. Although many are prepared to admit in private that this will relieve Serbia of responsibility for a politically troublesome and economically burdensome province, public discourse is full of resentment against the Albanians and the international community, held responsible for Serbia's loss of the territory which national mythology cherishes as the 'cradle' of Serbian identity and history. It is thus of no avail to try to persuade Serbia that in fact it would make much faster progress towards EU integration if it could only leave the 'Kosovo question' behind. No political leader in Belgrade has yet been willing, or felt able, to tell Serbian voters what most of them already know (as opinion polls show): that Kosovo was lost back in 1999 and will never be recovered. Since October 2000, when the ruthless and manipulative Slobodan Milosevic was removed from office in a 'democratic revolution' that recalled the mass popular uprisings of 1989 in Central Europe, expectations that Serbia would rapidly leave its past behind have proved illusory and, instead of leading the region's 'return to Europe' as by far its largest state, Serbia itself continues to pose a major threat to regional stability. Democratic development has been held hostage to an unrequited nationalism. The largest political party today is the Serbian Radical Party, with over 30 per cent support, while the democratic, moderate nationalist and pro-European political forces are deeply divided among themselves, potentially leaving the way open to the Radicals at the next elections. The next year or two will show what sort of state Serbia is to become – will democracy be consolidated after Kosovo is taken off the agenda, or will it revert to the nationalist semi-authoritarian isolation of the Milosevic era?

Concluding this section, we should note that questions of statehood and national identity were by no means absent from the transitions in Central Europe either: the Czechoslovak federation broke apart, and the Baltic republics broke away from the Soviet Union to form new nation-states closely tied to the majority ethnic identity. Resurgent ethnic minority demands in the region – particularly the Hungarian minorities' demands for territorial autonomy – seemed to raise questions about the stability of state borders. But there was no appetite for violence, and armed conflict between states did not occur. Why not?

One explanation has to do with the centrality of the idea of 'returning to Europe' to the Central European revolutions of 1989, which tempered popular nationalism and focused elite energies on proving their nations' 'European' credentials and getting into the EU and NATO. They were thus receptive to the EU message that no state could be accepted as a candidate for membership that had not first settled its relations with its neighbours and demonstrated respect for minorities. After unification in 1991, the new Germany moved swiftly to overcome the legacies of the Second World War in its relations with its Eastern neighbours, and won their trust by its vigorous support for their EU integration. The break-up of Czechoslovakia could be peacefully negotiated after 1989, because the two nations had no history of fighting each other and no mutual recriminations over territory or minorities. It was mutual indifference – rather than mutual fear and mistrust – that undermined the common Czechoslovak state. The Baltic States' recovery of their independence was more fraught on account of the adverse reaction of the Russian speaking minorities. Although Russia's rhetoric on their behalf often took on aggressive and threatening overtones, Russia refrained from armed intervention, because of its concern to remake its relationship with the West. And the Baltics' dependence on Western support (the United States and several other Western states had never recognised their annexation by the Soviet Union) at the same time constrained their anti-Russian nationalism vis-à-vis their minority populations.

By contrast, in the late 1980s and beginning of the 1990s, EU and other international players paid insufficient attention to developments in the former Yugoslavia, diverted by the overriding priority given to Central Europe and the crisis in the Soviet Union. It was simply taken for granted that Yugoslavia would follow the Central European pattern of peaceful democratization: the danger of war was not taken seriously. The SFRY was seen as having a head start in transition, because its decentralized 'self-management' model was already quite market oriented and had for decades been much more open to the West than communist-era Central Europe. Huge numbers of Yugoslavs freely travelled, worked and lived in Western Europe. The Yugoslav communist authorities placed few restrictions on the publication and dissemination of Western media and culture. The Adriatic coast had been one of the most popular tourist destinations for West Europeans, and Yugoslav trade and economic cooperation with Western Europe was extensive.

But the complacent expectation that Yugoslavia could be left to manage its mounting internal problems by itself was fatefully misplaced. Although the SFRY had stood apart from the two Cold War power blocs in Europe, its survival in fact heavily depended on its position between the blocs. When that division between the blocs began to melt away, SFRY began to implode as Yugoslavia's national-communist leaders no longer felt constrained by their old fears of absorption into the Soviet bloc, and Western interest in the SFRY as an independent, Western oriented communist regime declined. After 1989, Yugoslavia did not seem to matter any more. Only too late was it realized that the country needed much more, not less attention than before.

Stabilization of the new postwar order of states in the Western Balkans will continue to depend heavily on the EU's commitment to the region. In Central Europe in the 1990s, EU conditionality provided guidance and support to states, which often represented a deep intrusion into their internal domestic affairs by tightly constraining the range of policy choices for decision makers. In the case of the Western Balkans today, EU involvement is even more far-reaching. The limited capacity of the regions' states to reform and take on the obligations of EU membership means that the EU's role is not just a matter of setting conditions and providing incentives, but helping to *build* the very states themselves so that they will be capable of responding to incentives and complying with conditions. This has worked so far in Macedonia, but the stability and functionality of BH and Kosovo will continue to depend for some time on international, mainly EU, political supervision backed by military and police missions.

The future evolution of Serbia will continue to represent a major challenge for the stabilization of the region, not just because it is by far the largest state, but because of unrequited Serbian nationalism. The case of Croatia shows clearly how the tempering of ethnic nationalism to make it compatible with a basic orientation towards European integration depends on first achieving basic security of the territory and its borders. This was achieved in Croatia in 1995, after the forcible dismantling of rebellious secessionist Serbian minority enclaves. For Serbia, however, the borders that it finds itself left with after the collapse of Yugoslavia leave large numbers of Serbs outside in neighbouring countries (chiefly BH, Croatia, Montenegro, and Kosovo) more or less dissatisfied with their lot and looking to Belgrade to support them. Reorienting Serbian nationalism presupposes not only the readiness of Serbia to come to terms with its own statehood and accept the new borders, but also the readiness of Serbian communities outside Serbia to come to terms with the states in which they now live, to rebuild trust and reach mutually acceptable terms of coexistence with their fellow citizens (see Batt, 2006). Here again, close EU attention will be demanded – experience shows that such profoundly sensitive and potentially explosive political processes cannot be left to the parties directly involved to manage by themselves, but needs strong external political support.

Breaking with the past: transition in war-torn societies

In the Western Balkans, 'leaving the past behind' and moving on to the new agenda of reform and EU integration is proving more difficult than in Central Europe, and not only due to the lingering problems of nationalism and statehood in the region. Making a clean break with the communist past is also complicated by the fact that the regions' previous communist regimes were to a large extent 'home-grown'. Communism was by no means the first choice of the majority of people, but the Yugoslav and Albanian communist regimes were independent of Soviet control and developed largely in opposition to it. Communism in Central Europe, on the other hand, was overwhelmingly imposed from outside by Soviet force, and so could more readily be rejected as an alien implant. Without Soviet backing, these regimes could not survive, so when the Soviet leader, Mikhail Gorbachev, decided in 1988–89 that Central Europe could 'go its own way', the communist regimes ceded without a fight and the former communist parties rapidly adjusted to the new conditions, reinventing themselves as 'social democrats'.

The 'home-grown' character of Yugoslav and Albanian communist regimes – to some extent comparable with communism in Russia, Ukraine, Belarus, and Romania in the period of Ceausescu's dictatorship – meant that they penetrated, and became much more firmly embedded in, the respective societies and developed powerful internal mechanisms to sustain their rule. The vested interests attached to these (in the state apparatus, the economy and, crucially, the military and security sectors) have been, correspondingly, much harder to dislodge. One cannot help noticing that the transition from communism in all these countries has been slower, more contested, chaotic and threatened by violence, than was the case in Central Europe. Social resistance to communism was weaker and alternative non-communist elites struggled to emerge. Intellectuals were heavily dependent on the regimes, and both communist and nationalist ideological currents were much more powerful than liberal democratic ideas.

War had a devastating impact on the economies and societies of the region: key professional and managerial elites fled abroad, Western countries imposed visa regimes to stem the tides of emigrants and asylum-seekers, and tourists stayed away. Self-centred, obsessive nationalism led to political introversion and estrangement from the rest of Europe. External economic ties were cut as economies geared up for war, and, in Serbia's case, an international economic embargo was imposed. Recovering from war is not just a matter of making good the damage to property and infrastructure – restoring the material *status quo ante* – but of tackling its deeper impact on patterns of political economy and social psychology.

The transition away from the peculiarly dysfunctional system of Yugoslav self-managed socialism towards a market economy had already begun by the time war erupted, and continued in erratic fits and starts alongside the reorientation of economies to a war footing. In this unpromising context (greatly compounded in Serbia by the impact of Western economic sanctions), economic transition was diverted into very damaging blind alleys. Economic dislocations and shortages vastly inflated the profits of black-marketeers, who turned into local 'warlords' with a vested interest in sustaining ethnic conflict and undermining formal peace agreements still today: privatization was exploited by powerful individuals with close ties to the ruling elites and to the burgeoning security apparatus. War set the stage for a variety of 'crony capitalism', dominated by narrow self-serving coteries. This went much further than in Central Europe, where corrupt 'insider' privatization was constrained by more robust legal and institutional checks and competition from foreign investors.

The state itself in Western Balkan countries was distorted by the growth in power of the military and security forces during the wars. Corruption reached such dimensions that the state was 'captured' and thoroughly perverted by association with organized crime. The formidable challenges these forces could subsequently pose to new democratic elites seeking to undo the damage were tragically illustrated by the assassination of the pro-Western and reformist Serbian Prime Minister Zoran Djindjic in March 2003, in revenge for the arrest of Milosevic and his transfer to the International Criminal Tribunal for the former Yugoslavia in the Hague, where he was subsequently put on trial for war crimes (and died in March 2006 of heart failure while still in custody). The Polish leader Lech Walesa once pithily explained to Western audiences that the transition from socialism back to democratic capitalism would be like trying to turn a fish soup back into a tank of live fish. For many Western Balkan economies, the fish tank was smashed and the fish just rotted during the war years.

Wholly new spawning grounds are gradually emerging, but so far these are producing only small fry – small-scale private businesses, overwhelmingly in trade and services rather than productive industry. Much of this private sector is unregistered, so provides no revenue for the state. It has no chance of access to domestic capital for development, and provides little additional employment. In the absence of large inflows of foreign investment (deterred by the continued instability of the region), an unprecedented pattern of deindustrialization has taken hold in parts of the region, as large-scale industry collapses, and individual workers turn back to the countryside for survival, supplemented by unregistered earnings in the 'grey' economy.

The impact on society has of course been devastating, most of all for the sizeable numbers of refugees and displaced persons whose fate still remains to be settled. There are, thus, serious questions to be asked about the social capacity to withstand and respond positively in future to the shocks that the restarted economic transition will bring. Polish, and even more so Romanian, workers and consumers had taken a battering in the last years of communism, but exhaustion and frustration in thepostwar Balkans run much deeper. Most West Balkan economies are still only at the early stages of economic transition – restructuring and privatization of large public enterprises is only now beginning, yet unemployment levels are already at least 35 per cent, and in some countries may be as high as 60–70 per cent. Balkan societies have shown extraordinary resilience and resourcefulness in coping with the impact of war, but survival has entrenched some informal economic practices – such as the black market, tax evasion, smuggling, and conspicuous consumption instead of reinvesting profits – that are hardly conducive to rapidly reaping the benefits of democratic and market reform.

The most salient political legacies are profound mistrust of politicians of all hues and systematic evasion of the state. These are quite rational responses where politics is still a pretty dirty business and near-bankrupt states have little to offer citizens. But mass 'internal emigration' undermines the capacity of new democratic elites to build legitimacy, and deprives them of the self-confidence needed to implement the necessary reforms – hence the tendency to revert to ethno-nationalist prejudices in elections, instead of offering a 'vision of the future' that would have to include programmes of painful reform.

Societies are fragmented into small informal 'networks' based on personal trust, at the expense of the formation of robust social movements and parties capable of calling leaders to account. 'Civil society', where it exists, is mainly confined to cities and almost wholly dependent on foreign 'democracy-promotion' financial assistance, which may alienate it from wide swathes of 'real' society. Thus, would-be democratic elites find it hard to muster the courage – let alone the resources – to present a credible programme of reform to voters struggling in conditions of acute poverty and economic stringency.

This context offers ample opportunities for populist demagogues to keep ethno-nationalism on the boil, which suits the interests of shadowy, criminalized interests whose roots are still in the past. A key part of breaking with the past is bringing those involved in war crimes in the 1990s to justice. Serbia's new democratic Prime Minister Zoran Djindjic took a first bold step in this direction by arresting Slobodan Milosevic and delivering him to the International Criminal Tribunal for the former Yugoslavia (ICTY) in The Hague in March 2001. But after Djindjic's assassination in 2003, his successors have either lacked the political courage or the will to continue. Key ICTY indicted wartime leaders – notably, the Bosnian Serb leaders Radovan Karadjic and General Ratko Mladic – remain at large, sheltered by supporters linked to the old military and security apparatus, financially backed by organized criminal interests. Serbia's unsatisfactory compliance with the ICTY then led to the EU suspending SAA negotiations in May 2006, and may also hold up the SAA process in BH, where Republika Srpska is still sheltering war criminals. Cooperation with the ICTY is unpopular and deeply divisive: many people continue to revere these individuals as 'war heroes', while others see them as murderous criminals. Thus, both reconciliation among the peoples of the region, and progress towards EU integration are held up, if not completely blocked, as long as the past is allowed to overshadow present needs and reorientation to the future in political life.

Conclusion

To return to our original question: how far are the challenges of transition that the countries of the Western Balkans face today comparable to those surmounted in Central Europe after 1989? In a broad sense, once the war is over, there is much in common – all the states of the region are now democracies, and committed to EU integration. But they are starting out on this path after a delay of ten years of devastating war that has made the starting point of transition much less favourable in many respects, hence the weakness of the internal drivers of reform. Moreover, some major issues of statehood in the region that were at the heart of the wars of the 1990s have yet to be resolved: the viability of BH, the final status of Kosovo, and, last but not least, the reorientation of Serbian nationalism and the reconciliation of the Serbs to the new territorial dispensation in the region. At the same time, the EU, as the key external driver of reform, seems to be less wholeheartedly committed to the Western Balkans than it was to the Central Europeans in the 1990s, as several EU member states have lapsed into a bout of 'enlargement fatigue' since 2004. Yet it is widely recognied that the EU cannot abandon the Western Balkans, which, with the accession of Romania and Bulgaria in January 2007, has become a region wholly surrounded by EU member states. Neither the EU, nor the states of the region, really has much choice but to work together – in their common interests – on the long haul towards the promised land of EU integration.

Chapter 6

The East Europeans: Ukraine, Belarus and Moldova

Andrew Wilson

Ukraine was convulsed by the 'Orange Revolution' in November and December 2004. The eventual victor, new President Viktor Yushchenko, has since lurched from crisis to crisis; and in August 2006 was forced to accept Viktor Yanukovych, the man he had defeated two years earlier, as prime minister. There was no 'electoral revolution' in neighbouring Belarus in March 2006, only further consolidation of the country's isolationist authoritarianism. In Moldova, the Communist Party has been in power since 2001, and, having apparently converted itself into a pro-European force, comfortably won re-election in March 2005. Do the three countries therefore have anything in common? What similar dilemmas do they face?

Patterns of history

Ukraine and Belarus are both East Slavic nations, originally part of the condominium state of Kievan Rus' from the ninth to thirteenth centuries AD. The Mongol invasion in 1237–40 divided Rus', but affected Belarus least – one possible origin of the prefix Bela-, meaning 'white'. Some Belarusian historians claim that subsequent Lithuanian rule over their territory involved only nominal pre-eminence over an extant Slavic culture, even after union with Poland by the Treaty of Lublin in 1569. The 'more European' Belarusians also adopted the Greek Catholic faith, until this was suppressed under Russian occupation in 1839. The more Russophile version of history depicts a still Orthodox culture that looked to Russia under Lithuanian then Polish rule, and then developed in an all-Russian direction after the final Partitions of Poland in 1793–95. The Bolsheviks established a Belarusian Soviet Republic in 1919 (briefly merged with Lithuania), after an alternative nationalist 'Belarusian People's Republic' had lasted barely a month in

1918, but lost the western territories to the new Poland, before temporary 'reunion' in 1939–41 and then again in 1945.

Ukraine, on the other hand, developed a vigorous alternative Orthodox culture, independent of Moscow, in the seventeenth century. After the Cossack Rebellion of 1648, a 'Hetmanate' was established in central and Left Bank Ukraine, which, despite a loose alliance with Moscow established by the Treaty of Pereiaslav in 1654, survived as a quasi-state until 1785. Moreover, unlike Belarus, almost all of whose modern territory was absorbed by Russia in the late eighteenth century, west Ukraine fell under Habsburg rule in 1772, where a powerful nationalist movement developed by 1914. Ukraine therefore witnessed two independence movements in 1917–20, one in central and one in western Ukraine, while the east and south, where urbanization and industrialization were largely a product of late Tsarist and Soviet rule, either supported the Bolsheviks or Whites, or went its own way. Internal conflicts produced territorial re-division. The Bolsheviks established a Ukrainian SSSR at the third attempt. West Ukrainian territories were awarded to the new Polish, Czechoslovak and Romanian states, until annexation first in 1939–41 and then again in 1945.

Moldova was an independent medieval principality, at its strongest under Stephen the Great (1457–1504), before falling under Ottoman rule after his death. Eastern Moldova or Bessarabia, the land between the rivers Prut and Dnestr (Nistru in Romanian), was annexed by Russia in 1812. Moldovan territory west of the Prut united with Wallachia as Romania in 1859. Both territories were part of Greater Romania after 1918, but the Soviets established a rival 'Moldavian SSR' in 1924 east of the Dnestr as part of Soviet Ukraine. The Moldavian SSR was then expanded to swallow most of Bessarabia in 1945, however, with Romania now also in the socialist camp, less emphasis was placed on the cultural distinctiveness of the region (the theory that the Moldovans were descended from a mixture of Dacians and Slavs, Romanians from the Vlachs, hence their languages are different). Nevertheless, the leaders of the Soviet republic always came from the Dnestr territory rather than Moldova proper, or were outsiders, until 1989 (King, 2000).

All three Soviet republics developed opposition movements in the late Soviet period, but in all three there was a mixture of centrifugal and 'Russophile' forces. The Belarusian People's Front was by far the weakest of the three, and was forced to concentrate on cultural issues. The Ukrainian movement 'Rukh' won a quarter of the seats in the March 1990 elections, in western and urban central Ukraine, and declared itself in favour of independence at its second conference in October 1990. The People's Front of Moldova also originally won just over a quarter of seats, but the previously powerless communist ruling group in Bessarabia joined forces, and flirted with the idea of reunion with Romania, prompting a rebellion in the territories now calling themselves 'Transnistria', which was therefore caused as much by elite manoeuvring as by 'ethnic tensions' (King, 2000).

All three countries are ethnically diverse. Ukraine and Moldova are also marked by strong regional identities (Katchanovski, 2006). Both states have therefore found it hard to build strong governments with coherent reform programmes. In Moldova, the 'Transnistrian' region in the east established its *de facto* autonomy after a brief but bloody war in 1992. The 150,000 Gagauz (ethnically Turkish, Orthodox in religion) in the south have also claimed self-determination – rather more peaceably – and Gagauz Yeri has been a 'national-territorial autonomous unit' since 1995. According to the 2004 census, boycotted in Transnistria (where the population is supposedly 34 per cent Moldovan, 29 per cent Ukrainian and 29 per cent Russian), Moldovans make up 76 per cent of the population. Ukrainians are the largest minority with 8 per cent, Russians just under 6 per cent, Gagauz 4 per cent and Romanians 2 per cent. The Transnistrian problem is therefore more regional than ethnic. Almost as many Russians (108,000) live in the Moldovan capital Chisinau (formerly Kishinev) as in Transnistria. As a further complication, many Moldovans are Russian speaking.

Ukraine is a resolutely unitary state, with the exception since 1991 of the 'Republic' of Crimea, but there are considerable historical differences between the former Habsburg west and the rest, and also between the largely Ukrainian speaking west and centre and the largely Russian speaking east and south. Ukraine's historic ethnic minorities (Poles, Jews and Germans) had all shrunk to less than 1 per cent by 2001, although 248,200 Crimean Tatars had returned from exile, mainly since 1989. The Russian population stood at 17 per cent, down from 22 per cent in 1989, and the Ukrainian majority at 78 per cent. Linguistically, Ukraine is more equally divided between speakers of Ukrainian and speakers of Russian, although language competences and preferences overlap.

Regional differences, however, are more profound than ethnic ones. In elections in the 1990s, the most salient divide was between the west and the rest, with the nationalist former Habsburg territories in a distinct minority, although in the highly polarized 1994 election the divide was on the river Dnipro. Voters in the west and some in central Ukraine (45 per cent of the total) bought the argument that independence should trump economic difficulties; further to the east (52 per cent) they considered salvation lay in restoring ties with Russia. New

President Kuchma's highly eclectic approach to the national question bought stability for a time, while the opposition that emerged under Viktor Yushchenko after 2001 de-emphasized cultural nationalism and consolidated their appeal in central Ukraine.

In both the 2004 and 2006 elections, therefore, the main divide mirrored the border of the old Polish Commonwealth: that is, that between the historical west Ukrainian and Cossack heartland and the Russian-speaking territories of the south and east that were largely developed under late Tsarist and Soviet rule. The Orange forces won the 2004 election decisively. The outcome in 2006 was less clear, with the return of Yanukovych to government being depicted as the 'revenge of the east'.

In theory, Belarus is more united, ethnically, linguistically and regionally. The 1999 census reported that 81 per cent of the population were Belarusians; the main minorities are Russians (11 per cent), Poles (4 per cent) and Ukrainians (2 per cent). It also recorded 74 per cent claiming Belarusian as their native language, and 37 per cent claiming to use it at home. Regionally, there is gradation rather than division. In the 2001 election, for example, (for which the figures are relatively meaningful), the more pro-European opposition candidate Uladzimir Hancharyk scored better in the west (15.7 per cent in Brest, 15.1 per cent in Hrodno) than in the east (8.3 per cent in Homel, 9.8 per cent in Mohilev), but the most significant divide was between the capital Minsk (30.5 per cent) and the rest.

In practice, however, all the above figures mask a consensus assigning low status to Belarusian culture, and a dominant model of nested national identity, where Belarusian identity is assumed compatible with what President Lukashenka bizarrely but perhaps accurately terms 'Soviet-Orthodox' identity. His foreign policy trajectory since 1996 – closer to but not uniting with Russia – reflects the preferences of most Belarusians.

The development of political systems

Both Belarus and Moldova adopted their present constitutions in 1994, Ukraine in 1996; the last post-Soviet state to do so. Moldova, however, became a parliamentary republic with an indirectly elected presidency in 2000; Belarus adopted key amendments to change state symbols and strengthen the president's power in 1995–6 and 2004; while a package of constitutional reform negotiated at the height of the Orange Revolution in December 2004 turned Ukraine into a parliamentary–presidential republic in January 2006.

All three states have suffered from over-mighty presidents abusing their powers: as with Lukashenka after 1996, and even more so after 2006, Kuchma in his second term and the Moldovan president Lucinschi in 2000. However, politics in Moldova have become more consensual since 2001, and in Ukraine since 2006, although the new more 'balanced' constitution is struggling to contain the tensions that have developed since 2004.

Politics in Ukraine – early steps

Ukraine's first president Leonid Kravchuk (1991–94) led the 'national communist' group that had embraced the idea of sovereignty in 1990 and, belatedly, independence in 1991, but his term was beset by economic difficulties. His successor Leonid Kuchma at least achieved a semblance of economic order on taking office, and a new currency and constitution by 1996. But his second term (1999–2004) was marked by political drift, a reversion to semi-authoritarianism and corruption at the highest levels. Former Prime Minister Pavlo Lazarenko (1996–97) fled the country in 1999, accused of embezzling at least $114 million. Other 'oligarchs' became super-rich on the back of corrupt privatizations and rake-offs from energy deals. Kuchma's second term was also notorious for the 'Gongadze scandal', after the headless body of an opposition journalist (the editor of a campaigning internet site, Hryhoriy Gongadze) was discovered in a forest outside the capital Kiev in November 2000. The scandal led to Ukraine's *de facto* diplomatic isolation by the West, after secret tapes were released on which Kuchma was heard ordering Gongadze's beating or kidnapping – if not apparently his actual murder.

The protest campaign to force Kuchma's removal was initially unsuccessful in 2000–01, but it empowered a new opposition. A sort of 'pluralism by default' (Way, 2006) has existed in Ukraine since 1991 due to its weaker state, divided elites and stronger regional identities, at least in comparison to Russia. Paradoxically, a reform government had attempted to clean up the economy at the same time as the Gongadze affair, and its leaders, Viktor Yushchenko, prime minister until April 2001, and his deputy Yuliya Tymoshenko, were the main beneficiaries of the protest vote at the parliamentary elections in March 2002. Yushchenko's Our Ukraine bloc topped the poll with 23.6 per cent, Tymoshenko's bloc won 7.3 per cent, and the Socialist Party, whose leader Oleksandr Moroz had led the criticism of Kuchma during the Gongadze affair, took 6.9 per cent. The two main pro-Kuchma parties, For a United Ukraine and the Social-Democratic Party (United), the latter actually the party of the corrupt Kiev business elite, won only 11.8 per cent and 6.3 per cent respectively.

The opposition was unable to take control of parliament, however. The Communist Party won 20 per cent, and was under the influence of pro-government parties based in east Ukraine. Moreover, the election was fought using a dual system: half of the 450 seats were elected by proportional representation, half in local constituencies, where government 'administrative resources' and outright vote-buying had a much stronger effect. Most of the 83 independents originally elected were also pressed to join the government's ranks. As this still did not produce the numbers that were needed, bribery and intimidation thinned the opposition's ranks as well.

The authorities therefore controlled the resources of parliament in the run-up to the key presidential election in 2004. But it was clear the contest would be a close one.

The Orange Revolution

The authorities toyed with various options in the run-up to the election. In December 2003, the Constitutional Court was persuaded to rule that Kuchma could stand for a third term, but he was too unpopular and often too ill. In April 2004, the authorities tried to change the constitution, so that any incoming president would have much less power. The attempt fell only six votes short of the two-thirds majority required in parliament, with 294 rather than 300 votes out of 450. The third option for the regime was to impose a single candidate on its disunited supporters. The choice fell on the sitting prime minister, Viktor Yanukovych, who represented the strongest regional clan, the Party of Regions from Donetsk. He also represented the region's considerable financial resources and frequently thuggish political culture, which alienated many in the ruling elite.

Yanukovych also won the backing of Russia, which endorsed a populist campaign: a doubling of pensions, promises to upgrade the status of the Russian language and attacks on the USA and NATO, designed to appeal to voters in east Ukraine – which it did, but voter intimidation, manipulation and fraud were also embedded in Donetsk political culture. The Yanukovych campaign also used 'political technology', particularly the covert sponsorship of extreme nationalists to campaign 'in [unwanted] support of' Yushchenko. The opposition was harassed, and most notoriously, in September 2004 Yushchenko was poisoned at a secret meeting with the heads of the Security Service of Ukraine.

The authorities expected one or more tactic to deliver a knockout blow, but had not reckoned with the growth in opposition sentiment and civic organization since 2000. Their attempts to divide the opposition were also unsuccessful. Yushchenko looked like a winner, and even the highly ambitious Tymoshenko stood aside in his support. The Socialists also joined his coalition after the first round of voting in October (see Table 6.1), although at the price of forcing Yushchenko to commit to their pet project of constitutional reform. The centrist leader of the 'Industrialists' Party', Anatoliy Kinakh, also backed Yushchenko. The Communists, both the 'official' party led by Petro Symonenko and the more radical version backed by the Party of Regions and led by Oleksandr Yakovenko, backed Yanukovych, as did another left-wing firebrand paid to demonize Yushchenko, Nataliya Vitrenko.

The authorities had expected to win with minimal fraud, but, despite manipulating the first-round vote count for ten days, Yushchenko still ended up officially ahead. They therefore resorted to fraud that was exceptionally crude, even by Ukrainian standards in the second round three weeks later, over a million extra votes were added to the count overnight, mainly in Donetsk, where turnout supposedly soared from 78 to 97 per cent. When people went to bed, they were told 78.7 per cent had voted nationally. When they woke up, it was 80.7 per cent. The corrupted Election Commission attempted to declare that Yanukovych had won by 49.5 to 46.6 per cent. However, a massive exit poll, with 15,000 interviewees, indicated that Yushchenko had won by 53.7 to 43.3 per cent.

However, even the opposition had not expected the torrent of protest unleashed by the fraud. Given that many in the regime were

Table 6.1   *Ukrainian presidential election, 2004 (percentages)*

Candidate	First round, 31 October 2004	Second round, 29 November 2004	Third round, 26 December 2004
Viktor Yushchenko	39.9	46.6	51.2
Viktor Yanokovych	39.3	49.5	44.2
Oleksandr Moroz	5.8		
Petro Symonenko	5.0		
Nataliya Vitrenko	1.5		
Anatoliy Kinakh	0.9		
Oleksandr Yakovenko	0.8		
Others	1.7		
Against all	2.0	2.3	2.3
Invalid votes	3.0	1.6	1.5

uneasy about the roughhouse tactics used by the Donetsk group, they were outmanoeuvred by the sheer numbers who poured onto the streets of Kiev and elsewhere – over 100,000 by the end of the first day, over 500,000 by the third day. Radical repressive measures were apparently not considered until a week into the protests. Many of the richer oligarchs were already hedging their bets.

The divided regime was soon tempted to compromise. More surprisingly in retrospect, so was the opposition. Tymoshenko and the youth group Pora urged more radical measures, namely the occupation of government buildings rather than their encirclement. Others were mindful of the mistakes made during the failed protest campaign of 2000–1 that had allowed Kuchma to survive and the authorities to crack down. This time, the crowds stayed in Kiev's streets, but stayed peaceful.

The compromise 'package' adopted by parliament on 8 December opened the way to a repeat election on 26 December in return for constitutional reforms – very similar to those that had failed in April – to take effect after a year's delay on 1 January 2006. A new Prosecutor was appointed, actually the old one, Svyatoslav Piskun, who had previously served in 2002–03, amid rumours that a private deal had been reached guaranteeing the ruling elite safety from prosecutions. The 'third round' vote was remarkably similar to pollsters' estimate of the real vote in the second round, with Yushchenko beating Yanukovych by 51.2 to 44.2 per cent.

The aftermath

Yushchenko was finally inaugurated on 23 January 2005. He respected a secret agreement to appoint Tymoshenko as prime minister, but sought to balance her power by installing one of his business allies, Petro Poroshenko, as head of an expanded National Security Council. The two were soon at loggerheads, as Poroshenko represented the Our Ukraine financiers who now expected payback from the new government. Arguments also raged over Tymoshenko's allegedly 'populist' economic policy: including her promise to fulfil both Yushchenko's and Yanukovych's campaign pledges (the former on welfare payments and state salaries, the latter on pensions), a misguided attempt to control the prices of meat and petrol, and above all her campaign to right some of the wrongs of the Kuchma era by 'reprivatization' – meaning first the nationalization and then the resale of industries that had been corruptly privatized. As the list was open-ended, business confidence was severely affected and domestic investment collapsed, although in the end only one reprivatization was conducted in 2005, that of the Kryvorizhstal steel mill, sold to two of Ukraine's biggest oligarchs

(Viktor Pinchuk, close to Kuchma, and Rinat Akhmetov, close to Yanukovych) for $800 mn in 2004, but now reaching a price of $4.8 bn from Mittal Steel.

Each side accused the other of corruption. Poroshenko was said to be running a shadow government to pursue his business interests, and Tymoshenko to be skewing the reprivatization process to favour 'her' oligarchs. Most damagingly, several of those close to Yushchenko, including his chief of staff, Oleksandr Tretyakov, were accused of maintaining and profiting from the corrupt RosUkrEnergo scheme, set up by Ukrainian and Russian oligarchs in 2004 to siphon off profits from the gas trade.

In September 2005, Yushchenko took the surprisingly radical step of sacking all those involved. However, his first attempt to appoint a new and reassuringly business friendly government headed by the centrist Yuriy Yekhanurov on 20 September fell three votes short, with only 223 rather than 226 votes (half of parliament's 450 members). Yushchenko then signed a hugely controversial 'memorandum' with none other than Viktor Yanukovych to secure the necessary extra votes, declaring 'the impermissibility of political repressions against the opposition', in other words making public the immunity promise for the old regime. The memorandum even included an amnesty for election fraud. Yekhanurov won 289 votes at the second attempt on 22 September 2005, but Tymoshenko now moved into vocal opposition.

Even the fragile unity of the new arrangement was broken in January 2006. Russia temporarily reduced gas supplies to Ukraine, but just as European consumers downstream were complaining loudly enough to force Moscow to back down, Ukraine signed a curious deal which both accepted higher prices and increased the role of RosUkrEnergo. The Yekhanurov government was formally censured but limped on. Disillusioned Orange voters switched to the Tymoshenko camp.

The 2006 elections

The parliamentary elections in March were doubly important because the constitutional changes that took effect on 1 January 2006 had transferred so many powers to parliament (see below). They would also be the first elections to be decided wholly on the basis of proportional representation.

The political crisis since September allowed Yanukovych's Party of the Regions to make a strong comeback (see Table 6.2). However, surprisingly perhaps, voters in central and western Ukraine were prepared to give the three Orange parties a second chance. Yushchenko's Our

Ukraine block came a poor third, but Tymoshenko's surprisingly strong second place meant that a new Orange coalition was possible, even likely. Together, Tymoshenko's Bloc, Our Ukraine and the Socialists had 243 out of 450 seats. Several attempts by Kuchma era politicians to convince voters they had changed their spots – the People's Party led by parliamentary chair Volodymyr Lytvyn, the 'liberal' party Viche, the Social-Democrats reinventing themselves as Ne Tak! ('No to Yes!' – 'Yes' being Yushchenko's slogan in 2004) – were failures. Smaller Orange parties – the remnants of Rukh led by Yuriy Kostenko and Ivan Plyushch, the youth protest movement Pora – were also squeezed out.

Nevertheless, negotiations dragged on for over three months, because Our Ukraine's business wing was reluctant to see the return of Tymoshenko as prime minister. Our Ukraine's leaders began to contemplate a shock deal with Regions instead, despite the message from their voters. Yushchenko's insistence on pushing Poroshenko as chair of parliament provoked a crisis on 6 July, when the Socialists sensationally defected to form an alternative 'anti-crisis coalition' with Regions and the Communists. Socialist leader Oleksandr Moroz would be chair of parliament, but Regions insisted on its leader Yanukovych as prime minister. Hopelessly outmanoeuvred, Yushchenko's one

Table 6.2   *Ukrainian parliamentary election, 2006*

Party	Vote (%)	Seats
Party of the Regions	32.1	186
Tymoshenko Bloc	22.3	129
Our Ukraine	13.9	81
Socialists	5.7	33
Communists	3.7	21
People's Opposition (Vitrenko)	2.9	–
Lytvyn Bloc	2.4	–
Kostenko/Plyushch	1.9	–
Viche	1.7	–
Pora/Reforms and Order	1.5	–
Ne tak!	1.0	–
Others	7.0	–
Against all	1.8	–
Invalid votes	1.9	–

Note: the barrier for representation was 3 per cent.

crumb of comfort was the 'Universal of National Unity' signed on 3 August, which nominally committed the new government to maintaining Ukraine's post-2004 course towards democracy and European integration. Six Our Ukraine ministers joined the new coalition, although only 30 out of 81 of its deputies could bear to vote for Yanukovych. By October, Our Ukraine gave up its attempts to establish a formal 'grand' coalition, four out of six of its ministers quit, while Yanukovych tested his new constitutional powers to the limit. Tymoshenko remained in angry opposition; the Socialist Party looked likely to split; the Orange Revolution seemed over.

Politics in Belarus

From 1991 to 1993, Belarus was run by parliamentary chair Stanislaw Shushkevich and other former communists who had made their peace with the Popular Front opposition. The latter, mainly composed of cultural activists, have never held the reins of power, but retrospectively this was the period when they exercised most influence. Their constituency at this time was even more limited than that of the Ukrainian opposition. Without a natural geographical base, they had won only 8 per cent rather than 25 per cent of the seats in the 1990 elections. They were not even strong enough to provide the ruling nomenklatura with a cover story to justify their retention of power. The introduction of a presidential system in 1994 therefore opened the door to the populist Alyaksandr Lukashenka whose attacks on both official corruption and 'nationalists' struck a chord with voters. The old guard was also split between supporters of Shushkevich, who won 9.9 per cent in the first round, and the ambitious leader of the more Russophile nomenklatura Vyacheslaw Kebich, with 17.3 per cent. Zyanon Paznyak won 12.9 per cent for the Popular Front. Lukashenka won 44.8 per cent, and triumphed over Kebich in the second round with 80.1 to 19.9 per cent.

Lukashenka quickly moved to consolidate his power. A first referendum in May 1995 restored Soviet symbols and established 'equal status' for the Russian language with the Belarusian. Elections for a new parliament in 1995 went less well for Lukashenka. The Popular Front was wiped out, but 28 seats (out of 198) went to centrist parties, and 95 were independent, while most seats went to the Communist (42) and Agrarian (33) parties, Lukashenka's rivals as Russophile populists. A second, allegedly fixed, referendum in November 1996, actually contained four questions set by Lukashenka and three set by parliament, but Lukashenka ignored the latter and focused on the official 70.5 per cent approval for his version of the new constitution (turnout was 84 per cent). He then circumvented a negotiated solution, imposed his new constitution, and replaced parliament with a docile 'Palace of Representatives', to which he shifted loyalist MPs, and extended his five-year term to seven.

Opposition to Lukashenka was now demoralized and divided. Some chose exile or boycott, such as the Popular Front; others were selectively repressed or disappeared, particularly pro-Russian liberals like Henadz Karpenka, Yuri Zakharanka and Viktar Hanchar, or had their parties cloned with loyal, pro-Lukashenka versions, as with the Communists and Agrarians. Attempts to hold a presidential election on schedule in 1999 were frustrated. Only 'official' parties, most notably the pro-Lukashenka versions of the Communists and Agrarians, and the Liberal-Democrats, were allowed into the new Palace of Representatives elected in October 2000, as also with its successor in 2004 (eight tame Communists, three Agrarians and Syarhey Haydukevich for the Liberal-Democrats, plus 98 'independents'). In 2001 Lukashenka stage-managed his re-election with 75.7 per cent against 15.7 per cent for Uladzimir Hancharyk, a trade union leader, the 'united candidate' of the remaining opposition, and 2.5 per cent for Haydukevich, leader of the fake opposition Liberal-Democratic Party.

Lukashenka steered through the creation of a 'union state' with Russia from 1996 onwards (see below), but his relations with the Kremlin were more complicated after Putin took over from Yeltsin in 2000, particularly after the Belarusian president broke a private promise to open up the economy to Russian capital after the 2001 election. In his second term (2001–06), Lukashenka moved towards a stricter authoritarianism, particularly after Ukraine's Orange Revolution in 2004 (Silitski, 2005). In October 2004, he orchestrated another referendum, which approved the elimination of the constitutional limitation of any president to two successive terms. Lukashenka was able to silence Russian rumblings by reinventing himself as a bastion against 'coloured revolutions'. In December 2005, the day after he had met Putin in Sochi, he wrong-footed the opposition by announcing early elections in March rather than September 2006.

The election then became something of a test case in 'counter-revolutionary technology'. The opposition was kept off elections committees, foreign observation was kept to a minimum, and real exit polls were replaced by fake polls that echoed the official result. Alyaksandr Milinkevich, a quiet technocrat, was the only real opposition candidate allowed in the race. Haydukevich stood again, his real function being to demonize Lukashenka's opponents as a supposed 'neutral'. The opposition was also divided by the candidacy of Alyaksandr Kazulin of the Social Democratic Party, who was backed by some exiled businessmen and rumoured to be close to Russia.

Table 6.3   *Belarusian presidential election, 2006*

Candidate	Vote (%)
Alyaksandr Lukashenka	82.6
Alyaksandr Milinkevich	6.0
Syarhei Haydukevich	3.5
Alyaksandr Kazulin	2.3

The official result, on an official turnout boosted by four days of unsupervized early voting to a supposed 92.6 per cent, was designed to steamroller all possible opposition, with a mammoth 82.6 per cent claimed for Lukashenka. Protests were inevitable, but never drew more than 5,000. Attempts to set up a tent city in Minsk were frustrated. The authorities bided their time until most of the international media had left after six days, and then used an apparent provocation to justify a crackdown on 25 March. Opposition activists, who had hoped to use the campaign to change the political climate rather than win actual victory, were severely disappointed by the scale of the subsequent repression, with scores arrested, including even Kazulin (Marples, 2006).

Politics in Moldova

Until the Communists took power in 2001, Moldovan politics was characterized by extreme instability. The pro-Romanian Popular Front took power in 1990, followed by the nomenklatura dominated Agrarian-Democratic Party in 1994 and the three-party 'Alliance of Democracy and Reform' in 1998. Moreover, none of the three saw out a solid four-year term, suffering various splits and recombinations instead. Moldova's first two presidents also had unstable single terms. Mircea Snegur (1991–6) abandoned his original allies in the Popular Front. Petru Lucinschi (1996–2001) was initially more pro-Russian, but foundered when he attempted to modify the constitution and increase his powers as president. All governments have been beset by the *de facto* secession of Transnistria, which as a 'de facto state', has become a hotbed of corruption (Lynch, 2003).

Moldova became a parliamentary republic in 2000, but the parliament originally elected in 1998 was unable to choose a president. Lucinschi miscalculated again by calling early elections in February 2001, at which the Communist Party of the Republic of Moldova (PCRM), led by

Vladimir Voronin, triumphed with 50.1 per cent and 71 out of 101 seats, and routed both Snegur's (the Party of Rebirth and Conciliation, 5.8 per cent) and Lucinschi's supporters (the Braghis Alliance, 13.4 per cent and 19 seats) and the remnants of the Popular Front (the Christian-Democratic People's Party or CDPP, 8.2 per cent and 11 seats).

Voronin proved pragmatic in office, keeping on some of Lucinschi's ministers and absorbing some of his business supporters. Moldova joined the WTO in July 2001, and the PCRM actually continued with privatization in some areas, notably wine and tobacco, home to some of its more commercially minded supporters. Initially, Voronin tried to appease his more Russophile voters, but proposals to make Russian the second state language and the introduction of more 'Moldovan' (rather than pro-Romanian) history text books provoked demonstrations led by the CDPP in 2002, and Voronin's acceptance of a compromise sponsored by the Council of Europe that placed a moratorium on the first proposal. But the biggest break came with Voronin's rejection of the 'Kozak Memorandum' in 2003 (see below), and his adoption of a pro-European course thereafter.

Russia therefore turned sharply against Voronin. However, its hopes that he might be ousted by a pincer movement involving the far left parties Patria-Rodina ('Homeland-Motherland') and Ravnopravie ('Equal Rights') and the motley centrists (Braghis *et al.*) regrouped in Democratic Moldova were rebuffed at the next elections in February 2005 (see Table 6.4). The PCRM has prospered by turning itself into a populist champion of Moldovan identity and interests, and because many of its rivals, particularly some of the leaders of Democratic Moldova, are perceived as corrupt (March, 2005). It also co-opted the 'Orange contagion' by adopting the pro-European agenda as its own (March and Herd, 2006).

Table 6.4 *Moldovan Parliamentary Election, 2005*

Party	Vote (%)	Seats
Communist Party of the Republic of Moldova (PCRM)	46.0	56
Democratic Moldova	28.5	34
Christian-Democratic People's Party (CDPP)	9.1	11
Patria-Rodina	5.0	-
Social-Democratic Party of Moldova	2.9	-
Ravnopravie	2.8	-
Others	5.7	-

Note: the barrier for representation was 6 per cent.

Voronin needed 61 votes to be re-elected president, but secured a comfortable 75 after the opportunistic Democratic Moldova alliance quickly dissolved into its constituent parts: Our Moldova with 22 seats, the Democratic Party with eight and the Social-Liberal Party with four. Even the CDPP provided some votes for the new 'pro-European' Voronin.

Current issues

Outstanding political problems

Moldova still has to deal with its internal regional tensions, and Ukraine with the institutional compromises made in 2004. The Russian-sponsored 2003 Kozak Memorandum would have turned Moldova into a federal, arguably even confederal, state, with Transnistria, which only has 12 per cent of the population of Moldova as a whole, having equal veto powers over state policy. Chisinau therefore endorsed a rival plan drawn up by Ukraine's President Yushchenko instead, in June 2005, which argued that the 'three Ds' – democratization, demilitarization and decriminalization – should precede federalization in the region. After years of rampant smuggling, Ukraine also began trying to impose a proper customs regime in March 2006. Russia meanwhile preferred to pressurize Chisinau, imposing punitive trade barriers on Moldovan wine. The authorities in Transnistria rushed into unrecognized elections on December 2005, in which Igor Smirnov's 'Republic' movement (13 out of 43) and the business group 'Renewal' (23) won most seats, and followed up with an unofficial and unrecognized referendum on 17 September 2006, when 97.1 per cent backed independence and the option of eventual union with Russia, and 94.6 per cent rejected the alternative of reunification with Moldova. A 'presidential' election took place at which Smirnov was comfortably re-elected was scheduled to follow in December 2006.

In Ukraine, argument continued to rage over the constitutional amendments introduced in January 2006: whether they were a necessary compromise or a sell-out to the old guard, whether they deprived Yushchenko of the fruits of victory, whether they would help embed democracy in the longer term, and whether the new arrangements actually worked. Legislative stability was the key aim of the reforms. Parliament would now sit for five years rather than four; dissolution would only be possible if it failed to fulfil its functions, for example by failing to assemble. All seats would be elected by proportional representation to strengthen the role of parties (though the barrier for entry was reduced from 4 per cent to 3 per cent), these parties would have to

form a formal 'majority', and deputies would serve a so-called 'imperative mandate'; that is, if they left their party, as had happened so often
in the past, they would cease to serve. The 'majority' would now select
the prime minister and government, though the president still directly
appointed the ministers of defence and foreign affairs and the heads of
the National Bank and Security Service. Ironically, the main beneficiary
of the new system was Viktor Yanukovych, seemingly secure in office
after August 2006.

The agreements made in the summer of 2006 allowed the Constitutional Court, inquorate since October 2005, to resume functioning –
and possibly to question the reforms. At the same time, however, the
constitutional changes increased the controversial powers of the chief
prosecutor, a political appointee who had often politicized the law in
the past. Moreover, the Party of the Regions failed to maintain the
spirit of both the new constitution and the August 2006 agreement
once in office, running a sustained campaign further to curtail
President's Yushchenko's power, questioning his rights over decrees
and the appointment of local governors, and even encroaching on the
'reserved' foreign policy sphere.

The economy

All three states suffered severe depression and inflation in the 1990s.
Belarus' post-Soviet output collapse was shorter and shallower, with
positive growth returning in 1996. Ukraine and Moldova only
resumed GDP growth in 2000.

Belarus claims its relative success is based on a unique 'Belarusian
model' that has maintained state ownership and subsidy, restored trade
interdependency with Russia and prevented the emergence of 'oligarchs' by avoiding corrupt privatizations. But Belarus has also free-
ridden on Russian assistance, especially cheap energy and trade credits,
equivalent to a claimed 30 per cent of GDP, and on unusually high
investment levels in the late Soviet period. Recovery was particularly
impressive in Lukashenka's second term (2001–06), with average GDP
growth topping 7 per cent per annum (on official figures), and the
average monthly wage rising from $70 to $270. However, Russia signalled a much tougher stance immediately after Lukashenka's re-election in 2006 (see below).

Ukraine forestalled economic collapse when new President Kuchma
launched an emergency stabilization plan in October 1994, but thereafter drifted into an unhealthy equilibrium of partial reform, 'state
capture' by oligarchs and increasing corruption. As prime minister
from December 1999, Yushchenko cleaned up corruption in the energy

sector and kick-started economic growth, but Ukraine's powerful oligarchs were able to force his ousting in April 2001. GDP growth accelerated over the next three years, reaching a heady 12 per cent in 2004, but largely thanks to over-performing export sectors, especially in chemicals and steel. Growth fell under the Tymoshenko government, but rose again under Yekhanurov, making only 2.6 per cent for 2005 as a whole. The failure of Tymoshenko's bid to return as prime minister in 2006 was assumed to kill off the reprivatization issue, but the Ukrainian economy remained dominated by oligarchs, the richest of whom, Rinat Akhmetov, was the main financier of the Party of the Regions. State capture, or recapture, particularly at the local level, was a real fear as the party tightened its control of the main financial sinews of the state in the summer of 2006. Nevertheless, GDP growth in 2006 accelerated back to 6.5 per cent.

The EU only became Ukraine's biggest trading partner with the addition of the new members in 2004. Russia is still Ukraine's largest single state market, and the temptation to join the Single Economic Space first proposed in 2003 has been great. Russian economic pressure since the Orange Revolution has reinforced fears of dependence. After the 'gas war' of January 2006, Ukraine settled for a price of $230 per thousand cubic metres, supposedly reduced by RosUkrEnergo's admixture of Central Asian input to $95. Moldova agreed to $110, rising to $160 over three to four years. Belarus was still paying $47 per thousand cubic metres.

Moldova's equivalent of the Yushchenko government was the short-lived administration headed by Ion Sturza in 1999, which at least moved the issue of market reforms onto the agenda, but at a time when the region was badly hit by domino currency crises. Due to its lack of natural resources, Moldova has plenty of criminals but no real oligarchs, although President Voronin's son Oleg, head of FinComBank, is one of the country's most prominent businessmen. Transnistria is notoriously a transit territory for drugs, armaments and people smuggling – in both directions, as 're-export' to Ukraine avoids customs duties.

Moldova is the poorest of the three countries, with remittances from nationals working abroad making up almost 30 per cent of GNP, and remains reliant on agricultural markets in the CIS. It was therefore badly hit by Russia's energy price hike and wine ban in 2006, after a belated recovery in GDP growth had accelerated to 7.1 per cent in 2005. Despite being a Communist, Voronin was deemed market oriented enough for the IMF to resume funding in 2006.

Foreign policy

All three states have had a 'pendular' foreign policy since 1991. Since 2004, all fall, in theory, within the 'European Neighbourhood Policy' rather than the zone of likely EU expansion. In all three, residual Russian influence is still strong. Nominally 'multivector', foreign policy sometimes swings closer to Russia, sometimes to the West. Belarus reoriented most decisively with the election of Lukashenka as president in 1994. Moldova has paradoxically swung Westward under Voronin since 2003. Ukraine has been most inconsistent; even the Orange Revolution failed to establish a more single-minded pro-European approach.

The 'Community of Russia and Belarus' was established in 1996, and upgraded first to the 'Union of Russia and Belarus' in 1997–98 and then the 'United State of Russia and Belarus' in 1999. The last treaty, as yet unimplemented, envisages joint political institutions, a common currency and citizenship, and a common defence and foreign policy. However, to most politicians on both sides it mainly serves a declaratory purpose. Lukashenka once dreamt he could rule both states. An equal union between two states so unequal in size, however, is a non-starter; Putin has disingenuously proposed that Belarus's six regions should simply be added to the Russian Federation's 88 *oblasts* and other administrative units. Lukashenka's personal relations with Putin are not as good as those he enjoyed with Yeltsin, however, and Russia under Putin has pursued its economic interests more aggressively. Arguments over gas flared in both 2003–04 and 2006–07. After supporting Lukashenka again in the 2006 election, the Kremlin is less likely to forgive the promises made to open up to Russian business that Lukashenka made, and broke, in 2001. Gazprom will push aggressively to win control of BelTransGaz, which controls the main pipeline network across Belarusian territory to Central Europe. Relations with the EU have remained frozen at the pre-PCA (Partnership and Cooperation Agreement) stage since the political crisis of 1996. The USA has taken a more aggressively anti-Lukashenka approach, with Congress passing the Belarus Democracy Act in 2004.

In Moldova, the issue of independence was decisively settled by the referendum in March 1994, when 95.4 per cent rejected union with Romania. The Transnistrian problem has acted as a brake on any putative western orientation, however. Moldova was the first former Soviet state admitted to the Council of Europe, in 1995, but it also signed the CIS Customs Union in 1994. On the other hand, Moldova helped set up GUAM, the loose alliance of Georgia, Ukraine, Azerbaijan and Moldova, the CIS states most distant from Russia, in 1998. Voronin skilfully played the Soviet nostalgia card at the 2001 elections, but his prioritization of domestic problems was apparent after his rejection of the Kozak Memorandum in 2003. Moldova's subsequent (and most decisive) westward turn was also encouraged by the Orange Revolution in Ukraine and the simultaneous election of Traian Basescu as Romanian president in December 2004, who has downplayed historical and linguistic disputes in favour of practical economics, and promised to serve as Moldova's 'advocate' within the EU after Romania's entry in 2007. An EU Border Assistance Mission has helped to curb smuggling through Transnistria since 2005.

Ukraine's explicitly 'multi-vector' foreign policy was most successful in the mid-1990s. The denuclearization agreement signed with Russia and the USA in January 1994 removed Soviet nuclear weapons stationed on Ukrainian territory, and helped Ukraine temporarily become the third largest recipient of US aid, with $228 million in 1996. Ukraine signed a Charter on Distinctive Partnership with NATO in 1997 and a Partnership and Cooperation Agreement with the EU in 1994, coming into operation in 1998. Russia recognized Ukraine's independence and borders in a Treaty on Friendship, Cooperation and Partnership in 1997. Agreement on joint ownership of the Soviet Black Sea fleet and basing the Russian share in Crimea was also reached in 1997, although the agreement only lasts for twenty years.

Ukraine had fewer successes in Kuchma's second term. The Gongadze affair left Ukraine cold-shouldered by the West and more dependent on Russia. Relations with the EU in particular failed to develop, though Ukraine declared its intention to apply for NATO membership in 2003. A window of opportunity to improve relations after the Orange Revolution was missed by the time the EU constitutional treaty was rejected by French and Dutch voters in May–June 2005, even though the new Action Plan was signed at the height of post-Orange euphoria in February 2005. On the other hand, Ukraine agreed an 'Intensified Dialogue' with NATO in April 2005, and the USA was pushing hard for the granting of a Membership Action Plan until the formation of the Yanukovych government scuppered the prospect. His call for a 'pause' in Ukraine–NATO relations when visiting Brussels in September 2006 led to little concrete being offered to Ukraine at the Riga NATO summit in November 2006.

Conclusion

The foreign and domestic policies of all three states are shaped by the same factors in differing combinations: the legacy of Russian/Soviet rule, historical regional, ethnic and linguistic divisions, and authoritarian legacies balanced by a natural geographical desire to be 'more European'. Belarus is clearly the outlier of the three, and is indeed atypical of the Central and East European region as a whole, given President Lukashenka's increasing tendency towards autocracy and autarky. The underlying factors Belarus shares with its southerly neighbours may reassert themselves in time, but only once the regime's carapace begins to crack. Moldova and Ukraine have more in common than one might expect, with both making muddled progress towards markets, democracy and Europe. In Ukraine's case this is disappointing, given the high expectations raised by the Orange Revolution. In Moldova's case it is surprising, given President Voronin's pro-European volte-face in 2003. After 2007, Moldova gained the advantage of Romanian sponsorship inside the EU. This was, however, offset by intensifying troubles in Transnistria. Ukraine was rebuffed in both its EU and NATO ambitions, and the Party of the Regions government threatened democratic gains made at home. The economy, however, was rebounding strongly.

Chapter 7

Central and Eastern Europe and the EU

Heather Grabbe

The European Union has had a profound transformative impact on Central and Eastern European (CEE) politics. Ten CEE countries applied for membership in the early 1990s – Bulgaria, Czech Republic, Estonia, Hungary, Latvia, Lithuania, Poland, Romania, Slovakia and Slovenia – while Croatia and Macedonia put in applications in the early 2000s, and more Balkan countries are likely to join the list in future. Eight of these countries joined the Union in 2004, along with Malta and Cyprus, and Bulgaria and Romania entered in 2007. In 2005, Croatia and Turkey began negotiations for accession, while Macedonia gained candidate status – although no date for starting negotiations will be set until further reforms are complete. The EU has promised eventual membership to all of the former Yugoslav republics and Albania, but on no fixed timetable.

In all these cases, both past and future, the EU started influencing domestic policy making and many aspects of their political development in would-be members long before they actually joined or will join. This chapter investigates how the EU enlargement process influenced the CEE countries that joined in 2004 and 2007, and how it is likely to affect other countries, particularly those in South-Eastern Europe (SEE). It starts with a discussion of the conditions for accession. The second section considers in detail how the accession process works, setting out EU conditionality. The third section considers the potentially transformative effect of the EU on would-be members, past and present. The fourth section then discusses the limitations of the accession process. The final section draws some preliminary observations from the new members' experience in the EU in the first couple of years after accession.

How the EU accession process works

The accession bargain and the EU's leverage

When the EU accepts a membership application, it offers would-be members an explicit political bargain: if the country can meet the accession conditions, it will be allowed to join. Over the past 15 years in particular, the EU has developed an elaborate process to incentivize and assist potential members to meet its conditions (discussed below).

However, the impact of this political bargain on domestic policies, institutions and politics depends on a number of variables. On the EU side, the power of the conditionality is strongly affected by how credible it is in offering rewards or threatening sanctions for particular adjustments. The external incentives provided by the EU are particularly effective at getting countries to adopt EU rules and regulations. However, if the EU's commitment to eventual accession or to the delivery of interim rewards or sanctions is uncertain, then its conditionality is less powerful (see Grabbe, 2006).

In the countries that are seeking to join, a number of other factors are in play. Their initial conditions at the start of post-communist transition strongly affect how far their respond to the democratic conditionality, particularly the costs of adopting EU norms and veto player structures (see the conclusions drawn by Schimmelfennig and Sedelmeier (2005) from contributions to their volume). Political will – the internal drivers of reform – may be lacking, as in the case of the Western Balkans (see Chapter 5). The quality of domestic political competition can explain some of the differences between the CEE countries' responses to EU conditionality in the 1990s, because it affected the willingness of political elites to adopt liberal reforms that were promoted by the EU (Vachudova, 2005). However, the quality and capacity of state institutions are also critical to explaining differences in countries' responses, as are other factors levels of economic development and political traditions. For example, the state administration can fail to meet EU conditions even if the political will is strong, if lacks the resources and organization to adopt EU norms (see Grabbe, 2005, on the adoption of the Schengen *acquis*).

Therefore, EU conditionality does not work just through an asymmetrical power relationship, but rather through a complex and dynamic interaction between multi-level actors, perceptions, interests, temporal factors, institutional and policy factors (Hughes *et al.*, 2004). This chapter explains the framework of the accession process established by the EU and summarizes the broad range of effects so far observed in CEE and SEE.

The stages in the accession process

The EU first set out accession criteria to join in 1993, specifically for the post-communist countries to meet. For several years after these conditions were first set, it was not clear exactly which elements of the political and economic conditions had to be fulfilled for an applicant to be admitted to which benefits. But by the turn of the century, a clear progression had emerged of stages in the accession process:

1 Privileged trade access and additional aid;
2 Signing and implementation of an enhanced form of association agreement (Europe Agreements for the Central and East European countries, Stabilisation and Association Agreements for south-eastern European countries);
3 Candidate status (this became a separate stage in 2005, when the EU granted it to Macedonia);
4 Opening of negotiations, which has been explicitly dependent on a candidate's meeting the democracy and human rights conditions since 1999;
5 Opening and closing of the 36 chapters in negotiations;
6 Signing of an accession treaty;
7 Ratification of the accession treaty by national parliaments and the European Parliament, and referenda in some countries;
8 Entry as a full member.

Delays can occur between any of these stages, but the stickiest points are between stages 2 and 3, and 3 and 4. The EU prefers not to give countries the status of negotiations – or to conclude negotiations – until it is fully satisfied it will be able to accept the country as a member. For this reason, the Union delayed offering negotiations to Turkey for many years.

What comes after a positive assessment from the EU?

The first hurdle that any would-be member state has to jump is having its candidacy for membership accepted by the EU. The Union can turn a cold shoulder immediately, as it did to Morocco in 1987 and initially to Turkey. A would-be candidate needs to be fairly sure of getting a warm reception from the EU, because a premature application can turn member states against the idea of accepting it. For example, Croatia got a favourable reception in 2003 when it applied, but the same country would have received a frosty response had it applied just a few years earlier while still under the rule of Franjo Tudjman. The EU's member states are easily scared by a country that says it wants to join, but is far from having the basic requirements of political stability, territorial security and economic growth in place. For this reason, it is unwise to apply too early, as that can prejudice the EU against a country that might have received a warmer response had it applied later.

Once the member states have decided to respond favourably to an application, the European Council (comprising the heads of state and government) asks the European Commission to draw up an 'opinion' (or *avis*) on the country's application, usually the following year. This document sets out the Commission's assessment of the country's suitability as an EU member, and usually recommends whether or not the EU should begin negotiations with the country in the near future:if this opinion is accepted by the European Council, the Commission then begins a process called 'screening', in which Commission officials go through the country's legislation to assess its compatibility with EU law and point out major discrepancies. The European Council has only once rejected the Commission's opinion, in 1976, when it decided to begin accession negotiations with Greece, overruling the Commission's recommendation that the country was not ready.

The opening of negotiations is usually greeted with celebration in the applicant country. Turkey waited for that moment for nearly four decades after applying; accession negotiations finally began in 2005. But, in fact, the start of negotiations is one of the hardest parts of the process to manage politically, because it is the moment when political realities begin to sink in: the political classes, the business community and the public begin to realize what EU accession is all about. Not all of the news they receive will be welcome. The conditions for accession may look innocuous and welcome on first reading; however, meeting them entails stringent requirements that require the would-be member to undertake measures that are often unpopular at home.

The EU's membership conditionality

The EU set three conditions for membership at the Copenhagen European Council in 1993: 'Membership requires that the candidate country has achieved stability of institutions guaranteeing democracy, the rule of law, human rights and respect for and protection of minorities, the existence of a functioning market economy as well as the capacity to cope with competitive pressure and market forces within the Union. Membership presupposes the candidate's ability to take on the obligations of membership including adherence to the aims of political, economic and monetary union.'

These conditions were designed to minimize the risk of new entrants becoming politically unstable and economically burdensome to the existing EU. They were thus formulated as much to reassure reluctant member states as to guide the candidates, and this dual purpose of the conditionality has continued to play an important role in the politics of accession within the EU.

The Copenhagen conclusions also stated that 'The Union's capacity to absorb new members, while maintaining the momentum of European integration, is also an important consideration in the general interest of both the Union and the candidate countries'. This last consideration reflected member state anxieties about the impact that enlargement might have on EU institutions and policies because of the increase in numbers and diversity, apart from the specific problems that CEE members might bring in.

All of the accession conditions are general, leaving the EU with a lot of room for interpretation. As the Commission elaborated what constituted meeting them in the 1990s for the CEE applicants, it progressively widened the detailed criteria for membership. It added new conditions and redefined old ones as the Commission itself had to develop a new policy for preparing post-communist countries for membership for the first time. When the accession negotiations began in 1998, the EU found new issues of concern for which it then added specific requirements, such as closing down nuclear power plants in Bulgaria, Lithuania and Slovakia, and improving the treatment of children in state care in Romania.

Because of their general nature, it is very difficult to pinpoint exactly when each of the accession conditions has been met. As a result, the European Commission has had a degree of discretion in reporting on the candidates' progress, both for the 2004 and for subsequent enlargements. The Copenhagen conditions do not provide a checklist of objectives; neither do they specify the means to achieve stated goals. They are not like the conditions set by the IMF, where there are quantitative targets for macroeconomic performance. Nor are they like the development goals set by other organizations such as the World Bank. This is unsurprising, because the EU's rules and requirements were never designed as a development agenda for third countries; instead, they are the result of hard-fought agreements between the member states on common rules for themselves. Moreover, in some policy areas where the EU has little role, such as minority protection, the member states have diverse policies and the EU has no common standards to apply to candidate countries.

The first two Copenhagen conditions require definitions of what constitutes a 'democracy', a 'market economy' and 'the capacity to cope with competitive pressure and market forces', all highly debatable and slippery concepts. The EU has never provided an explicit definition of any of them, although there are implicit assumptions about their content in the Commission's 'Opinions' produced on each candidate's readiness for membership and the annual reports it has published on the candidates' progress since 1998.

This third condition on the 'obligations of membership' is concerned with the *acquis communautaire*, the whole body of EU rules, political principles and judicial decisions. Up until the 1995 enlargement, the Commission had defined these obligations as lying solely in the implementation of the *acquis communautaire*, which amounts to around 100,000 pages of legislative texts already. However, the *acquis* keeps growing as the EU develops new policies and issues new directives, declarations and jurisprudence. For the 2004 enlargement, the *acquis* was defined more broadly as 'all the real and potential rights and obligations of the EU system and its institutional framework' (Gialdino, 1995).

This formulation is also open to minimalist and maximalist interpretations, and these in turn affect the demands made on CEE applicants. So far, the EU has generally presented a maximalist interpretation to the applicants. Candidates cannot have opt-outs on monetary union, Schengen or defence policy, even though member states such as Britain, Denmark, Ireland and Sweden have had them.

Moreover, the conditions are a moving target as the EU agenda becomes more detailed and demanding because the Union itself develops new policies and responsibilities during the period while the candidates are preparing themselves for membership. Since it set the accession conditions in 1993, the EU has added new policy areas to its activities, such as justice and home affairs, and the Schengen area of passport-free travel; a common foreign and security policy, with a defence identity; and a common currency. All of these developments add to the requirements that the candidates have to meet before accession. The candidates also have to take on much of the EU 'soft law' of non-binding resolutions and recommendations.

Aspirant members have to become like the EU in certain areas viewed as essential to the future functioning of the EU. Regulatory alignment with the Single Market – which involves the removal of all trade barriers and meeting EU product and process standards – is non-negotiable, and it was the first set of priorities presented to the CEE candidates by the EU. Ultimately, an applicant is ready to join when member states are convinced that the new member will behave like a good citizen in the EU. A potential member state has to show a certain style of operation – in its public policy making and state administration – that looks familiar to member states if it is to be acceptable. A country's capacity to implement and enforce EU inspired legislation effectively is an increasingly important part of meeting the conditions too.

The *acquis* is divided into different 'chapters' for the purpose of negotiations – 31 for the 2004 enlargement, and 36 for Croatia and Turkey, because the *acquis* had already grown so much by the time they started negotiations. Because progress in closing the chapters is one of the few clearly measurable parts of the process, candidate countries usually concentrate their efforts on getting chapters provisionally closed, and opening new ones, in order to demonstrate their progress. But closing chapters does not necessarily guarantee an earlier date for accession. Moreover, provisionally closed chapters can be re-opened later in negotiations, so the deal is not final until the accession treaty is signed.

How will the conditions evolve for the countries of south-eastern Europe?

Over the years ahead, the EU is likely to add further refinements to its accession conditions. It will undoubtedly add more requirements to the list, as its own policies develop after the 2004 enlargement, and in order to tackle particular problems posed by the countries of SEE.

For future aspirants to membership, implementation and enforcement will be key. The Union is getting more and more fussy about compliance with its standards, especially after the 2004 enlargement. The new member states have better track records at implementing laws and enforcing regulations on average than the old EU15 countries. But a 25-member Union is harder to govern than one of 15, so standards will matter more. To keep the EU functioning, the Commission will no longer be able to turn a blind eye to member states' misdemeanours in implementing single market rules, and the Council will demand that all countries guard their external borders more effectively. That raises the stakes for potential members too.

When Turkey and Croatia started negotiations in 2005, the EU changed the basis for closing the chapters in accession negotiations. Previously, the candidates had given commitments to rectify problems in order to close chapters, whereas now they had to show evidence of implementation of the promised measures. In future, candidates will also have to prove their ability to enforce EU laws over a sustained period before they are allowed to join. This change has slowed down the process of negotiations, and also increased EU leverage, giving both the Commission and the member states more opportunities to object to a candidate's progress towards accession on the grounds of insufficient readiness.

The reason for this change in the logic of negotiations was the lessons learned from previous enlargements, when the Commission found that towards the end of the negotiations, the candidates still had a great deal of homework to do on provisionally closed chapters. The Commission also learned that it took longer for the countries to work on some key tasks, such as reform of the judiciary, building the capacity of state institutions, and setting up systems to handle EU funds, than expected, so would-be members needed to start this work much earlier in the accession process. Bulgaria, and particularly Romania, had to make an enormous effort to deal with these issues in the last two years before they joined in 2007, under huge pressure from the EU with the threat of a one-year delay to their accession. For South-Eastern Europe, the Commission has started this process much earlier, urging the candidate and potential candidate countries to undertake institutional and systemic reforms even when they are many years away from being ready to join.

The EU has also elaborated additional conditions for the SEE candidates; in particular, the Union demanded that the former Yugoslav countries achieve full cooperation with the International Criminal Tribunal in the Hague, by handing over fugitives indicted for war crimes, as well as improving regional cooperation, in order to meet the political conditions – which are the prerequisite for starting negotiations. Over the years ahead, the EU is likely to keep emphasizing the need for improvements in governance; reductions in levels of corruption, organized crime and trafficking; and more substantive policies for the protection of minorities.

Opportunities: the potentially transformative effect of the accession process

Joining the EU requires a profound transformation of a country's laws, institutions, policies and foreign policy orientations. Gaining entry to the Union is therefore much more difficult and complex than is joining NATO, which essentially requires political commitment and changes to the armed forces. It is also much more difficult to join the EU now than it was for Greece, Ireland, Portugal and Spain in the 1980s. The EU itself was less complex before the creation of the Single Market and the establishment of a common currency, so the candidates had fewer adjustments to undertake. Moreover, in past enlargements, the EU allowed the candidates to negotiate long transitional periods and it provided much more aid to them after accession than to the post-communist countries. It was partly the experience of relatively expensive previous enlargements and very slow adaptation by poorer countries such as Greece that caused the EU to impose such tight conditions for the countries that applied after 1989.

EU membership now requires changes to a huge range of policies, and the reshaping of many of a country's public institutions. EU members have developed some form of coordination, harmonization or common rules in almost every area of public policy – although the extent of harmonization and the burden of adjustment vary greatly. The effects of the accession process range widely, from the creation of market regulators to civil service reform, from border controls to hygiene standards in abattoirs. Moreover, the political and economic conditions are new in this enlargement, so the EU has an influence in the candidate countries' domestic politics that goes beyond the Union's remit for its current member states.

The EU and its member states become involved in shaping political institutions too, through the creation of new agencies and new coordination procedures within and between government agencies, as well as in transferring policies. The EU has an impact on the reform of the civil service, public procurement, budgetary procedures, and regional self-government. The accession process puts direct pressure on three sets of relations between different parts of the state: the relationship between the executive and legislature; the emergence of a privileged accession team in the executive; and the relationship between central and regional governments (see Grabbe, 2006).

These effects emerge from the conditions and the way that the accession process works. But they also stem from a paradox. The stability of democratic institutions is one of the three general conditions for accession, and the EU has promoted the involvement of political institutions beyond the executive to implement and enforce the *acquis*. Yet, at the same time, the incentives and constraints created by the accession process support the emergence of a core national executive at the expense of other branches and levels of government – including the legislature and regional actors. The way the accession process is structured encourages the emergence of a strong, central team to manage it, because the conditionality is based on implementing a vast array of legislation and procedural rules in order to comply with EU standards, which in turn depend on reporting from the centre of government to Brussels.

This can create an 'executive bias' in the accession process, because of the structure of negotiations and the fact that EU actors mostly see the process of adopting EU norms as an administrative exercise. This bias can in turn exacerbate centralizing tendencies in applicant countries – as happened in CEE – which were already evident owing to the previous decades of state socialism. If mishandled, this approach could erode public support and involvement in European integration. Negotiations between bureaucracies do not necessarily contribute to the development of shared values as a basis for new structures of government. This has implications for the future behaviour of the applicants as member states: if candidate countries' governments invoke 'EU standards' as the reason for imposing centralized governance frameworks, the administrative bias of the accession process can impede the development of a wider debate on forms of governance in the country.

The accession process also affects party competition. Pressures from the EU interact with domestic debates about both policies and governance. The interaction between EU pressures and domestic processes can be seen clearly in centre-regional relations as well, where there is 'triadic engagement' between the EU, national governments and subnational administration (Hughes *et al.*, 2004). That engagement between Brussels and regional governments can appear threatening to countries that are sensitive to any potential threat to their territorial integrity.

An appeal to 'Europe' was a constant feature of the domestic debate in CEE prior to accession (see Fowler, 2001, on Hungary), and it is rapidly becoming one in SEE. All sides and all political parties can make this appeal, yet the EU is a confusing model because of the diversity of the member states in handling issues such as constitutional reforms and minority rights. Political actors in candidate countries can therefore point to the various examples of how different member states run their affairs and implement EU policies in some areas. Diversity within the EU can thus undermine its efforts to export particular models of governance, and the accession process itself sometimes presents conflicting demands. This can provide ammunition for many different sides in domestic political battles.

Limitations: what the EU accession process cannot do

We cannot assume that the perspective of EU accession will have the same transformative effect on SEE that it did for the Central European candidates. On the EU side, the Union is currently unable to provide models in some of the areas where SEE candidate countries might need them most. When it comes to the most sensitive and difficult issues in the region, such as the status and treatment of minorities, human rights, corruption, organized crime and constitutional reform, the EU has no detailed policy guidance to offer. Although potential members have to meet the political conditions, the EU has no democratic *acquis* on which to draw to provide guidance to the candidates. The member states themselves have diverse policies on issues such as provision of bilingual education for the children of ethnic minorities, or on tackling corruption in the public sector. Although the members form part of a community of nations and share norms on what is and is not acceptable behaviour on the part of the state the trickiest dilemmas of democracy often cannot be solved by drawing on a codified guidance set down in EU law.

On the other side, in the SEE region, some of the key prerequisites for taking advantage of what the EU has to offer are simply not in place in many of the countries. Judging by the experience of the CEE countries, the most important prerequisites for using EU conditionality to transform a country are:

- a well-functioning state administration
- a cross-party consensus on the importance of joining the EU and the need for reforms to succeed in doing it
- inflows of foreign direct investment, to achieve a virtuous circle working between reforms, economic growth and EU accession prospects.

In order to respond to the incentives that the EU has to offer, countries need to have fairly strong states. The EU negotiates with a small executive team, which it expects to co-ordinate the process of preparing for membership. This team needs strong political backing so that it can override the priorities of other ministries, and it needs to be highly competent in the approximation of laws – often overriding parliamentary objections too. And the judiciary needs to be able to enforce EU inspired laws, or they simply foster a culture of non-compliance. Weak states – such as the Balkan countries – find it difficult to take advantage of the twinning projects that the EU organizes between member state and candidate country civil services, as well as the financial aid and technical assistance that the EU offers to assist preparations.

Where these prerequisites are absent, there are two dangers: the first is that the EU accession process might engender a split bureaucracy, where the best officials are attracted to work on EU matters, but the rest of the civil service gets no better. The second is that an implementation gap will open up, whereby the preparations team ensures that EU inspired laws reach the statute books, but there is little implementation or enforcement of them. If that happens, the likely EU response is to slow down the country's progress until it improves its institutional capacity.

A basic cross-party consensus is also essential, to ensure consistency of policy on the EU across governments. Otherwise, the efforts of one government are wasted, and the country gains little benefit from the painful reforms already undertaken if the next government reverses them – causing further disillusionment among voters.

Foreign direct investment (FDI) is the grease that keeps the wheels turning towards the EU, by bringing the country capital, skills and expertise, employment and hope. Countries that undertake economic reform and gain FDI in consequence can start a virtuous circle where their efforts are rewarded, they achieve approbation from the EU, which encourages more foreign investors, and enables them to undertake the next phase of reforms. Investors feel more confident about putting their money into a country if it has been given the EU seal of approval.

But if the country attracts little FDI, problems of de-industrialization and lack of competitiveness can get worse; as a result, access to the EU single market may bring the country little benefit because it has little to export that EU consumers want to buy. When other SEE countries apply to join, they are also likely to find that their progress towards EU membership helps to encourage reforms, while loss of support for the reform process is detrimental to FDI inflows. Consequently, a loss of reform momentum would damage FDI receipts, and might well exacerbate a vicious circle of reduced investment and slower reform. So putting in an application prematurely is a bad idea if there are likely to be many disappointments and long years before membership, because it can lead to a loss of popular support for key reforms and also undermine the confidence of foreign investors.

In sum, we cannot assume that a direct cause–effect relationship between the accession process and success in domestic reforms will operate in SEE the way it did in CEE, if these key factors are not in place. Aspirant members can only use an application to join the EU as a route to economic success if they already have both widespread political support for the necessary reforms and also adequate institutional resources to implement the measures demanded by the EU. The EU is no panacea for weak institutions and a lack of political consensus. This section outlines two ways in which the EU could tailor the process to take account of these constraints.

The strength of EU commitment as a motivation to stick to reforms

The most important effect of the prospect of EU membership is its role as an anchor to the reform process. The drive to join the EU can be one of the most powerful incentives for undertaking major reforms in the right circumstances, as explained above. Through the tasks set annually by the European Commission in its 'Partnership' documents for the countries, the EU puts a fairly consistent external pressure on successive governments, helping to ensure continuity of reform efforts. The reform anchor role offered by the credible prospect of membership is then reinforced by the tangible benefits that the EU links to progress in reforms; such as additional aid, trade access and political support.

Can these benefits be used to guide SEE countries during a long period of difficult and painful reforms? Only if the EU sticks to its promise that the countries will be rewarded if they make progress. If the prospects for EU membership recede, it will be much more difficult to overcome domestic political opposition to difficult reforms by justifying hard choices in the name of EU requirements. Slower reform, in turn, would have a direct negative impact on performance, and an adverse impact on foreign direct investment. Therefore, the EU needs to maintain a very clear commitment to eventual accession – even if it is many years away – in order to keep the countries on the right track. Any waning of its commitment will immediately reduce the effect of its conditionality.

The experience of Bulgaria and Romania over the past decade carries important lessons for South-Eastern Europe, because they had to scramble to catch up in the last years prior to accession, having wasted time in the 1990s. The EU can help governments to overcome opposition to unpopular measures, but the Union has few sanctions that can be applied to unwilling governments: it can only encourage, not coerce. For Bulgaria and Romania, enormous EU pressure when they were very close to membership had a remarkably motivating effect in key areas such as judicial reform. But other countries should be careful not to follow their example of wasting time earlier in the process. And the EU needs to sharpen its structure of incentives from the start of the accession process, to ensure that countries start to respond to its conditionality at an earlier stage.

The relationship between accession requirements and development needs

Future aspirants need to recognize the opportunity costs of EU accession preparations. For countries that are unlikely to join the EU within the next ten to twenty years, it is unlikely to be optimal to expend enormous efforts in meeting EU standards and harmonizing with EU policies designed for established market economies, if this is at the cost of more immediate policies to establish sustainable economic growth. EU policies are often cumbersome to administer and implement.

For countries that have a good chance of joining the EU within a decade, however, the overall benefits of EU membership certainly outweigh the short-term costs of adopting possibly sub-optimal policies and regulatory regimes. But countries that have little hope of meeting the conditions in full for many years might be better advised to use the eventual prospect of membership as an incentive to undertake basic reforms, rather than concentrating on the detail of EU policy models. For these countries, the EU could develop a 'core *acquis*' which can be used to guide reforms, rather than presenting its rules and regulations as a monolith.

The EU accession process of the 1990s and 2000s was essentially based on the model for previous enlargements, rather than being designed specifically to assist and encourage economies undergoing post-communist transition. As a result, the structure of incentives and constraints that it imposes on economic and regulatory policies may be inappropriate for countries facing acute development and/or recon-struction problems. EU policy makers tend to assume that accession and transition require the same policies. However, although many accession related policies are also required for successful economic transformation, applicants have to take on numerous EU policies that were developed for advanced, industrialized economies. They were not designed for countries in transition, and they often require a complex institutional structure for implementation that is little developed in many parts of South-Eastern Europe.

Moreover, some EU policies are inappropriate for less developed economies, such as its agricultural policy, and the expensive parts of its environmental and social regulations. This is unsurprising, as the EU is not a development agency, but rather a members' club. But perhaps it ought to establish a more explicit development policy to help some of its neighbouring countries – including the least developed of the coun-tries that have an accession perspective – to catch up faster.

What happens after accession?

Other chapters in this volume consider developments in the domestic politics of the new member states since they joined the EU in 2004. For many, the first years of membership were a turbulent period at home. Not a single incumbent prime minister who went to the polls in the first two years after accession held onto his post. In 2006, Poland and Slovakia elected governments that were widely viewed as stridently nationalistic, populist and anti-EU. The Czech Republic and Poland underwent many months of political uncertainty before new govern-ments could be formed, leading to confused and inconsistent positions in EU decision making.

Many reasons lay behind this trend, most of which lie in domestic processes of post-communist transition (see Chapters 3 and 4 in this volume, and the contributors to Schimmelfennig and Sedelmeier (2005)). But the anti-reform and anti-elite backlash has also included an anti-EU backlash, which is unsurprising, given the EU's role, for more than a decade before accession, in constraining policy choices and demanding oftenpainful reforms. After accession, voters had nothing to lose in electing populists who would have jeopardized chances of membership in previous years. The pro-EU and economically liberal parties could no longer frighten voters with the idea that their more nationalistic opponents would lead to ostracism of their country by the rest of Europe. People were also fed up with hearing that many policy options were impossible because of EU demands, and that more painful reforms were still required.

Some voters were disappointed that membership did not immediately lead to improved living standards – or, indeed, better politicians. One interesting exception was the farmers, who had been effectively mobilized, particularly in Poland, to oppose accession by tall tales of how their interests would be harmed. After joining, they found that they received larger subsidies (funded by the Common Agricultural Policy) and the market adjustments were not as dramatic as many had feared. Even though their receipts from EU agricultural policy were only a quarter of those paid to their French counterparts, the CEE farmers gained a major boost to their income.

However, the consequences of electing populists were probably greater than most voters realised. Their countries had less influence in EU decision making than their size or interests suggested they should. Poland's experience is particularly striking; as the largest new member to join in 2004, with a population of 40 million, it was expected to have a major impact on EU policy making (see Grabbe, 2004). But the widespread perception in Brussels is that Poland has punched significantly below its weight, at least in the first two years.

One reason was the disorganization and lack of clear policy lines that afflicted ministries during the periods of political chaos following changes of government, especially when the party taking power did not have clear policy preferences on much EU business. The ministries could run on autopilot for a short period in taking positions in the Council of Ministers, but when controversial issues arose that attracted attention at home, the Brussels based diplomats and officials would find their country's position suddenly changed. This made it very difficult for national officials based in Brussels to find allies among the other member states, and to build the cross-country coalition deals which are key to influencing EU decision making (see, among others, Wallace *et al.*, 2005). This problem led to a few high profile confrontations – such as when Poland opposed a decision on value-added tax, alone among the 25 member states, in February 2006 – but also many more ineffective attempts to change EU decisions that never hit the headlines.

Another problem was that new governments elected on anti-EU rhetoric and the promise of aggressive defence of national interests were not taken very seriously by their peers. Again, they found it difficult to build the all-important alliances with other member states, even through the party groupings in the European Parliament and the Council of Ministers. Party political allegiances and sympathy for national difficulties are key ingredients in finding consensus in the EU. If a country fails to use these tools effectively, the other 24 members tend not to take its concerns and interests into account.

This lack of influence can lead to a vicious circle: populist governments find that they are losing influence in Brussels, contrary to their election pledges to protect national interests more strongly, so they resort to more confrontational stances at a higher political level. Their failures to influence outcomes are then even more visible to the public, and they are forced to wield their veto in the Council of Ministers. This is not a very effective tactic, given that votes are formally taken only on about 15 per cent of Council business (Hayes-Renshaw and Wallace, 2005). The government's failure to play the EU game effectively can then lead its leaders to condemn the whole EU system as being unfair – leading to further anti-EU rhetoric. This phenomenon is well known from other countries where Euroscepticism has been long established, such as the UK and Denmark (see George, 1998).

However, although domestic party competition became more turbulent in most of the new member states in the first years following accession, their state institutions performed well in meeting the obligations of membership, making their integration into the EU community of law and policies smoother than expected. For example, the new member states' record of compliance with EU laws was on average better than that of the old member states two years after accession (European Commission, 2006). This finding suggests that the accession process had deep and lasting effects in building state institutions that were both willing to meet, and capable of meeting, EU requirements – and which were robust enough to continue fulfilling this function in conditions of political uncertainty.

Conclusion

The issue of EU accession is not a yes/no question: 'Will this country get in or won't it?' Rather, it is a long and uncertain process that has clear stages, but a variable timetable. The process can have a profoundly transformative impact on a country's political systems, economies and legal frameworks, as it did in CEE and most of the previous enlargements. However, we cannot assume that the accession process in South-Eastern Europe will have the same transformative effect that it did in Central and Eastern Europe, especially if the extra-EU conditions of political consensus and economic growth are not in place first. The effectiveness of the accession process in changing domestic policies and structures depends on a wide range of variables in the countries striving to join, and also in how the EU manages the process. Thus, the more relevant question is: 'What effect will trying to join have on these countries, and how can they best use it to transform themselves?'

Chapter 8

Executive Leadership

Ray Taras

A distinguishing feature of the politics of post-communist Europe is the structure of executive leadership. Even though 'the institutional models of democracy are very few' (Przeworski, 1992: 99), nearly all post-communist European states have opted for a mix of parliamentary and presidential government. Executive power in these states has been distributed in different ways. But it is invariably the country's president, prime minister, the cabinet of ministers (or government), or some combination of these that is identified as the political executive. However constituted, an executive leadership is checked by the legislative and judicial branches of government.

What is the political executive?

This chapter examines the *executive* branch of government – the traditional core of a political system. Before there were parliaments, judiciaries, and bureaucracies, there was executive leadership. It took the form of absolute monarchs, emperors, strongmen, sultans and the like. In a modern political system, however, the political executive is expected to share power, in some measure, with other government branches, and has to submit to varying degrees of institutional checks. One of these checks (discussed below) is the existence of ministerial bureaucracies that are responsible for carrying out the will of the political executive. It is the political executive, however, that is responsible for discharging leadership and formulating policy – in short, for governing.

Significant differences in the nature of executive leadership exist across this region. For a start, there may be recurrent *intra-executive* conflicts, especially in recently constructed political systems (Figure 8.1). These invariably involve 'a political struggle between the president and the prime minister over the control of the executive branch' (Sedelius, 2006: 19). Far more familiar to us are *executive–legislative*

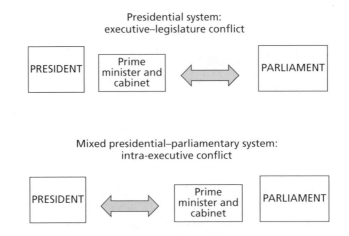

Figure 8.1   *Conflict in presidential versus conflict in mixed presidential-parliamentary systems*

conflicts between different branches of government, as occur in both the US presidential system and the parliamentary model. Political executives also differ; in terms of the circles from which they are recruited, the process by which they emerge, the powers they hold, and the policies that they pursue.

The simplest typologies of the political executive are based on two dichotomies: effective (the president of the Russian Federation) versus ceremonial (the king of Spain); and individual (the German chancellor) versus collective (the British cabinet) (Almond and Powell, 1983: 106). Executive power evolves over time, as in the case of the USA where a two centuries-old constitution has not prevented the president from enhancing the powers of the office. In Britain, too, the role of the prime minister has reached the point where the system is sometimes described as quasi-presidential.

It is no surprise, then, that since the collapse of communism different approaches have been taken to constructing executive power. Poland and Belarus are neighbours, for example, but the many constitutional, electoral, and political checks on the Polish president and prime minister contrast starkly with the virtual unaccountability of the political executive – the presidency – in the former Soviet republic. The limited powers of the presidency in the Czech Republic have characterized the office from the time of Vaclav Havel's presidency to the present. By contrast, in such Balkan states as Croatia and Serbia presidents have seen their powers steadily eroded.

There are three general types of executive government in modern democracies. The first is *cabinet government*, in which political leadership is entrusted to a prime minister and such colleagues as head the important departments of government. The composition of the cabinet reflects the balance of political power in the legislature, which, in turn, is the product of legislative elections. A test of whether cabinet government exists is whether it accepts collective responsibility before parliament for the policies it pursues. The Czech Republic, Hungary, Poland, Slovakia, and Slovenia are countries that qualify as systems of cabinet government in this sense. There have been examples of strong prime ministers in these new democracies (Vaclav Klaus in the Czech Republic and Janez Drnovsek in Slovenia were two) but no one has come close to building the prime ministerial system of government that Margaret Thatcher and Tony Blair did in Britain.

A second type of executive government is the *presidential system*. It is distinguished by the fact that there is a single head of the political executive who is elected to office directly by the people. In this model the president usually combines the roles of head of government and head of state – that is, effective and ceremonial roles. In a cabinet or parliamentary system, on the other hand, the head of state largely performs a ceremonial role and, as a corollary, the office is entrusted to a political figure of secondary importance, who nevertheless embodies the virtue of prestige or impartiality. In a presidential system the head of state appoints the key members of the administration who become an integral part of the executive. Belarus under Alexander Lukashenka, Ukraine before the Orange Revolution, Romania in the early 1990s, and Yugoslavia under Slobodan Milosevic had presidential systems of government.

These cases are sometimes classified as examples of super-presidential systems: 'a huge apparatus of executive power that overshadows other state agencies and the national legislature in terms of its size and the resources it uses; a president who controls most or all of the levers of public expenditure; a president who enjoys the power to make laws by decree ... a legislature that enjoys little real oversight authority over the executive branch; and a judiciary that is appointed and controlled largely by the president and that cannot in practice check presidential prerogatives or even abuse of power' (Fish, 2000: 178–9).

Super-presidentialism is a system favoured by the non-European former Soviet republics. Its attraction is that it can be distorted so as to incorporate quasi-democratic features while still avoiding the appearance of clearly anti-democratic practices. Thus, 'The main potential forms of postcommunist authoritarianism are personal dictatorships, one-party states, and military regimes' (Parrott, 1997: 7). Another undemocratic model is neo-patrimonialism, which involves 'the capture of the state by ruling clans' (Van Zon, 2001: 72). The non-European ex-Soviet republics – as well as the Russian Federation – have largely avoided these models and opted for super-presidentialism, which transfers enormous power to individual leaders who win largely uncompetitive elections (Fish, 2000: 178).

In Central and Eastern Europe presidentialism as a model of executive leadership has had much less appeal. Still, an ambitious president intent on reordering the balance of power between executive and legislative branches – such as Poland's Lech Kaczynski – reminds us that the nature of executive leadership is always subject to change.

A third type of executive system consists of assembly or *parliamentary government*. Here the elected legislature is politically dominant and is able, paradoxically, to wrest executive power from the executive branch. The classic example of such a system is the Third (1875–1940) and Fourth (1946–58) French Republics where the legislature was able to overthrow cabinets with consummate ease. If we take the turnover in prime ministers and their cabinets triggered by parliamentary crises – rather than electoral verdicts – as the measure of incipient parliamentary government, then Poland seemed headed for a parliamentary dominant system. But the simultaneous holding of the offices of president and prime minister by the Kaczynski twins in 2006 suggested a weakening of the powers of the Polish parliament. Today, assembly governments are rare anywhere in the world.

The preference for mixed political systems

We have highlighted both the fluidity and the hybrid nature of executive systems. A mix of presidential–parliamentary government is a safe choice, explained by a number of considerations.

A pure presidential system generates a zero-sum game. The winning candidate takes all and the losers receive nothing, as in Belarus under Lukashenka. A parliamentary system, by contrast, increases total pay-offs with many parties and their candidates gaining influence even while losing elections. Losers in this system have an incentive to stay in the parliamentary game because they are heartened by the prospect of expanding their representation or of obtaining positions of power next time around. Alteration of power among political elites is one of the defining characteristics of the politics of Central and Eastern Europe. The mixed presidential–parliamentary systems have produced a greater rotation of leaders – presidents, prime ministers, and cabinets – than a presidential one would have done.

The best example of a hybrid system is the semi-presidentialism found in the French Fifth Republic. In constitutional terms the president is a powerful executive. But when a party different from the president's commands a majority in the national assembly, the president's role is weakened. Indeed, a stand off between the presidency and parliament could lead to a constitutional crisis about who really embodies executive power. In practice, the Fifth Republic has weathered uneasy periods of 'cohabitation', such as between a socialist president and a conservative government (1986–88), and a conservative president and socialist prime minister (1997–2002). These episodes have established the convention that under cohabitation the strong presidency envisaged by the constitution will be set aside in favour of a diminished semi-presidential system.

Cohabitation in the more fragile and volatile conditions of post-communist Europe has not always worked as smoothly. Various issues – often the separation of powers itself – can produce intra-executive conflicts (Sedelius, 2006: 168), especially when executive office holders come from different parties. The election of a liberal democratic president in Bulgaria in 1996 precipitated a wave of anti-socialist demonstrations demanding the resignation of the socialist government – even though it had a mandate to rule for another two years. By contrast, in Poland a former communist, President Aleksander Kwasniewski, encountered few difficulties in working with a prime minister from the Solidarity camp between 1997 and 2001. In the Czech Republic, right-wing President Klaus, elected by parliament in 2003, was regularly at loggerheads with Social Democratic prime minister Jiri Paroubek during 2005–06; even the date for the 2006 parliamentary elections became a source of disagreement. The dead heat between leftist and conservative camps in that year's election provided Klaus with the opportunity to strengthen his position by subsequently nominating a prime minister from his own party.

Executive experimentation

Do these examples indicate that semi-presidential systems operating in Central and Eastern Europe have proved successful? Fifth Republic style semi-presidentialism requires the direct election of the president, which is not the case in Albania, the Czech Republic, Estonia, Hungary, Latvia, and Moldova after 1996. In these countries the president is selected indirectly, by parliament. In theory, then, executive power rests in the hands of the prime minister – usually the leader of parliament's largest party. But even the direct election of the president does not guarantee that he will exercise political – as opposed to formal – executive power. A case illustrating this point is Ukraine after the Orange Revolution. Even as voters were electing Viktor Yushchenko as president in 2004 in a free and transparent election, many of the powers of his office were being transferred to parliament. Ironically, by 2006, the head of the governing party in parliament and prime minister had become Yushchenko's archrival and defeated presidential candidate Viktor Yanukovych (see Chapter 6).

As in their French counterpart, Central and Eastern European presidents generally serve for five years (Romania's has a four-year term). As in the French National Assembly, their parliaments have a four-year mandate (the exception is Slovenia where it is five). The extra year in most presidents' terms is suggestive of semi-presidentialism in that it seems to privilege that office. But neither this, nor indirect election alone, accounts for semi-presidentialism. Rather, it is the president's political retreat when deadlock occurs with parliament that distinguishes this model in the new Europe.

Thus, the executive powers of Bulgaria's presidency dwindled in the mid-1990s at a time when its incumbent came from a different political camp than the country's prime minister. Poland moved towards a parliamentary dominant model following the passage of the 1997 constitution, which weakened the powers of the presidency. When Ion Iliescu regained the presidency in Romania in 2000, the office was very different from the one to which he had been elected in 1990 and 1992. Politically he could no longer exercise the extensive executive powers that he had wielded in his earlier administrations.

The Baltic republics are other examples of hybrid executive systems. Estonia and Latvia have chosen a presidential–parliamentary model while Lithuania appears more semi-presidential. The most dramatic shift from a presidential system to semi-presidentialism occurred in Croatia and Serbia. The end of the Tudjman and Milosevic eras led to the assertion in both countries of the powers of parliament, thereby recasting their political executives along the lines found in Slovenia – the very first state to have broken away from socialist Yugoslavia.

Ukraine and Yugoslav successor states such as Croatia provide the best evidence supporting the thesis that institutional flexibility and experimentation pay off. Efficient and adaptive institutions presuppose a society's willingness to abandon dysfunctional institutional arrangements. As Nobel Prize winning economist Douglass North emphasized, 'It is essential to have rules that eliminate not only failed economic organization but failed political organization as well'. The existence of such rules 'not only rewards successes, but also vetoes the survival of maladapted parts of the organizational structure'. It follows that 'the society that permits the maximum generation of trials will be most likely to solve problems through time' (1992: 81).

In the aftermath of regime change, one of the major dilemmas facing constitutional framers was resolving the tension between the imperatives of democracy and those of efficiency. The choice made directly affected the political executive because a preference for deliberative democracy would favour the legislative branch at the expense of the political executive; priority to the virtues of efficiency, management, and decisiveness would favour the executive branch. In each country, specific historical, economic, and social conditions – for example, an unfortunate interlude with dictatorship – affected the selection of institutional arrangements. To be sure, in a handful of states, particularly former Soviet republics outside the Baltic region, the deck was stacked about equally against both democracy and efficiency. Some leaders seemed to downplay the importance of regime change and preferred more muddling through to any combination of democracy and efficiency. Today, it cannot be said that any country in Central and Eastern Europe is guilty of institutional ossification.

Despite the rhetoric of democracy promotion used by outside actors, and of democratization employed by indigenous parties, no single formula or general law exists about how to constitute the political executive at a time of political transition. What we learn from the evolution of executive power in Central and Eastern Europe is the value of flexibility and experimentation in determining how constitutional authority should be exercised. If most states in the region gravitated, sooner or later, to variations of the French model while shunning the hyper-presidential systems being constructed in the United States and the Russian Federation in the early years of the twenty-first century, it was the result of a kind of institutional Darwinism, of natural selection.

The distribution of both constitutional authority and political power has changed markedly since 1989. We agree with Petr Kopecky that 'there is a trend towards a changing balance of power between executive leadership (and agencies) and their respective legislatures across the region'. But this trend has involved increasing legislative dominance over the political executive – not the converse as the author contends. Kopecky's argument is that 'the partial stabilisation of political parties and party systems, together with the institutional reforms of the core executive and the enlargement of the EU, have eventually led to a marked increase in the control exercised by political executives over parliaments in the region' (2004: 142). Yet, with the exception of Belarus, no all-powerful president or prime minister has emerged in Central and Eastern Europe. Instead, political power has been exer-

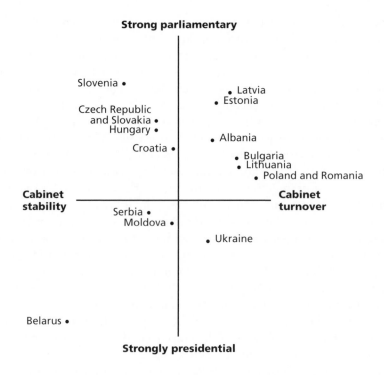

Figure 8.2   *Type of political system of cabinet turnover*

cised largely by prime ministers holding office for short periods of time and kept in check by parties, parliaments, and presidents (see Figure 8.2).

Over time there has been convergence around this structure by the states in the region. The pioneering countries that opened up the debate over institutional arrangements to the greatest number of participants (as at round-table talks) were able to choose from a multiplicity of institutional possibilities. For example, Hungary held a referendum on whether its president should be directly elected. But within a decade of communism's fall, institutional experimentation characterized the entire region. Approaching two decades since communism's collapse, the differences between institutional fast-starters and latecomers had become nearly meaningless. The general pattern discernible in the region about the design of the political executive was that those parts of the structure that were most maladapted, and therefore required elimination, were features of a strong political executive.

Factors shaping the political executive

During the transition years, Central and Eastern European states were faced with conflicting imperatives. On the one hand, they were expected to construct a system of checks and balances that would limit executive power, which had gone unchecked under communism. On the other, the new political systems had to ensure sufficiently strong leadership to govern over politically, and sometimes ethnically, divided societies, over disaffected social groups reeling from shock therapy, and over fragmented party systems. The choice of the structure of executive power has been credited with – and blamed for – many of the major developments that have taken place in the region from the 1990s on: Poland's successful transition to a market economy and Romania's reform failures; Czechoslovakia's velvet divorce and socialist Yugoslavia's violent end; the Baltic states' admission into NATO and the EU and Belarus and Ukraine's struggle to comply with Western rule-setting institutions such as the Council of Europe.

Many factors influenced the choice of model of political executive. Constitutions adopted in the 1990s reflected a backlash against communist authoritarianism and its centralized system of executive power, a new set of expectations about the role of civil society in governance, the different political traditions of the individual states, the individual preferences of actor-agents, and the international normative regime dominant at the time. Let us examine each of these factors.

Backlash against communism and new public expectations

The backlash against authoritarian regimes triggered by the harrowing experience of communism served as the catalyst for putting greater store in representative institutions than in strong rulers. Even accepting the controversial proposition that most Central and Eastern European societies historically had preferred being ruled by strong leaders, the political environment was very different when these societies enacted regime change in 1989 and after. Survey results from the 1990s onwards indicated that respondents increasingly prized a representative form of government over strong leadership. Some societies fully embraced representative democracy in 1989, in others democratic values grew on citizens.

Democracy presupposes that citizens support the institutions that are created and consent to the leaders who emerge. Put another way, 'constitutional forms are lifeless or irrelevant if they do not have the support of the people. That is why even though elites propose, the masses dispose' (Rose *et al.*, 1998: 8). If institutions are the hardware of democracy, what people think about them makes up democracy's software (Agh, 1996: 127). Democratic rule and efficient government are not irreconcilable, for 'The ideal democratic system is representative and has effective leaders. Logically, the two criteria can be mutually reinforcing, in so far as leaders may gain effectiveness by mobilizing popular support, and effective action increases a leader's popular support' (Rose and Mishler, 1996: 224). Of particular importance in designing the architecture of power, then, was setting up safeguards to control the actions of leaders. Otherwise, as one long-time analyst of Soviet politics conjectured, 'we can see the possibility of an authoritarian personality serving as leader in the regime of a constitutional democracy, and, conversely, of a democratic personality serving as the leader in an authoritarian system of rule' (Tucker, 1981: 68).

While public opinion can act as a safeguard against a return to authoritarian practices, it can also be manipulated to serve those in power. On the basis of a case study of Bulgaria, one author concluded that a decade after communism's collapse, 'political elites use opinion polls not to extend political power to citizens, but to concentrate it in their own hands' (Henn, 2001: 67–8). Instead of 'populist government' which pollster George Gallup had thought would result from elites knowing voters' preferences well, Joseph Schumpeter's notion of 'competitive elitism' – under which leaders acquire information about the electorate's views in order to obtain a competitive advantage over adversaries – has become a more common practice (Schumpeter, 1976).

Differing political traditions

Another factor influencing the emergence of executive structures is a country's prior experience with different forms of government. In Central and Eastern Europe the political structures of the inter-war period were particularly important in affecting thinking about new institutional designs. Baltic nations proudly looked back at their inter-war states and sought to build on them. In Czechoslovakia and Poland, advocates of a presidential system held up the examples of towering inter-war state builders such as Tomas Masaryk and Jozef Pilsudski. Yet, if Lech Walesa of Poland self-consciously strove to become a strong president, Czech president Havel was content to serve as moral authority and sometime political broker. In neither country was a presidential system created.

In the case of Hungary, no inter-war leader was dominant for sufficiently long to inspire nostalgia in the 1990s. It is true that the authoritarian inter-war leader Admiral Miklos Horthy was a controversial figure and some political circles, such as those opposed to the direct election of a president, invoked Horthy's name to highlight the dangers of a strong executive. Hungarians on the right, by contrast, supported his rehabilitation. Today, the Hungarian president is indirectly elected and has few powers. The succession of different prime ministers has indicated Hungarians' wariness of a strong executive. Significantly, when the ambitious Viktor Orban set out to redefine the office along the lines of the German chancellor, he was not re-elected to a second term in 2002. A few years later, another assertive prime minister, socialist leader Ferenc Gyurcsany, ran foul of many Hungarians after he admitted with brutal frankness that his party had won re-election by lying about the state of the economy.

The purportedly violent history of the Balkan states has received much comment. Both Bulgaria's and Romania's inter-war experience of illiberal politics and authoritarianism served as a negative model for post-communist state builders. By 1997, both had shaken off the vestiges of communism and, in the case of Bulgaria, had even catapulted the heir to the Bulgarian throne to the post of prime minister. In what used to be socialist Yugoslavia, South Slav nations took advantage of the collapse of communism to escape from a Serb dominated state. To do so Croatia, Macedonia, and Bosnia-Herzegovina initially established strong presidencies. Slovenia was exceptional in that its break from Yugoslavia in 1990 was relatively peaceful and swift and, as a result, it could afford to forego a powerful executive. Ironically, its prime minister, Drnovsek, ended up holding executive power much longer than the autocratic rulers of the other Balkan states.

Actor-agent preferences

The legal experts who write a constitution, together with the political actors in executive and legislative branches who ratify it, are the agents determining what executive power will look like. Their interests count, therefore, especially since 'The decisive step toward democracy is the devolution of power from a group of people to a set of rules' (Przeworski, 1992: 14). Taking this step is hardly a purely technical affair for 'Each political force opts for the institutional framework that will best further its values, projects, or interests' (ibid.: 80). Especially during a political transition, 'the chances of the particular political forces are very different under alternative institutional arrangements' (ibid.: 40).

The types of executive structures that emerged in the 1990s were the products of bidding and bargaining among interested parties – not merely rational outcomes arrived at by disinterested state builders. A few cases are illustrative. Those who favoured a strong presidency (such as Walesa in Poland) were often the politicians who were the strongest candidates for the office. Those who felt comfortable under cabinet government (such as Klaus in the Czech Republic) were usually adept party leaders who performed best in a parliamentary system where their bureaucratic, technical, and brokering skills counted most.

An instructive case of how quality of leadership resulted in different institutional outcomes was in the two constituent parts of the former Czechoslovakia. A study concluded that 'Rather than deep cultural differences between the two countries on the mass level, differences in economic performance, or a previous communist regime of different nature, it is the elite and political competition which function in a different way, and this is what accounts for the different political outcomes' (Kopecky and Mudde, 2000: 77). The Czech political elite united in support of fundamental democratic principles whereas their Slovak counterparts were deeply divided over how to promote national and regime identity. Leaders, their styles, and their personalities affect the character of a political system, then. Especially critical in a transition period is the emergence of 'leaders with the personality formation appropriate to democracy' (Lasswell, 1986: 196).

International norms

The global ascendance of liberal political and economic values in the 1990s was both a product of communism's defeat and a force promoting a normative shift towards democratic reforms. Political transition occurring in a period of unrivalled American power was bound to reflect the preferences of the then dominant state. It is surprising, then, that the American emphasis on individual freedoms and the allure of the US presidential system did not have a greater impact on constitutional framers. Even though individual freedoms could seamlessly be inserted into new constitutions, the powerful executive branch found in the US presidential system could not. The US system was predicated on the existence of federalism, a two-party system that pervaded politics from the national to local levels, and an executive office that was enmeshed in the legislative process. Such institutional arrangements had no real history in the former Soviet bloc.

The result was that constitutional framers looked to the political experience of Western Europe, which offered a more salient and viable model of institutional architecture while still being consistent with the norms of liberalism. A cabinet system of government appeared *de rigeur* in EU member states, which were exemplary in their political stability, social consensus, and prosperity. The Western European experience signified more than a particular kind of political system: it embraced liberal democratic values, free markets, and a transnational ideal of citizenship. Some observers therefore claimed that EU enlargement into Central and Eastern Europe would set off a process of 'executive Europeanization' that would help integrate both parts of Europe (Goetz, 2000).

Apart from institutional design and political values, the leadership culture of Western Europe evoked efforts at imitation by numerous politicians in the new democracies. In the early 1990s, the driven leadership style of British prime minister Margaret Thatcher was fresh in the minds of emerging conservative groups. The plodding but reassuring style of long-serving German chancellor Helmut Kohl, who had presided over unprecedented prosperity and political unification, had an appeal to politicians who lacked charisma but possessed resilience. Another admired German chancellor was Konrad Adenauer, who had consolidated the West German state and helped produce an economic miracle after the Second World War. For politicians with messianic aspirations – and there were many among those who had spearheaded the victory over communism – Charles de Gaulle of France, founder and centrepiece of the Fifth Republic, cut an imposing figure. For more authoritarian minded 'democrats', Spanish dictator Francisco Franco as well as Chilean dictator Augusto Pinochet, both of whom had crushed Marxism and set up virtual one-party states, became role models. The paternalism of US president Ronald Reagan also had widespread appeal in the early transition years. But the initial fascination with Western leaders faded fast as the difficult transition years led to growing disillusionment.

In the early years of transition other leadership styles were much in demand: political brokers and consensus builders, chief executive officers and anti-leaders, charismatic and traditional leaders. Executive leadership in the region could have evolved in ways that transcended institutional designs. Yet, that did not happen and leadership based primarily on charisma had, almost everywhere in the region, to take a back seat to leadership based on executive-legislative cooperation.

The background of Central and Eastern European leaders

Writers, movie directors, child film stars (and identical twins to boot), stunt pilots, electricians, economists, engineers, philosophers, geologists, and communist bureaucrats have served as political executives in Central and Eastern Europe since 1989. While occupationally diverse, they have been predominantly male and somewhat younger than the preceding ruling elite. The majority comes from a privileged *intelligentsia* background; that is, they are well educated, have professional and white-collar occupations, and are economically well off. Elite members have variously used free market, nationalistic, pro-Europe, social democratic, and more recently anti-EU rhetoric to get elected. They have almost never used political violence to stay in power. Most have learned to be expert in the art of coalition building.

An issue that might be regarded as crucial when selecting democratic leaders in Central and Eastern Europe is what these prospective leaders were doing during the communist era. It is surprising to find, then, that even today many leaders are linked to the old communist system:

> In virtually all post-communist countries, including those which have abandoned old political habits, familiar faces from the communist past dominate the landscape . . . Everywhere, individuals who have dropped out of the elite since the fall of communism are outnumbered by those who have maintained or improved their positions, by a ratio of almost nine to one in Russia and over two to one in Poland and Hungary. Until age attrition takes its toll, the best prospects for success under democracy will belong to those who were successful under communism (Liebich, 1997: 68).

Not surprisingly, in an effort to speed the demise of former communist officials, both Poland and Hungary launched vigorous new decommunization programmes around 2005 after the preceding campaigns of a decade earlier had stalled.

The ex-communists (or post-communists) who have attained leadership posts in the young democracies share attributes with post-totalitarian elites. Exemplified by presidents Iliescu of Romania and Milosevic of Yugoslavia, 'post-totalitarian leaders tend to be more bureaucratic and state technocratic than charismatic' (Linz and Stepan, 1996: 47) but owe power to their former communist constituency. By contrast, post-communist leaders such as President Kwasniewski in Poland and Prime Minister Gyula Horn in Hungary came to power after breaking with the communist apparatus. They tapped a broader political constituency to gain political office. As with post-totalitarians, they embraced bureaucratic leadership values but, unlike them, they accepted the rules of the democratic game. For rabid anti-communists, that was not enough to entitle them to participate in holding office.

There have been two sitting presidents in the region who were removed from power by extraordinary means and their association with communism was not the primary reason for their ouster. One was a communist, the other a liberal democrat. The Serb leader of

Yugoslavia in its death throes, Milosevic, refused to accept his electoral defeat in 2000 and resigned only after protesters stormed the parliament building in Belgrade. He was arrested soon thereafter and delivered to the International Criminal Tribunal for Yugoslavia to face charges of war crimes. In contrast, President Roland Paksas of Lithuania became the first leader in all of Europe to be impeached. In 2004, the Constitutional Court found that he had acted improperly in granting Lithuanian citizenship to a Russian arms dealer. Along with charges of a breech of national security, parliament voted to remove him from office. While other executive office holders in the region have had their communist pasts held against them, they have not been forced to resign for that reason alone.

Dissidents from the old communist regime have not been as successful in gaining power as the former communists. Winning elections requires different political skills and resources than winning out over communism. The list of political executives who were formerly communist party members is long, while only a few post-1989 presidents and prime ministers can 'boast' of having been incarcerated by communists. The most prominent were Hungary's first democratically elected prime minister – Jozsef Antall, Havel, and Walesa. It may seem puzzling that relatively few old warriors, hardened by years of struggle against communism, ever held power for very long in the new democratic systems. Some never could get away from their combative, ideological ways but others turned from politics to capitalism. Just as much of the communist nomenklatura sought to enrich itself, so many dissident intellectuals did the same (see Eyal *et al.*, 2000). The *desiderata* for leadership became possessing the right managerial and economic qualifications to govern. Leadership anchored in both Western liberal democratic values and Central and Eastern European culture was particularly well placed to promote the interests of the new democracies.

The rise of a professional political class also took place in the transition years. Many young professionals whose formative experience was of 'goulash communism' in the 1970s, when communists promoted a more Western oriented economic system, came to power after 1989. But regime transition should not be equated with generational change. Some very young politicians enjoyed meteoric careers (such as prime ministers Waldemar Pawlak in Poland and Orban in Hungary) but inter-war politicians such as Tudjman also did. In general, executive power in the formative years of the new democracies was assumed by members of the baby boom generation born, ironically, in the early years of the communist regime.

Regime transition did not bring about greater representation of women in the political executive. If women had been excluded from executive power under communism, they fared only marginally better in the democratic systems. The most notable 'success story' has been that of Vaira Vike-Freiberga of Latvia, who served two terms as president. Women are generally well represented in high office in the Baltic states - as deputy prime ministers, ministers of foreign and European affairs, justice, and even defence (in Latvia). The process of EU enlargement has, perhaps inevitably given EU norms on the issue, empowered women in ways that domestic policy processes have not. Qualities such as being a team player, paying attention to detail, and exhibiting patience – often associated with women more than men – may explain why many women in the region have spearheaded their countries' EU integration drives.

Women remain underrepresented in executive power, however, and an optimistic interpretation for this is that they prefer to 'express their presence and political will in ways that are different from those of men – or of their sisters in long-established Western democracies' (Szalai, 1998: 200). Not everyone would agree that women's absence from executive office holding is primarily the product of women's choice.

In the Baltic republics, but elsewhere too, a successful professional career in the West was an asset in seeking high office. Returning émigrés were appointed as presidents (Latvia's Vike-Freiburga had lived most of her life in Montreal), prime ministers (Simeon, the claimant to Bulgaria's throne who changed his name to Simeon Borisov Sakskoburggotski when he served as prime minister from 2001 to 2005, had lived in exile in Madrid), and defence, foreign, and finance ministers. It was said of one Polish government minister, Radek Sikorski – son of a prominent Second World War general – that he lived abroad except when he was serving as defence minister. Some émigrés were more nationalistic than native politicians (such as in Croatia and Slovakia) and supported right-wing causes, but this pattern faded two decades into the post-communist era.

Ministerial structures and the political executive

The real work of implementing executive decisions is carried out by bureaucracies; the operational appendages of the executive branch. In both democratic and undemocratic states the political executive appoints people who they expect will carry out policies consistent with their views as well as with laws that have been enacted. Public administration is therefore hierarchical in nature with the political executive at the top and various layers of civil servants below. Bureaucracies are supposed to be rule-bound, impersonal, and specialized, characterized by a division of labour, established routine, professionalism, and merit. But another way that bureaucracies have been staffed is through political patronage, nepotism, and social networks where merit is not a criterion.

In reforming the civil service, post-communist Europe confronted another dichotomy. Should communist era bureaucrats – especially high-level ones – be allowed to keep their jobs or should they be replaced as part of a policy of decommunization? Two extreme cases illustrate the dilemma.

The first post-communist government in Bulgaria was headed by Andrei Lukanov, himself a former communist, who served as prime minister in 1989–90. He quickly became aware that his leadership prospects were linked with those of high-ranking bureaucrats. 'There was a natural coalition between remaining old administrative cadres and politicians from the renamed Communist Party, based on political loyalty and the need for both politicians and civil servants to "survive" under the new conditions' (Verheijen, 1999: 96). Not surprisingly, Bulgaria was very slow to enact civil service reform.

On the other hand, the most sweeping purge of communist era civil servants was probably that undertaken in Slovakia in 1994 by the newly elected nationalist government of Vladimir Meciar. The first day of parliament was devoted almost exclusively to the dismissal of high-ranking civil servants and the appointment in their stead of political cronies. In addition, Slovakia – and Poland, too – expanded the size of their state bureaucracies. In contrast to the autonomy and stability of the Czech civil service, 'In a process of runaway state-building, these states grew without becoming more professional, effective, or autonomous' (O'Dwyer, 2006: 99).

About three years after Meciar's patronage excesses, as one of its criteria for membership the EU began to insist on 'administrative conditionality' – that is, the requirement that Central and Cast European states carry out civil service reform. As they entered into negotiations about EU membership, most of these states quickly adopted civil service legislation, even though rule adoption differed from one country to another (Dimitrova, 2005: 85).

The temptation to stack the higher echelons of state administration with fellow travellers and cronies did not go away, however. A study of Hungary that seems representative of much of the region concluded that even after repeated attempts at reform, 'governing parties have a deep reach into the ministries in that they can potentially exercise political control over the staffing of the entire ministerial civil service' (Meyer-Sahling, 2006: 294). Polarization of politics between the ex-communist camp and the anti-communist bloc has allowed party

patronage and politicization of the ministerial bureaucracy to continue
– notwithstanding the EU *acquis*. Thus 'governments of neither the left
nor the right can be assumed to have an incentive to offer major
support to the depoliticisation of the civil service' (Meyer-Sahling,
2004: 98). For its part, 'the senior bureaucracy has come to be dominated by officials whose tenure is bound to that of alternating government and whose career interest in commuting between public
administration, politics and the private sector contradicts efforts to
depoliticise post-communist civil services' (ibid.).

The stubbornness with which the region's political executives have
clung to patronage as a way of staffing senior civil service posts may be
familiar to citizens living in older democracies. Eurocrats themselves
are often the products of partisan politics, after all. A reassuring aspect
of changes in Central and East European state administration is that
the process of professionalization does not seem to have been derailed
by the persistence of patronage appointments.

Conclusion

In the early transition years, Central and Eastern European leaders did
not stay in office for long periods of time. A short election cycle characteristic of the early 1990s led to considerable executive turnover.
Since the mid-1990s, following greater political and institutional consolidation, elections have more often stuck to a four- or five-year cycle,
thereby producing less turnover of executive leadership. Getting re-
elected is still a skill that few leaders in the region have acquired but,
then, so is winning a majority in parliament in two successive elections
in Western Europe.

Holding executives accountable to representative institutions while
giving them the space to provide strong leadership is the perpetual bal-
ancing act of governance. Our analysis suggests that Central and East
European states have now reached a functional equilibrium. The skilful
construction of executive power has a lot to do with this achievement.

Chapter 9

Structures of Representation

Petr Kopecký

Parliaments – or legislatures – are core state institutions of modern democracy. Parliaments provide the forum for interaction of intermediary agencies: the parties, interest groups, or social movements that link them to society. Parliaments also link society with other democratic institutions, the executive, judiciary or state bureaucracy. In that sense, parliaments are the key structure of representation, encompassing a wide range of institutions, rules and procedures, as well as political organizations. They can thus be viewed as a focal point around which any crucial questions of political style, legitimacy and democratic accountability revolve. In addition, parliaments are multifunctional. They of course legislate: that is, they make laws. However, parliaments also socialize and train political elites, integrate diverse social strata and nationalities in one state, oversee national administration, and help to articulate societal interests.

Many studies of (West) European politics and government have for a long time advocated a thesis of parliaments in decline. Parliaments came to be seen no longer as supreme legislative and representational institutions but instead became stigmatized as rubber-stamping bodies, dominated by executives, bureaucracies and strong political parties (see Norton, 1990). The parliaments in non-democratic communist Eastern Europe fitted this pattern. Although none of the Eastern European countries abandoned parliament during the communist period, they were so subordinated to the Communist Party apparatus that their law-affecting activities and oversight functions were minimal, at least until the 1980s, when communist leaders began to lose their grip on their respective societies (see Nelson and White, 1982).

The wave of political change that swept across Eastern Europe in the early 1990s has therefore presented parliaments with a new opportunity to reassert themselves as important platforms in the political life of the newly emerging democracies in the region. They were almost overnight propelled from institutions with very limited autonomy in decision making to bodies that had initially become something of a linchpin of transition to democracy, in the eyes of political elites and publics alike. However, as this chapter shows, as with all other institutions in Eastern Europe, the parliaments too experienced numerous problems typical for new institutions. They lacked institutional resources, infrastructures and experienced members, which constrained their capacity to act. Moreover, the political context in which these parliaments operate has gradually changed as well. Indeed, as this chapter will also show, with the reassertion and development of both political parties and executives since the second half of the 1990s, the parliaments' centrality in political life may have waned further still despite a considerable stabilization of their internal life and procedures.

Institutional origins and profile of parliaments

Table 9.1 presents a basic profile of parliaments in Central and Eastern Europe. We can see, first, that the majority of legislatures are unicameral – a trend apparent in new democracies worldwide (see Woldendorp *et al.*, 2000). Second, or upper, chambers everywhere are usually established to represent territorial and/or functional interests. The representation of territorial interests is clearly the case of the second chamber in Bosnia-Herzegovina. It also includes the Polish Senate, which has been established to represent the country's various territorial-administrative units. An example of representation of functional interests is the corporatist second chamber in Slovenia (the National Council), to which councillors are (s)elected to represent economic, local, trading and other professional interests.

However, the second chambers are, in addition to their specific representational tasks, also established to provide a system of checks and balances, and to ensure horizontal accountability among the institutions of the state. This idea has strongly influenced the creation of upper houses in both the Czech Republic and Romania. Yet, it is only in Romania where the upper house – the Senate – exercises legislative powers that are on a par with those of the lower house – the Chamber of Deputies. In the Czech Republic, as well as in Slovenia and Poland, the second chambers have some legislative and appointive powers, but can mainly delay or suspend policies and legislation, rather than block them, or even propose them. In all these countries, we therefore talk about weak bicameralism.

The size of legislatures varies greatly across the region. Upper chambers are smaller than lower houses in all countries with bicameral parliaments, which is usual for legislatures in established democracies as

Table 9.1 A profile of Central and East European parliaments

Region and country	Chamber Structure	Election years (all elections)	Chamber names	Size	Term
Central Europe					
Czech Republic	Unicameral	1990 and 1992,	Czech National Council	200	2 (4)
	Bicameral	1996, 1998 and 2002, 2004 and 2006	Chamber of Deputies	200	4
			Senate	81	6
Hungary	Unicameral	1990, 1994, 1998, 2002 and 2006	National Assembly	386	4
Poland	Bicameral	1989, 1991, 1993	Sejm	460	4
		1997, 2001 and 2005	Senate	100	4
Slovak Republic	Unicameral	1990 and 1992	Slovak National Council	150	2 (4)
		1994, 19998, 2002 and 2006	National Council	150	4
Baltic States					
Estonia	Unicameral	1990	Supreme Council	105	4
	Unicameral	1992, 1995, 1999 and 2003	Parliament of Estonia	101	4
Latvia	Unicameral	1990	Supreme Council	201	4
	Unicameral	1993, 1995, 1998, 2002 and 2006	Saeima	100	4
Lithuania	Unicameral	1990	Supreme Council	141	2
	Unicameral	1992, 1996, 2000 and 2004	Seimas	141	4
Balkans					
Albania	Unicameral	1991	People's Assembly	250	4
	Unicameral	1992, 1996, 1997, 2001 and 2005	People's Assembly	140	4
Bosnia-Herzegovina	Bicameral	2000	House of Representatives	42	2
			House of Peoples	15	2
	Bicameral	2002, 2006	House of Representatives	42	4
			House of Peoples	15	4
Bulgaria	Unicameral	1990	Grand National Assembly	400	4
	Unicameral	1991, 1994, 1997, 2001 and 2005	National Assembly	240	4
Croatia	Bicameral	1992, 1993, 1995 and 1997	House of Representatives	138	4
			House of Municipalities	63	4
		2000, 2003	House of Representatives	152	4
Macedonia	Unicameral	1998, 2002 and 2006	Assembly of the Republic	120	4
Romania	Bicameral	1990	Chamber of Deputies	385	4
			Senate	119	4
	Bicameral	1992, 1996, 2000, and 2004	Chamber of Deputies	345	4
			Senate	140	4
Slovenia	Bicameral	1992, 1996, 1997	National Assembly	90	4
		2000, 2001 and 2004	National Council	40	5
Montenegro	Unicameral	2002	Assembly	75	4
Serbia	Unicameral	2003	National Assembly	250	4
Former USSR					
Ukraine	Unicameral	1994, 1998, 2002 and 2006	Verkhovna Rada	450	4
Moldova	Unicameral	1994, 1998, 2001 and 2005	Parliament	101	4

Sources: Olson (1998); Inter-Parliamentary Union (www.ipu.org).

well. The size of lower chambers ranges from 42 MPs in the House of Representatives in Bosnia-Herzegovina to a rather mighty 460 MPs in the Polish *Sejm*. Larger countries (Poland, Ukraine, Romania) have, not surprisingly, larger lower houses than the small or medium-size countries, such as is the majority in the region of Central and Eastern Europe.

Table 9.1 also shows that the parliamentary term is almost uniformly four years. This is especially the case for all lower chambers. Upper chambers are sometimes constituted differently from the lower houses. This can be seen, first, in electoral formulas, which differ between the two houses in the cases of, for example, the Czech Republic and Slovenia. The members of the lower house in the Czech Republic are elected by a PR electoral system based on party lists, while the senators contest elections in single-member districts; in Slovenia, the members of the National Assembly are elected by a PR system in multi-member districts, while the members of the National Council are indirectly elected by an electoral college. But it can also be seen, second, in the length of upper second chamber terms. For example, the National Council in Slovenia is elected for five years, in contrast to the National Assembly's four-year term. The Czech Senate is elected for a period of six years, in contrast to the Chamber of Deputies' four-year term; moreover, a third of the places in the Senate are the subject of electoral contest every second year.

Two further observations can be made on the basis of Table 9.1, concerning changes in the names of parliamentary chambers and, in many cases, initially shorter legislative terms of the entire parliaments. Both relate to the institutional origins of Central and Eastern European legislatures. The post-communist parliaments have not been built from scratch, but rather originated in the old communist legislatures. This explains changes in the names of various chambers in the early 1990s, as the new MPs and political elites tried to disassociate legislatures from their communist past. Thus, for example, the Grand National Assembly in Bulgaria became the National Assembly. In addition, countries such as the Czech Republic and Slovakia, as well as the Baltic states, which all emerged as new independent states after the breakdown of communist federal systems, elevated previously provincial level parliaments to the status of sovereign and supreme legislative bodies. There, too, renaming of legislatures was part and parcel of the creation of a new constitutional framework.

The short term of the first democratically elected parliaments relates to the major task these bodies faced after the demise of the communist regimes – writing and ratifying new constitutions. As we can see in Table 9.1, the first freely elected Czech and Slovak legislatures had their term deliberately shortened to a period of two years, in which they were supposed to draft a new constitution, which would then be followed by elections under a newly designed constitutional order. This was the case also in many other states, such as Estonia, Lithuania or Romania, where parliaments dissolved before serving a full term, after they had ratified new constitutions. In Romania, for example, the first free elections took place in 1990. The new constitution was agreed upon and ratified (by referendum) in December 1991. The constitution stipulated that both presidential and parliamentary elections had to take place a year after the ratification of the basic law and, indeed, the president and parliament were elected in the second free elections in 1992.

The shorter terms of first post-communist parliaments can, there-fore, be explained by the fact that they were endowed with the impor-tant task of drafting and agreeing new constitutions. It should be noted here that this has had major consequences for the institutional struc-ture in Central and East Europe in general, and the position of parlia-ments in particular. Since parliaments were the prime constitution makers, rather extraordinary powers have been vested in the legisla-tures, at least in comparison with the position of parliaments in West European countries that changed their constitutions, such as France in 1958 or Spain in 1978. Moreover, communist constitutions had usually endowed parliaments with sovereign powers, even if this was on paper rather than in reality. The strong constitutional position of parliaments thus happened to be the starting point of all negotiations on new constitutions in the early 1990s. This strong constitutional position was very unlikely to be removed, given that the same parlia-ments also became constituent assemblies.

Parliaments and representation

Parliaments are, perhaps above all, symbols of representation. They are sometimes deliberately set up to reflect socio-cultural diversity in society. Indeed, the communist legislatures deliberately aimed to ensure the equal representation of women, peasants, workers, and national minorities. In a liberal democracy, citizens elect their representatives to parliament, and these representatives, accountable to citizens through the electoral process, then hold the government to account. In most European democracies, such representation operates through political parties, which select and campaign for lists of representatives that sit on the parliamentary benches. However, links between parliaments and the electorate are also provided, especially between elections, by constituency representation, whereby individual MPs may choose to promote the interests of certain geographical areas, sectors of society or even individual constituents. The particular form in which models and modes of representation develop in any political system of course depends on many informal practices. Moreover, it also depends on a range of formal political institutions, most importantly the electoral system and the nature of political parties and party systems.

Parties and elections

Today, multi-party elections and multi-party systems are the norm across the Central and East European region. However, organized political parties have emerged relatively slowly and, indeed, parties were not the most prominent actors in the early years of democratization (see Chapter 11). Partly because of strong anti-party sentiments among the population and new political leaders alike, and partly because of the particularly oppressive nature of the communist regimes, the early transition period was dominated by broadly based anti-communist movements and umbrella organizations such as the Civic Forum and Public Against Violence in the former Czechoslovakia, the National Salvation Front in Romania, Sajudis in Lithuania and Demos in Slovenia. With a few exceptions, such as in Bulgaria, these movements also won the first freely contested parliamentary elections

Parties began to emerge only as these broad movements started to disintegrate in parliament during their first term in office. In that sense, parliaments performed one very important function in the early stages of post-communist politics: they became the arenas in which new political alliances were forged and new political parties were established. Given that most of the newly established parties were formed from above and consequently lacked links with wider society, their survival would have been unimaginable without the institutional, logistical and often also financial support that was provided to them by parliaments. In addition, parliaments provided the institutional framework within which the former communist parties were able to redefine and reconstitute themselves, allowing them to make spectacular comebacks to political prominence in many countries of the region, including Hungary, Poland or Albania.

However, the rapid and somewhat disorderly process of party formation also had negative consequences for the links between parliaments and the electorate. Many political parties disappeared during the parliamentary term and other parties were formed instead. For example, as against the initial eight parliamentary parties in the Federal Assembly in the former Czechoslovak federal parliament in 1990, MPs were organized in no fewer than 16 parliamentary parties at the end of 1991. In Slovakia, the 18 parties that registered for elections in 1994 in fact represented 31 parties and movements. In addition, electoral systems have often been changed in the region, most notably with respect to legal thresholds to enter parliament (see Shvetsova, 1999). For example, Latvia, Lithuania, Moldova, and Poland have all increased such barriers in order to reduce the number of parties in parliament. Slovakia has also manipulated the size of its electoral districts, actually making the whole country one electoral district. Together with the generally high organizational fragmentation of individual political parties, the frequent tinkering with electoral rules had one major effect: it made it difficult to establish stable and predictable patterns of representation or, to put it differently, clear and transparent links between the members of parliament and the electorate.

This all said, certain patterns are now emerging across the region, mainly in reaction to the relative stabilization of parties and party systems in some countries. Party system stabilization is still highly differentiated across the region (see Lewis, 2000). But it has progressed where democracy has become more firmly established and advanced beyond its rudimentary electoral phase, like in some of the Central European or Baltic states, as well as in Slovenia. There, political parties generally provide a key anchor for parliamentarians, not least because MPs now owe their career to political parties rather than to their own individual qualities and personalities. Electors too vote primarily for political parties, rather than for persons. Parties are thus the key agencies of representation, similarly to most countries in Western Europe. Research also suggests that some forms of constituency representation is a part of MPs' working routines in, for example, Slovakia (Malova and Sivakova, 1996) and Poland (van der Meer Krok-Paszkowska, 2000).

Members

Not surprisingly, a large number of deputies in first post-communist parliaments of Eastern Europe were drawn from the ranks of opposition movements. These movements themselves were largely composed of intellectual elites, independent professionals and artists, who constituted the backbone of anti-communist dissent. As a consequence, the early parliaments gained significant legitimacy in the eyes of the population, as former dissidents replaced the communist-era deputies and party officials. However, the gains in terms of democratic legitimacy were offset by the inexperience of these new members in operating in a large-scale organization. Moreover, former dissidents were elected alongside a sizeable group of prominent actors and musicians, which boosted the electoral lists of newly formed, and thus largely unknown, parties to lend them extra visibility and popularity. Although dissidents and artists often displayed considerable rhetorical talent in parliamentary debates, their organizational skills and loyalties to organizations such as parliamentary parties or parliamentary committees were much less impressive. Ironically, it was the deputies of the (ex)communist parties that often turned out to be more effective parliamentarians, since they had learned the necessary skills of negotiation, deal making and constituency representation under the previous regime.

Partly because of this pattern of membership of the first democratic parliaments in Eastern Europe, the turnover of MPs has been high in comparative terms: put simply, members of each successive parliament in the region are largely different persons, which undermines deputies' long-term specialization, and legislative continuity and stability. Many of the former dissidents, as well as the majority of expressive artists, did not conceive of their position as deputies as a life-long career and, consequently, did not seek re-election. Moreover, the organizational instability of political parties as well as a relatively high level of electoral volatility has meant that incumbency rates among East European parliamentarians remain relatively low, though perhaps not as low as in the early years of post-communist transformation.

The quotas for representation of various sectors of society are largely missing in the new parliaments of the region. There are several exceptions, such as Poland, Hungary and Romania, which introduced measures either to guarantee or to encourage representation of their respective ethnic minority groups (see Juberias, 1998). However, the representation of women has suffered in comparison with the communist period, even though the number of women deputies is not uniformly low across the East European countries if compared with the European average. As of June 2006, European countries, including the Nordic states, had an average of 19.2 per cent of women MPs in (both houses of) parliament (see www.ipu.org). In Eastern Europe, this number was, in the same period, exceeded by, for example, Bulgaria and Lithuania (both 22 per cent), Moldova (21.8 per cent), Croatia (21.7 per cent), Latvia (21 per cent) and Poland (20.4 per cent). Considering that Estonia (18.8 per cent) nearly matched the European average, it appears that all the Baltic states, with their close proximity to the Nordic European countries, do especially well on representation of women in the regional context. However, both Albania (7.1 per cent) and Ukraine (7.1 per cent) are well below the European average, as are Hungary (10.4 per cent) and Romania (11.2 per cent).

This having been said, the position of individual members of East European parliaments is increasingly affected by a general tendency

towards political professionalism. A move towards the creation of professional deputies and politicians has been promoted in the region by
significant increases in deputies' salaries, travel and accommodation
allowances, and general improvements in MPs' working conditions;
for instance, the construction of new parliamentary buildings. Croatia
is a good example of such dramatic developments, as the professional
full-time status for MPs, including full salaries, was introduced in
1992, shortly before the election to the second post-communist parliament. Until then, the deputies were entitled only to per diem payments
and other small compensations of costs.

This all means that being a deputy is now a lucrative job, especially
if we consider that parliamentary careers are often a stepping-stone for
even more lucrative careers in the higher echelons of both political life
and the public service. This has gradually increased the dependence of
parliamentarians on their party organizations, and also makes them
less likely to defect from the party, or even to vote against it. In addition, professionalism also empowers parliamentarians in the region to
perform their representative duties on a more consistent and enduring
basis. It thus improves conditions for serving both the non-geograph-
ical interests of various social, religious, professional, and sectoral
organizations, and the territorial interests of MPs' constituencies.

Executive–legislative relations

The relationship between parliaments, on the one hand, and the government and the president, on the other hand, are extremely important
in any democracy, let alone a new one. At the same time, these relationships are complex, depending on a range of formal and informal
practices. The constitutional prerogatives vested in legislatures and the
executives are, of course, most important because they define the
broad framework for interactions between the two powers. However,
numerous informal rules and conventions, such as the customs concerning the nomination of prime ministers following the election, are
equally important, especially given that formal documents such as constitutions cannot provide for every conceivable political situation.
Indeed, the lack of established customs and informal norms has
arguably been behind many conflicts between regions' prime ministers
and presidents (see Baylis, 1996, 2007).

Formally, the parliamentary system of government, with a weak
formal position of presidents (heads of state) and government's dependence on legislative confidence, is the dominant model of
executive–legislative relations in the region. Romania is an exception,

in that the country adopted a semi-presidential system of government, in which the head of state possesses significant powers vis-à-vis both the government and the parliament. Several states in the region, such as Poland, Croatia and Ukraine, had initially also chosen a semi-presidential system, modelled on the French Fifth Republic, but eventually adopted constitutional reforms (Poland in 1997, Croatia in 2000, and Ukraine in 2004) that also provide for a parliamentary system of government.

The new parliaments of Central and Eastern Europe enjoyed significant advantages over their respective governments in the early years of transition. This made legislatures appear stronger and more powerful in the matrix of executive–legislative relations than the same bodies in the established parliamentary democracies of Western Europe. First, the parties that formed governing coalitions in the region were seldom able to achieve or impose party loyalty among their MPs, making government support in parliament highly volatile. In addition, because of the high degree of political polarization, coalition partners often quarrelled among each other, sometimes to the extent that part of the government voted with the opposition in parliament. This did not necessarily lead to governmental instability, as in the Czech Republic (up to 1996) or Hungary, but this was only because parties in the opposition suffered even greater divisions than the parties of the government. However, in countries such as Estonia, Latvia, Poland, and Albania, governments lasted on average less than one year, a figure well below the European average of 1.9 years (see Blondel and Müller-Rommel, 2001).

Second, frequent conflicts between governments (prime ministers) and presidents undermined executive cohesion. The highly charged relationship between President Lech Walesa and several of the Polish governments between 1990 and 1995 are good examples (see van der Meer Krok-Paskowska, 2000). Arguably, these conflicts led the Polish political elite to return to the drawing board and change the so-called Little Constitution in a manner substantially curbing the powers of the president. Disagreements over political issues, personnel questions and executive powers had also been behind destabilizing conflicts between presidents Zhelev, Iliescu and Goncz and prime ministers Dimitrov, Roman and Antall in, respectively, Bulgaria, Romania and Hungary in the first half of the 1990s. The conflicts between the former president, Kovac, and the former prime minister, Meciar, in Slovakia between 1994 and 1998 led not only to a change of constitutional framework, but also to the implication of government in the kidnapping of the president's son (see Kopecky, 2001). Parliaments were, of course, the main beneficiary of these conflicts, because in the absence of cohesive executive leadership they were less vulnerable to ceding powers to either presidents or governments.

Third, state institutions in general, and bureaucratic structures in particular, were in a state of disarray, hardly able to provide the executives with sufficient support to draft and implement policies. Unfortunately, parliaments in general, and individual MPs in particular, were not endowed with administrative resources any greater than those of the executive (see Olson, 1997). This meant that not only were the governments initially unable to create and maintain the executive dominance typical of established democracies of Western Europe, but also that the overall quality of legislation has been poor, as exemplified by frequent amendments and changes of existing laws typical for the legislative process in the region. Nevertheless, the position of governments has gradually strengthened throughout the region, to the extent that the balance of power between the executives and legislatures has increasingly been tipped in favour of the former. There are several elements involved here.

First, parties and party systems in some countries have stabilized somewhat in comparison with the early years of transition. This has enabled political leaders to organize the relationship between the executive and legislative branches much better and to impose a degree of party discipline and cohesion.

Second, both parliaments and governments in the region have undergone a series of institutional reforms that have led to the creation of a core executive, which is centred on the head of government (or the president, in semi-presidential systems). This institutional reconfiguration has gradually enabled the executive to gain and consolidate its position around a set of powerful institutions, most notably council of ministers and finance ministers, but also including numerous advisory bodies, policy devising and implementing agencies and support staff units. As a result, the institutional and human resources at the disposal of the executive now often far outweigh similar resources in the hands of legislatures.

Finally, the position of governments in the region has been significantly strengthened in relation to parliaments by the introduction of fast track legislative procedures. These procedures were originally adopted in many countries in the region during the EU accession negotiations as a way of coping with the conditions specified by the European Commission, but often stayed in place even after many of the countries joined the EU in 2004 and 2007. The adoption of EU laws, contained in the so-called *acquis communautaire*, was a precondition of joining the club. The absorption of such a vast amount of laws would, of course, have been unimaginable if normal legislative procedures, notably those inherited from the past, were used.

Therefore, countries in the region aspiring to EU membership have amended their rules of procedure and treated EU related laws as a legislative priority (for example in Bulgaria), or even used extraordinary parliamentary sessions to speed up the adoption of laws (as in Slovenia). Consequently, the capacity of parliaments to challenge the legislation emanating from the executive has been reduced since, for example, the parliaments have been granted far less time for deliberation and legislative scrutiny.

Internal structures and procedures

The parliamentary standing orders represent for the parliament what the constitution represents for the political system as a whole. They are the basic rules regulating the internal functioning of parliaments. As with many constitutions in the region, the standing orders of new Central and Eastern European parliaments were inherited from the communist legislatures of the previous era. They provided some basic rules to regulate political conflicts and to offer rudimentary internal organization, but because they both lacked legitimacy and were designed for a different political system, the standing orders were subject to even more frequent changes than the constitutions. The capacity of parliaments to organize themselves and to react to policy demands placed upon them was thus limited, at least in the immediate aftermath of the collapse of communist rule.

Parliamentary committees

Specialized parliamentary committees, consisting of a small group of deputies, are in general critical to the deliberative powers of parliaments. Parliamentary committees also condition effective parliamentary influence in policy making because they enable parliamentarians to develop a degree of specialization in specific policy areas and to acquire the necessary information to challenge the government. Parliaments in the region have all developed such system of committees, though their precise numbers and internal structures vary considerably between the countries. However, since most communist era legislatures had some type of committee system, the internal organization of parliaments was, in this particular aspect, generally less problematic than the organization and functioning of parliamentary parties (see below), or the organization of parliamentary support staff.

In common with practice in continental European countries, there has been attempt in the region to establish a system of permanent legislative committees whereby their structure parallels the structure of the ministries, with the aim of ensuring the supervisory and controlling power of the parliament over the executive. However, parliaments in the region have also offered some innovation in institutional design; for example, by establishing legislative committees. These committees, variously named in different legislatures, were charged with the responsibility of ensuring the legal compatibility of laws with the constitution, and co-ordinating the work of different committees. They considered all bills, and thus acquired the status of very powerful and prestigious committees. Their existence is a direct result of the complexity of the legislative process in new post-communist democracies and, most importantly, of the sheer amount of legislation that the parliaments in the region have had to process within a short period. The Macedonian parliament, for instance, held 123 sessions between 1991 and the first half of 1996, during which it dealt with 1,820 topics on the agenda and adopted 1,133 laws! (Mircev and Spirovski, 1998).

The volume of bills that has gone through Central and East European parliaments since the fall of communism partly explains why committees did not quite develop a strong position from which to challenge their respective governments. Indeed, the committees in the region initially enjoyed a relatively powerful position, free of much of the external control experienced by the committees of West European parliaments. Again, this was mainly because political parties were unable to control their own members on committees. As a result, committees frequently introduced important amendments to government legislation, even though they were also obviously limited by a shortage of time for deliberation, and the pressure from governments that they consider the bills urgently.

Committee membership in the region also usually reflects the party composition of parliament, in that both members of committees, as well as the committee chair positions, are distributed among parties according to their share of seats. Committees thus can hardly renounce their party political character and, as parties themselves began to reassert themselves over individual MPs, the conflicts correspondingly began to be structured between party lines rather than across them. In addition, some countries have seen attempts to curtail the power of committees by changes in their institutional status. In the Czech Republic, for example, committees now consider bills only in their 'second reading', after the broad principles have been agreed upon in a 'first reading' on the floor of the parliament. This still leaves committees with considerable scope to amend the details of the bill, but it is certainly more difficult to do so than when committees were considering bills before they reached the floor debate.

Parliamentary parties

Parliamentary parties, or parliamentary party groups, in the parliaments of the established democracies of Western Europe are the key means by which the parliamentarians organise themselves to manage the collective affairs of the legislature (for example, Heidar and Koole, 2000). This has not always been the case in Central and Eastern Europe. Parliamentary parties have frequently changed in composition: several members either defected to another parliamentary group, or became independent. The parties themselves often fractured into several sub-groupings or disappeared altogether, and party leaders struggled to enforce a party line on their parliamentary party colleagues (see Gillespie *et al.*, 1995; Karasimeonov, 1996; Kask, 1996; Malova and Krause, 2000). Cases of individual MPs introducing their own legislation, often against the wishes of their own party or the government coalition they represented, were thus also more common than in more established parliaments. Parliamentary party groups acted more like 'clubs' of individual deputies, who met each other to discuss issues and make decisions, but were often unable to agree upon common action (Agh, 1994; Remington, 1994; Longley and Zajc, 1998).

However, as with many other areas of parliamentary life in the region, there have been important developments in these respects over recent years, at least in some countries. First, the number of parties that actually enter the parliament has been decreasing, as a result of both the effect of (many times) increased thresholds to enter parliament, as well as a stabilization of voting behaviour at the mass level. The internal organization of parliament has thus gradually become more stabilized. Second, the institutional context in which parliamentary parties operate has firmed up, so that it is now increasingly more difficult for individual deputies to defect from their party and/or to set up wholly new parties. In Hungary, for example, the number of MPs needed to form a parliamentary party, and thus to receive a financial subsidy and other forms of support from the parliamentary budget, has been increased from ten to 15 (Ilonszki, 2000). Similar measures have been introduced in the Czech Republic where, in addition, parliamentary parties that are formed anew during the legislative term do not receive financial subsidies (Kopecky, 2001).

It is perhaps no coincidence that it is Hungary and the Czech Republic that show the greatest stabilization of the internal workings of parliament and where, for example, only a few deputies leave their parliamentary party groups after the election (Millard, 2004). It is also in these two countries, and in Estonia and Slovenia, that largely the same parties continue to survive over several successive elections

(Lewis, 2006). There, the pattern of flux and instability typical of the first democratic parliaments has gradually changed towards a pattern characterized by the emergence of distinct parliamentary cultures, settled institutional structures, and parliamentary routines.

However, more restrictive institutional rules have not produced similar results elsewhere. In the Polish *Sejm* – the parliament that had perhaps the most notorious fragmentation of parliamentary parties – the minimum number of MPs for the formation of a parliamentary party (*klub*) has also been increased, from the previous three to 15 deputies. It was also in Poland, during the second legislative term, that several MPs from all but one parliamentary party were expelled; for example, for breaking voting discipline (van der Meer Krok-Paszkowska, 2000). Yet, the Polish *Sejm* elected in 2001 had the same high levels of parliamentary party fragmentation as its predecessors (Lewis, 2006), while the 2005 elections brought in a number of entirely new parties.

Conclusion

The post-communist parliaments in the early years of transition experienced a paradox between high opportunity and low capacity (Olson, 1998). Compared with the legislatures of established democracies, they were significantly less under the external control of established political parties and powerful interest groups, or the dominance of strong executives. At the same time, they were constrained in their action by their own unsettled internal procedures, the presence of inexperienced members, and the fragmented nature of parliamentary parties. In addition, all parliaments in the region had to function initially under a provisional or highly disputed constitutional framework.

The parliaments of the second post-communist decade are somewhat different. Their capacity to act has significantly improved as the process of institutionalization has progressed. Their internal structures and procedures are now more defined and settled. Legislative tasks are increasingly performed as routines. A system of parliamentary committees is in place. Large groups of MPs have now served for one or more parliamentary terms. This, together with generally improved conditions for deputies' work, has enhanced stability and continuity in the legislative process. Parliamentary parties too have become a more accepted means by which parliament in general, and individual MPs in particular, can organize the functioning of the legislature. Although changes of institutional structures still occur, major constitutional conflicts seem to have been resolved in the region.

However, the increased institutional capacity of parliaments should be seen in a changed external context in which legislative bodies now function, most notably in the context of increasingly powerful governments and better organized political parties. Both the institutional reforms of core executives, as well as the EU enlargement process, have also reduced parliaments' independent input into the policy-making process. This does not mean that parliaments are completely impotent in contemporary post-communist Europe. And it certainly does not imply that these institutional developments have taken place uniformly. Rather, it means that parliaments throughout the region have begun more closely to resemble their sister institutions in established democracies, both in terms of their internal organization and procedures as well as in terms of the external constraints that are normally placed upon such institutions in a modern democracy.

Chapter 10

Electoral Systems

Sarah Birch

Elections are widely recognized as the keystone of representative democracy, and electoral systems are a central feature of the institutional set-up of any democratic polity. Not only do electoral systems channel popular preferences, they also play an important role in shaping political party development and in structuring the style of politics in a country. Furthermore, comparative research has shown that electoral systems are one of the most important factors influencing the composition of governments. These general findings are highly relevant to the Central and Eastern European context.

Electoral system design has played an important role in Central and Eastern European politics since the transitions from communism in the late 1980s and early 1990s. Elections have been the terrain on which many of the most significant debates in the region have played themselves out, and the rules of the electoral game have been intimately associated with deliberations over the nature and role of political institutions in the post-communist setting. There has thus been considerable diversity in the choices made in the region's various states, as well as in the effects of these choices. There have nevertheless been a number of common trends in post-communist electoral institution design that stem from the specific features of the communist system and perceptions about what needed to be done to dismantle it. The aim of this chapter is to provide an overview of the causes and consequences of electoral system design in post-communist Europe, and to assess the main features of the electoral systems in the region.

The overall story of recent electoral system development in Central and Eastern Europe has been initial reform (mostly in the direction of proportional representation), followed by relative stability in overall electoral system architecture, but considerable tinkering with the details of the system. There are notable exceptions to this general rule – states such as Ukraine and Macedonia have already experienced three different electoral system types over the post-communist period – but Central and Eastern Europe has, on the whole, been free of the frequent radical overhauls of electoral institutions that some had predicted in the early stages of the transition.

Before proceeding to more detailed analysis of electoral systems in post-communist Europe, a word is in order about what is meant by this term. Strictly speaking, the term 'electoral system' can be taken to refer to many elements of electoral legislation, from registration procedures and boundary delimitation methods to electoral commission composition, campaign finance regulations and dispute adjudication mechanisms. In the academic literature, however, the term 'electoral system' is generally taken to refer to the aspects of electoral legislation relevant to the conversion of popular preferences into elected representatives – namely, the options available on the ballot, constituency delineation, and the formula for converting votes into seats. It is mainly in this sense that the term will be used in this chapter, though reference will also be made to other aspects of electoral system design broadly understood.

This chapter will be concerned with the design of electoral systems for lower (or only) houses of parliament, as these are the institutions that are generally recognized as having the greatest impact on the political configuration of a state. The three main electoral system types that have been employed in Central and Eastern Europe are: (i) the single-member district (SMD) systems in which the territory of the state is divided into a number of constituencies, and one member of parliament is elected from each (either by plurality, as in the UK 'first-past-the-post' system, or by absolute majority, as in the French two-round system); (ii) list proportional representation (PR, employed throughout most of Western Europe), in which voters choose party lists, and members are elected to parliament from these lists in proportion to the votes cast for each; (iii) mixed systems that combine SMD and PR, generally by giving voters two votes, one for an SMD member and one for a party list. Most of the post-communist mixed systems are designed such that the two votes represent two separate and unconnected elections (in other words they are what is sometimes referred to as 'parallel' systems).

Reframing Central and Eastern European electoral systems

In order to understand the motives behind electoral system reform in Central and Eastern Europe, it is necessary to make a brief diversion into the electoral institutions that were in force in the region during the communist period. The communist states of Europe used elections to maintain and legitimate their systems, rather than to select the political direction a country was to take. Elections held during the communist period were universally held under absolute majority electoral systems that, in theory, required a second round of voting if no candidate achieve at least 50 per cent support in the first round. In practice, however, it was rare that run-off ballots were conducted, as pre-selected candidates almost always won the posts for which they were standing. Voting took place in multi-member constituencies in Poland and the German Democratic Republic; elsewhere single-member districts were employed.

During the communist period, elections were the object of various forms of subtle and not-so-subtle manipulation by the authorities. Though voting was nowhere formally compulsory, heavy pressure was exercised on voters to encourage them to vote, generating turnout figures of well over 90 per cent in most cases. And while there was in no case a direct ban on competitive candidacies, a variety of mechanisms were employed to ensure that the electoral options available to voters did not represent genuine political alternatives (see Furtak, 1990). In some cases (the USSR, whose experience lies outside this book but is relevant to it, and Czechoslovakia) the communist party took charge of nomination procedures and ensured that there was but one name on the ballot. In the USSR, for example, voters had the 'choice' of either depositing the ballot in the box unmarked (thereby indicating a vote in favour of the single name thereon) or crossing out the name of the candidate to indicate a vote against that person. In order to indicate a 'negative' vote of this type, they had the option of using a screened-off polling booth, but given that the vast majority of voters deposited their ballots in the box unmarked, the very fact of resorting to use of the private polling booth was potentially seen as a sign of political disloyalty.

In other cases, such as Poland and Bulgaria, non-communist parties remained in existence throughout the communist period and won seats in parliament, though such 'satellite parties' formed part of communist-led 'fronts', and were allocated a share of seats in advance of each election. In such cases, voters thus had no more real choice than they did in states where there was only one party. In Yugoslavia, voters did have real choice at election time, but this was restricted to a selection of individuals, rather than a political choice between competing policy platforms.

In the late 1980s, a number of communist states began to experiment with offering voters greater choice at elections (see White, 1990). Hungary and the USSR began to use multiple candidacies along Yugoslav lines as a means of encouraging voters to select those with the most desirable personal qualities, though partisan competition was still not allowed. At the same time, a grassroots movement in Poland led to election boycotts, which significantly reduced participation. All in all, however, there was remarkable uniformity in the form elections took under communism and the ends to which they were used by communist regimes. Rather than being institutions for gauging popular preferences and selecting between policy options, elections were devices designed to mobilize the population and to make it complicit in the decisions of the communist parties that were in charge of making policy. They thus served as instruments of manipulation, popular control, and legitimation of communist rule.

The consequences of the collapse of communism were nowhere more evident than in electoral practices, whose role and meaning changed dramatically in the first genuinely competitive electoral events held, in most cases, shortly after the transition was initiated. It is, therefore, not surprising that reform of electoral institutions played a prominent role in the transition process. It was a central topic of debate in the round-table negotiations held in Poland, Hungary, Czechoslovakia, and Bulgaria, and electoral reforms were in each case among the most important outcomes of these events (see Elster, 1996). In most other cases, electoral reforms were decided through the normal parliamentary process shortly after the initial transitions (the exceptions are Romania (1990) and Russia (1993), where electoral laws were issued by decree). In all cases, the most important actors were the emerging democratic elites, together with former communist holders of power. Ordinary citizens played very little part in electoral reform, and advice from established democracies of the West was hardly more influential (Birch *et al.*, 2002).

Following the electoral reforms that accompanied the initial transitions, electoral legislation continued to be a hot topic of debate in virtually all of the Central and Eastern European states. Large-scale reforms have been relatively rare, however, and most of the changes in electoral legislation have been a matter of tinkering with the details of the electoral process. Thresholds have been raised and lowered, constituencies have been redrawn, and electoral administrative practices have been revised, but most of the Central and Eastern European states have stuck with the electoral systems they adopted immediately following transition. Furthermore, the changes that have taken place have been exclusively in the same direction.

Since the collapse of communism, there has been a general trend toward the introduction of more proportional elements to Central and East European electoral systems. Some countries made the transition to proportional representation at the time of transition from communist rule, while others initially adopted mixed electoral systems, most of which have subsequently been replaced by full-scale PR. A few states – Albania, Belarus, Macedonia, Ukraine – stayed with their single-member district absolute majority systems for the first post-communist elections, but with the exception of Belarus, these were all abandoned in favour of mixed systems (subsequently to be replaced by full PR in Macedonia and Ukraine). Belarus thus remains the only state in the region to have a single-member district system.

There are a variety of reasons for the shift to more proportional electoral systems. The aim of reformers was, in all cases, to ensure, first, that elections would be conducted on a multi-party basis and, second, that they would be free of manipulation by the communist authorities. PR was associated by post-communist reformers with multi-party politics, as it institutionalizes competition between parties and strengthens partisan organization. Single-member districts, on the other hand, were associated with localized politics that focuses on individuals (often based on patronage networks established by well-known communist leaders under the previous system), and were for this reason widely viewed as being less democratic. List PR was seen as a means of embedding political competition on a multi-party basis and preventing backsliding into one-party politics. It was also perceived as a means of strengthening parties as institutions; when parties rather than people became the object of election, fledgling political organizations had an incentive to build strong party organizations in order to attract the popular vote. Voters, for their part, have an incentive to investigate the policy platform that the party stands for, rather than thinking of it simply in terms of the individuals who make it up. PR was thus, first and foremost, a means of shifting political competition from personalized to programmatic competition, in other words, from competition between individuals to competition between ideas.

In this sense it was the party list element of PR, rather than the proportional outcome it generated, that was most attractive to Central and Eastern European reformers. It is perhaps for this reason that non-list forms of PR or semi-PR were hardly considered. The single transferable vote (STV) was employed briefly in Estonia in 1990 under the influence of Estonian emigre and electoral law specialist Rein Taagepera, but it was soon abandoned and has not been seriously considered elsewhere (Ishiyama, 1995). Other semi-proportional systems such as the single non-transferable vote have hardly been contemplated in any post-communist state.

The move toward PR did not take place immediately in all the region's countries, however, and variations of the speed of adoption of PR can be explained largely with reference to the political role of former communists in the immediate post-transition years (Elster *et al.*, 1998; Kitschelt *et al.*, 1999). In states such as Belarus, Ukraine, and Albania, where communist elites still held substantial power following the transition, the communist era single-member district system was retained with only minor revisions for the first post-communist elections. By contrast, states such as Poland, Czechoslovakia and Slovenia, where communists were ejected from power swiftly and completely at the time of transition, PR was adopted straight away. The overall story of post-communist electoral reform has thus been a move away from majoritarian election in single-member districts towards list proportional representation; this move has been swiftest and most complete in states where former communist power-holders fell from power most abruptly.

Electoral systems in Central and Eastern Europe today

The most striking feature of current electoral system design in Central and Eastern Europe is the general similarity in key elements of institutional design with those of the established democracies of Western Europe. There are, to be sure, more mixed electoral systems in the eastern portion of the continent than the western but, all in all, the fifteen years following the communist collapse have witnessed a considerable convergence between East and West in the area of electoral institutions. The dominant feature of electoral system design in both parts of the continent is list proportional representation. Yet, this generalization masks a variety of complexities that need to be taken into consideration in any detailed analysis. These include: the overall architecture of the system governing parliamentary elections in a state, districting procedures, ballot format, and thresholds of representation. It is worth considering each of these in turn.

Architecture

Four of the 20 post-communist European states employ mixed systems, one (Belarus) a relatively unreconstructed form of absolute majority SMD, and the remaining 15 states have list proportional representation. Thus, though list PR is unquestionably the dominant electoral system type in the post-communist region, it is worth noting the relative frequency of mixed systems. Prior to 1990, mixed electoral systems were a rarity on the global electoral systems scene, Germany being the only prominent example in the postwar world. Since the collapse of communism, however, mixed systems have spread rapidly in diverse parts of the world including Latin America (Bolivia, Mexico, and Venezuela), Africa (Lesotho, Senegal, and Tunisia) and East Asia (Japan, the Philippines, South Korea, Taiwan, and Thailand), as well as sub-national bodies in Western Europe such as the London Assembly and the Scottish parliament (see Reynolds *et al.*, 2005). The adoption of mixed electoral systems in a number of Central and East European states immediately following the collapse of communist rule was one of the events that sparked this wave of electoral reform, thereby providing a useful set of experiences that were closely studied by electoral engineers in other parts of the world. It is fair to say that in the field of mixed electoral systems, post-communist Europe served as both a pioneer and a laboratory, and that the series of electoral reforms that swept Central and Eastern Europe in the early 1990s represented a fundamental shift in global thinking about electoral systems.

Districting

The post-communist mixed systems follow the standard pattern of superimposing single-member constituencies (elected through plurality or absolute majority; see Table 10.1) on to a single, state-wide constituency through which party list seats are distributed. The states employing proportional representation typically divide the state into a number of relatively large multi-member constituencies, though Moldova, Slovakia and Ukraine distribute seats in a single, nation-wide constituency.

Ballot format

With the exception of Albania, the mixed systems in the post-communist region require voters to cast two separate votes, one for a candidate in a single-member constituency and one for a party list. Most of the post-communist PR systems elect parliamentarians on the basis of 'closed' lists, where the parties decide the composition of the list and the order of the candidates on them (and hence which individuals are elected), though several Central European states – the Czech Republic, Estonia, Latvia, Poland, Slovenia and Slovakia – allow voters to vote also for individual candidates (in other words, the lists are 'open'), and thereby influence the order in which a party's candidates are elected.

Thresholds

Post-communist thresholds of representation – the level below which parties in list PR systems are formally excluded from winning seats –

are generally high by Western standards. They range from two per cent in Albania to six per cent in Moldova (and seven per cent in the new Russian electoral system to be used for the 2007 *Duma* elections). Most of the states in the region have thresholds of either four or five per cent (an overview of the key elements of electoral system design in 20 post-communist states is provided in Table 10.1).

As far as other elements of electoral system design are concerned, post-communist Europe is one of the only regions of the world where

Table 10.1   *Electoral systems in Central and Eastern Europe (most recent lower house elections)*

Country	Year of most recent election	Size of chamber	Electoral system	Single-party threshold (first tier PR seats)[a] %	Prefer-ences in PR list voting?	Success require-ment in single-member seats
Albania	2005	140	Mixed (29% PR)	2[a]	No	Abs. maj.
Belarus	2004	110	SMD	–	–	Abs. maj.
Bosnia-H.	2006	42	PR	None	Yes	–
Bulgaria	2005	240	PR	4	No	–
Croatia	2003	152	PR	5	No	–
Czech Rep.	2006	200	PR	5[a]	Yes	–
Estonia	2003	101	PR	None[b]	Yes	–
Hungary	2006	386	Mixed (54% PR)	5	No	Abs. maj.
Latvia	2006	100	PR	5	Yes	–
Lithuania	2004	141	Mixed (50% PR)	5	No	Plurality
Macedonia	2006	120	PR	None	No	–
Moldova	2005	101	PR	4[a]	No	–
Montenegro	2006	81	PR	3	No	–
Poland	2005	460	PR	5[a]	Yes	–
Romania	2004	327 (+18 minority seats)	PR	5[a]	No	–
Serbia	2003	250	PR	5	No	–
Slovakia	2006	150	PR	5[a]	Yes	–
Slovenia	2004	90	PR	4	Yes	–
Ukraine	2006	450	PR	3	No	–

Notes: a = graduated threshold structure; higher levels for coalitions; b = a 5 per cent threshold is imposed for seat distribution in the upper tier.
Sources: Birch, 2003; www.electionguide.org; www.ipu.org.

compulsory voting is totally absent. This is undoubtedly due to the impact of transition from communism, which entailed various forms of pressure designed to secure the highest possible turnout. Yet, a number of the states in the region (notably those that were formerly part of the Soviet Union) employ an unusual type of 'collective compulsory voting' in the form of turnout requirements, which had been common under communism. In Lithuania and Hungary, 25 per cent of voters must have voted for a parliamentary election to be considered valid, while in Belarus and Moldova the figure is 50 per cent. Though entire elections have never been invalidated due to low turnout, these stipulations have resulted in individual constituency races having been rerun in a number of cases.

Electoral system effects in Central and Eastern Europe

Electoral systems have a variety of effects on both the style of politics in a state and on political outcomes. In the post-communist setting, electoral systems have been shown to have a number of the same impacts as they have in established democracies (with important exceptions). But the post-communist setting differs from that of established democracies in one crucial respect: party systems developed in their current form only following the introduction of competitive politics after 1989; the party systems of Central and Eastern Europe are therefore largely the products of transition. Electoral systems shaped party systems in important ways (as well as being shaped by them).

Given that there is only one SMD system in the region – Belarus – and given that this state is generally recognized as being less than democratic, it makes sense in the analysis of post-communist electoral systems to focus mainly on the distinction between mixed and fully proportional systems.

Research has found that Central and East European PR systems are generally associated with larger party systems (as is the case in established democracies), except where the party system is not nationalized. In this case, election in SMDs can lead to considerable party system fragmentation and weakening (Moser, 1999; Birch, 2003). We observe this phenomenon, for example, in Belarus and Russia where SMDs have led the election of large numbers of independents (see Table 10.2). In Russia (and also in Ukraine prior to the adoption of a fully proportional system), SMD elections also spawned many small parties, whereas the PR component of the ballot in these mixed systems was a consolidating force. Overall, however, proportional representation electoral systems are associated with larger party systems than their

Table 10.2   *Electoral System Effects in Central and Eastern Europe (Most Recent Lower-House Elections)*

Country	Year of most recent election	Electoral system	Turnout (as percentage of registered voters)	Proportion of votes excluded from representation %	'Effective' number of parliamentary parties[a]
Albania	2005	Mixed (29% PR)	49.23	9.14	3.68
Belarus	2004	SMD	90.14	N/A	1.95
Bosnia-H.	2006	PR	51.59	14.23	7.17
Bulgaria	2005	PR	55.76	8.91	4.81
Croatia	2003	PR	61.65	12.90	3.20[b]
Czech Rep.	2006	PR	64.47	5.97	3.10
Estonia	2003	PR	58.24	5.00	4.67
Hungary	2006	Mixed (54% PR)	67.57	.0	2.40
Latvia	2006	PR	60.08	11.38	6.00
Lithuania	2004	Mixed (50% PR)	46.07	5.22	5.46
Macedonia	2006	PR	55.98	8.96	4.06
Moldova	2005	PR	64.84	16.42	2.31
Montenegro	2006	PR	72.05	N/A	3.16
Poland	2005	PR	40.57	10.93	4.26
Romania	2004	PR	58.51	11.97	3.01[b]
Serbia	2003	PR	58.75	14.23	4.80
Slovakia	2006	PR	54.67	11.97	4.81
Slovenia	2004	PR	60.64	7.70	4.90[b]
Ukraine	2006	PR	67.13	22.34	3.41
Average	–	–	59.48	10.75	3.92

Notes: a = the effective number of parliamentary parties is calculated by taking the inverse of the sum of squares of the seat percentages won by each party. Seats won by independent candidates are excluded prior to the calculation of seat shares. In Belarus, the figure was 98 of 110, making the effective number of parties a figure of doubtful significance; b = excludes minority representatives, who are separately elected.

Sources: Birch, 2003; www.electionguide.org; www.ipu.org; www.electionworld.org; 'Republic of Albania Parliamentary Elections 3 July 2005: OSCE/ODIHR Election Observation Report', Warsaw: OSCE/ODIHR, 7 November 2005; Central Electoral Commission of Bosnia and Herzegovina website at www.izbori.ba; Central Electoral Commission of Latvia website at www.cvk.lv.

mixed counterparts. Using the common measure of the 'effective' number of parties (a measure that weights parties by their level of support; see Table 10.2 for details), we find that in the most recent elections in the region, elections held under PR led to party systems with an average of 4.24 'effective' parties, whereas elections held under mixed systems generated on average 3.47 such parties. But while more proportional electoral systems have a mildly fragmenting effect on party systems, they also work to strengthen individual parties, by privileging collective party identity and ideology over individual politicians and the politics of personality often associated in the post-communist region with patronage and clientelism.

Another relevant feature of electoral systems is their propensity to include voters in the representative process. Electoral systems where every vote goes toward the election of a parliamentarian are the most inclusive, whereas those that result in a large number of votes being 'wasted' suffer from a lack of inclusiveness. In general, more votes are 'wasted' under SMD rules than under PR, due to the high natural threshold for representation that results from the application of plurality or absolute majority rules. But interestingly, the mixed systems of post-communist Europe are associated with higher levels of inclusion than their PR counterparts; on average 7.38 per cent of voters voted for parties that failed to achieve representation in the most recent election in states with mixed systems, whereas the corresponding figure is 11.64 for the PR states. This is most likely due to the fact that mixed systems offer two channels to representation, thereby multiplying the means through which votes can be made to 'count' and increasing the chances that the choices made by any individual voter will contribute to the election of a representative.

Electoral systems have also been found to have an impact on rates of electoral participation in Central and Eastern Europe. One of the most notable features of electoral politics in the region is the dramatic decline in turnout that has characterized the post-communist period. There are a variety of reasons for this decline, having to do with socio-economic conditions, election timing and other factors (see, for instance, Kostadinova, 2002), and there is little evidence that the decline is being reduced as the post-communist states 'consolidate' their political systems. The most recent round of parliamentary elections in the region exhibited several dramatic further decreases, turnout falling in Bulgaria from 66.8 per cent in 2001 to 55.8 per cent in 2005, in Lithuania from 58.6 per cent in 2000 to 46.1 per cent in 2004, in Macedonia from 71.9 per cent in 2002 to 56.0 per cent in 2006, and in Slovakia from 70.1 per cent in 2002 to 54.7 per cent in 2006.

Electoral systems have, in most cases, remained relatively stable in recent years, and they cannot therefore explain such election-on-election declines. But electoral systems have been found to be a significant predictor of rates of electoral participation as well as the overall propensity of these rates to decline over time in the Central and Eastern European region; turnout has remained highest in those states that have made a rapid transition to PR, and it has fallen most in states that have used the greatest number of single-member districts (Birch, 2003). This trend is evident in the data contained in Table 10.2. In the states with full PR, turnout averaged 59.0 per cent in the most recent polls, whereas in those elections conducted under mixed systems average electoral participation was only 54.6 per cent.

Finally, it is worth considering the influence of electoral systems on the integrity of the electoral process, which has been an important touchstone in debates about Central and East European elections. With the so-called 'Bulldozer Revolution' in Serbia in 2000, the 'Rose Revolution' in Georgia in 2003, and the 'Orange Revolution' in Ukraine in 2004, world attention also turned to the quality of electoral processes in Central and Eastern Europe. There is evidence to suggest that SMD systems are associated with higher levels of electoral manipulation and abuse than PR systems (Birch, 2007). Possible reasons for this may be the incentives individuals face under SMD systems to cultivate personal votes, as well as the fact that fewer votes need be altered in SMD systems to change the outcome of the election, thus making abuse more 'efficient' than is the case under PR.

All in all, electoral systems can be seen to have a variety of important effects on party system configuration and political competition in post-communist Europe. Whereas proportional representation systems have a tendency to increase the size of party systems slightly, systems that include single member districts are associated with lower levels of electoral participation as well as increased levels of electoral manipulation and abuse. It is therefore unsurprising that democratization in the Central and East European region has been accompanied by a gradual shift to greater proportionality in electoral system design, and that those states that have proved themselves to be most democratic have a larger proportion of parliamentary seats elected through PR. There are, of course, exceptions to these general tendencies: Hungary and Lithuania are among the most democratic states in the region, yet they have both held tenaciously to their mixed electoral systems. The general association between more democratic forms of government and greater proportionality in electoral system design nevertheless remains one of the most striking features of contemporary Central and East European politics.

Conclusion

Institutions are but one of the factors that influence political developments in transitional and post-transitional contexts, and electoral systems are but one type of institution. A wide variety of other forces have played a large role in shaping political developments in the post-communist world since the momentous events of 1989, including economic change, cultural shifts and events specific to each individual state. Nevertheless, electoral system design has played a central role in political developments in Central and Eastern Europe since the late 1980s. Not only have debates over electoral systems been a forum in which key elements of state identity have been thrashed out, but also the systems implemented have played a significant role in shaping the course of political change.

The trajectory of Central and East European electoral system design has in many ways mirrored political developments in the region more generally. As political parties have become stronger, electoral systems have become increasingly dominated by list proportional representation mechanisms for distributing seats. Yet in those parts of the region where politics has remained most personalized (particularly the former Soviet republics), there has been considerable support for maintaining the single-member districts that are favoured by well-known local bosses. This highlights the fact that electoral systems have been evaluated in post-communist Europe not only in terms of their likely impact on specific parties, but also on the basis of their expected effects in shaping the basic forms of political contestation. The struggle for electoral reform in Central and Eastern Europe has been a struggle to put parties and programmatic politics above individual and personalized political competition. The most important lesson to be learned from the recent history of electoral system design in post-communist Europe is perhaps, therefore, that institutional design options 'mean' different things in different contexts; whereas debates over electoral systems in Western Europe revolve mainly around issues of fairness and benefit to individual parties, in Central and Eastern Europe similar debates focus on which type of political entity is to be the basic building block of politics.

Chapter 11

Political Parties

Paul G. Lewis

Political parties are an indispensable component of modern liberal democracy, and the outcome in Central and Eastern Europe (CEE) in terms of democratization and party activity overall has been a positive one. The achievements of the new democratic parties generally provide a favourable testimony to the region's political development. At the end of 2005, of the region's 18 states, 13 were identified as being free in terms of their ranking for political liberties and civil freedom, four were partly free, and only Belarus was placed in the unfree category. Further, 16 were classed as electoral democracies, with only Bosnia-Herzegovina and Belarus being excluded from this more inclusive category (Piano *et al.*, 2006: 893–5). The region as whole thus provides extensive scope for competitive party activity. Its strengthening democratic identity suggests that the actual role of parties has become increasingly prominent and that fertile ground exists for their further growth.

Origins and functions of CEE parties

Whatever the character of the actual institutions and the range of functions they are able to perform in CEE, it is generally the case that parties of some kind play a prominent part in the reasonably free elections that are held in nearly all the countries of the region. The case of Belarus, the authoritarian characteristics of whose regime strengthened through the 1990s and remained a consolidated authoritarian regime in 2006, is a singular one. Conditions there have provided few opportunities for the development and activity of democratic competitive parties. Elections held in 2000, whose validity was seriously questioned, saw 'independents' (nearly all loyal to President Lukashenka) taking 74 per cent of parliamentary seats. After the elections of 2004, just 11 per cent of seats were occupied by representatives of parties – none of them opposed to the government (White and Korosteleva-

Polglase, 2006: 158). In Ukraine, another former Soviet republic, two thirds of the vote also went to independent candidates in 1994. But after new constitutional arrangements came into force in January 2006 and transferred many presidential powers to the parliament, all seats were won by representatives of parties in the elections held the following March (see Chapter 6). In all other CEE countries, parties also fully dominate the electoral process and now act as the primary agents of parliamentary representation. As Enyedi points out, democratic politics in post-communist states now generally equals party politics – although whether this is a blessing or curse is a matter of further judgement (Enyedi, 2006: 236).

Parties play an overwhelmingly dominant role in government formation and the conduct of government throughout the region. In terms of basic party functions, the main questions at issue are how solid parties are as the main components of government formation and how effectively they perform their role as agents of political representation. In the first case, the situation in CEE is different from that found in some established democracies – and certainly from established Anglo-American practice – in that governments are rarely formed by a single party. Coalition governments are the rule, a natural consequence of the relatively large number of parties elected to many parliaments and the lack of capacity on the part of any one organization to secure a parliamentary majority.

While this is not a particular CEE characteristic (and is also seen in many West European democracies), it does reflect the specific conditions of post-communist change and the weakness of many of the new parties that have been established or brought back to active political life since 1989. The early parliaments in post-communist CEE were often fragmented and subject to major flux as numerous new and old parties battled for representation. In the early years, highly proportional electoral mechanisms that lacked any threshold for entry to parliament were sometimes introduced. This gave a wide range of political forces their own seats in the legislature. General conditions for party development and institutional growth in the early post-communist period were not at all favourable, either. Little organized political opposition to communist rule in CEE was able to develop prior to its collapse, and even a powerful independent social movement such as that organized by the Solidarity trade union in Poland during 1980–81 was effectively neutralized for much of the following decade. Only in Hungary was there a pattern of evolutionary regime change. Proto-parties came into being well before the end of communist rule, with the Hungarian Democratic Forum (MDF) being established in September 1987 and registered as a party the following year (see Chapter 2).

The Emergence of parties in CEE

As a rule, parties were established after or during the first democratic elections. They had not been prominent in the early stages of regime change, and they did not channel the pressures that helped bring about the end of communist rule. It was generally within a social movement or under an umbrella organization sheltering a number of diverse political groups and orientations that the newly formed opposition groups and infant democratic forces entered the newly liberated CEE political arena. If parties as institutions are not popular in Western democracies and are little trusted, such suspicions are yet more prominent in CEE, where parties command even less public confidence.

Even in the more rapidly democratizing countries of Central Europe, where the early anti-communist movements broke up quite rapidly, it took some time for the different political tendencies to become identified and for separate political parties to be formed. Patterns of party development were, therefore, quite complex and differed considerably both among the countries of the CEE region and between the contrasting sectors of the newly expanded political arena of each post-communist state (Lewis, 2000: 32–48). Groups on the anti-communist right in Poland found it particularly difficult to organize effectively and act within a common institutional framework. A number of them regrouped under the Solidarity banner in 1996 and won the election held the following year. The coalition government it formed ran into increasing difficulties, however, and in 2001 the Solidarity group failed to gain any parliamentary seats at all (see Chapter 3).

The Civic Democratic Party (ODS) formed in 1990 by Vaclav Klaus on the basis of the Czech Civic Forum, on the other hand, has played a prominent role in the country's political life since that date. Right-wing forces have also been strong in Hungary, although Fidesz has replaced the MDF as the main party on that side of the spectrum. The main centre-right organizations in Romania and Bulgaria took several years to gain effective power and also failed to sustain their role as the main competitor to leftist parties for more than one parliamentary term. The Democratic Convention of Romania (CDR) lost power to a social-democratic alliance in 2000 and was eclipsed by the nationalist Party of Great Romania (PRM) as the main party of opposition. The coalition headed by the Christian-Democratic Union of Democratic Forces (SDS) lost power in Bulgaria in 2001, and was succeeded by a diffuse populist movement headed by Simeon II as the last occupant of the Bulgarian throne. This in turn was eclipsed by a socialist coalition in the 2005 elections.

Alongside socio-political movements such as Solidarity in Poland

and Civic Forum in Czechoslovakia that acted as birthplace and nursery for one group of new parties, there was also a major evolution of former ruling communist parties. But not all on the left moved in the same direction. Those in Poland and Hungary transformed quite rapidly and with considerable success into a fair approximation of Western social-democratic parties. These new socialists won elections in Poland in both 1993 and 2001, and achieved an equivalent success in Hungary in 1994, 2002 and 2006. The Polish socialists suffered a dramatic loss of popular support in 2003–04, however, and retained only a quarter of their parliamentary seats in the 2005 election. The Lithuanian Democratic Labour Party won a similarly striking electoral victory in 1992 and maintained a significant, though declining, electoral presence through to the 2004 elections. The Communist Party of Bohemia and Moravia (KSCM) in the Czech Republic, on the other hand, has retained its traditional identity and remained a significant, if marginal, political force in successive elections, although in 2002 it did gain 18.5 per cent of the vote. The Slovak Party of the Democratic Left has suffered another fate and showed that extensive reform of a former ruling party is no guarantee of subsequent electoral success.

A further group of parties has emerged and followed a path of development related to, but still distinct from, both these models. Poland's United Peasant Party enjoyed a formal though marginal existence throughout the communist period as a junior partner of the ruling party. In 1990, it aligned itself with groups emanating from the prewar and immediate postwar period and established itself as a significant post-communist political force, although its strength has declined in successive elections. Other parties of an 'historic' character trace their roots directly to parties of the pre-communist period, and have developed separately from both communist and active anti-communist forces. The Czech Social Democratic Party (CSSD) is the most striking example of such an organization while a Hungarian agrarian party, the Independent Party of Smallholders (FKGP), for some years built successfully on prewar foundations.

Ethnic minority parties have also emerged on the basis of durable social divisions and played a significant role, often as coalition partners, in the party systems of several states. This has been the case with the Turkish minority in Bulgaria, Hungarians in Slovakia and Romania, Russians in Latvia and Albanians in Macedonia and the Kosovan portion of Serbia. Some of these parties as well as nationalist/populist movements have gained momentum in recent years; the latter often gaining strength in opposition to those seeking to defend and promote the rights of minorities (see Chapter 12). Such sentiments have fuelled the rise of *Ataka* in Bulgaria and sustained the momentum of Slovak Nationalists and PRM, as well as underpinning the electoral dominance of the Serbian Radicals, who gained the single largest share of the vote in the 2003 election (see Chapter 5). An extreme case even in the West Balkans, this party was formed during the hostilities of the early 1990s and its leader, Vojislav Seselj, held under arrest from 2004 and finally brought to trial at the War Crimes Tribunal at The Hague in November 2006.

The evolution of party politics

One problematic feature of the early post-communist period was the relatively large number of weak parties elected to the newly democratized parliaments, which then showed a high degree of fragmentation. Such problems should not be overemphasized as the divisions within many early CEE parliaments were not that pronounced, but fragmentation has nevertheless declined over time as a number of major parties have became established and electoral mechanisms have been progressively refined (see Chapter 10). Indicators of this process are often expressed in terms of the 'effective' number of parties engaged in the electoral process. This is not just a count of all those participating but an index of the overall pattern formed by the organizations taking part that gives more weight to larger parties.[1] It is generally assumed that a smaller number of 'effective' parties leads to better government. In many countries (Poland, Estonia, Slovenia, Romania, Hungary, Bulgaria, and the Czech Republic) the effective number of parties indeed declined between 1992 and 2000, although it is a trend not seen in other countries such as Slovakia, Latvia, and Lithuania. The average effective number of parties continued to decline after the turn of the century in the fourth cycle of post-communist CEE elections.

In terms of democratic performance, however, overcoming problems of parliamentary fragmentation is linked with the need to achieve adequate representation for most of the electorate. There is often a distinct trade-off between securing a reasonably low effective number of electoral parties and making sure that not too many voters are left without representatives in parliament. The problems of a highly fragmented electoral process such as that of Poland, nevertheless, diminished considerably through the 1990s while the system succeeded in maintaining a high degree of voter representation. The effective number of parties

---

1. It is derived by squaring the percentage of the vote taken by each party, adding the totals and inverting the result (i.e. $1/x$) to arrive at the measure of 'effectiveness'.

fell from 14.7 to 4.6 per cent between 1992 and 2000, but the proportion of voters left unrepresented (that is, those whose vote was 'wasted' because their favoured party did not enter parliament) only rose from 10.3 to 11.8 per cent. In Estonia, Slovenia, Romania, Hungary, Bulgaria and the Czech Republic, on the other hand, there was a fall in both the effective number of parties and the proportion of voters whose vote was wasted. The general trade-off between the formation of a less crowded electoral arena and adequate voter representation thus developed positively through the first post-communist decade, although those excluded from political representation by their 'wasted' vote remained far higher than in the democratizing states of other regions. Volatility has also remained at very high levels and generally increased in recent elections (Bielasiak, 2005: 338, 342).

Electorates have often had volatility forced on them by the short lives and high rate of turnover seen in the case of many parties. Some coalitions have been very cumbersome creations that did not survive the pressures of government (the CDR and Solidarity Electoral Action – AWS – in Poland), and the rate of new party creation has also been high. While a high rate of party creation would be expected to occur at the beginning of the post-communist period, signs of the intensification of the process some ten years into the democratic period is more surprising. The most meteoric political trajectory was that of Simeon II, who returned to Bulgaria in 2001 and founded the National Movement (NDSV), which won 42.7 per cent of the vote in an election held little more than two months later. A less rapid, but nevertheless striking, ascent was that of *Res Publica* in Estonia, which carried a parliamentary election and supplied the prime minister for a coalition government fifteen months after it was founded in 2001 (Taagepera, 2006: 78). These were not isolated cases. In Lithuania, a relative stability seemed to be emerging towards the end of the 1990s that was destroyed as the New Union–Social Liberals (NS/SL) and Liberal Union emerged to take nearly 45 per cent of parliamentary seats in 2000. Yet another new organization, the Labour Party, emerged in 2003 to win the election with 28.6 per cent of votes the following year. Equally, New Era emerged to win the 2002 Latvian election, while Poland saw four new parliamentary entrants in 2001 that went on to win 70.5 per cent of the vote between them in 2005.

But not all are convinced that this electoral and organizational fluidity is attributable to a high rate of party formation and the capacity of new political forces to capture a major part of the CEE vote. The different measures of volatility are by no means uncontentious and the frequency of splits, mergers and coalitions between existing organizations means that apparently new parties are often not as authentic as they seem. The impact of genuinely new parties, which do not just represent a rebranding of existing structures and are not just a different vehicle for established political figures, may be far less strong (Sikk, 2005a: 392–9). There is considerable resistance to new entrants from incumbent parties, their median support is only around the 10 per cent level and they have only limited success in gaining and retaining parliamentary representation.

Structure and organization

The problems involved in developing effective democratic parties in post-communist CEE have generally been associated with their thin membership base, weak organizational structure and the slender resources at their disposal. The resources available to CEE parties can be analyzed under several headings.

Membership

In comparative terms, CEE post-communist party membership levels have generally been low. Central European parties were estimated to have enrolled between 4 and 1.3 per cent of the adult population by the mid-1990s in contrast to 15–16 per cent in countries such as Austria and Sweden. But membership in the UK and the Netherlands, at 2.5 and 2.1 per cent respectively, was in the same range and, while CEE levels were relatively low, they were not markedly out of line with those of some countries of Western Europe. Later research presented another different perspective on membership issues confirming not just the low – and generally declining – membership levels in Central Europe but also pointing to a more dramatic fall in party membership in Western Europe in the context of growing disengagement from established parties (Mair and van Biezen, 2001: 14).

The main point here is not so much that CEE parties have few members but that this is not a surprising state of affairs in the light of broader European experience. The conclusion to be drawn from this comparison is that party membership is often low and declining in many European countries – but that the fall has been more pronounced in some Western countries than in the east, and that Western party membership levels in some cases were already low to start with. At the end of the 1990s levels of party membership were thus higher in Slovakia, Hungary and the Czech Republic than in either France or the UK. There is some evidence that party membership is higher in small polities than large ones, but the analysis on which this is based does not cover the relevant cases of the Baltic States (Weldon, 2006: 473). Existing knowledge suggests that there might be a significant association, as Lithuania has had an above-average index of party membership (at least on one count) while membership in Estonia has also steadily risen.

The highest levels of membership in Central Europe are still seen in the old communist parties of the region, their reformed successors and allied organizations. The KSCM still claimed more than 100,000 members in 2005, the Polish Democratic Left Alliance (SLD) 80,000, and the Hungarian Socialists some 37,000 (Kopecky, 2006a: 133; Szczerbiak, 2006: 116). High levels of party membership were also seen in former communist allies such as the Polish Peasant Party (PSL: 120,000), while the Hungarian FKGP – another agrarian party – still claimed 60,000 in 1998. Whether the latter totals bore much relation to contemporary reality was a matter of some doubt, as the parties' electoral support had declined quite dramatically – to less than one per cent in 2002 in the case of the FKGP. Attempts to halt the process of membership decline seemed to bear little fruit in the Czech Republic; for example, Kopeckyy (2007). There have been signs recently, however, that the decline in overall party membership and persistence of low levels of party adherence has been reversed – at least in some of the more dynamic and electorally successful parties of Hungary, Estonia and the Czech Republic – as well, more surprisingly, in Romania. Whether these changes have had any influence on the effectiveness of party activity or on the quality of democratic practice overall is by no means clear, as membership levels in CEE do not necessarily have direct implications for party strength or weakness nor for the consolidation of democratic party systems.

Structure

The conditions of contemporary party activity, elitist attitudes held by many CEE party leaders and the reluctance of much of the public to join them have all combined to give the members the parties did enrol a relatively marginal role in the organization as a whole. This has also been reflected in the restricted institutional development shown by many parties and the relative weakness of party structure. In many cases, there seems to have been little conception of how a rank-and-file membership could be organized or what it was actually for in the first place. There has, too, been little correlation between the development of organizational structure and party success at the polls. It was one of the paradoxes of the Polish election of 2001 that the party that had paid most attention to questions of institutional development and put most effort into organizing a national structure – the Freedom Union –

actually failed to reach the electoral threshold and lost the parliamentary representation it had maintained since its formation in 1990. In Bulgaria, on the other hand, the NDSV won the 2001 election with virtually no members and minimal organization – a deficiency that made itself felt when the party performed dismally in the 2003 local elections (Spirova, 2005: 608). Questions of inner-party democracy have also often been ignored and rarely perceived to be much of an issue in party life at all. Post-communist politics and the practice of liberal democracy are generally understood to operate most effectively at national level and within the narrow confines of the political elite. This often involves a very limited conception of the political party, and provides few incentives for developing a party's organizational network or much of a sub-national structure (Toole, 2003: 112).

In line with patterns of party membership, it has been possible to identify some national differences in party structure and organizational development. With more members on the ground, for example, Czech parties have shown a greater capacity for development as autonomous units. They have had some power to manage their own affairs, settle management and leadership issues on their own account, and control their own finances. In Hungary, on the other hand, the resemblance of the new parties' structures to those of the former ruling communist party was remarked on at an early stage, the growth of professionalization and bureaucratization only leading to the emergence of a sharply restricted and elitist democracy. But there were signs at the time of the 2002 election that Fidesz was beginning to succeed in mobilizing greater numbers of anti-communist activists, a process that may have had some bearing on the violent protests that broke out against the re-elected Socialist government in 2006 (Enyedi and Toka, 2007). The trajectory taken by Bulgaria from communist rule had a different effect, as the continuing dominance of the successor party through much of the 1990s established a model of political success that placed a premium on institutional strength and party organization (Spirova, 2005: 612). In Poland, it was once again the parties such as the SLD and PSL, organizations with roots in the former regime, that had stronger local networks and were better represented at the grass roots. In other cases, local party structures were very weak and in keeping with the low level of party membership nationally.

But the organizational assets inherited from the communist regime by successor parties have also tended to diminish. As membership of the once all-powerful KSCM dropped away – falling by over half between 1992 and 1999 – a similar decline could be seen in the party's network of local organizations, although in comparative regional terms its network is still quite dense: lack of organization has not always been perceived by parties as a source of political weakness. The Civic Platform that emerged after the 2000 presidential contest in Poland and scored a reasonable success in the 2001 parliamentary election fell prey to considerable internal dissension when the development of its organizational structure was subsequently discussed. Some were fearful of excessive dominance by the parliamentary faction and argued for strong grassroots democracy; others argued for a 'light' organizational touch and saw the party primarily as an electoral body. In the 2005 elections it was, further, beaten to second place by the Law and Justice party (PiS) whose membership was the lowest of all six parliamentary parties and whose organizational model was emphatically that of a cadre, leadership vehicle.

The prominence of other leader dominated parties such as that of Meciar's Movement for a Democratic Slovakia (HZDS) for much of the 1990s, a model replicated in several Balkan countries and former Soviet republics, was facilitated by control over state resources and the capacity for extensive patronage; conditions that were clearly more prevalent in the less democratized CEE countries. Elements of clientelism can certainly help sustain the position of a party leader under such conditions, and they have often been linked with diffuse appeals to nationalism as a cover for such sectional interests. These features were present in Croatia until Tudjman's death in 1999, as well as in some other Balkan states. The clientelist path taken by traditionally dominant parties in the former Soviet Union distinguishes them sharply from the post-communist line of development and emergence of more Europeanized social democratic structures in the old socialist and workers' parties in Hungary and Poland – although the Polish SLD also went into political free fall in 2003–04 following allegations of extensive corruption. The emergence of distinctive European political entrepreneurs in recent years, typified by Berlusconi's *Forza Italia*, has also found CEE parallels in new business/firm party structures such as Karic's Strength of Serbia, Slovak media magnate Pavol Rusko's ANO and the Lithuanian Labour Party founded by Russian businessman Viktor Uspaskich. The latter party scored a stunning electoral victory little more than a year after it was founded in 2003, although Uspaskich's career in government soon ended when he was removed from parliament and sought refuge in Russia as a series of financial scandals came to light.

Funding

The weak base of many CEE parties and their leadership emphasis is also reflected in funding patterns. Membership dues played, naturally enough, a considerably larger role in the finances of communist and successor social democratic parties than in most liberal and right-wing organizations. In the mid-1990s, the Czech communists and Hungarian and Polish socialists drew from 20 to 43 per cent of their income from their members. None of the other main Hungarian parties drew more than 10 per cent of their income from members, and patterns of funding were little different for the leading Polish organizations (with the exception of AWS, which had little official income on its own account and was dependent on the resources of the trade union for much of its activity). Precisely where the balance of the funds used to fund party activity has come from is not always very clear, although national legislation generally provides for the regular publication of party accounts and full transparency of the parties' financial dealings.

The distribution of state property and other assets at the end of the communist period gave some parties substantial material assets and left them with major advantages over their competitors. Such resources provided parties with more than 80 per cent of their annual income in some cases. Diverse forms of 'economic activity' were a category that provided 88 per cent of PSL income in 1998 and 91 per cent in 1999. It still meant that the Peasant Party derived only 11.9 per cent of its income from the state in 2003 (Szczerbiak, 2006: 114). This marked advantage was to be phased out after amendments to the Law on Political Parties excluded investment as a source of party finance (Jasiewicz, 2007). Direct state funding for parties in Hungary and the Czech Republic was quite generous from the early years of post-communist rule, and the Hungarian Free Democrats obtained 91 per cent of their funds from this source in 1995. The Hungarian Socialists also drew on substantial state funds to supplement the sizeable income it already derived from its members. The situation in Poland was rather different, as there was no direct funding of party activity (apart from the reimbursement of election expenses) until 1997. But Polish parties soon followed the strong regional tendency to depend on the state for their income (a facility still not provided in Latvia, though), and by 2003 three of the six parliamentary parties depended on this source for more than 90 per cent of their income.

The issue of how party activity should best be financed – as well as how party politicians' relations to financial resources should be regulated in general – remains a live and contentious issue in many countries of the region. Finance is clearly an important condition of effective party activity, although it is not particularly clear how important it is for the quite large numbers of new parties that continue to break through and gain entry to the parliamentary arena in a number of countries. A general impression is that finance is not a prime condition for political success, and that the continuing fluidity of the political constellation offers diverse opportunities and various points of access to the political arena. There are, however, some indications that the pattern of state funding in new CEE democracies is rather different from that in recently democratized Southern European regimes – and that the tendency for funds to flow more strongly to the parties' central offices than to their parliamentary leadership may have major consequences for their patterns of development (van Biezen, 2003: 199–201). There is also some evidence of a distinction between the Central European and Baltic countries on the one hand, and other post-Soviet and Balkan countries on the other (Kopecky, 2006b: 263). The near-universal principle of state support in the former group fosters a more egalitarian distribution of state resources and seems to encourage a more inclusive form of party competition.

The media

The importance of the media in party competition in modern democracies and the substantial costs they involve suggest that access to the media may be a significant link between a party's material status and its chances of political success. The Polish record showed, however, that expenditure on the media was a limited element in party outgoings in election campaigns – little more than 20 per cent as a rule (although they may be more substantial in the personalized competition seen in presidential contests). Intensified censorship and stronger government control of the Ukrainian media, too, did not preserve the establishment parties in 2002 or prevent the onset of the Orange Revolution (Dyczok, 2006). That, of course, is not to argue that media and television resources are not of great importance in new democracies, where many parties are competing to construct and project a distinctive political identity, where members are thin on the ground and unable to spread the parties' message by word of mouth, and where party organizational networks fail to penetrate many local communities. 'Visibility' was a major factor in the success of *Res Publica* – and this did not just mean paid advertisements. Intensive use of e-mail was another important factor in the party's growth – and perhaps its decline as well (Taagepera, 2006: 86–8).

Television in particular plays a major role in projecting party leaders and securing critical shifts in a party's image as a condition for electoral success. TV presentation during the 2001 election campaign in Poland projected Self-Defence (SO) leader Andrzej Lepper from the margins of political life, where he played a lively but limited role as organizer of peasant blockades, to a central position, by developing a more statesmanlike image that appealed to far broader sectors of the electorate. Similar examples could be drawn from most countries of the region. The interplay of media and party politics takes other forms than politicians simply exploiting the opportunities that television offers. Those controlling major media outlets can use the position to launch their own political careers. The influence of the owner of Poland's major TV satellite channel, Zygmunt Solarz, was reported to have extended to over thirty parliamentary deputies who helped promote his interests. Supporters of the Polish Catholic station, Radio Maryja, equally helped ensure the strong showing of the League of Polish Families (LPR) in the 2001 elections, and then helped PiS to power in 2005. In Slovakia Pavol Rusko founded ANO in April 2001 and clearly had hopes of winning over a substantial segment of the 40 per cent of Slovaks who watched the news programme broadcast by his station. Having won 8 per cent of the vote in 2002, though, his support fell to 1.4 per cent in 2006.

Europeanization and the CEE party spectrum

One distinctive influence on the development of party identity has been the requirement of democratic conditionality for the eight countries that joined the European Union (EU) in 2004, as well as similar demands placed on the current CEE candidates and continuing expectations of those with more distant prospects of EU membership (see Chapter 7). Confirmation of the democratic credentials and institutional identity of a post-1989 party by one of the major international groups or federations was often a major advantage in stabilizing its position and enhancing its status over competitors in the same area of the political spectrum – as well as rewarding it with financial and other material advantages. Major CEE parliamentary parties affiliated with the party groups in the European Parliament (EP) are listed in Table 11.1. In terms of its resemblance to the range of political families seen in Western Europe, the CEE party spectrum shows an increasing degree of development in terms of identity formation and ideological correspondence with European norms.

Several categories of party experienced problems in developing a European identity and affiliating with any of the EP groups. One group consisted of parties that derived directly from the ruling institutions of the communist period and had undergone little change in the intervening period. This originally concerned quite prominent organizations such as the Czech KSCM, which is now a member of the European United Left (GUE-NGL) group, but still includes the parties of the former Soviet countries of Moldova, Ukraine and Belarus, who have no prospect of EU membership in the foreseeable future and do not therefore have even observer status within the EU. Countries with more distant prospects of EU membership, such as Serbia, Montenegro, Macedonia, Bosnia and Albania also have a minority of parliamentary parties allied with EP groups. Nationalist parties, some of which have played a central role in the political system of their country, such as the HZDS, PRM, Slovenian People's Party, as well as the more recently formed *Ataka* in Bulgaria, have remained outside the EP party groups. Agrarian organizations such as the PSL also found it difficult to find an appropriate West European partner. Many of these parties just seemed to be *sui generis* in CEE terms and did not fit well with West European patterns for this reason.

Most major parliamentary parties in the EU member states now have some affiliation with EP party groups, although there are some exceptions like the newly resurgent Slovak National Party, Slovene Nationalists and HZDS. Neither of the nationalist parties has EP representation, though, so that incentives to integrate more fully with its party groups are also lacking. Major parliamentary parties in Latvia like the Harmony Centre, Latvia's First and the Centre Party – Latvian Peasants' Union also lack such links. Somewhat more striking is the position of some Polish parties, as SO is formally non-affiliated although two of its six MEPs joined the Group of European Socialists (PES) in December 2004. The PSL is officially affiliated with the dominant right-wing European People's Party–European Democrats (EPP-ED), but three of its four MEPs joined the Union for Europe of the Nations (UEN) in 2005. The position of the LPR is also ambiguous in terms of its link with the Independence and Democracy (IND/DEM) group, as most but not all of its MEPs are listed as members. The League is, indeed, the only CEE party to have any affiliation with that maverick party group.

Just two parties, from Slovenia and the Czech Republic, are members of the European Greens–European Free Alliance (EFA) group, and the two relatively unreconstructed Communist Parties have joined the GUE-NGL. The great majority of major parliamentary parties are thus linked with the leading EPP-ED, Socialist and Association of Liberals and Democrats for Europe (ALDE) groups. Most EU member and candidate countries have a representative in each of these groups, although the Czech Republic (relatively strongly polarized between the right and left) does not have any liberal representation and the Polish representatives (Freedom Union) no longer have national parliamentary representation. In states with less immediate prospects of EU membership fewer parties have any affiliation with the EP party groups. As is the case with the member countries,

Table 11.1 Affiliation of major CEE parliamentary parties with groups in the European parliament
Note: the barrier for representation was 3 per cent

	EPP-EDD	PES	ALDE	Greens–EFA	GUE–NGL	UEN	IND/DEM	Unaffiliated
Czechia	Christian and Dem. Union ODS	CSSD		Green Party	KCSM			Freedom Union
Estonia	*Res Publica Pro Patria*	Social Democrats	Centre Party Reform P.			People's Union		Constitution Party
Hungary	FIDESZ MDF	Socialist Party	Free Democrats					Christian Dem. Peoples' Party
Latvia	New Era People's Party	Social Democratic Workers'	Latvia's Way			Fatherland and Freedom		People's Harmony Latvia's First
Lithuania	Fatherland Union	Social Democrats	Labour, NS/SL Liberal and Cent. Union			Liberal Democrats Peasant Nationalists		Polish Alliance
Poland	Civic Platform	SLD				PiS, PSL	LPR	Self-Defence
Slovakia	Democratic and Christian Union Hun. Coalition Ch. Democrats	*Smer*	ANO		Communist Party			National Party MDS
Slovenia	Dem. Party New Slovenia People's Party	Social Democrats	Liberal Democracy	Youth Party				National Party Dem. Pensioners

Table 11.1 Continued

	EPP-EDD	PES	ALDE	Greens-EFA	GUE-NGL	UEN	IND/DEM	Unaffiliated
Bulgaria	SDS Democrats for Strong Bulgaria People's Union	Coalition for Bulgaria	NDSV Rights and Freedoms Movement					*Ataka*
Romania	Democratic Party Hungarian Alliance	Social Democrats	National Liberal Party					Conservatives PRM
Croatia	Dem. Union Peasant Party Dem. Centre	Social Democratic Party	People's Party Soc.Liberals Istrian Assembly					Liberal Democrats Liberals Croatian Rights Pensioners
Albania	Dem. Party Reformed Democrats		Democratic Alliance			Republican Party		Socialist Party Social Democrats Integration Movement
Bosnia	Party of Dem. Action Croatian Community Dem. Progress	Social Democrats Independent Social Democrats						Serbian Democrats Party for Bosnia and Hercegovina
Macedonia		Social Democratic Union	Liberal Party Lib-Dems					National Unity Party Socialists
Serbia	Democratic Party of Serbia G17 Plus							Radical Party Democratic Party Serbian Renewal

those without links are generally found amongst nationalist parties, ethnic groupings and socialists whose democratic credentials are yet to be established. Increasing numbers of mainstream parties, particularly amongst the region's democratic leaders, are thus forging stronger links with the leading European party federations and becoming more 'European' in their own right.

The impact of Europe

Nevertheless, any process of 'Europeanization' is not uniform or one-directional in its effects (Lewis and Mansfeldova, 2006). While main-stream parties forge closer links with counterparts in the EP and elsewhere, high rates of electoral volatility and weak party institution-alization give considerable scope for the emergence of new, often unconventional parties and populist movements beyond and often in opposition to the Euro-consensual political centre. Major new parties emerged and took power throughout the region in the first years of the new century (Bulgaria, Poland, Slovakia, all three Baltic states, as well as the forces driving the Orange Revolution in Ukraine). Such develop-ments sometimes emerge outside the pro-EU establishment consensus that has prevailed in many countries but they are by no means uncon-nected with it. One of the first steps taken by the new *Smer* govern-ment was the abolition of the flat-tax system that underlay Slovakia's radical neo-liberal economic policy designed to anchor it firmly within the global capitalist system. More contentious was its decision to form a governing coalition with the extremist National Party, which led to *Smer* being excluded in October 2006 from the key activities of the Party of European Socialists (see Chapter 4). Similarly, the great bogeyman of the PiS-led coalition in Poland was Leszek Balcerowicz, architect of Poland's economic shock therapy and, for many concerned Western observers, guarantor of the country's economic rectitude.

Such populist responses to Western, EU-sponsored development strategies were not in themselves surprising – more of a shock was the opportunistic ease with which former Europhobes like SO and the LPR changed their tune once the country had gained EU membership (and began to receive its benefits) and they found themselves in positions of power. Such *volte-faces* reflected the continuing political fluidity seen throughout much of the region, consequences of the low level of insti-tutionalization of party activities and the weak party systems found in many countries – although to the extent that such parties were com-mitted to nationalist principles it could now be argued (as did SO) that the Polish national interest was indeed well served by the country's membership of the EU. The overall picture now is a very mixed one.

The new enthusiasm of SO for the EU accompanies the reassertion of national interests by the PiS-led government in ways that contradict the former consensus for increased European integration. Such views are echoed by Czech leaders although, as in other countries, the apparent Euroscepticism of some politicians is considerably stronger than the continuing pro-EU sentiments of the bulk of the population.

None of these tendencies should be over-emphasized. At a relatively early stage, empirical research showed a relatively high level of pro-grammatic crystallization of parties and party systems in Central Europe and a lower one in more problematic democracies like those of the Balkans, typified in this instance by Bulgaria (Kitschelt *et al.*, 1999). These, nevertheless, provided no guarantee that existing regional characteristics in terms of the path and character of party development would disappear or that a uniform model based on West European patterns was likely to emerge. Overall the party spectrum of contemporary CEE is sufficiently complex and fluid to resist easy definition and effective analysis through the prism of any single classification system – although a clearer view of the party landscape can be gained by distinguishing between the different parts of the region. Central Europe saw a rapid evolution from the Soviet model, with party relations characterized by extensive and effective competition, distinctive arenas of programmatic competition and relatively frequent alternation of party government. Europarties and national political foundations, particularly German ones like the Ebert and Adenauer Foundations, were influential in Europeanizing CEE parties by creating and operating channels of cultural transmission that facilitated institutional development and by creating positive perceptions of the EU both among the elite and in the broader public arena. But only in some countries have there been signs of significant party system development: no more than Hungary, Slovenia and the Czech Republic – as well as Estonia in certain respects. The absence of stable parties has been seen as a primary factor in the absence of party system consolidation (Lewis, 2006).

For a lengthy period the post-Soviet republics of Ukraine, Moldova and Belarus continued to be strongly influenced by the character of the former regime. If they were no longer actually dominated by the institutions of communist rule, then they were certainly still strongly influenced by their style and the procedures through which they operated. But developments here have also now taken divergent paths. Since the Orange Revolution of 2004 Ukraine has taken major steps towards a party-based democracy and received considerable support from countries that are now EU neighbours, while Belarus has further strengthened its authoritarian regime. Party arrangements in the Balkans lie somewhat between these two models (such as they are), and saw either the lengthy dominance of a partially reformed communist establishment with relatively weak democratic party opposition (Romania and Bulgaria) or the rule of authoritarian right-wing parties whose democratic credentials were no more convincing than those of their neighbours (Croatia). The rump Yugoslavia under Milosevic managed to combine elements of both these models in a distinctive form of national authoritarian and aggressive rule. Bulgaria and Romania have now opted decisively for the democratic European mode. Both Croatia and post-Milosevic Serbia have also moved away from the non-democratic path of transition taken in the 1990s, but the development of effective democratic parties has been far more successful in Croatia where the Europeanization of the Croatian Democratic Union under Ivo Sanader brought it major political advantages and has taken the country as a whole to the threshold of EU membership.

Conclusion

A number of complex issues have been raised in this discussion, and any conclusions that can be reached are necessarily tentative and often ambiguous. As a very broad generalization, however, parties have developed with a fair degree of success in most countries of the region, some steps have been taken towards the emergence of viable party systems, and a growing Europeanization of party processes in many CEE countries can be identified. In many countries party turnover and electoral volatility remain high, though, and even amongst democratic leaders membership levels are low and party organization rudimentary. But many of the characteristics and apparent defects are increasingly evident in Western Europe, too, and CEE party development certainly appears to be adequate to sustain continuing democratic development. Whether this will continue to be case with the continuing prevalence of 'flash' parties that erupt on the political scene and sometimes decline just as quickly, and in the light of the continuing strength of diffuse and often extremist populist forces remains to be seen. It might, however, also be argued that these features reflect processes increasingly seen in Western Europe and that the Europeanization of CEE party structures and systems is continuing – albeit in somewhat unexpected ways.

Chapter 12

Citizens and Politics

Krzysztof Jasiewicz

It is conventional wisdom that the Central and East European revolution was won on the streets of Prague and Timisoara, Belgrade and Kiev, in the shipyards of Gdansk and steel mills of Cracow. This point of view hardly can be disputed, but it is also true that this revolution was won in voting booths across the region. Sometimes, as in Poland, Hungary, and Czechoslovakia of the 1980s, mass street demonstrations and strikes initiated the change, to be followed by competitive elections – the real turning point in the process of political transition. In other cases, as in Yugoslavia in 2000 or Ukraine in 2004, spectacular street demonstrations followed fraudulent elections and were an expression of the will of the people who, unlike their rulers, were determined to treat democracy seriously. Yet, as the October 2006 events in Hungary indicate, mass demonstrations and street violence may break out even in countries that, seemingly, have already completed their democratic transitions. Hence the obvious question to be addressed in this chapter is the one of maturity of post-communist democracies. We will examine this issue looking at various forms of citizens' involvement in politics.

Popular revolts and elections are but extreme forms of this involvement. Citizens interact with the political system and its elements in a rich variety of ways. People join political parties or other organizations, come to meetings and rallies, collect – and make – monetary contributions, write letters of support to political leaders. People go on strike, occupy public buildings, boycott commercial organizations or political events (such as elections), or sign petitions in protest at political decisions. Forms of political participation are, virtually, countless. Scholars consequently analyze political behaviour in many ways, looking at everything from individual motivations, to patterns of interaction (between individuals, groups, and/or institutions), to eventual outcomes (those desired and those unintended). For the purposes of this chapter, we will use a simple typology of political action, based on two criteria: (i) whether it engages its participants on a universal or a particularistic basis, and (ii) whether it follows established conventions (cyclical or perpetual routines) or involves protest politics in sporadic/transitory acts of mobilization (for more on this criterion, see Dalton, 1988). Of course, there are many other possible criteria to classify political actions: they can be legal or illegal, overt or clandestine, peaceful or violent, successful or ineffective, and so forth. We believe, however, that the typology proposed here is helpful in exposing specific features of citizens' involvement in politics in post-communist Central and Eastern Europe (CEE).

In democracies, elections – presidential, parliamentary, local – take place with a certain regularity (every two, four or five years, or whatever is the constitutional requirement), and follow prescribed procedures; even exceptions to this cycle – such as early elections in parliamentary systems – are covered by established rules. Mass upheavals or rebellions, on the contrary, happen suddenly and seldom; no one can predict their occurrence with any accuracy and very few people can participate in such an event more than once in their lifetime.

Yet, dissimilar as they obviously are, national elections and revolutionary upheavals do have something in common: they tend to involve and engage all citizens of a nation-state – and to engage them *as citizens*, not as members of any particular group. Even if some people do not participate in elections (because they decided to boycott the act or because they are too apathetic to take part) or ignore the call to join a rebellion (out of fear or out of rejection of rebellion's goals), the outcomes of these universal (at the national level) events in all likelihood will be relevant for their lives.

By contrast, when people join political, economic, or cultural organizations (sometimes making a lifetime commitment), or when they decide to participate in an industrial strike, road blockade, or act of civil disobedience, they usually act because they are motivated by some particular group interest. In any democracy, platforms of aggregation of particularistic interests (such as class, professional, ethnic, religious, regional, gender or age based) as well as forms of collective action are potentially countless. Just as universal actions, particularistic actions tend also to coalesce into two types, conventional (usually long-lasting) and protest (usually transitory and sporadic).

Schematically, the intersection of the two ways of looking at political behaviour can be presented as follows:

Types of political action	Universal	Particular
Convention	Elections	Organizational membership
Protest	Rebellions, revolutions, upheavals	Strikes, riots, demonstrations, petition drives, and so on

It should be emphasized that this scheme is a typology, not a classification of forms of political actions, which means that certain specific
actions cannot be unequivocally labelled as representing a given single
type. For instance, an organization, such as a trade union or a political
party, can be established one day and dissolved soon after, making it a
sporadic phenomenon rather than a part of any routine (although the
sporadic emergence and disappearance of political organizations has
become a *routine* in many CEE states). Some actions launched to secure
particular interests may over time develop into nationwide upheavals:
such was the case of a strike in the Gdansk Shipyard in 1980 that eventually gave birth to the Solidarity movement. Some upheavals last but a
few days, other evolve into social movements active for months or even
years and, over time, gaining resemblance to formal organizations
(again, Solidarity is a striking example). Certain groups (such as intellectuals) can make a legitimate claim that protection of their particular
interests (such as freedom of expression) has a universal, and not just a
particularistic value. Still, when discussing the involvement of citizens in
politics in Central and Eastern Europe today, we can focus on the four
types presented above, without ignoring important issues. We will begin
with mass upheavals, moving then clockwise over the adopted scheme
to elections, organizational membership, and various forms of protest
actions motivated by particular interests. We will conclude with a brief
examination of mass political attitudes – the cognitive and affective
foundations of political behaviour.

Mass upheavals

Why do people rebel? When do they rebel? Why are some rebellions
successful and others are not? These and similar questions have been
addressed in a vast political, historical, sociological, and psychological
literature on revolutions, collective action, collective violence, and
social movements (see, for instance, Smelser, 1962; Brinton, 1965;
Moore. 1966; Huntington, 1968; Davies, 1971; Gurr, 1971;
Eisenstadt, 1978; Tilly, 1978; Skocpol, 1979; Kimmel, 1990). So far,
scholars engaged in reflections on this subject are far away not only
from any consensus on the causes and mechanisms of mass popular
upheavals, but even from establishing a common terminology. We can
agree here that the concept of revolution can be applied (albeit not
always without reservations or qualifications) to the complex processes
that entailed the collapse of communist regimes and the establishment
of viable pluralist democracies and market economies in Central and
Eastern Europe in the 1980s and 1990s.

Despite local variations, the process of political change in all the Central and East European countries occurred according to the same general pattern, from polarization to fragmentation: a united opposition faced the old regime in a stand-off (at round-table negotiations and/or during elections), but remained united only until the apparent defeat of the communists. But post-communist revolutions shared several other common features. In almost all cases, the upheavals were launched, or at least preceded, by a spectacular, massive display of national unity, in defiance of the formal rules and/or informal expectations of the communist system. In Poland, such a display came in June 1979 during John Paul II's first visit to his native land after becoming Pope, when millions attended open-air masses and services in an orderly fashion and a joyful mood, with the communist coercive apparatus nowhere to be seen. The subsequent events, from the Gdansk Shipyard strike to the June 1989 elections, reinforced this effect time after time, in spite of serious setbacks on the way (notably the introduction of martial law in December 1981). In Hungary, the reburial of Imre Nagy and his associates (leaders of the failed 1956 revolution) on 16 June 1989, attended by hundreds of thousands, gave additional impetus to the process of negotiated transition already under way. In the Baltics, the human chain of people holding hands joined the three capitals, Vilnius, Riga, and Tallinn, on 23 August 1989 – the fiftieth anniversary of the Molotov–Ribbentrop pact (the act that had sealed Soviet domination of the region). Only a decade earlier, such a display of solidarity would have been unthinkable: very few people, if any, would have been ready to pass the threshold of fear, as the response of the Soviet regime would have been swift and ruthless. In Romania, the crowd that the regime assembled in Bucharest's central square on 21 December 1989 to cheer Nicolae Ceausescu delivering an address to the nation instead booed him in front of TV cameras, transmitting live the image of a falling dictator to all Romanian households and to the world. Massive demonstrations on Wenceslas Square in Prague in November 1989, and in several East German cities in late 1989, as well as those in Belgrade (2000) and Kiev (2004) played a similar role.

All these events played a dual function. First, they helped to draw clearly in peoples' minds the line separating 'us' (the people) from 'them' (the old regime). Second, they exposed the impotence of the old regime, unable or unwilling to 'restore order' and punish people for violating the prescribed routines of mass behaviour allowed in communist systems. In an apt metaphor, Kenney (2002) compares Central European revolutions to a carnival – a period of suspension, or even a reversal, of the usual rules in society. Consequently, the movements sparked by those events acquired a specific aura of charisma: a shared belief that 'the people', acting in solidarity, can accomplish goals that, until that moment, were at best only in the realm of political dreams (for the notion of a charismatic social movement, see Jowitt, 1992 and Cirtautas, 1997). In most cases, this belief has become a self-fulfilling prophecy.

Central and East European revolutions had also their charismatic leaders – although in the light of hindsight their role seems often more ambiguous than it appeared at the time. Still, Poland would not be the same without Lech Walesa, nor the Czech Republic without Vaclav Havel, Lithuania without Vitas Landsbergis, or Bulgaria without Zheliu Zhelev. For that matter, Croatia would not be the same without Franjo Tudjman, Slovakia without Vladimir Meciar, Albania without Sali Berisha, or Serbia without Slobodan Milosevic. More recent upheavals displayed the charismatic qualities of Viktor Yushchenko and Yulia Tymoshenko (Ukraine), and Mikhail Saakashvili (Georgia). On the other hand, several transitions in the region took place without the strong imprint of a charismatic leader, at least one whose fame would extend beyond national boundaries. All in all, the dynamics of the leader–followers relationship tend to be idiosyncratic and hence create only a limited basis for region-wide generalizations, much less universal theoretical statements.

The 'charismatic moment' associated with spectacular events usually, if not always, had its impact not only locally, but also across the region (and sometimes beyond). Solidarity's spectacular electoral victory in June 1989 and the subsequent creation, in defiance of the Brezhnev doctrine, of a grand coalition government with only token communist representation, emboldened opposition leaders and the wider popula-tion in neighbouring countries. Then, the ensuing developments in East Germany, Czechoslovakia, and Hungary fuelled each other until the ultimate collapse of the old regimes. Bulgaria, Romania, Albania soon followed suit. Similarly, the 1989–91 events in Lithuania, Latvia, and Estonia gave inspiration to national liberation movements not only mutually among the three Baltic States, but also in Ukraine, Georgia, and other Soviet republics: this quick diffusion of revolutionary ferment was undoubtedly facilitated by the modern media of mass communication, in particular television. Images such as the fall of the Berlin Wall, the trial and execution of Nicolae and Elena Ceausescu, or Boris Yeltsin commanding resistance to the August 1991 coup trans-mitted a sense of defiance and victory across the region. (Patterns of emulation are sometimes strange. When in London, in March 1990, youngsters opposing Margaret Thatcher's poll tax waved Union Jacks with a hole in the middle, they followed, unconsciously, the example of the December 1989 Bucharest demonstrators, who had cut the dis-

graced communist insignia from the middle of the Romanian tri-
colour.)

In addition to the demonstration effect, in some instances popular
upheavals were aided in more direct and tangible ways. The underground Solidarity in the 1980s covertly received significant financial
and logistical support from abroad, mostly from Western trade unions.
In the 1990s, pro-democracy movements in Yugoslavia or Ukraine
were overtly aided by international NGOs, which supplied 'democratic
know-how', in addition to printing presses, radio transmitters, and
similar equipment. Furthermore, as Bunce and Wolchik (2006) point
out, 'graduates' of one 'electoral revolution' were often instrumental in
facilitating another one in a neighbouring country (see, for instance,
the Serb, Georgian, Polish, Czech, and Slovak contributions to the
Orange Revolution in Ukraine).

Yet, the access to information and the mobilizing force of the
demonstration effect cannot alone account for the fact that it was not
until 1989 that the success of a rebellion in one country (Poland)
launched a domino effect across the region. An old saying, attributed
to Vladimir Lenin, says that revolutions happen when 'the masses do
not want the old ways anymore and the regime is unable to maintain
the old ways anymore'. In the late 1980s, all Central and East
European communist regimes faced – although most of them failed to
recognize it – a crisis of legitimization (Rigby and Feher, 1982; Rychard,
1992). Since their rise to power after the Second World War, the communists of Central and Eastern Europe based their rule on 'legitimisa-
tion through utopia': a promise to create an ideal system of social,
political, an economic institutions, guaranteeing all citizens equal
rights and equal access to the benefits of the welfare state; a system
that would eventually generate an affluent society, free of exploitation
and conflict. By the late 1980s this mechanism of legitimization had
exhausted its potential. The promise of a better, more just political
system and society was never fulfilled, and even the communist leaders
occasionally had to admit this: but, above all, the countries of Central
and Eastern Europe experienced economic crisis, or, at the very best,
stagnation. The gap between their 'economies of shortage' (Kornai,
1980) and the affluent market economies of Western Europe in North
America became wider than ever. The people responded with disbelief
to the official statistics on economic growth, which were themselves
much less impressive than in the 1950s or 1960s.

Hence, the course of Central-Eastern European revolutions seems to
confirm the analyses of those theorists, who, following Alexis de
Tocqueville (1966), point to the importance of relative deprivation
(Gurr, 1970) or a widening gap between popular expectations and the

actual fulfilment of needs (Davies, 1969) as factors leading to revolutionary ferment. Indeed, the 'masses' of the region did not want the old ways anymore.

On the other side of the equation, governments could not continue to act in the old ways either. Not only were they unable to keep up with the pace of economic growth in the West; even more importantly, in the summer of 1989 they lost another tool of legitimization – the Brezhnev doctrine. They could no longer count on Soviet 'friendly assistance'; they could not even blackmail their own populace by using the spectre of a Soviet intervention. Subsequently, they lost, gradually or suddenly, the allegiance of intellectuals, the unity within their own ranks, and the will and determination to use coercive means in protection of their rule (the mechanisms outlined theoretically by Crane Brinton, 1965). Even where the top leader did not hesitate to resort to coercion (Ceausescu in Romania), the defection of his lieutenants made those efforts fruitless.

This leads us to another common feature of Central and Eastern European revolutions: their non-violent character. With the notable exception of Romania, these revolutions were remarkable in the commitment of their participants to use civil disobedience and peaceful demonstrations, rather than any violent means, in their quest for victory. Unlike in previous instances (Hungary 1956, Poland 1956, 1970, 1976, 1981), the national communist authorities this time also refrained from using violence, even if only out of impotence. Another interesting case – with potentially significant theoretical implications – is the one of Yugoslavia (or rather, Serbia). The October 2000 demonstrations (not entirely non-violent) led to the collapse of the Milosevic regime. Yet, only four years earlier, between November 1996 and February 1997, another wave of massive street demonstrations, night after night, shook Belgrade and other Serbian cities – to no avail. The precipitating factor was the same (electoral fraud by the regime), so was the scale of involvement and determination of participants. Why, then, was Milosevic able to outwait the protestors in 1997 but not in 2000? Did the violence applied by some demonstrators who, in 2000, stormed the parliament building tip the scales? Or did Milosevic's resolve weaken after the NATO bombing campaign in defence of Kosovo Albanians in 1999? Or were numerous defections from the regime camp the decisive factor here? An answer to these and similar questions is important not only for journalists and historians, but also for those who try to make general, theoretical statements about revolutions, rebellions, and popular upheavals.

While the revolutions in CEE seem to confirm some theoretical approaches (such as those of de Tocqueville and his followers, or

Crane Brinton) and disconfirm others (Karl Marx, with his emphasis on absolute deprivation), they remain, almost two decades later, understudied within mainstream sociological and political theory. Sure enough, the literature covering particular cases is vast and contains important theoretical contributions (see, for instance, Touraine, 1983; Garton Ash, 1985 and 1993; Dahrendorf, 1990; Ost, 1990; Jowitt, 1992; Bernhard, 1993; Kubik, 1994; Ekiert, 1996; Tokes, 1996; Cirtautas, 1997; Kenney, 2002, to name just a few), yet those scholars whose substantive interest is not in the region but in theory, seldom utilize the available evidence from Central and Eastern Europe.

Elections and voting behaviour

In his essay *Reflections on the Revolution in Europe*, Ralf Dahrendorf made the following prediction about the course of reforms in the region:

> I suspect that ... in East Central Europe ... the pendulum of normal politics will have to swing once in the liberal and once in the social direction before you feel that you have made it. The liberal direction ... involves the jump start of economies ... Opposition to this process is bound to arise, and it will be about the social cost of economic growth. At some point, in four or even eight years' time ... other groups will take over. They may even be called Social Democrats (Dahrendorf, 1990: 71–2).

In several countries of the region, the electoral pendulum swung in the social direction, often earlier than the four or eight years Dahrendorf had predicted. The victorious parties were called social democrats, socialist, or 'democratic left'. With only one exception (the Czech Social Democrats), they were reformed (more or less) communists.

The electoral resurgence of former communists constitutes one of the most fascinating aspects of democratic consolidation in Central and Eastern Europe. The 'Dahrendorf hypothesis' has been commonly accepted as the main explanation of the pendulum effect in Central European electoral politics (Brown, 1994; Mason, 1996; Holmes, 1997). This point of view is based on the presumption that societies undergoing a rapid social and economic change bifurcate into winners and losers, haves and have-nots, causing massive feelings of relative deprivation, which in turn generate political populism. The hardships of transition feed retroactive sentiments – longings for the times of full employment and a reliable if also a minimal social safety net. Such reasoning hardly defies the common sense and seems at least reasonable. As Mateju *et al.* point out: these processes 'create conditions for the strengthening of class-based voting behaviour and the crystallization of the "traditional" left-right political spectrum' (1999: 235).

Many other authors have accepted a similar point of view, while trying to incorporate other, ideological and/or cultural factors. Szelenyi *et al.* have observed that many intellectuals have interpreted the political developments of the 1980s and 1990s in Central Europe in terms of a conflict between conservative and liberal values, dismissing the role of the socio-economic, or left-right dimension. On the basis of empirical evidence from Hungary and Poland in the early 1990s, they suggested as the more appropriate a 'theory of two axes', pointing out that '[w]hile the Liberal/Conservative cleavage is created by differences in values, the Left/Right axis is based on economic interests' (1997: 205). Herbert Kitschelt (1992) suggested that, with the progress of transition, the orthogonal relationship between these two dimensions would be displaced by a parallel one, with the ends of the political continuum defined, as in Western Europe, by a libertarian and distributive left and an authoritarian and pro-market right. Evans and Whitefield (1993), on the contrary, argued that economic and cultural liberalism would remain associated with each other in East Central Europe, hence specific issue dimensions would be defined by redistributive, authoritarian, anti-West attitudes vying with pro-market, liberal, cosmopolitan ones. All the cited authors agreed that, as the transition to market economy progressed, the economic cleavage would gain a more prominent role in determining the actual choice the voter makes in the voting booth.

Such hypotheses, obviously, can be (and have been) tested empirically. The available data seem to confirm that two major cleavages are particularly relevant for voting behaviour in post-communist Europe: a socio-economic cleavage between the supporters of a free-market/free-enterprise economy and those preferring welfare oriented state interventionism (in short, the classical left–right cleavage), and a cultural cleavage between particularism and universalism. The latter may, at specific times and places, express itself as a conflict between the traditional and the modern, the confessional and the secular, or between exclusive nationalism and a more inclusive, pan-European orientation. It may also still reflect the attitudes towards the communist past of a given country. The data suggest further that the dominant role of the value-based cleavage lasted at least until the end of the 1990s. For instance, the constituencies of the post-Solidarity parties and the post-communist Democratic Left Alliance in Poland did not differ from one another in terms of their views on the economy and social welfare (which is hardly surprising, given the strong trade union component of both movements); what set them apart were views on such issues as abortion or the public role of the Roman Catholic church (Jasiewicz, 2003). Similarly, religiosity was the best predictor of voting preferences in Hungary (Szelenyi, Fodor and Hanley, 1997). Ethnic issues (such as policies towards ethnic minorities) have greatly influenced patterns of voting behaviour in the Baltics (the Russian minority in Latvia and Estonia), the Balkans (Albanians in Macedonia, Turks in Bulgaria, Hungarians in Romania and Serbia, Serbs in Croatia, not to mention the situation in Bosnia or Kosovo), and in Slovakia (Hungarians). Across the region, political parties based on ethnicity have remained much more common than those based on social class (such as the Polish Peasant Party).

Still, the cases of successful resurgence by the former communists in the mid-1990s may be attributed, at least in part, to the social costs of economic growth. The hardships of the transition (which often reached the point of absolute pauperization), whether caused by the ultimately successful 'shock therapy' (as in Poland), or by a 'shock without therapy' (as in Lithuania or Bulgaria in the 1990s), caused widespread popular dissatisfaction and gave a competitive advantage to political actors promising quick and easy solutions. The former communists were as eager as anyone else to make such promises. Having also the additional advantage of control over the assets of their predecessors (from material resources to connections in the media), they were able to mobilize electoral support sufficient to win, either as a single actor, or as a senior partner in a coalition. They could be prevented from scoring such a victory by certain idiosyncratic factors, which fell into three general patterns (see Jasiewicz, 1998): a relatively smooth transition without a dramatic decline in standards of living (Slovenia, the Czech Republic), the presence of an external threat associated with the communist past (Latvia, Estonia), or an effective non-liberal alternative (the semi-authoritarian regimes in Croatia and Slovakia in the 1990s, the Radical Party in Serbia). But there were no quick and easy fixes for the ills of transition, and the victorious reformed communists were either forced to continue the reform policies of their predecessors (Poland, Hungary, Lithuania), or simply wasted time and national resources (Bulgaria). As in any democracy, the scrutiny of unfulfilled and fulfilled promises came at the time of the next free and fair general elections, in which the post-communists were defeated. They were among the first to use populism as a tool to enhance their chances in elections; after their period in government they have become perceived as the part of the establishment, the rascals that must be thrown out. Consequently, at the turn of the century, the electoral pendulum in several countries began to swing neither to the left nor the right, but altogether away from the left–right dimension. Various anti-establishment and even anti-system parties and movements began to score well in elections: suffice it to mention the National Movement Simeon II in Bulgaria (for the period 2001–05, the former Tsar Simeon II of the House of Saxe-Coburg-Gotha became Prime Minister as Simeon Saxekoburggotski), a Polish anti-system party, Self-Defence, and its demagogical leader Andrzej Lepper, or the Smer-SD (Direction-Social Democracy) party in Slovakia, which under the charismatic leadership of Robert Fico won the 2006 general election.

Political populism – understood here as a political discourse that calls for protection of the 'man in the street' from economic misfortunes (allegedly caused by reforms introduced for the benefit of narrow elites), usually coupled with ethnic or religious particularism or even xenophobia (again, in the name of protection of the in-group against alien forces and foreign schemes), has been present in East Central European politics ever since the beginning of the transition (and before). Almost all East Central European countries have aspired to join the European Union; eight (the Czech Republic, Estonia, Hungary, Latvia, Lithuania, Poland, Slovakia, and Slovenia) accomplished this goal in 2004, while two more (Bulgaria and Romania) joined in 2007. Central European populists see in the European Union the epitome of their fears: free markets, open borders, supranational political institutions. The public debate on EU membership has brought to the forefront the cleavage between particularistic and redistributive (and, in their extreme version, outright xenophobic-populist) attitudes and universalistic, liberal, pro-European attitudes. This cleavage typically combines the economic dimension (the losers versus the winners in the process of transition) with that one stemming from the differences in values, and runs roughly along the lines predicted by Evans and Whitefield. It has a potential of superseding other cleavages: the re-emerging traditional left–right, or the liberal–conservative. The electoral resurgence of political populism has also recently taken place in several old member states of the EU (France, Austria, the Netherlands). This obviously opens up avenues for most odd political alliances and configurations. At the very beginning of the new millennium, politics in Europe (not only Central or Eastern Europe) seem to have entered a new (but not quite unexplored) territory.

The sudden emergence of new parties – and, as the electoral ups and downs of the former communists illustrate, perhaps the most spectacular feature of the electoral process and voting behaviour in post-communist CEE – brings with it the perils of incumbency. As a rule, the governing parties (be it a single party government or a coalition) do worse in the elections at the end of their term than in those that had brought them to power. According to Kieran Williams (2003), in ten CEE states classified as parliamentary democracies (Bulgaria, Czech Republic, Estonia, Hungary, Latvia, Lithuania, Poland, Romania, Slovakia, and Slovenia), during the period of 1990 to 2002, of 59 Prime Ministers only Janez Drnovsek of Slovenia (three times, in 1992, 1996, and 2000), Vaclav Klaus of the Czech Republic (1996), and Mikulas Dzurinda of Slovakia (2002) were re-elected to a consecutive term. Since 2002, all these states have undergone another election cycle; only three more prime ministers have been able to secure re-election: Algirdas Brazauskas in Lithuania (2004), Ferenc Gyurcsany in Hungary (2006), and Aigars Kalvitis in Latvia (2006).

Equally striking are data about the percentage of the popular vote gathered by incumbent parties. According to Williams, for the parties that formed a ruling coalition after one election, their vote share in the next election diminished, on average, by nearly 17 per cent (again during the period 1990–2002). This number reflects, among other factors, the high losses suffered in the second post-transition election by the original umbrella movements, such Public Against Violence in Slovakia in 1992 (37 per cent). Above all, however, it is influenced by the popular will to 'throw the rascals out': citizens, disappointed with the hardships brought in by economic reforms in general and the performance of a given government in particular, are receptive to the populist rhetoric of opposition parties – often only to turn against them at the time of next election. Perhaps the most telling is the case of Poland, where parties that in 1997 had formed the ruling coalition, the Electoral Action Solidarity (AWS) and the Freedom Union (UW), four years later not only suffered the highest loss in vote share recorded in CEE since 1990 (39 per cent), but did not even manage to win a single seat in the new parliament (this applies, however, to the parties running under their original banners; certain splinter groupings in this election did quite well). Yet, the coalition of the post-communist Democratic Left Alliance (SLD) and the Labour Union (UP), which delivered this devastating blow to the AWS and UW in 2001, in the following (2005) election experienced its own humiliation, losing nearly 30 per cent of its vote share. Pre-election promises tend to turn against the victorious parties, if they repeat the mistakes of their predecessor, which in CEE is more often a rule than an exception. Only in a handful of cases (Estonia 2003, the Czech Republic 1996 and 2006, Slovenia 1996, Hungary 2006, Slovakia 1994, Latvia 2006) were the ruling coalition parties able to increase their vote share. Those gains were always only minimal, in no case exceeding 5 per cent; one of the largest, the 3.8 per cent gained jointly by the Centre Party and Reform Party in Estonia in 2003, proved insufficient to keep this minority coalition in power. The amplitude of the 'anti-incumbent' pendulum swing differs from country to country; it tends to be relatively high in Poland, Slovakia and Lithuania, and relatively low in the Czech Republic, Hungary and Slovenia. All in all, voter volatility remains high, with many voters choosing, often at the very last moment, to cast a vote for the 'highest bidder': a party or a candidate who is the most critical of the current government and promises the easiest solutions for the future.

Furthermore, as the vicissitudes of transition continued, the failures of political elites to resolve important problems, coupled with incompetence, corruption and cronyism, have brought about the general disillusionment and apathy of the electorate. Most strikingly, turnout in elections has declined, sometimes dramatically. Williams, in his article, gives the average turnout in ten parliamentary democracies as 76.1 for 1990–96 and 62.9 per cent for 1997–2002. The *Global Report on Voter Turnout Since 1945*, published by the International Institute for Democracy and Electoral Assistance (IDEA) in 2002 (Pintor and Gratschew, 2002), points out that citizens of post-communist CEE tend to participate in elections at a lower rate than the inhabitants of the established democracies in Western Europe, North America, and Oceania. In Table 12.1, we present data on voting turnout in parlia-

Table 12.1   *Turnout in parliamentary elections, 1945–2001*

Country	Vote/voting age population
Albania	92.4 (4)
Bulgaria	76.1 (43)
Croatia	77.2 (41)
Czech Republic	82.8 (25)
Estonia	53.5 (123)
Hungary	68.1 (67)
Latvia	60.3 (98)
Lithuania	56.9 (111)
Macedonia	48.4 (134)
Moldova	61.6 (93)
Poland	51.4 (128)
Romania	72.2 (58)
Slovakia	82.9 (24)
Slovenia	77.9 (40)
Ukraine	70.8 (61)
As compared with	
United States	47.7 (138)
United Kingdom	73.8 (53)

mentary elections between 1945 and 2001 measured as a ratio of those participating in elections to the voting age population, with the world-wide ranking (out of 169 states) given in parentheses.

It should be noted that the low participation rates recorded for Estonia, Latvia, and Moldova are influenced by the presence in these countries of ethnic Russians, who have not qualified for citizenship and, hence, for voting rights. In states that choose their presidents by popular vote (Bulgaria, Lithuania, Macedonia, Moldova, Poland, Romania, Slovakia, Slovenia, Ukraine), turnout in presidential elections tends to be slightly higher than in parliamentary ones; on the other hand, municipal elections – as well as super-national ones (European Parliament) – tend to attract fewer voters. The IDEA data do not include Serbia, where low turnout led to a constitutional crisis in 2003–04, when three consecutive attempts to elect a president failed due to turnout falling below the legally required 50 per cent. Consequently, the law was changed and Boris Tadic was elected president in June 2004, with the turnout still below 50 per cent.

The decline in voting participation, while universal across the board, was the steepest in the former Czechoslovakia: in the Czech Republic from a high of 96.8 per cent in 1990 to a low of 58.0 per cent in 2002, in Slovakia from 95.4 per cent in 1990 to 54.7 per cent in 2006. Consistently, the lowest turnout has been recorded in Poland. While elsewhere in the region the first election (which everywhere was more of a referendum on communist rule than anything else) brought about a massive mobilization of the electorate (usually well above 80 per cent), in Poland in June 1989, for the election that launched the process of change across the region, a mere 62.1 per cent showed up at the polls. Two years later, the turnout in parliamentary elections in Poland fell to 43.1 per cent; it later stabilized at about a half of all eligible voters, to fall again to a mere 40.6 per cent in 2005. This apparent indifference is difficult to explain. A young Polish scholar (Czesnik, 2006), in a comparative analysis of Poland and other CEE states, tested three hypotheses: institutional (peculiarities of electoral law), structural (specific features of social stratification), and historical-cultural (patterns of behaviour shaped by unique historical factors), and found that none of the three provided a compelling explanation of different levels in voter turnout. All in all, the varying patterns of electoral participation in CEE still await a thorough empirical analysis and a convincing theoretical interpretation, in a broader context of citizens' involvement in politics.

Membership in political organizations

The apathy of the Polish electorate might be surprising to anyone who has studied the history of civic resistance against communism in CEE. As noted by Padraic Kenney, 'As a result of the Solidarity experiment, there were far more people in Poland than elsewhere with experience in independent political activism – perhaps by a factor of 100' (2002: 15). Not much of this activism remains today, if as a measure we use the membership of political parties and other politically involved organizations. A mere 1.5 per cent of the Polish adult population, or somewhere between 400,000 and 450,000 individuals, carry a party card of any kind (Szczerbiak, 2001). But in this respect Poland is no exception: party membership in the Czech Republic, Slovakia, Hungary, and Ukraine, even if slightly higher than in Poland, oscillates around 2.5 per cent, and at any rate does not exceed 3.0 per cent (see Webb and White, 2007). Even these numbers, given their provenance (self-reporting by parties and estimates based on public opinion polls), are more likely to exaggerate than to understate actual party membership nationwide. In other states in the region, party membership is in all likelihood even lower, but too difficult to estimate with any accuracy, due to the questionable reliability of party statistics. It is not a coincidence that this issue is not covered in any systematic or exhaustive way even in the best recent studies (see, for instance, Lewis, 2001; Kostelecky, 2002).

One plausible explanation of the low membership levels may be found in the rapidly changing nature of mass communication at the turn of the century. Parties may simply have no use for mass membership anymore. Their finances come from state subsidies and other sources (often of dubious legality) and they would not be able to sustain themselves from members' dues alone, no matter how massive the membership. Also, card-carrying members ceased to play an essential role in electoral campaigns, as these are taken over by professional organizations and narrow groups of volunteers, while party leaders can communicate directly with potential voters utilizing broadcast media, in particular television. One can agree with David Olson's observation that parties in Central European new democracies do not emulate the patterns of party development in the West, but rather 'leapfrog directly into the mass communications video age' (Olson, 1998: 445).

Yet, the low membership of political parties, when examined against the backdrop of more general patterns of participation in secondary organizations, becomes a symptom of another problem common to all post-communist polities, often referred to as 'the weakness of civil society'. Obviously, civil society – a complex, multi-dimensional phe-

nomenon – cannot be equated with membership in formal organizations alone (see Chapter 13). Still, people's willingness to get engaged in
voluntary associations remains a decent indicator of the strength and
quality of social bonds in a given place at a given time. Marc Morjé
Howard (2003: 69) in his analysis of 13 CEE polities (his sample
includes East Germany, but excludes Poland, Moldova, and several
post-Yugoslav states) compared with ten post-authoritarian polities
(such as Spain or Brazil) and eight 'old' democracies (among them the
United States and Scandinavian countries) points out that the average
number of organizational memberships in post-communist CEE is, at
0.91, significantly lower than in two other groups (post-authoritarian
1.82, older democracies 2.39). Furthermore, his statistical analysis indi-
cates that the communist past has a significantly stronger influence in
determining this number than other factors, such as economic development, the current scope of civil liberties, or historical traditions associated with Western civilization (Howard, 2003: 83–4).

Almost a generation after the collapse of communist rule, its legacy
remains strong. The communists attempted to replace the natural horizontal ties of civil society with vertical ones, with party-state agencies
playing at least an intermediary – if not leading – role in all public (and
often also in private) social relations. The mass upheavals of the late
1980s and early 1990s restored grass-roots-level social bonds, but only
temporarily. At its pinnacle in 1981, Solidarity had almost ten million
members; today, the entire trade union membership in Poland is just a
fraction of this number. Elsewhere in CEE the situation is not any better
(see Crowley and Ost, 2001). Weak trade unions find their match in
underdeveloped business associations. The tripartite (labour–government–business) arrangements that have been instrumental in steering
socio-economic development in many West European states have played
no significant role in East Central Europe. The absence of strong formal
organizations contributes to – and in turn results from – the growing role
of informal ties and the blurring of lines separating politics from business.

Consequently, corruption, cronyism and nepotism spread out and
hamper the re-emergence of civil society. The Corruption Perception
Index (CPI) published annually by Transparency International
(http://wwl.transparency.org.cpi/) gives ECE much lower marks than
those recorded by their West European counterparts. Furthermore,
these marks, in both absolute and relative sense, have not been
improving over the past decade. East-Central Europeans, so apt at
getting organized at times of crisis, seem indifferent, if not helpless,
when it comes to managing their day-to-day affairs. Social atomization
and anomie, induced along with the introduction of communist
regimes decades ago, remain in place.

Protest politics

In September 2006, six weeks before the fiftieth anniversary of the tragic Hungarian Uprising, the people of Budapest took to the streets again. This time their goal was more limited than a half-century before: not the abolition of a hated Soviet-installed regime, but the resignation of a prime minister who only six month earlier had managed to win re-election (a rare feat in CEE these days, as we have noted). A leaked tape revealed that Prime Minister Gyurcsany, during the campaign, had cynically misled the electorate about the real state of the Hungarian economy. The 2006 Budapest riots are, certainly, an exception from the patterns common for the entire region, even if only because of the high stakes involved and the level of violence used by both the angry mob and the riot police. Yet, these stunning events illustrate, through their exceptionality, a truly remarkable phenomenon: the transition to democracy and a market economy in Central and Eastern Europe has been, by and large, surprisingly peaceful. As we observed above, in the early stages of systemic transformation it was expected that economic hardships might fuel class-based voting and promote electoral populism. For the same reasons, many expected high levels of industrial unrest: from work stoppages and strikes to street demonstrations and riots. Developments of this kind seemed likely because of the expected increase in the class-consciousness of workers who had been deprived of the special position given to them by communist ideology and threatened by rationalization of industrial production and employment. Indeed, as Branko Milanovic points out, the cuts in wages in CEE in the 1990s have been 'larger than those experienced by labor in major countries during the Great Depression' (1998: 30). Crowley and Ost compare economic contraction in Poland in the early 1990s and in Russia in the mid-1990s 'to that of Germany in the four years preceding Hitler's rise to power' (2001: 1). Yet, as noted by Ekiert and Kubik (1999), even in Poland, where instances of 'contentious collective action' have been in recent years (as in the past) more frequent than elsewhere in the region, at no time did they pose a serious challenge to the process of democratic consolidation.

Certainly, there have been many cases of industrial unrest across the region, from countries with a strong tradition of organized workers' movements and independent trade unions (Poland) to those where trade unions had been completely under communist party state control (Ukraine): in some instances, workers' rage at hardships was cynically used by politicians trying to outmanoeuvre their rivals. Such was the case when in 1990 and 1991, President Ion Illiescu of Romania 'invited' Jiu Valley miners to come to Bucharest, first to disperse pro-democracy student demonstrations, and then to force out the reformist prime minister, Petre Roman. Also, 'economic anger' is not specific to workers alone, as evidenced by road blockades set up periodically by Polish farmers (but only until 2004, when they became eligible for EU agricultural subventions). Yet, the overall frequency of economically motivated strikes and demonstrations in CEE does not deviate much from analogous instances in other democracies (see Welz and Kaupinnen, 2005). Even more importantly, nowhere in the region did industrial unrest so far rise to a point or assume forms that would significantly alter the nature of democratic politics.

In ways parallel to the patterns of voting behaviour, sporadic political mobilization in CEE may also be instigated by non-economic (cultural) factors, such as ethnicity, religion, lifestyle, or simply the expression of certain values (for instance, pro- or anti-democracy). Sporadic political actions of this sort are surely not uncommon across the region. Some have gained a certain level of fame – or notoriety: suffice it to mention the controversies stirred by the wall raised in the Czech city Usti-nad-Labem to separate neighbourhoods inhabited by the Romani (Gypsy) population from the well-to-do middle-class Czechs, or by decisions of certain mayors in Poland to ban gay parades in their cities. Also the recent Budapest demonstrations seem to have been motivated more by outrage over violations of democratic principles than by any immediate economic hardships. But again, political actions stemming from cultural factors, while sometimes causing local disruptions of public order, have not so far undermined the fundaments of democracy.

To sum up: young democracies in Central and Eastern Europe have experienced the challenge of grass-roots political activism at a moderate level, at most. They have managed to cope with this challenge remarkably well. They have been able to establish political mechanisms that help to diffuse and absorb political discontent and usually allow it to flow through the channels of electoral competition. In that respect, they are performing, on the average, no worse than typical old democracies or post-authoritarian polities.

Popular attitudes and democratic consolidation

Juan Linz and Alfred Stepan in their classic work on democratic transition and consolidation have this to say about the question of attitudes: 'Attitudinally, democracy becomes the only game in town when, even in the face of severe political and economic crises, the overwhelming majority of the people believe that any further political change must emerge from within the parameters of democratic formulas' (1996: 5). Indeed, if communism failed because it did not fulfil its promise of an efficient, prosperous economy and a fairer just society, the same supply-and-demand approach can be used to assess democratic regimes. Policies that alienate significant segments of population may not only bring down an unpopular government, but also undermine popular support for democracy itself. In the first half of the twentieth century democracies across the region gave way to various authoritarian governments precisely because they failed to meet popular expectations. Will history repeat itself?

Opinions about governments' performance fluctuate greatly over time and from place to place. Yet, as Linz and Stepan point out, what really matters here is not the evaluation of particular governments, but the level of support for democratic procedures and institutions as the most appropriate way to organize collective life. If people who have personally experienced the shortcomings of both democratic and undemocratic regimes (the fate of older and middle-aged Central and East Europeans) opt in favour of the former, then one can be assured of durability of democracy in the region. This issue has been addressed in several comparative and comprehensive research projects conducted in the mid-1990s (Plasser *et al.*, 1998; Rose *et al.*, 1998). The general conclusions stemming from these projects are moderately optimistic. Democracy seems to have taken root in Central and Eastern Europe, and to prove more attractive than its alternatives. Furthermore, while support for the current (democratic) regime is still tied to the assessment of economic performance (another attitudinal, hence volatile, variable), rejection of non-democratic alternatives is more solidly rooted in structural factors, such as education, urbanization, and income (see Rose *et al.*, 1998: 193). In Central Europe (the Czech Republic, Hungary, Poland, Slovakia) almost half of the population can be considered what Linz and Stepan (1996: 226–7) call 'confident democrats' – individuals who believe that democracy is both legitimate (preferable to other forms of government) and, by and large, effective in solving major social and economic problems. Still, this number is lower than the 70 per cent in neighbouring Austria (Plasser *et al.*, 1998: 191); comparable estimates among post-authoritarian regimes are close to 80 per cent for Southern Europe (Spain, Portugal, Greece), but for Latin America they are on levels similar or lower than these in CEE (Linz and Stepan, 1996: 229).

The cited data come from the mid-1990s; there are some indications (unpublished data from the 2004 European Election Study) that support for democracy in all Central European states has somehow eroded since then, but there has been a similar experience in several

West European polities (Austria and Portugal among them). Democracy is, by its nature, a tiring and unruly – often outright messy – enterprise. Arguably, Central European political elites do little to spare their people exposure to democracy's discontents. But, across the region, support for non-democratic alternatives does not approach threatening levels (if we set aside the genuinely undemocratic regime in Belarus). If anything, popular dissatisfaction with democracy is expressed by apathy and anomie, as discussed throughout this chapter. Democracy might be 'the only game in town', but many potential players prefer to stay home rather than join in.

None the less, once again, Winston Churchill's famous bon mot finds its confirmation: 'democracy is the worst form of government except all the others'.

Chapter 13

Civil Society

Cas Mudde

No concept has been so central to the discussions on Central and East European politics than that of civil society. Whereas the 'democratic revolutions' of 1989 were seen as the victory of a flourishing civil society, the period of post-communism has generally been considered as one of a particularly weak civil society. While there has been some debate over the alleged effects of this 'fact' on the state of democracy in the region, notably the Havel–Klaus–Pithart debate (see the *Journal of Democracy*, January 1996), the general consensus in academia and politics alike is that the poor development of civil society in post-communist Europe is one of the main causes of the assumed lack of democratic consolidation (in terms of a deepening of democracy) in the region.

This chapter will critically assess the claim of the weakness of civil society in Central and Eastern Europe on the basis of concepts, empirical evidence and theories. First, we will briefly highlight the key problems in defining the concept of civil society. Second, we will present a necessarily rough empirical account of the state of civil society in the region, based on a variety of indicators, and compare it to other regions in the world. Third, we will debate the issue of civil society in its larger political and social context, addressing some of the key issues and relationships involved. Fourth, and finally, we will revisit the weakness of civil society thesis, arguing that the situation is more nuanced than is generally stated.

Definition: who is in, who is out?

Civil society is most commonly defined as a set of organizations that operate between the state, the family (individual; household) and economic production (market; firms). Individuals and families are excluded because of their orientation to their own private ends and firms because of their orientations towards profit making (Keane,

1988; Cohen and Arato, 1992; Kopecky and Mudde, 2003). While the exclusion of economic society is widely accepted among contemporary authors, it constitutes a significant break from the western traditions of both the (Scottish) liberals and the Marxists (see, for instance, Szacki, 1995).

Influential authors have distinguished not only between civil society and economic society, but also between civil society and political society (see, for instance, Linz and Stepan, 1996; Kubik, 2000). In fact, many academics and activists in the region exclude political parties from the realm of civil society, because they pursue political power and thereby become part of the state. Some even imply the existence of a zero-sum relationship between political parties and civil society; that is, the strength of the one leads to the weakness of the other, sometimes equating political parties and the state. This argument is also linked to the specific weakness of political parties in Central and Eastern Europe, which are still mainly cadre parties with very weak links to society (incidentally, similar critiques are voiced in respect of so-called cartel parties in Western Europe; see Katz and Mair, 1995).

A group that is explicitly excluded on the basis of normative criteria is so-called 'uncivil society'; that is, organizations that are (considered as) either non-democratic or non-liberal. Even if such organizations actually operate between the state, the family, and economic production, they are not accepted as part of civil society. The argument is that while nationalist or communist groups might be part of associational life, they are not 'civil'. As this chapter employs a non-normative definition of civil society, both political parties and 'uncivil' organizations are included under the heading of civil society (cf. Kopecky and Mudde, 2003). As will be discussed later, this inclusion has consequences for the relationship of civil society to democracy and democratization.

The state of affairs

It is received wisdom that civil society in Central and Eastern Europe is underdeveloped and weak. In fact, some authors even deny outright the existence of a real civil society in the region, instead referring to 'an illusory civil society' (Mokrzycki, 2000: 65). Roughly all studies on civil society in Central and Eastern Europe are based on highly impressionistic accounts. They suffer from various flaws: (i) an exaggeration of the strength of civil society in the last phase of communism, often implicitly generalizing the unique case of Poland; (ii) a narrow operationalization of civil society (excluding 'uncivil' groups); and (iii) an absence of empirical evidence for their claims.

The most popular dataset used in studies on democratization in Central and Eastern Europe is that constructed by Freedom House (see Table 13.1). In these studies, the variable 'civil society' is constructed on the basis of the following question: 'Assess the growth of non-governmental organizations, their organizational capacity and financial sustainability, and the legal and political environment in which they function; the development of free trade unions, and interest group participation in the policy process' (Karatnycky *et al.*, 2002: 9). In essence, this indicator is largely constructed on the basis of institutional and legal variables (such as organizations and legal framework), and therefore correlates strongly with the overall assessment of (procedural) democracy in the country.

Table 13.1   *Freedom House scores for civil society in Central and Eastern Europe, 1997–2005 (1 = highest, 7 = lowest)*

Country	1997	1998	99–00	2001	2002	2003	2004	2005
Albania	4.25	4.25	4.00	4.00	3.75	3.75	3.50	3.25
Belarus	5.25	5.75	6.00	6.25	6.25	6.50	6.75	6.75
Bosnia	—	5.00	4.50	6.00	4.25	4.00	3.75	3.75
Bulgaria	4.00	3.75	3.75	3.50	3.25	3.25	3.00	2.75
Croatia	3.50	3.50	3.50	2.75	2.75	3.00	3.00	3.00
Czech Rep.	1.50	1.50	1.50	1.50	1.75	1.50	1.50	1.50
Estonia	2.25	2.25	2.50	2.25	2.00	2.00	2.00	2.00
Hungary	1.25	1.25	1.25	1.25	1.25	1.25	1.25	1.25
Latvia	2.25	2.25	2.25	2.00	2.00	2.00	2.00	1.75
Lithuania	2.25	2.00	2.00	1.75	1.50	1.50	1.50	1.50
Macedonia	3.75	3.75	3.50	3.75	4.00	3.75	3.25	3.25
Moldova	3.75	3.75	3.75	3.75	4.00	3.75	4.00	4.00
Poland	1.25	1.25	1.25	1.25	1.25	1.25	1.25	1.25
Romania	3.75	3.75	3.00	3.00	3.00	2.75	2.50	2.25
Slovakia	3.25	3.00	2.25	2.00	1.75	1.50	1.25	1.25
Slovenia	2.00	2.00	1.75	1.75	1.50	1.50	1.50	1.75
Ukraine	4.00	4.25	4.00	3.75	3.75	3.50	3.75	3.00
Yugoslavia*	—	5.00	5.25	4.00	3.00	2.75	2.75	2.75

Note: * Yugoslavia changes during this period and from 2004 is only the score of Serbia.
Source: adapted from www.freedomhouse.org.

On the basis of an overview of all post-communist countries for the period 1997–2005, Freedom House data show the following trends (Goehring and Schnetzer, 2005: 28): among the new EU members the average score has improved from 2.00 to 1.53, in 'the Balkans' it has improved even more, from 3.85 to 3.06, but in the 'non-Baltic former Soviet republics' the score has remained at 4.88 (despite annual variations). As the intermediate scores are unspecified, it is difficult to evaluate these changes, but they seem fairly small. In summary, the three sub-regions are stable in their differences: the new EU members have a highly developed/free civil society, the Balkans a moderately developed/free civil society, and the non-Baltic former Soviet states a poorly developed/free civil society.

A similar, if somewhat more insightful, indicator is the 'sustainability index' of the United States Agency for International Development (USAID, 2006). Constructed on the basis of seven separate if interdependent variables – legal environment, organizational capacity, financial viability, advocacy, service provision, infrastructure, and public image – the index provides a comprehensive indicator of the state of (formal) civil society in Central and Eastern Europe and Eurasia. In 2005 USAID considered NGO sustainability as 'consolidated' in all but one of the Central European countries that joined the EU in June 2004 (the exception was Slovenia). The other countries in the region were in 'mid-transition', as most of Eurasia, or in 'early transition'; that is, the clearest non-democracies (Belarus, Turkmenistan, and Uzbekistan).

More in-depth empirical accounts of civil society in the region generally use one of two indicators: the number of non-governmental organizations (NGOs) or the level of participation of individual citizens. Although the thesis of the weakness of civil society is popular in both fields, it is particularly with regard to the latter indicator that desperation is expressed. In fact, in terms of the number of NGOs Central and Eastern Europe seems to have a fairly vibrant civil society. While reliable comparative data are lacking, even the scattered information that is available shows a plethora of NGOs in all countries in the region: for example, Hungary had almost 50,000 organizations in 2000, while Poland had a little under 100,000 in 2002 (Rose-Ackerman, 2005: 169). Particularly popular fields of activity are minority rights, ranging from Roma to women, environmental protection, and corruption and good governance. Not surprisingly, given the dependence of local civil society organizations on extra-regional funding, these are all topics considered to be of major concern in the donor countries in the West (see below).

Nowadays, most experts agree that the impressive number of registered NGOs provides a fairly poor indicator of the real state of civil society in the region. A majority of these 'organizations' exist either in name alone, or as one-person businesses. And even the NGOs that are established as active participants in the political realm of their country tend to have little contact with the wider population, let alone a significant grass-roots base. The comparative data collected by the Johns Hopkins Comparative Nonprofit Sector Project puts all of the Central and Eastern European states included in its study among the bottom countries in terms of percentage of paid staff and volunteers in the nonprofit sector in relation to the active workforce in the country.

A more positive picture is painted by the research conducted by Civicus, the World Alliance for Citizen Participation. According to their survey of civil society organizations, the situation in Central and Eastern Europe is not that bad. Though some problems remain, particularly with regard to corruption and transparency, the civil society organizations, on average, are reported to be internally democratic, gender balanced, tolerant and non-violent. One has to treat these findings with some caution, however, as the organizations surveyed seem to be a particular subsection of civil society – that is, groups that are integrated into what is increasingly labelled 'global civil society' (see, for instance, Keane, 2003).

It is particularly with respect to mass participation in associational life that the weakness of civil society in Central and Eastern Europe has been demonstrated. Irrespective of the datasets used, notably the World Values Studies (WVS) or European Values Surveys (EVS), the degree of activity and membership of civil society organizations in Central and Eastern Europe is extremely low, both in absolute and relative terms (see, for instance, Bashkirova, 2002; Howard, 2003; Rose-Ackerman, 2005). For example, according to the New Europe Barometer of winter 2004–5 the percentage of the population belonging to 'any sports, arts, community or charitable organization' ranged from an acceptable high of 46 per cent in Estonia to a dramatic low of 3 per cent in Romania. The average of the eleven Central and Eastern European countries included was only 16 per cent (Rose, 2005). When compared to other regions of the world, either established or newly democratic, the post-communist region shows a markedly low development of civil society activism. In the words of Marc Morje Howard:

post-communist citizens have significantly and consistently lower levels of membership and participation than citizens of most other democratic countries, particularly when compared to citizens of post-authoritarian countries that have similar levels of economic development and political rights and civil liberties (2003: 147).

And while Central and Eastern Europe fares better than the post-Soviet space, the general conclusion remains valid.

In various Central and Eastern European countries, environmental movements were among the few non-party civil society organizations allowed to function during the last decade of communism. While environmental concerns were important to most groups, many people joined the environmental protests as covers for more overt anti-communist dissidence. After the fall of communism, environmentalist groups lost their prime position within civil society in the region, but they remained among the most numerous. For example, Hungary alone counted 973 environmental organizations in 1998 of which 141 (14 per cent) had been founded before 1990 (Rose-Ackerman, 2005: 175).

At first sight then, the situation seems very good. The region still counts an abundance of environmental groups. The Danish Cooperation for Environment in Eastern Europe (DANCEE) lists a staggering 2,700 environmental NGOs in 15 Central and Eastern European countries. Still, Central and Eastern European citizens remain marginally active in environmental groups: even according to the 1990 World Values Studies, only 2.6 per cent of Central and Eastern Europeans participated in environmentalist groups, compared with 6.2 per cent of the West Europeans (Dalton and Rohrschneider, 2002).

Despite the relatively successful development of gender studies in the region, it is impossible to get a reliable empirical account of the strength of women's organization in post-communist states. There are many different databases available on the web, but all are different in their focus and criteria of inclusion. The Regional Women's Directory Database lists 543 'woman's groups and initiatives' in 11 Central and East European countries, ranging from 130 in Serbia and Montenegro to 12 in Hungary. Clearly, this list is very much biased towards the former Yugoslav republics, probably as a consequence of the better knowledge of the situation in that region of the scholars involved (the project is based in Croatia).

Most scholars note that women's organizations used to have more members under communism, but that they were no more than 'transmission belts' of the ruling party. After 1989, these women's organizations lost most of their members and relevance, despite shedding their communist ideology, yet various new organizations were founded. The net result is that participation levels are comparatively low: 1.9 per cent of Central and East Europeans participated in women's groups, according to the 1990 World Values Study, compared to 3.7 per cent of Western Europeans (Dalton and Rohrschneider, 2002). Overall, women's movements are considered to be active but relatively powerless, in part because of the very low proportion of women in (party) politics.

In line with the strongly normative inclination of civil society scholars, most research on women's movements focuses exclusively on feminist groups, in spite of the fact that many of the groups are either not feminist or even explicitly anti-feminist (see, for instance, Wolchik, 1998). Moreover, in certain cases these anti-feminist groups are far more entrenched and relevant in domestic politics and societies than the feminist groups: this points to a broader problem in the study of civil society in the region – it often ignores activities and groups that do not share liberal democratic values but that do have a significant grass-roots following.

An extreme example of such a sector of 'uncivil society' that flies below the radar of traditional studies of civil society in the region is the neo-Nazi skinhead subculture. Although groups and individuals of this kind tend to eschew formal organizations, partly out of fear of state repression, various Central and East European countries are home to relatively vibrant subcultures. Particularly in countries such as the Czech Republic, Poland, and Slovakia, skinheads number in the thousands and are active in the organization of rock concerts and street demonstrations. In fact, in relative terms Central and Eastern Europe houses more Nazi skins, and a more active subculture, than Western Europe or the United States (see Mudde, 2005).

Key relationships

To achieve a better understanding of the complexities of civil society in Central and Eastern Europe, as well as the varied views of scholars on its development, we will now address some of the key relationships of civil society (and specifically organizations). Of particular interest is the relationship between civil society and both the institution of democracy as well as the process of democratization in the region.

The state

If there is one border of the amorphous concept of civil society that is generally accepted, it is that with the state. The state is *not* part of civil society. That being said, the most fruitful relationship between civil society and the state is a topic of heated debate within academic and political communities. Different models existed in the West at the time of the democratic transitions of Central and Eastern Europe; notably, a relationship of close cooperation (such as neo-corporatism) in much of Western Europe and one of strict separation in the United States. Leading East European dissidents and their Western supporters had pushed for a different model: that of complete opposition. Importantly, this opposition model of 'antipolitics' was not just supported because of the particular context of communist dictatorship; civil society was believed to be inherently anti-state, irrespective of the nature of the regime. As Gyorgy Konrad (1994: 231) clearly stated:

> If the political opposition comes to power, antipolitics keeps at the same distance from, and shows the same independence of, the new government. It will do so even if the new government is made up of sympathetic individuals, friends perhaps; indeed, in such cases it will have the greatest need for independence and distance.

In fact, sympathetic individuals and friends did become leading political figureheads in several Central and East European countries in the first years of transition, exemplified by Vaclav Havel and Lech Walesa, presidents of Czechoslovakia (later the Czech Republic) and Poland, respectively. Some authors were so carried away by this that they claimed civil society was now in power and that this was the ultimate victory for democracy. Others, such as Tomas Mastnak, remained loyal to the idea of fundamental opposition, and argued that 'the unification of civil society and the state in the post-communist polis is the structural destruction of civil society' (Corrin, 1993: 193).

In truth, the grip of civil society on the Central and Eastern European states was never really strong. While a few former dissidents did become leading state figures, most state offices were filled by people who were either not associated with anything or who had been associated with the state under the former regime. This notwithstanding, many leading activists of the generally fairly weak civil societies in the region did take up state (sponsored) positions, leading to the factual beheading of civil society in the region (Dryzek, 1996). This was as much the result of the strength of the new state, at least in terms of being an attractive employer, as of the general weakness of pre-transition civil society.

Today, the intellectual tradition of the anti-state position of civil society remains strong in the region. In most of the cases that victories of civil society are claimed, for example in the 1998 elections in Slovakia or the 2000 'revolution' in former Yugoslavia, it involved at the very least an opposition to the regime. At the same time, various regional political leaders see civil society as a nuisance at best and a 'national' threat at worst. Consequently, cooperative relationships between state and civil society organizations remain scarce in the region, though (the desire for) EU membership has strengthened cooperation in some sectors (see, for instance, Rose-Ackerman, 2005).

Contentious politics

One of the most surprising aspects of post-communist politics is the lack of large-scale political protest (Greskovits, 1998). Social science traditionally associates large outbursts of (violent) political protest with processes of rapid and substantial change, and arguably no region has undergone such profound change over the past decades as Central and Eastern Europe. Whether it has been a double, triple or even quadruple transition, the region has been going through a massive economic, political, and social transformation with all the insecurities and upsets that involves. Moreover, given the anti-state tradition of civil society, and the successful model of contentious politics of the democratic 'revolutions' fresh in mind, the lack of large-scale contentious politics in the region is even more puzzling.

While 'contentious politics' and 'new social movements' have become hot topics in the study of comparative West European politics since the late 1970s, these topics feature scantly in the study of Central and Eastern European politics. Though much research has been done on feminism, and initially some on environmentalist movements, few studies relate them to the new social movements (literature) of Western Europe. And while contentious politics was hailed as ultimately democratic during the transition, many authors consider it un- or even anti-democratic (and thus 'uncivil') in times of post-communist democracy.

The few empirical studies of contentious politics in the region substantiate the impression that the levels of contention are very low (for example, Szabo, 1995; Ekiert and Kubik, 1998). The only exception is Poland, not surprisingly home to the only mass dissident movement under communism (Solidarity), although even there contentious politics is not at the same level as in much of Western Europe (Ekiert and Kubik, 1999). While the lack of much contention by new social movements is not that puzzling – one could argue that during the first decade or so Central and Eastern Europe had not reached the conditions of 'the silent revolution' (Inglehart, 1977) – yet the almost complete paralysis of 'old' social movements such as trade unions is more surprising.

The decline in membership of trade unions was phenomenal during the first years of democratic transition, not unlike that of the communist (successor) parties, but they still remained among the biggest civil society organizations in the region (for example, Crowley and Ost, 2001; Kubicek, 2004). Yet, even the successful model of *Solidarnosc* (Solidarity) and the massive effects of economic transformation could not change the fact that the trade unions are 'among the weakest institutions of the new civil society' (Ost and Crowley, 2001: 1). While the key explanation may be their tainted legacy of the past, the institutional and organizational consequences might have long-lasting effects on the trade unions' (in)ability to organize mass protests.

Though contentious politics is largely absent from day-to-day political life in Central and Eastern Europe, there have been occasional outbursts reminiscent of the democratic 'revolutions' of 1989. At the end of the last century, various civil society bodies organized massive mobilization campaigns in Croatia and Slovakia, thereby raising electoral turnout and overthrowing the semi-authoritarian regimes in their countries. And at the beginning of this century even more dramatic 'revolutions' took place in Ukraine and former Yugoslavia thanks to continuing protests organized by civil society organizations such as Otpor (Resistance).

Foreign support

'Civil society provides the lifeblood of liberty; its creative chaos of associations gives people the chance to live their lives without having to go begging to the state or to other powers' (Dahrendorf, 1997: 50–1). This optimistic statement needs some qualification, as people might not have to beg of the state, but civil society organizations in many regions, including Central and Eastern Europe, are highly dependent on other powers. While it would go too far to speak of 'foreign-made democracy' (Zielonka, 2001b: 511), there is no doubt that the democratization process in the region has been heavily influenced by foreign pressure and support. International organizations such as the European Union and the World Bank have had a crucial effect on the process of economic transition, while the EU and USA were also heavily involved in supporting the development of democratic transition. Foreign organizations such as USAID and the Open Society Institute (OSI) have played a crucial role in the shaping of local civil society through their massive funding.

Paradoxically, while many civil society organizations in the region are highly sceptical about funding by their own state, out of fear of cooption, they do not seem to have the same inhibitions about funding by foreign states. The EU and USA are among the main donors of civil society within Central and Eastern Europe; even though the percentage of the budget for democratic assistance earmarked for civil society specifically is not particularly high (Raik, 2006). Similarly, despite the fact that many of these organizations are highly sceptical about the effects of capitalism and neo-liberal globalization, the Hungarian-American global speculator and philanthropist George Soros is one of the main funders of civil society in the region. In the year 2005 alone his OSI spent a staggering $13.8 mn on specific civil society projects in Central and Eastern Europe. Most money was spent in Poland ($2.3 mn), while the $1.3 mn that was spent in Hungary constituted 75 per cent of the entire annual budget of the national OSI branch.

Many authors have heralded the undeniable successes of the 'Western project' (Smith, 2001: 31), and particularly the role of the European Union (for example, Vachudova, 2005). Still, the effects have not been exclusively conducive to the development of a vibrant local civil society. According to Zielonka (2001b: 524):

> Western aid to East European NGOs has strengthened the basic pillars of each democracy – namely civil society. However, aid has also stalled the spontaneous emergence of indigenous NGOs in these countries. NGOs have thus become a symbol of foreign dependence rather than of grassroots initiative.

This has been particularly problematic given the erratic and short-term nature of the financial support that is provided by international organizations and foreign states. Moreover, the foreign connection has made many of these NGOs, among them key human rights and minority organizations and sometimes the whole idea of 'civil society', an easy target for nationalist attacks, sometimes condoned or even instigated by the state (for example, Croatia under Tudman and Slovakia under Meciar).

In the end, however important foreign influence might have been, it is important to remember that 'international and transnational factors may condition, constrain, catalyze, and induce developments in the course of democratic consolidation; they rarely if ever ultimately determine them' (Pravda, 2001: 15). This applies also to the specific case of post-communist civil society, whose relative weakness is at least as much a reflection of domestic circumstances as of foreign factors. Among these domestic circumstances are the frequently antagonistic relationship between the state and civil society, low levels of interpersonal trust, and the comparatively limited number of people involved in voluntary organizations (a point made strongly in Howard, 2003).

Democracy

It has long been received wisdom that an active civil society is good for democracy. The argument is that civil society fosters democracy in a number of ways: most notably, by dispersing power and thereby keeping a check on the state ('controlling the controllers': Miszlevitz, 1999: 61), and by developing 'social capital' (Putnam, 2000), with ordinary people increasingly involved in the daily affairs of their own society. In fact, many authors even go a step further and argue that an active civil society is a necessary condition for a 'real' democracy. This position was reinforced by the myth of the democratic revolutions of 1989; that is, that 'actually existing' socialist systems had been toppled by an active pro-democratic civil society. While the democratic revolution thesis has become a source of academic dispute in the 1990s (see the range of opinion reported in *East European Politics and Society*, Spring 1999), the consensus on the thesis that real democracy needs active civil society remains strong.

Recently a growing group of scholars have come to challenge this 'civil society determinism' (Li, 1999) on the basis of new insights from contemporary and historical studies. For example, several scholars have showed that Weimar Germany had a relatively thriving civil society, and that the Nazi takeover was largely a result of its strength in civil society (see, for instance, Berman, 1997; Tenfelde, 2000). Similar tensions between an active (un)civil society and flawed democratization have been noted in parts of contemporary Eastern Europe and the Islamic world (see, for instance, Berman, 2003; Kopecky and Mudde, 2003).

But even democratic civil society organizations can have negative effects on democracy or democratization. For example, some observers argue that the various successor organizations of the famous Polish anti-communist social movement Solidarity have hindered the development of a truly pluralist civil society and have played an important role in the continuing polarization between 'communists' and 'anti-communists' in Polish politics and society after 1989 (see, for instance, Arato, 1991; Curry and Pankow, 2001). Similarly, the short-lived Czech pro-democratic civil initiatives 'Impuls 99' (Impulse 99) and 'Dekujeme, Odejdete' (Thank You, Time To Go), which were active at the turn of the century, undermined the development of civil society in the Czech Republic (Dvorakova, 2003).

By contrast, participation in alleged uncivil groups can be conducive to democratic behaviour, as suggested in the social capital thesis (see Putnam, 2000). Natalia Letki found that 'social capital, conceptualized as the interaction between social trust and associational membership, is largely irrelevant for political engagement in East Central Europe' (2003: 2), but that former membership of the Communist Party was positively related to political participation in post-communist democracies.

One of the explanations for this complex relationship could be the different forms of trust involved in these associations. Empirical studies have already shown that 'unqualified trust' is not strongly related to the strength of civil society or democracy, as argued by Francis Fukuyama and others. If anything, it is 'generalized trust' – trust in people who are different – which is positively related to association and democracy. However, over fifty years of communism have undermined generalized trust at the expense of small scale experience-based trust; for example, through the 'economy of favours' (*blat* in Russian), and 'particularized trust' – trust of one's own kind. Associations in Central and Eastern Europe are mostly based on particularized trust, such as ethnic bonds, which means that '(c)ivic engagement may create a less civil, and less trusting, society' (Uslaner and Badescu, 2003: 226). Interestingly, in the 1990 WVS Central and East Europeans underperformed in generalized groups (such as the environment and women), yet outperformed the Western Europeans only in one group, the more particularized 'community groups' (see Dalton and Rohrschneider, 2002).

This tension between civil society and liberal democracy is neither surprising nor new to the region. As Ralf Dahrendorf (1990: 98) noted early on about the famous chant of 1989, ' "We are the people" is a nice slogan but as a constitutional maxim it is a mirror image of the total state which has just been dislodged.' In the discourse of both some dissidents under communism and some civil society activists of post-communism, the opposition against the regime/state crosses the borders of pluralism to take on a distinct populist content: 'we', the homogeneous pure people, against 'them', the homogeneous corrupt elite (see Mudde, 2001; see also Glenn, 2001).

According to a number of observers, the tension between civil society and democratization is even inherent to their relationship. Andrew Milton, for instance, argues that 'the process of democratization both encourages and discourages the advancement of civil society by empowering political actors to participate, but, also use or exploit state and civil society institutions to advance particularist claims that can sometimes undermine both democracy and civil society' (2005: 12). Others take a more neutral stand, arguing that civil society reflects rather than creates a democratic culture (see, for instance, Rossteutscher, 2002; Zakaria, 2003). In both cases, the development of a democratic civil society will, to a large extent, depend on the actions of the state, ironically seen as the major enemy by many of its participants in the region.

Legacies of the past

With the growing popularity of path-dependency theories in democratization studies, it comes as no surprise that the weakness of civil society has often been explained by the region's past. A popular explanation is that whereas in the West political society grew out of civil society, in the East political society preceded civil society and thereby kept it weak (see, for instance, Bunce, 2000). However, this argument is flawed on both conceptual and empirical grounds. Conceptually and empirically, the distinction between civil and political society is problematic: for example, where do trade unions fit in? Moreover, in the various pillarized societies of Western Europe political parties were often not the most powerful parts of the subculture. In fact, in the socialist pillar most power traditionally resided in the trade unions, while in the religious pillars the churches were the source of the key leadership.

However, whereas the past might not explain the strength or weakness of civil society, it could leave an important legacy in terms of the forms and strategies of mobilization that are chosen. For example, when Czech civil society activists wanted to express their dissatisfaction with national politics, they founded a group by the name of 'Impuls 99' that presented a public petition signed by a number of public intellectuals – a clear copy of the famous anti-communist dissident movement 'Charter 77' led by Vaclav Havel and others (Dvorakova, 2003). And Samoobrona's successful combination of a radical trade union and an electoral political party (see Krok-Paszkowska, 2003) undoubtedly profits from the positive image of the similar combination of Solidarity under communism.

Civil society: an assessment

There is no doubt that Central and Eastern European countries do not harbour vibrant civil societies. Even where a fairly developed civil society existed at the beginning of the twentieth century, as arguably in the First Czechoslovak Republic (1918–38), five to seven decades of communist rule had almost completely eradicated all independent activity outside state control (with the notable exception of Solidarity in Poland and churches in some countries, notably the GDR and Poland). Not surprisingly, the 1990 WVS showed that Central and Eastern Europeans were less active in civil groups than their Western counterparts. Moreover, 'NGOs are often weak factors in their local culture; they focus more on issues of importance to people outside their community than on the needs of those nearest to them' (Mendelson, 2002: 233). This is a structural concern for the region, as many NGOs are highly professional non-profit businesses that depend fully on foreign funding and are thereby able to ignore grass-roots support.

Still, while the weakness of the civil society thesis is true in its general form, it is often overstated in the academic literature and the domestic and foreign media. This is the consequence of three wrong approaches that are applied in the literature: (i) the overestimation of civil society under communism (the 'revolution' thesis); (ii) the underestimation of post-communist civil society (the 'uncivil' thesis); and (iii) the skewed comparisons (the 'Western' thesis).

Many accounts of contemporary Central and Eastern Europe compare the current situation with a mythical civil society alleged to have been active in the last decade of communist rule. Not taking anything away from the brave anti-communist dissidents of that time, in virtually all communist states they were isolated intellectuals organized, at best, in *ad hoc* structures such as Charter 77. And although the impact of Solidarity far exceeded the borders of its native Poland, it was only in that country that a vibrant dissident civil society could and did develop.

Contemporary accounts of civil society also underestimate its strength because of the exclusion of so-called 'uncivil' groups. Far too much attention is paid to NGOs with a 'Western' agenda, which often count only a few fully paid professionals and lack any grass-roots support (though see Stark *et al.*, 2005). In sharp contrast, nationalist and Orthodox religious groups constitute true mass movements in many countries in the region. For example, much of the mass mobilization in Poland has been linked to 'uncivil' groups such as Radio Maryja and Samoobrona. Similarly, illiberal and nationalist organizations have been highly active in the 1990s in most countries of the Balkans.

Finally, even when the situation in post-communist Europe is not compared to a mythical past, it is contrasted with an ideal or ideal-typical present. In short, the region is compared to how the West is, was, or should be. Obviously, civil society in Central and Eastern Europe cannot compete with an ideal typical situation, which is sometimes the way that Western Europe is depicted. But even if the accounts of Western Europe do have an empirical basis, they often refer to a situation that no longer exists – as has been demonstrated most famously in Robert Putnam's seminal study *Bowling Alone* (2000). This notwithstanding, civil society in Western countries is still considerably stronger than in Central and Eastern Europe.

When the situation is compared to some other areas, however, Central and Eastern Europe does not always measure up that badly. As a case in point, the 1990 WVS showed that Central and Eastern European citizens were as, or even more, active than the citizens in the still relatively new democracies of Southern Europe. This seems to strengthen the claim of those who argue that civil societies have to grow and that time rather than institutions is the key factor in this process. Moreover, if it is indeed true that the communist experience explains much of the lack of participation from Central and East Europeans, future generations should show more similar patterns of civic activity to those of their generational peers in Western Europe (for example, Howard, 2003).

For this to happen though, the continuing legacy of an anti-state position of civil society must be overcome in Central and Eastern Europe. To cite Dahrendorf again (1990: 96), 'Both are needed, civil society and the state, but they each have their own *raison d'être* and their own autonomous reality'. Only when the new generation of civil society activists embraces the state as their protector, and political leaders see civil society as a supporter rather than an adversary of parliamentary democracy, will a truly vibrant civil society of whatever shape or form be able to develop in the region.

Chapter 14

Constitutional Politics

Kataryna Wolczuk

The collapse of communism brought about a revival of constitutional politics in Central and Eastern Europe (CEE). Even though constitutions existed in communist states, it was only after communism collapsed that they regained their essential functions to constitute, structure, and limit political authorities. Thus, changes in the exercise of political power have been reflected in and driven by constitutional politics; that is, the politics of constitution making and living under refurbished constitutions. The expectation was that post-communist constitutional engineering would deliver 'an enduring, stable framework facilitating rule-governed elite interaction' (Ganev, 2001: 202–3).

A constitution is a written document (or, seldom, a set of laws) containing the fundamental rules of the state. Constitutions tend to be framed as a special type of contract, expressing the consent of the governed and their acceptance of state power as legitimate as long as this power is exercised in accordance with the constitution. A constitution defines the institutional framework of the state and describes the mechanisms for citizens' participation in public affairs. Usually it also lists civic and human rights, and some may also include social and economic entitlements such as state education and social welfare. Because of its role in codifying the institutions of a democratic and law governed state, the constitution is the supreme legal act of the polity. This special status is reflected in strict rules on interpreting and changing the constitution. This interpretation tends to be delegated to a specific body named in the constitution itself (such as a constitutional court), while the rules for making amendments are stricter than those for ordinary laws in order to ensure the stability of the 'rules of the game'.

This chapter will focus on constitutional politics in terms of, first, the process – the context, time framework and main challenges of constitution making – and, second, the outcome; that is, the product of constitution making. The second part of the chapter will address the following questions: Why did so many post-communist countries opt for a directly elected presidency with executive powers? How can post-communist constitutions be classified in terms of role they assign to the presidency? And what are the consequences, if any, of constitutional design for democratization and political stability?

Constitutions and change: tribulations of constitution making

All communist states had written constitutions. However, this is not synonymous with the notion of embracing constitutionalism – the doctrine that the exercise of power is constrained by law. Communist constitutions incorporated a bill of civic rights and stipulated interactions between 'representative' institutions such as parliaments, local government, collective heads of state and so forth. Yet, in fact, constitutions were a facade behind which the communist parties controlled the levers of power. The locus of sovereignty was not in the people, but in the party, which claimed to play a 'leading role' in the construction of socialism in the name and interests of the people. Effectively, the party as the supreme political authority was above – rather than subordinated to – the constitution and laws, thereby deviating from the doctrine of constitutionalism. As a result, there were no 'checks and balances' capable of thwarting the party's will, or, in the terms of the ruling political ideology, that could have held back the overriding goal of 'building socialism'. Under communism, the gulf between the written constitutions and actual exercise of power rendered the organizing and limiting function of the constitution a fiction.

The crumbling of the communist system culminated in immediate changes to constitutional frameworks. In Hungary and Poland, important amendments were made to constitutions in the course of negotiations between governments and organized opposition in 1989. The constitutional norm that legitimized the party's 'leading role' was removed, putting the party on an equal footing, in legal terms, with all other political actors. Thus, from the outset of the transition, a profound change in the mode of exercising political power was reflected in constitutional reform. Constitutions regained their central role in defining the political life of CEE. The aim was to imbue the constitution with real meaning so that constitutional practice (also referred to as a 'real constitution', to emphasise that it embodied the actual functioning of the political system) developed on the basis of the written constitution.

Besides striving for limited government, there was also the more immediate need for the state to continue to function after the demise of the previous ruling parties. Once the non-constitutional means of the party's rule had been abolished, much confusion permeated the process of government. Thus, new constitutions had to disentangle the paralyzing confusion of functions, and clarify the distribution of powers between state institutions. This happened at the very time when the countries were experiencing profound socio-economic upheaval and a challenging international situation. Adopting a new constitution became an urgent priority.

In line with the idea of the 'return to Europe' (see Chapter 7), there has been a tendency to look towards West European institutional templates that have been successfully tested for their effectiveness in safeguarding civic liberties, preventing the usurpation of power and delivering 'public goods' to citizens. Yet, there is no uniform matrix of governmental design in Europe. While the separation of powers, judicial review, and checks and balances are general guiding principles, they can take very different forms, such as the Westminster model nurtured by British customs and traditions on the one hand, and the French semi-presidential or German chancellor-based systems, on the other. The doctrine of constitutionalism defines the goals, such as the inviolability of constitutional rights. But it does not provide guidelines on how to craft the institutional framework to reach those goals.

While rejecting the communist constitutions and reorienting themselves towards Western models, it was not immediately clear to post-communist constitution drafters what should replace them. Countries with pre-communist constitutional traditions were eager to instil some sense of historical continuity, though most decided again resuscitating their pre-communist models. Only Estonia and Latvia opted for a wholesale restitution of their constitutions from the early twentieth century. In these two cases, assertions of historical longevity and the restoration of sovereignty took priority over the more immediate concerns of constitution drafters.

However, the plurality of models was not the only difficulty in post-communist constitution drafting. The constitutional process took place under the 'old', communist era rules – partially and inadequately adapted for the changed circumstances, and amidst fierce conflicts over competencies and policies. Elster (1993: 171) has compared constitution making in post-communist states with 'rebuilding the boat in the open sea'. This metaphor captures both dimensions of the process. First, the refuge of the dry dock in which a full-blown constitutional refurbishment could take place was not available. New constitutions therefore emerged as an amalgam of old and new elements – many old institutions were simply 'given a new coat of paint' while the 'ship of state' was already at sea. Second, it was the sailors themselves who had to rebuild the ship: the political actors had to redefine the constitutional 'rules of the game', while themselves playing that game. Frequently it was parliaments that were given the task of drafting a constitution, as, having been popularly elected, they had the most obvious claim to legitimate authority. But they were far from the detached, politically neutral 'law giver' envisaged by Rousseau. With ordinary legislatures taking on the extraordinary role of constitutional assemblies, the task of drafting the rules of the game was assigned to the same bodies that were to be governed by what they produced.

The case of the Polish upper chamber of parliament, the Senate, illustrates this point. The common wisdom was that there was no compelling rationale for a Senate – a second, upper house of parliament – as Poland, a unitary, homogeneous state, had no need for the kind of regional representation that a Senate might offer. Yet, when the Polish constitution was drafted in the early 1990s, the Senate already existed as a result of the 1989 round-table agreement. Moreover, it had historical legitimacy: the institution existed in inter-war Poland and was only abolished by the communist government. Crucially, the Senate had a key role in constitution making, because it had to approve the new constitution, together with the lower chamber or *Sejm*, in a joint session of the National Assembly. And so, it is hardly surprising that the upper chamber was preserved in the 1997 constitution of Poland: the Senate was hardly likely to legislate itself out of existence.

Passing new constitutions is 'the quintessential political act, by which countries make choices concerning the most fundamental concepts of political life: power and authorities, representation and legitimacy, liberty and equality' (Elgie and Zielonka, 2001: 25). Even though fundamental laws are adopted for decades to come, their passage tends to be heavily politicized and reflects the political circumstances of the time. In particular, multiple partisan interests come into play in the process of reassigning powers between the branches of the state: many interests and identities are still in flux, adding complexity and uncertainly to actors' preferences and motivation. As pointed out above, life did not come to a standstill during constitution drafting in Central and Eastern Europe. In fact, political actors were not only working on new constitutions but were simultaneously tackling other momentous issues of the post-communist transformation, including fundamental social and economic reforms, and international realignment. Moreover, institutional design was not the only contentious matter that was involved in constitution making: the role of religion in post-communist Poland, or state language and symbols in Ukraine, led to vigorous and protracted debate. Constitution making thus became entangled in multi-issue bargaining, in which trade-offs, compromises and deals were made and unmade that had direct implications for the coherence and integrity of the final constitutional documents. This complex bargaining, against the backdrop of the communist-era institutional landscape and selective use of pre-communist traditions, accounts for the diversity of institutional configurations that can be found in the post-communist states.

How did the post-communist countries go about drafting their new constitutions? Did they settle for a quick-fix constitution or engage in lengthy constitution deliberations? Was it more important to end political uncertainty quickly or deliver a quality product that would have a longer life? The length of the constitution-making process, in practice, varied greatly across the region. It took Bulgarians only twelve months to draft and adopt their Fundamental Law. By contrast, it took Poland almost eight years to do the same and, in the meantime, the country was governed by an interim 1992 'Little Constitution'. Most new constitutions in the region had been adopted by 1994, with the exception of Ukraine (1996), Poland (1997), Albania (1998), and Hungary, which had already amended its 1949 constitution in 1989–90. Two broad generalizations can be made about explaining the length of the process: the mode of regime change and newness of statehood.

Countries that experienced a clear rupture with the old regime moved swiftly to adopt a new constitution, either through pluralistic bargaining as in the Czech Republic (1992) or by a dominant group imposing it. It is worth emphasizing that the rupture did not necessarily result in the demise of communist-era actors. In the cases of Albania, Romania, Bulgaria, and Serbia, the dominant group that drove constitution making consisted of former communists who had remained in power (von Beyme, 2001). Paradoxically, the countries that were at the forefront of dismantling the communist system, such as Poland and Hungary, were much less radical in seeking wholesale constitutional change. This reflected the negotiated nature of the political change in those countries, which slowed down the pace of constitutional reform. In the most extreme case, Hungary has so far failed to adopt a new constitution and is governed by several amended acts.

The second factor was the break-up of the communist-era federation. States that (re-)gained sovereignty on the collapse of federations had a stronger incentive to adopt a new constitution as a manifestation of sovereign statehood (on the role of constitutions in state building see Batt and Wolczuk, 1998). For example, Slovakia and Lithuania swiftly adopted new documents. However, as already mentioned above, Latvia and Estonia, while eager to leave behind the communist-era constitutions, put a premium on historical continuity and restored the pre-communist constitutions, which had been abolished following the Soviet annexation in 1940. Not all states found it easy to assert their statehood through the passage of the new constitution. In Ukraine, the multitude of contested issues, ranging from institutional design to notions of nationhood, hampered constitution making up until 1996 and Ukraine was one of the last post-communist states to adopt a new constitution, despite the compelling need to overcome paralysis and confusion (Wolczuk, 2002).

Despite some concern over hastily drafted quick-fix constitutions, the outcome of lengthier constitutional deliberations did not always result in a better outcome. Elgie and Zielonka have asserted that a 'lengthy constitutional process failed to produce more consensus on the constitutional draft than was the case in countries that experienced a brief constitution-building period. . . . [while] "quick-fix constitutions" (that is constitutions adopted in a relatively brief period) proved to be remarkably effective, durable and beneficial' (2001: 37).

Case study: Poland

In many post-communist states – as pointed out above – drafting new constitutions proved to be protracted, and the outcome was not necessarily determined by the quality of the product alone. The Polish case study illustrates how precarious the process and outcome of constitution making can be. It took eight years in Poland to pass a fully revised new constitution. The early start in the summer of 1989 was not necessarily advantageous as the early initiatives suffered from a lack of legitimacy. Soon the form of government became a thorny issue as no obvious foreign and historical model could accommodate all institutional interests that had a stake in the outcome. In the final stages of constitution making, the passage became entangled in an electoral campaign – so the constitution was ratified amidst bitter protests, with question marks over its legitimacy. In the event, however, the final document survived the test of time and has served well under very testing conditions.

The process of constitution drafting was launched by the parliament elected in the only partially free competitive elections of the summer of 1989. The lack of democratic legitimacy of that assembly was a stumbling block (65 per cent of the *Sejm* had been nominated by the Communist Party as part of the round-table agreement that had allowed the elections themselves to take place, and only the upper chamber, the Senate, had been elected in free elections). Then, after the genuinely free elections of 1991, an interim 'Little Constitution' was adopted in 1992, which clarified some of the ambiguities in governmental relations, but added a few others. The 'Little Constitution' firmly placed Poland in the club of semi-presidential systems, which to a large degree reflected the ambitions of President Lech Walesa and the respect in which he was held. At the same time, a special constitutional commission of members of parliament was delegated the task of drafting a brand new constitution. After four years' work, this commission tabled its final draft in 1996.

Although Poland has a long constitutional history, Polish traditions hardly provide a viable model for a modern constitutional democracy. These traditions date back to 1791 when the so-called Constitution of 3 May was adopted to prevent a slide into anarchy in the face of external threats. The poorly designed 1921 constitution and the authoritarian 1935 constitution were followed by the Stalinist constitution of 1952. Thus, in the 1990s the problem of agreeing on a new form of government – a presidential or a parliamentary democracy – was the central issue in constitution making.

However, protracted constitution making was not without its benefits. It allowed plenty of consideration of constitutional solutions and options, even allowing them to be tested in practice. President Walesa took advantage of every ambiguity of the 'Little Constitution', stretching its provisions to extend presidential prerogatives. This led to a 'war of laws' between the anti-communist President and a parliament dominated by former communists. After such a trial of strength, Aleksander Kwasniewski, as the head of the parliament's constitutional commission, advocated the trimming of presidential powers. One of these powers was the president's right to veto parliamentary law, which could only be overridden by a qualified, two-thirds majority in the *Sejm*. In order to eliminate any ambiguity leading to possible 'uses and abuses' of the constitution by a 'pro-active' president, in the new constitution a presidential veto over laws can be overruled by three fifths of all deputies, and interactions between the parliament, president and prime minister were regulated in great detail.

The resultant semi-presidential form of government in Poland was the product of an overarching compromise rather than the transplant of any foreign template or revival of a historical model. The juxtaposition of various interests guided final choices, amongst which institutional ones featured prominently as the President, the *Sejm* and the Senate all vied to expand their respective powers. As was argued above, having participated in constitution making, the Senate ensured its survival even though many questioned the rationale for the upper house of parliament in a unitary state such as Poland.

Furthermore, the constitution is a fundamental law of the land and hence, while dealing with the basic organizing principles of the state, it has to enjoy not only procedural but also moral legitimacy. In Poland, a particularly contentious issue in constitution making – state–church relations – significantly undermined the legitimacy of the constitution on moral grounds. The Catholic Church, oppressed and yet vibrant under communism, was in the vanguard in bringing down the communist system. The Church itself equated the demise of an 'evil regime' with a return (by default) to a traditional, Christian way of life, which, in its view, the Polish state should promote or, at least, not oppose. In turn, the social democratic parties (mainly ex-communists) and the liberal centre – who became the constitution drafters – propagated a secular, liberal version of the constitution, giving priority to the rights and freedoms of the individual. The constitutional debate in this way touched upon the issue of national identity at its deepest level. The Church hierarchy and the right-wing, nationalistic parties strongly favoured an exclusive notion of the national community based on traditions, culture and Catholicism as the fundamental attributes of the Polish nation. Thus, the liberal-individualist concept of constitutional democracy clashed with the organic notion of nationhood and Christian values as a superior moral order. In the event, the new constitution reflected a compromised, ambiguous relationship between these two conceptions of the state, based on different sets of fundamental principles and values (although not that many concessions were made to the right). Eventually, a compromise was negotiated between the four main parties in parliament (the Social Democracy of Poland, the Polish Peasants' Alliance, the Union of Freedom and the Party of Labour), which then closed ranks behind the draft, while the right-wing opposition (mostly not represented in parliament), with the backing of the Church, proposed its own alternative 'citizens' draft'. They opposed, on the one hand, the liberalism embedded in the official constitution and its allegedly 'anti-national' and 'anti-Christian character'. On the other hand, they questioned the moral right of former communists in the Social Democracy of Poland, now the leading party in parliament, to draft and adopt the first post-communist constitution.

Elster, as we have seen, compares the drafting of a constitution in these circumstances with making a boat in the open sea. In the Polish case, it became entangled in the electoral campaign and, accordingly, became a victim of electoral politics. The intention was to ratify the constitution in 1996. After both houses of the National Assembly had, in a joint session, adopted the law by a constitutional majority (451 voted in favour, 40 against and 6 abstained), a constitutional referendum was to endow the constitution with popular legitimacy. However, the referendum took place only in May 1997, four months before the parliamentary elections were held, and as a result of this approval of the Fundamental Law became part of a bitter and polarizing electoral campaign. The referendum formally ratified the constitution: 53 per cent voted in favour, and 46 per cent against. However, with a turnout of only 43 per cent, the constitution had hardly been overwhelmingly endorsed by Polish society. Furthermore, the right-wing opposition, with the prospect of a strong presence in the new parliament, declared its intention of amending the constitution once in power. The stability of the new constitutional order in Poland seemed far from assured.

However, despite political instability instigated by the high turn-over of parties at elections as well as public discontent with the socio-economic situation and corruption amongst politicians, the constitutional framework not only survived but, still more importantly, passed the quality and durability test. No doubt, Kwasniewski's restrained style of presidency in comparison with Lech Walesa's (up to 1995), as well as detailed constitutional norms regulating institutional interactions, facilitated the stability of the constitutional order. Constitutional practice, developed on the basis of constitutional norms, effectively channelled political conflicts through constitutional channels. Through stable constitutional practice the written constitution acquired legitimacy, something it initially lacked, making it difficult for any political actor in Poland to challenge the constitutional framework on the grounds of either its ineffectiveness or its illegitimacy. As in other post-communist countries, the constitution has become an important reference point for all political decisions; violating it is no longer a costless action (Elgie and Zielonka, 2001: 47).

From process to outcome of constitution making: form of government

We will turn our attention to the outcome of constitution making by examining the institutional design of legislative–executive relations. These relations are of pivotal importance in any democracy as they determine representation, policy making and accountability. Under communism, most states in the region had collective and nominated bodies that performed the functions of the head of state, which in Western Europe tends to be vested in presidents or monarchs. These collective head of state institutions performed ceremonial and symbolic functions, being effectively 'rubber stamp' institutions. In virtually all post-communist states, they were replaced with presidencies. But often these presidencies were not designed as mere figureheads – they were vested with important executive powers and a popular mandate, thereby turning them into powerful political actors.

Semi-presidentialism: a compromise solution

Why did so many post-communist countries opt then for a stronger, directly elected presidency? As in France, which introduced a semi-presidential system in 1957, crisis management and power maximization of actors involved in constitution making played a prominent role across CEE.

First, under the conditions of profound political, socio-economic changes, the presidency carried the promise of a stern leadership capable of fast and effective decision making. Even though parliaments, after decades of acting as mere 'rubber stamps', were vested with significant authority, they could hardly be expected to perform all functions effectively. They lacked the capacity and experience, and were characterized by fragile, volatile and fragmented party systems. A president could compensate for the un(der)development of democratic institutions during the chaotic days of political and economic transformation, and counteract divided and weak parliaments and governments. A charismatic, popular president could provide a sense of unity and direction during turbulent days of post-communist reforms and thereby compensate for the weakness of representative institutions.

Second, those involved in constitution making tend to adopt constitutional solutions to suit their own institutional interests in order to exercise political power to the greatest possible extent. Elster (1996a) argues that new institutions reflected the preferences of the bodies involved in constitution making. Favouring a stronger presidency was the natural preference for parties and personalities who believed that the institution was within their reach. In Central Europe, semi-presidential regimes resulted from a compromise between ex-communists, who favoured parliamentary models, and the former opposition, which supported a stronger presidency, while (still) enjoying strong public support. At the same time, parties and movements were more influential than incumbent presidents in constitution making, and this prevented presidents from dominating the whole process to the same extent as in the former Soviet republics.

Where presidents directly influenced constitution making, as in Ukraine and Russia, the emerging constitutions tended to grant them extensive powers. In the former Soviet Union, presidents were amongst the 'constitutional fathers' and, moreover, they enjoyed the powerful backing of ex-communist elites. These elites, even though they eschewed formal ideology and organizational structures, remained in power and saw the presidency as a guarantee of their continuing hold on power. This was because they believed that presidents were easier to control than parliaments, despite the introduction of competitive elections. In particular, presidencies were envisaged as a kind of protection against any possible attempts to review the acquisitions that had been made during an opaque process of privatization and through other forms of 'asset stripping'.

Before considering the implications of institutional choices, a basic typology of forms of government is required in order to understand the role of the presidency. The key differentiating factors are (i) popular mandate, and (ii) executive powers. In a parliamentary system, there is one directly elected agent of the electorate: the parliament. Parliament is responsible for the formation of the government (the Cabinet of Ministers). There are two main models (depending on the type of electoral system): (i) the Westminster model, in which a first-past-the-post electoral system tends to produce a majority (one-party) government; and (ii) a proportional representation (PR) model in which a coalition of parties tends to form the government (see Chapter 10). The best example of the former is the United Kingdom, whereas parliamentarism with coalitional governments is common in Western Europe. Regardless of the electoral system, however, all parliamentary systems rest on the principle of mutual dependence of government and legislature as the government has to be supported by a majority in parliament. The head of state (presidents, monarchs, and so on) performs mainly representative, ceremonial and symbolic functions.

In semi-presidential systems, by contrast, the two key institutions are directly elected: the parliament and the president. In addition to performing the functions of head of state, the presidency has some executive powers. As a result, the executive branch is effectively split or bifurcated: the president shares power with a prime minister. The terms of the president and parliament are fixed and tend not to be contingent on mutual confidence. However, there is still a mutual dependency between the government and the legislature, which means that the government is accountable to the legislature. In essence, in semi-presidential systems the president has more constitutionally defined competencies than in parliamentarism but does not fully control the executive branch (as in the US presidential system). In semi-presidential systems, executive presidential powers tend to vary but they can be broadly categorized into three main groups:

(i) *Political*
Formation of the Cabinet of Ministers
Dismissal of the Cabinet of Ministers
Appointment to official positions (such as judges, prosecutors)

(ii) *Legislative*
      Proposal of legislation
      Decree-making powers
      Legislative veto
(iii) *Dissolution of the parliament*

How can post-communist constitutions be classified in terms of the role they assign to the presidency? Semi-presidential systems have caused significant confusion but, on the basis of the above three types of powers enshrined in the constitution, Shugart and Carey have provided a helpful classification. According to them, two main types of semi-presidential systems can be identified: premier–presidential and presidential–parliamentary. In premier-presidential systems, the president is popularly elected, has significant powers and coexists with a prime minister whose cabinet is subject to parliamentary confidence (Shugart and Carey, 1992: 23). Significantly, the president does not possess the power unilaterally to dismiss ministers who have parliamentary confidence. This particular competence characterizes a president–parliamentary system, where the cabinet is subject to both parliamentary and presidential confidence. Thanks to the control over the cabinet in a president–parliamentary system, the president is, as a rule, more powerful than in the premier–presidential system.

Following Shugart and Carey's typology, out of the 27 post-communist countries (including Central Asia and Mongolia) only nine adopted a classic parliamentary system in the 1990s, while the rest opted for a semi-presidential system (eight premier–presidential and ten president–parliamentary). A clear regional pattern could be discerned by the 1990s. Parliamentary and premier–presidential systems were dominant in the post-communist states that were not part of the Soviet Union, whereas president–parliamentary systems dominated in the former Soviet republics. Of the 15 former Soviet republics, Lithuania and Moldova are the only two that initially adopted a premier–presidential system (Ukraine joined them in 2006), while Croatia (until the constitutional reform of 2000–1) was the only president–parliamentary system outside the former USSR (see Table 14.1). In a nutshell, post-Soviet states opted for stronger presidencies.

The consequences of semi-presidentialism

The proliferation of different constitutional frameworks in CEE has encouraged researchers empirically to validate arguments in lively debates about the merits and perils of different institutional designs. This research agenda has had not only empirical aims but also norma-

Table 14.1   *Types of constitutional systems in Central and Eastern Europe*

Parliamentarism	Semi-presidentialism	
	Premier–presidential	*President–parliamentary*
Albania	Bulgaria	Belarus
Czech Republic	Croatia (from 2000–1)	Croatia (till 2001)
Estonia	Lithuania	Ukraine (till 2005)
Hungary	Moldova (till 2000)	
Latvia	Poland	
Macedonia	Romania	
Moldova (from 2000)	Ukraine (from 2006)	
Slovakia		
Slovenia		

tive implications. The debates on constitutional design have also been inspired by a desire to identify the optimal form of government for democracy and socio-economic development (Sedelius, 2006).

Already, before the emergence of executive presidencies in the region, a number of charges had been made against it (see, for example, Linz, 1990a, 1990b; Lijphart, 1991, 1992) that were frequently reiterated throughout the 1990s. Presidents tend to personalize political power. With weak 'checks and balances', popularly elected presidents can claim that their formal powers do not reflect the popular mandate they have received from the electorate. By capitalizing on their legitimacy and faced with weak parties and parliaments, they can easily dominate the political scene to the detriment of political stability and the consolidation of other institutions indispensable for democratization. A strong presidency should compensate for weak institutions, but in practice it exacerbates rather than alleviates the problem. With direct elections, the presidency may become the highest political prize, and thereby weaken the standing of political parties.

Many of these arguments have resonated in Central and Eastern Europe. Kitschelt *et al.* (1999) have argued that Lech Walesa's presidency was instrumental in preventing the reunification of the fragmented Solidarity camp in the early 1990s by pursuing a 'divide and rule' strategy and undermining the role of political parties. Moreover, presidents found themselves locked in protracted interactions with parliaments, parties and the cabinet of ministers, thereby unable to deliver, or at least contribute to, effective and strong government. In many cases, such as Romania under Constantinescu in late 1990s, the president became embroiled in intra-executive conflict – a political struggle with the prime minister over control of the executive branch.

The limits of constitutional engineering

The analysis of the consequences of the adoption of various constitutional models, however, throws up the question of the extent to which developments in post-communist states can actually be explained by focusing on constitutional design alone.

In Belarus, President Lukashenka, through constitutional amendments in 1996, created a system subordinated to the presidency that was never meant to foster democracy. So, under the formally semi-presidential constitution, Belarus developed a presidential authoritarian system. The second term of Kuchma's presidency (1999–2004) in Ukraine displayed a similar tendency. On the other hand, in Bulgaria, where the premier–presidential constitution of 1991 was closest in design to parliamentarism, the presidency has limited itself to performing a ceremonial figurehead role. Bulgaria has, in practice, become a parliamentary republic. Poland under Kwasniewski evolved in a similar way. In contrast, however, in Romania and Moldova, the presidents have assumed a central role on the political stage. Under Romania's premier–parliamentary system, the presidents (Iliescu, Constantinescu, and Basescu) have been closely involved in day-to-day politics on both foreign policy and domestic matters (Sedelius, 2006: 147). In Moldova, despite the shift from a premier–presidential system to parliamentarism in 2000, President Voronin has dominated policy making thanks to his control of the communist majority in the parliament.

These developments make clear how difficult it is to separate the effects of constitutional design from other institutional factors. Presidents do not operate in a vacuum and numerous institutional features – such as the party system, the electoral system, the composition of the parliament, the role of the judicial branch in conflict adjudication and so forth – ultimately determine their capacity to exercise their constitutional powers.

Constitutions acquire life through actual constitutional practice, which is woven from a rich texture of formal rules and unwritten norms, routines and habits in responses to specific political events and circumstances. Frequently, it is not the formal constitutional provisions but how institutions actually function that generates a parliamentary or presidential label for a political system (for an example of this approach, see Chapter 8 in this volume).

Even though some inherent features of semi-presidential systems fuel conflict and rivalry, constitutional frameworks alone are not sufficient to account for political instability and/or authoritarian tendencies. Other more durable systemic – rather than constitutional – factors may mitigate against democratization. In Ukraine and Belarus, the authoritarian presidencies of Kuchma and Lukashenka can be viewed as a consequence rather than a cause of democratic failure, which can be better explained by other causal factors – such as elite continuity, socio-economic decline, a weak party system and the political culture. In other words, strong presidencies can easily abuse their constitutional powers against the backdrop of weak or non-existent conditions for democracy.

By the same token, the safer design of a parliament-centred system has not been a magic bullet against authoritarianism and bad government. President Berisha imposed dictatorial rule over Albania despite his relatively weak constitutional powers. In Bulgaria, a balanced and respected constitutional framework served as a mere platform for rent seeking, corruption, and rapacious profiteering amongst the political elites in the 1990s. The constitution provided an effective channel for non-violent elite rivalry but did not restrain politicians from exploiting political power for personal gains (Ganev, 2001: 210).

Conclusion

The collapse of communism has given fresh impetus to the study of constitutions and institutional arrangements as political scientists have explored the process of laying down the foundations of statehood and democracy in CEE.

During constitution making, there was no ready-made template that could simply be appropriated as a guarantee against autocracy and instability. Instead, post-communist constitutional drafters were confronted with a bewildering range of momentous choices. Even though many political scientists referred to post-communist constitution making as 'institutional engineering', the resulting constitutions were hardly the products of a detached wisdom and precise crafting in pursuit of the 'public good' and 'general interest'. Rather, constitutional frameworks were outcomes of intense and complex elite-level bargaining, deeply embedded in a particular cultural, social and historical context. The amount of time spent on crafting constitutions did not seem to make a difference to the quality of the product.

Central and Eastern Europe has provided a rich new seam of empirical data for the study of the origins and consequences of constitutional arrangements. In particular, the region offered a testing ground for theories of 'institutional engineering', according to which some institutional designs – such as those with executive presidencies – are less conducive to democratic survival. The former (non-Baltic) Soviet republics opted for stronger presidencies while the former Soviet satellite states were more cautious about vesting presidents with executive powers.

However, the evidence is not clear-cut. Executive presidencies cannot be held solely responsible for democratic failures and instability, although they are often implicated. Even though the aim of constitutional making was to organize and limit the use of political power by creating a stable framework for rule-governed elite interactions, this has not always been the outcome. This is because constitutional frameworks are intertwined with cultural, historical and economic factors to the extent that the actual functioning of political systems is not determined by, and thus cannot be attributed to, constitutional design alone. As Ganev has argued, 'Bad government does not necessarily result from fatal flaws in institutional design – it is a large-scale initiative that bounces off and meshes with a multitude of factors at work within a concrete social environment' (2001: 208). With the exception of outright authoritarian states, the experience of CEE shows that analyzing written constitutions is a necessary starting point – but not a sufficient condition – for explaining the functioning of political systems.

Chapter 15

Managing Transition Economies

D. Mario Nuti

The fall of the Berlin Wall on 9 November 1989, leading to *de facto* German reunification, is usually taken as the symbolic date of the collapse of the Soviet-type economic system, and the beginning of the post-socialist transition to capitalism. A better date might be 4 June 1989, when in Poland the first (partly) contested elections since the end of the Second World War gave the government coalition of peasant and communist parties not a single seat – except for the uncontested 60 per cent of the seats in the Lower Chamber (*Sejm*) which had been expressly reserved to them in the Memorandum of Understanding agreed in April of the same year between the government and the Solidarity opposition. Thus, in September 1989, the first non-communist government since the Second World War took over, and a domino effect followed throughout the area. Iconic of the transition is the Warsaw Palace, built with bricks contributed by communist party members. Until 1990 it had housed the party headquarters then; in April 1991, it became the Warsaw Stock Exchange.

This chapter discusses the main economic aspects of the transition in Central and Eastern Europe, dealing only in passing with Russia and the Asian republics. A sketch of the old economic system, and the reasons for its collapse, is given in the first section for a better understanding of the transition to (a form of) capitalism; it is followed by an account of the progress and diversity of the transition process in different sectors and countries. The specific issues of gradualism versus shock therapy are discussed in the third section. The transition was accompanied by an unexpected, deep and often protracted recession, whose very extent and possible causes are controversial; these are considered in the fourth section, together with other aspects of economic performance. The fifth and final section draws some lessons and considers current prospects, including issues of European integration.

The Soviet-type system: its reform and collapse

The model of a centrally planned economy with public ownership and enterprises was consolidated in the Soviet Union in 1928–32. After the Second World War, it spread with minor variations to other countries including most of Central and Eastern Europe. Such a system, as we have seen in earlier chapters, is characterized by the political monopoly of the Communist Party (alone or in coalition with similar parties), strengthened by the prohibition of factions within the party, its 'leading role', and so-called 'democratic centralism' – in theory, the central execution of democratic decisions; in practice, totalitarian rule. The party is omnipresent at all levels of the state, economy, and society in such a system, duplicating and dominating all command structures.

The whole economy is organized as if it were a single enterprise, according to a detailed central plan drawn up in both physical and monetary terms by a Central Planning Commission. Plan execution is compulsory for enterprises and for the state ministries on which they depend. The enterprise is managed by a director – 'one-man management' – in collaboration with trade unions and the party (the 'troika'); bonuses are awarded for plan fulfilment and over-fulfilment, and there are penalties for under-fulfilment. The state has the exclusive ownership of productive resources in the most important sectors (what Lenin called the economy's 'commanding heights'), next to other forms of public ownership such as cooperatives, municipal enterprises or – in Yugoslavia – socially owned enterprises, with a private sector that was either absent or, at most, limited to agriculture, construction, retail trade, handicraft, and some minor services.

Money circulated in two separate circuits – cash (or means of payment convertible into cash) for the payment of wages, the purchase of consumption goods and other transactions involving the public; and bank money exclusively for inter-enterprise transactions sanctioned by the plan. Joseph Berliner (1957) used the label 'documonetary' to characterize such an economy, where, in order to acquire productive resources, firms needed a central allocation document as well as a means of payment of the right kind. Thus money, besides the usual functions, performed an important function of control. However, as long as financial means were necessary to fulfil and over-fulfil the plan, they were always available under the guise of subsidies or credits, thus subjecting firms to the 'soft budget constraints' theorized by Janos Kornai (1980), who also noted the propensity of such a system to over-investment.

Money prices were fixed administratively by the centre, primarily on the basis of distributive considerations. In theory, the quantities supplied of the various goods should have corresponded to the quantities demanded at those prices. In practice, quantities supplied were always less than demand. Planned prices were kept at an artificially low level by the well-meaning but tragically misguided intention of avoiding inflation, which was regarded as a major evil of capitalism. Price controls simply repressed inflationary pressure, instead of avoiding it, causing shortages, queues, waiting lists, and re-trading at higher prices in grey or black markets. Interest rates on savings were symbolic, and could not be raised to absorb demand for fear of creating a rentier class, living off their ownership of property.

A generalized, permanent and endemic state of excess demand, for both consumption and production/investment goods, became an integral part of the system, not by design but by default, as the necessary implication of inflation avoidance at all costs. So much so that Kornai (1980) could entitle his two-volume treatise on that system *The Economics of Shortage*. Full employment, indeed over-full employment (an excess demand for labour) prevailed and was maintained simply as a by-product of excess demand for goods, due to the insatiable demands both by the centre (for public consumption, investment, military expenditure, aid to allies, space conquest and so forth), and – at artificially low prices – by consumers and enterprises.

Foreign trade was also a state monopoly in this system, exercised by large foreign trade organizations specializing in the import and export of broad groups of products; they operated on their own account, not on behalf of enterprises. Exchange rates were usually overvalued in terms of gold or convertible currencies but had a purely accounting role, as domestic currencies were not convertible, not even within the bloc. Foreign exchange was surrendered by exporters to the central bank, which allocated it centrally to importers. Subsidies or taxes equalized domestic and external prices and foreign trade organizations' profits or losses were transferred to the state budget, while enterprises were largely insulated from the world market. The system had an autarkic bias, which facilitated central planning but was a source of gross inefficiency, even within the Council for Mutual Economic Assistance (CMEA or Comecon), the trading bloc established in 1949 (see Kaser, 1967; Lavigne, 1985).

This system realized important initial achievements: industrialization and accelerated growth, urbanization, victory in war, military might and space conquest. Already by the second half of the 1950s, however, these economies registered a growth slowdown, in spite of a rising share of investment in national income, due to the exhaustion of extensive sources of growth (reserves of labour and natural resources: see Kalecki, 1969). Towards the end of 1980s, the slowdown turned into a slow decline, accompanied by large-scale imbalances: growing inflation, first repressed and then also open (Nuti, 1986), public budget deficits and current account deficits. External debt rose from virtually zero in the early 1970s to critical levels in the course of the 1980s; Poland defaulted in 1982; with the exception of Romania, which repaid its debt before it was due through a brutal deflation implemented in 1987–88 by Ceausescu, all other countries increased their debt.

Repeated attempts at reforming this Soviet-type system were made from the mid-1950s. They were first directed towards improving the system, through forms of decentralization (regional, as in the USSR in 1957, or sectoral, as in the German Democratic Republic); increasing enterprise autonomy (as in Poland 1956, USSR 1965, Hungary 1968, Poland 1980–81), introducing net value indicators including profits in place of gross physical indicators, making some use of interest rates, rent and international prices; utilizing mathematical methods in central planning (what was called 'perfect computation' rather than 'perfect competition'). But the fear of losing economic and political control led the authorities to suppress the more advanced attempts (in the GDR in 1954, Hungary in 1956, Czechoslovakia in 1968, and Poland in 1981). Reforms were often inconsistent and not sufficiently radical; the basic system design remained unchanged. Yugoslavia, soon after its break with Moscow in 1948, took the road of so-called 'associations', giving enterprises significant autonomy and workers the power of self-management and distribution of net value added; the system, however, was similar to the planned economy, through monetary control rather than administrative means (Uvalic, 1992).

In the 1980s, some countries – notably Hungary with its New Economic Mechanism, Poland and, towards the end of the decade, the Soviet Union with reform designs never fully implemented – moved from system improvement towards the construction of 'market socialism', combining public ownership and enterprise with the market benefits of efficiency and automatic adjustment. But such an attempt was incompatible with the maintenance of a permanent excess demand, under which no system using money and prices, not even the traditional central planning system, could function properly. The system collapsed under the weight of (i) increasing excess demand, which exploded into open inflation when prices were liberalized in the transition; and (ii) increasing inefficiency due to domestic prices being out of line with international prices, with opportunities of substitution in production and consumption, and with equilibrium between demand and supply. The irresistible force of inflationary pressure met the immovable object of price stability, and the system was caught in the middle and crushed.

The collapse was delayed by the rise in oil prices in the mid-1970s, which benefited the Soviet Union as a net energy exporter, the East European countries because of subsidized access to Soviet oil, and the whole socialist bloc from the ability to borrow petrodollars at low interest rates. The subsequent rise in interest rates, the growth of debt, the fall in the price of oil (accompanied by its delayed increase for East European importers of Soviet oil), and the cost of the invasion of Afghanistan turned this opportunity into a trap. The only road that remained open was capitalist restoration. What used to be said in Moscow at the end of the 1980s – that 'socialism is the longest way from capitalism to capitalism' – came true.

Progress and diversity of post-socialist transition

Transition began in January 1990 in most of Central and Eastern Europe (with a few years' lag in the Balkans), and in January 1992 in the former Soviet Union, whose 15 member states split (after the failed coup of the preceding August) in an attempt to proceed towards their own target model at their own speed , thus splitting the rouble area.

The first step in the move to a market economy was macroeconomic stabilization. Here, it is essential to distinguish between price liberalization on the one hand – that is, the price rise necessary to bring about macroeconomic equilibrium, transforming the monetary overhang existing at administered prices into a burst of open inflation spreading throughout the economy, and, on the other hand, the subsequent disinflation – that is, the abatement of the initial burst of inflation (occasionally hyperinflation) down or close to single-digit inflation. The first was absolutely necessary, and there was nothing to be gained from delay. Market clearing prices were reached on day one of the transition – with few exceptions such as Romania, or in housing, energy, and public services. Annual inflation rates, reflecting earlier financial repression, were, in 1990, 586 per cent in Poland, 549 per cent in Slovenia, 333 per cent in Bulgaria, and 1526 per cent in Russia in 1992. Subsequent disinflation, associated with various degrees of fiscal and monetary restraint, on the contrary gave governments the choice between gradualism or speed, including the possibility of controlling inflation with government subsidies, with costs and benefits attached to each option. By 2001, all Central Eastern European countries had single-digit inflation rates except Romania (which reached it in 2005) and Serbia and Montenegro, which hovered just above 10 per cent.

The establishment of market clearing prices created an environment in which other changes could be introduced effectively. Foreign trade was open to all enterprises and individuals, instead of being a state monopoly. To make this effective, foreign exchange transactions were legalized, thus making the domestic currency convertible for current account transactions, under diverse exchange rate regimes – from freely floating to crawling pegs at a pre-fixed rate, within bands of variations, to fixed or hyper-fixed (that is, currency replacement or currency boards issuing domestic currency exclusively in exchange for foreign currency at fixed rates). Comecon was officially dissolved in September 1991 but was already withering by the start of 1990. Capital account convertibility was soon introduced almost everywhere. Foreign trade was redirected towards the West, and especially the European Union.

Private ownership and enterprise were legalized, preparations were made for the privatization of state property, first of small productive establishments (shops, restaurants, hotels, construction), small plots of land and housing – 'small' privatization; then the 'large' privatization of state enterprises, converted into share companies under the control of their ministry or the treasury and to be subsequently sold by various methods, such as partial liquidation, sales of entire enterprises directly or following corporatization (transformation into joint stock companies), sales to managers and employees. In view of the general wish to restrain acquisitions by foreign investors (with the exception of Hungary), and of the pulverization of domestic liquid assets in the first bout of inflation, privatization could take place quickly only if state enterprises were given away to the population. This is what happened with mass privatization, an unprecedented form of institutional engineering, consisting in the large-scale distribution of free or symbolically priced vouchers convertible into privatized state assets. Competition was introduced, somewhat more slowly. The new private enterprises – especially those in the hands of foreign investors – undertook the restructuring of their finances and productive capacity, and so to some extent did many state enterprises.

A number of countries – including Hungary, Poland and the Soviet Union – had already set up an independent central bank as part of their radical reform; commercial banking functions formerly vested in the traditional, omnipresent central bank were transferred to other banks. Other countries were now following. Foreign capital began to flow in, in the form of both foreign direct investment (FDI) in productive capacity, and financial investment. The demise of the old economic system was accompanied by the collapse of the ruling party, often outlawed and expropriated, which brought down much of the state structure with which it was intertwined, with adverse implications for the rule of law, public administration, and tax collection.

In truth, 'transition' is a misnomer: it is a profound, complex and very rapid Great Transformation. The idea of transition suggests a linear movement in a uni-dimensional space from point A to point B, both common to all the countries in question, with the various 'transients' differing only in the beginning and the speed of the journey – with the presumption that the faster the transit the greater will be the net advantages. On the contrary, transition countries have had different starting points and final targets, in a multidimensional space, with a movement neither linear nor uniform, and not even uni-directional nor consistently followed, with possible intermediate stops and regressions, and various degrees of progress reached over time in different fields and countries, which have not all reached or even approached their target.

Seventeen years later – 15 for the Former Soviet Union – post-communist countries in 2006 exhibit the most profound and complex diversity. An authoritative 'expert' evaluation, though totally subjective, is provided by the Transition Scoreboard of the EBRD (the European Bank for Reconstruction and Development, set up to help finance the transition), in their *Transition Report* published annually since 1994 (and recently back-traced to 1990). The 2006 Scoreboard is reproduced in Table 15.1.

For each of the EBRD countries of operation, now 28, ten indices are estimated by officials of the Bank's Chief Economist's Office: the share of the private sector in GDP and nine scores on as many aspects of the transition. These are: small and large scale privatization; enterprise governance and restructuring; price liberalization, foreign trade and exchange rate regime; competition; banking reform and interest rate liberalization; financial markets; infrastructure reform. The scores on these nine aspects range from 1 for little or no change with respect to a fully centralized planned economy to 4+, which is the standard of advanced and internationally open market economies, such as OECD members.

Table 15.1 shows in an immediate and lucid way the sectors and countries where the transformation is proceeding more slowly: almost everywhere sectors such as company governance, competition, banking reform and financial markets' development, as well as infrastructure reform. In these areas, and in foreign trade and ownership regimes, the distance between the starting and target models had been greatest, but in the last two of these the speed of change had been surprisingly rapid. Foreign trade liberalization had benefited from earlier reforms, from pre-existing contacts with Western partners, who could take the initiative in identifying and proposing mutually profitable transactions, from the greater facility with which markets can be set up for foreign exchange with respect to other markets for goods and services and for capital. Privatization lent itself to being accelerated with the free or

Table 15.1 *Progress in transition in Central and Eastern Europe, the Baltic States and the CIS*

Country	Private sector share in % of GDP, mid-2006 (EBRD estimate per cent)	Enterprises			Markets and trade			Financial institutions		Infrastr. reform
		Large-scale privatisation	Small-scale privatisation	Governance and enterprise restructuring	Price liberalization	Trade and foreign exchange system	Competition Policy and interest rate liberalization	Banking reform	Securities markets and non-bank financial institutions	
Albania	75	3	4	2+	4+	4+	2	3-	2-	2
Armenia	75	4-	4	2+	4+	4+	2+	3-	2	2+
Azerbaijan	60	2	4-	2	4	4	2	2+	2-	2
Belarus	25	1	2+	1	3-	2+	2	2-	2	1+
Bosnia-Herze.	55	3-	3	2	4	4-	2-	3-	2-	2+
Bulgaria	75	4	4	3-	4+	4+	3-	4-	3-	3
Croatia	60	3+	4+	3	4	4+	2+	4	3	3
Czech Republic	80	4	4+	3+	4+	4+	3	4	3	3+
Estonia	80	4	4+	4-	4+	4+	4-	4	4	3+
FYR Macedonia	65	3+	4	3-	4+	4+	2	3-	4	2
Georgia	70	4-	4	2+	4+	4+	2	3-	2+	2+
Hungary	80	4	4+	4-	4+	4+	3+	4	4	4-
Kazakhstan	65	3	4	2	4	4-	2	3	3-	3-
Kyrgyzstan	75	4-	4	2	4+	4+	2	2+	2	2-
Latvia	70	4-	4+	3	4+	4+	3	4-	3	3
Lithuania	75	4	4+	3	4+	4+	3+	4-	3	3

Table 15.1   *Continued*

Country	Private sector	Enterprises			Markets and trade			Financial institutions		Infrastr. reform
Moldova	65	3	4-	2	4	4+	2	3-	2	2+
Mongolia	70	3	4	2	4+	4+	2	2+	2	2
Montenegro	65	3+	3	2	4	3+	1	3-	2-	2-
Poland	75	3+	4+	4-	4+	4+	3	4-	4	3+
Romania	70	4-	4-	3-	4+	4+	3-	3	2	3+
Russia	65	3	4	2+	4	3+	2+	3-	3	3-
Serbia	55	3-	4-	2+	4	3+	2-	3-	2	2
Slovakia	80	4	4+	4	4+	4+	3+	3+	3	3-
Slovenia	65	3	4+	3	4	4+	3-	3+	3-	3
Tajikistan	55	2+	4	2-	4-	3+	2-	2+	1	1+
Turkmenistan	25	1	2	1	3-	1	1	1	1	1
Ukraine	65	3	4	2	4	4-	2+	3	2+	2+
Uzbekistan	45	3-	3+	2-	3-	2	2-	2-	2	2-

Note: The transition indicators range from 1 to 4+, with 1 representing little or no change from a rigid centrally planned economy and 4+ representing the standards of an industrialized market economy. For a detailed breakdown of each of the areas of reform, see the methodological notes in the 2006 Transition Report: 198.

Source: European Bank for Reconstruction and Development data, used with permission.

The private sector share of GDP is calculated using available statistics from both official (government) sources and unofficial sources. The share includes income generated from the formal activities of registered private companies as well as informal activities where reliable information is available. The term 'private company' refers to all enterprises in which private individuals or entities own the majority of shares.

The accuracy of EBRD estimates is constrained by data limitations, particularly in the area of informal activity. EBRD estimates may, in some cases, differ markedly from official data. This is usually due to differences in the definition of 'private' or 'non-state sector'. For example, in the CIS, the 'non-state sector' includes collective farms as well as companies in which only a minority stake has been privatized.

subsidized disposal of state capital. By contrast, financial markets were missing completely in the old system, where their functions were implemented by redistribution via the state budget and credit planning, thus starting from a blank sheet rather than capacity restructuring. The greater time required for the construction and reconstruction of institutions and behaviour has slowed down the development of financial markets, competition and legality.

Transition progress varies not only by sector but also by countries. The front-runners are those countries that first began negotiations to accede to the European Union, the so-called Luxembourg group: Hungary, Poland, the Czech Republic (the first to join the OECD), Slovenia and Estonia; as well as the initially lagging Helsinki group (from the capitals where the summit deciding to open negotiations had taken place) of Slovakia, Latvia and Lithuania, which joined the EU on 1 May 2004, and the more delayed Romania and Bulgaria, which joined on 1 January 2007. The very process of negotiating entry has been a powerful engine of institutional change and of legal and economic convergence with the EU. They are open market economies, with developed financial markets, a solvent banking sector, competition and corporate governance. A second group includes countries that have only just begun their negotiations for EU access, such as Albania, plus the more advanced among the CIS republics, headed by Russia, as well as the former Yugoslav republics. They leave much to be desired in the areas of financial markets, banking and governance, and external opening. A third group includes the least advanced of the CIS republics, such as Belarus, Uzbekistan and Turkmenistan, also in terms of privatization and price liberalization; for them perhaps we should not speak of transition other than for their optimistic assimilation, by way of analogy, with other countries where the process is much more advanced.

Even accepting the EBRD indicators, the scale from 1 to 4+ exaggerates transition progress in that no progress rates 1 out of 4+, rather than zero. Moreover, some indicators seem over-optimistic; their reversal over time signals not so much a transition regress but a prudent reconsideration of earlier overestimates; there is no notion of a transformation critical mass, at least in terms of a minimum level that each indicator should reach before we can talk of transition to a market economy. On the whole, EBRD indicators err on the side of optimism.

Gradualism versus shock therapy

Initially the dominant approach, both in the transition countries and in international circles, was that these absolutely unprecedented transformations were easy to implement, relatively painless and necessarily very rapid. The so-called 'Washington Consensus', represented by the Bretton Woods institutions (the IMF and the World Bank) and the American Treasury (see Kolodko and Nuti 1997), can be summarized in the belief that:

(i) both macroeconomic stabilization and transition to the market economy can and should be implemented at a stroke, as 'shock therapy', 'cold turkey' or 'big bang';

(ii) it is sufficient to liberalize prices and international trade, and liberalize the economy, for the automatic realization of the new system; in the words of Jeffrey Sachs (1993), 'As soon as central planners move out, markets move in';

(iii) the superior efficiency of the new economic system, though perhaps after a brief, minor economic fall, would have rapidly and amply compensated for the possible gross losses due to the reallocation of resources as well as the possible adverse effects on the distribution of income and wealth (in Poland, for instance, Finance Minister Balcerowicz in 1990 expected a decline of 4–5 per cent of GDP for a couple of months, if not weeks – instead of which he lost 18 per cent of GDP over two and a quarter years).

These positions, strongly contested at the time by a minority of 'gradualists', have been shown, on the whole, to be factually wrong and more generally misguided. Certainly – as we have argued above – equilibrium prices had to be reached quickly. A gradual move towards equilibrium, possibly with small steps at a pre-announced rate inadequate to reach equilibrium as in the Soviet Union in 1989–91 or Romania in 1990, was inefficient and inflationary and would not balance markets. There are also other measures that cannot wait, such as the legalization of private ownership and enterprise, and universal access to international trade with a convertible currency. At the other extreme, there are measures of economic policy and, especially, of institutional transformation that cannot be hurried – such as the introduction of economic legislation, measures for its implementation, the accumulation of jurisprudence, the setting up of financial markets, the creation of reputations and the building of trust. In these areas, it is costly and often dangerous to proceed as if these aspects of transformation could be instantaneous. There is only a handful of intermediate measures that can be instantaneous or more or less gradual, and in those cases there is no a priori reason for speed over gradualism, only costs and benefits whose net effect depends both on the trade-off actually offered by the economy, and on the weightings employed by the government in their valuation.

Thus, bringing down inflation from hyperinflationary rates to single digits can be tackled gradually or rapidly; the benefits of price stability must be offset against the costs of associated unemployment. External tariffs can be eliminated rapidly and unilaterally, or negotiated more slowly. The positive impact on competition and prices must be offset against the possible adverse effect on government revenues and unemployment: it is no accident that countries that opened trade fast, as did Poland, Czechoslovakia and Hungary, subsequently back-pedalled and reintroduced tariffs and surcharges. Subsidies can be eliminated gradually (as in the Czech Republic, in spite of Vaclav Klaus' hyper-liberal rhetoric) or quickly (as in Poland); the benefits in term of inflation control must be offset against the claim on government expenditure. Currency convertibility on capital account can be introduced quickly, gaining from capital inflows but risking their volatility (which caused a currency and financial crisis in the Czech Republic in 1993), or slowly, avoiding both benefits and risks. Finally, it is possible to privatize at different speeds, with different positive and negative effects on efficiency, equity, access to new investment and managerial resources, and government revenue.

Even without the benefit of hindsight, clearly a generalized and unconditional 'shock therapy' approach is facile and superficial. Just as for Lenin in December 1920 'communism = electrification + Soviet power', we can say that for the initial Washington consensus 'transition = liberalization + privatization'. Both equations have doubtful theoretical foundations and have yielded poor results.

Performance: the transformation recession

The move from a Soviet-type system – notoriously inefficient, inert, imbalanced and cut off from the global market – to an open market economy with all the incentives associated with private ownership and enterprise, was expected to bring rapid benefits in terms of GDP, living standards and growth. Instead of which, all transition economies experienced a recession varying from about 20 per cent in Poland to 40 per cent on average in the former USSR, with peaks of about 65 per cent GDP decline in Georgia and Armenia. The picture is clearly summarized in Figure 15.1, where the 1989 GDP level is equal to 100.

By 2005, all the new EU member states from Central Eastern Europe had exceeded the 1989 GDP level by an average of 33 per cent, except for Bulgaria (94 per cent) and Lithuania (98 per cent). South Eastern Europe was still on average at 97 per cent of the 1989 level, the CIS on average at 87 per cent (Russia at 88 per cent), with an overall average

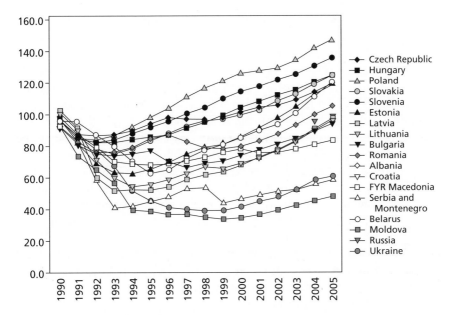

Figure 15.1 *Real GDP Index (1989 = 100)*

for transition economies still below the 1989 level at 97 per cent. The picture was more encouraging if GDP was measured at exchange rates corresponding to purchasing power parity (PPP) in terms of a common representative consumption basket, reflecting the real appreciation of their exchange rates, starting from a grossly undervalued base at the start of transition. Thus, for instance, from 1990 to 2004, Poland's GDP per head rose from $5,980 to $12,974, Hungary's from $9,040 to $16,814, Russia's from $8,340 to $9,902 in US dollars expressed in purchasing power parities.

Confronted with the disturbing evidence of a 'transformation recession', observers' first reaction was one of incredulity: recession – it was argued – was a statistical mirage. In the old system there was a tendency to exaggerate economic achievements in order to obtain bonuses from plan over-fulfilment; all productive units were subject to compulsory reporting; goods were not available at the official prices, and often involved negative value added. In the new system, producers tend to understate their output and incomes in order to avoid tax; reporting is not compulsory and samples are used instead; a large 'informal' or grey/black sector is neglected; price increases often reflect quality improvements and should not be used to deflate monetary values; in any case, consumers are better off because supplies are now, at last, plentiful at current prices. Years later, commentators such as Anders

Aslund (2001) were still speaking of post-communist recession as a 'myth'.

While, undoubtedly there was an element of truth in these qualifications, they can easily be exaggerated. The informal sector was already present before the transition and now began to surface, actually boosting official figures instead of depressing them. The reduction of negative value-added output should have raised GDP instead of reducing it. Not all loss-making enterprises should necessarily be closed down, as happened often at the beginning of the transition, but only those producing less positive value added than could be obtained in alternative uses. Consumer surplus from goods availability has never been reckoned to be a part of GDP and there is no reason to start with transition economies. An observer above suspicion, Nobel laureate Bob Mundell (1997), writes that the transformation recession was not only real but, indeed, worse than the 1929 worldwide recession and at least as serious as the Black Death recession of five centuries previously, with the difference that the plague at least reduced not just output but also population, thus preserving living standards.

Moreover, the transition has been accompanied by the rapid emergence of labour unemployment, converging to similar average values and dispersion typical of European Union countries. The many queues for goods typical of the old system have been replaced by a single, but much longer, queue for jobs (see Table 15.2). Income distribution has become more unequal; the most common measure of inequality, the Gini coefficient (0 for absolute equality, 1 for absolute inequality) has increased everywhere from 1989 to 2004, from about 0.25–0.30 to around 0.35–0.40 (except for the Czech Republic, where it was and is lower, but still has risen from 0.198 to 0.235, a similar trend for Belarus, and Slovenia where it has fallen slightly from 0.265 to 0.243 from 1991 to 2004; see UNICEF, 2006). Poverty has also increased, before falling again with the resumption of economic growth according to World Bank figures.

The unexpected 'transformation recession' can be attributed to several causes:

(i)   trade shocks; that is, the disintegration of large commercial blocs – Comecon, the USSR, Czechoslovakia, the Yugoslav federation – and the monetary areas associated with them, aggravated by the move to world prices and settlement in convertible currencies;

(ii)   a systemic vacuum in the switch from the old system which is no longer there, to a new system not yet fully in position;

(iii) gross mistakes in economic policy, such as the unintended credit shock from targeting monetary variables in nominal terms in the

Table 15.2   Annual registered unemployment rate (average per cent of labour force)

	Note	1989	1990	1991	1992	1993	1994	1995	1996	1997	1998	1999	2000	2001	2002	2003	2004
Czech Republic	a		0.3	2.6	3.1	3.0	3.3	3.0	3.1	4.3	6.0	8.5	9.0	8.5	9.2	9.9	9.5
Hungary	a	0.4	0.8	8.5	12.3	12.1	10.4	10.4	10.5	10.4	9.1	9.6	8.7	8.0			
Poland			3.4	9.2	12.9	14.9	16.5	15.2	14.3	11.5	10.0	12.0	14.0	16.2	17.8	18.0	19.1
Slovakia			0.6	6.6	11.4	12.7	14.4	13.8	12.6	12.9	13.7	17.3	18.2	18.2	17.8	15.2	14.3
Slovenia		2.9	4.7	8.2	11.5	14.4	14.4	13.9	13.9	14.4	14.5	13.6	12.2	11.6	11.6	11.2	10.6
Estonia						3.9	4.4	4.1	4.4	4.0	3.7	5.1	5.3	6.5	5.9	5.3	
Latvia					0.9	4.6	6.4	6.4	7.0	7.5	7.6	9.7	8.5	7.8	8.9	8.5	8.7
Lithuania			0.3	1.3	4.4	3.8	6.1	7.1	5.9	6.4	8.4	11.5	12.5	11.3	10.3	6.8	
Bulgaria					13.2	15.8	14.0	11.4	11.1	14.0	12.2	13.8	18.1	17.5	17.7	14.3	12.7
Romania	a			3.0	8.2	10.4	10.9	9.5	6.6	8.9	10.4	11.8	10.5	8.8			
Albania		7.0	10.0	9.0	27.0	22.0	18.0	12.9	12.7	13.9	17.8	18.4	16.8	14.5	15.8	15.0	14.4
Bosnia-Herzegovina	b									39.6	39.3	39.1	38.9	39.8	42.5		
Croatia		8.0	9.3	14.9	15.3	14.8	14.5	14.5	16.4	17.5	17.2	19.1	21.1	22.0	22.3	19.2	18.0
FYR Macedonia	a	22.6	23.0	24.5	26.0	27.7	30.0	35.6	38.8	41.7							
Serbia and Montenegro	c	17.9	19.7	21.4	22.8	23.1	23.1	24.6	25.7	24.5	25.1	26.1	26.4	27.5	29.5		
Belarus	a			0.1	0.5	1.4	2.1	2.9	4.0	2.8	2.3	2.1	2.1	2.3	3.0	3.1	1.9
Moldova					0.1	0.7	1.1	1.4	1.5	1.5	2.0	2.0	2.1	2.0	1.9	2.0	1.8
Russia	a			0.1	0.8	1.1	2.2	3.3	3.6	2.9	2.9	1.7	1.4	1.6	2.1	2.3	2.6
Ukraine	a				0.3	0.3	0.4	0.4	1.3	3.0	3.7	4.3	4.2	3.7	3.8	3.7	3.5

Notes: (a) end-of-year; (b) data refer to Federation of B-H; (c) data for Kosovo for 1998 is an SMSO estimate; 1999–2002 exclude Kosovo.

Sources: derived from UNICEF data and the TransMONEE Data Bank, accessed 26 December 2006.

presence of higher inflation than anticipated, or 'overshooting' the initial fiscal squeeze (as in Poland in 1990 under Balcerowicz as finance minister). Moreover, interest rates were raised to higher than usury levels (over 200 per cent in real terms in Russia in 1994) thus depressing employment via low investment and an overvalued currency, and encouraging demonetization and barter (also caused by not making payments from the state budget, in a misguided attempt to hold down inflation – a form of financial repression similar to the monetary overhang of the old days).

In the second half of the 1990s, a 'New Washington Consensus' gradually emerged, stressing not only private ownership and liberalization but also competition, corporate governance, the social costs of unemployment and income distribution, the role of state regulation in economic life, and generally the importance of developing and consolidating economic institution (see, for instance, Kolodko and Nuti, 1997).

Lessons and prospects

As Western politicians have taken to remarking, 'Nobody said it was going to be easy, and nobody was right.' Somebody had evidently equated the task of transition to the transformation of a fish soup back into an aquarium. To some extent the transition had to be a messy affair, as any complex, unprecedented process, with international ramifications and ridden with conflicts within and between groups and countries. In evaluating the costs and benefits of the transition, comparison should not be made with the past, but with what the alternative would have been over the same period of time without transition.

It may be the old system might have evolved – eventually – into a new model of market socialism capable of surviving, if not thriving. After all, the laggards in the transition process – such as Belarus or Uzbekistan – have performed better than the keener reformers – such as Russia – although not as well as radical reformers such as Poland, Hungary or Slovenia. But, unlike Belarus or Uzbekistan, the other pre-transition socialist economies failed to introduce market-clearing prices that would have enabled markets to function, and failed to exploit the opportunities of international trade. We will probably never know whether the old system might have survived in some form. Its political features, such as those of Belarus and Uzbekistan, were sufficiently unattractive not to be missed. In any case, the point is that the system did not evolve in that direction; without transition its performance would have been worse than it was in the transition.

Just as the earlier successes of communist economies were built on the sacrifices of the populations and in particular workers, so were the successes of the transition. There is no doubt that much of the cost could have been avoided if only the process had not happened to occur at the time of the dominant hyper-liberalism of Reagan and Thatcher. The market economy model implemented in the transition was more fundamentalist than any modern capitalist model in existence. The principle of central bank independence, for instance, gave rise to some of the most powerful central banks in the whole world (Poland), creating a costly failure of coordination with fiscal policy. The dogma of a positive real interest rate, unsupported by any economic theory, was taken to very costly extremes, effectively turning the interest rate into a centrally administered price rather than an expression of market forces. Central banks made significant quasi-fiscal losses (appearing in their balance sheets as lower profits but materializing as lower transfers to the state budget) in order to sterilize the expansionary impact of capital inflows, borrowing back from the public excess funds at higher interest rates than they got on their reserves.

The principle of market sovereignty was not applied to the labour market, which was subjected to widespread wage ceilings and punitive taxes (as in Poland in 1990). The welfare state, which in these economies was to a large extent the responsibility of state enterprises, was dismantled without being reconstructed at the central level. The pension system was transformed, or is being transformed, almost everywhere from a 'pay as you go' or distribution system, whereby pensioners are funded by the contributions of current employees, to a capitalization system with pensions paid out of accumulated past contributions, making a submerged pension debt emerge and creating a vast, unnecessary hole in government accounts. The speed of privatization cost government revenue and opportunities for injections of new investment and management; it also created unprecedented opportunities for the self-appropriation of state assets by managers and party officials, and straightforward corruption (as in the 'loans for shares' scheme that gave a few Russian banks a large stake in privatization at rock bottom prices). The process led to 'state capture' by private investors rather than simply state assets privatization. The marginalization of the state led to delays or gaps in market regulation, especially in financial markets (as in the disastrous spread of banking pyramids in Russia, Romania, Albania, Serbia, Macedonia and elsewhere), for the protection of shareholders and more generally for corporate governance. This list could be extended.

Usually the International Monetary Fund and the World Bank are either praised or blamed for their part in imposing economic policies and institutional transformations in extreme forms through the conditionality of their financial assistance, whose effects are multiplied by other public and private institutions in turn making their assistance conditional on an IMF programme. Sometimes Western advisors have been blamed for recommending policies that they would not have dared propose to their own governments. But the ultimate responsibility for the policies actually adopted must be attributed to sovereign governments that have accepted those policies, and often have been only too pleased to conform to the requests of international institutions and the advice of Western consultants.

Nevertheless, current economic prospects for the entire group of transition economies are buoyant, especially for the ten new members of the European Union. Economic growth is driven by exports, domestic investment and foreign direct investment (FDI). While, in the early 1990s, Hungary was the only transition economy receiving significant FDI, in the second half of the 1990s foreign investment flowed into Poland, the Czech Republic, Slovakia, the Baltic States and, in more recent years, investment inflows have increased throughout the transition economies, rising from US$20–30 bn a year in 1998–2003 to $39 bn in 2004 and an estimated $48 bn in 2005 (Svejnar, 2006; UNCTAD, 2006).

The 'gravitational pull of the EU' over the 15 years before accession has helped transform Central and Eastern Europe from communist regimes with central planning and public ownership and enterprises into modern, well-functioning democracies with open market economies and dominant private ownership and enterprises. In 1993, the EU indicated that those transition countries with which it had been signing Europe Association Agreements since 1991 could be considered as potential candidate members if they fulfilled the conditions of being a stable democracy with the rule of law, able to respect human and minority rights, with a competitive market economy and willing and able to fulfil the obligations of membership (the so-called *acquis communautaire*), subject to the EU's ability to absorb them. By the time of accession, a considerable institutional convergence had taken place, a free trade area had been established by 2001 for 85 per cent of bilateral trade, so that there was no trade shock. To recall eight countries joined on 1 May 2004 (the Czech Republic, Hungary, Slovakia, Slovenia, Poland, Estonia, Latvia, Lithuania); Bulgaria and Romania on 1 January 2007. Membership of the eurozone is one of the obligations of new members (unlike the UK and Denmark, and rather like Sweden); Slovenia introduced the euro on 1 January 2007 and Lithuania, Latvia and Estonia are lined up for early entry. Candidate countries are Croatia, the former Yugoslav Republic of Macedonia;

Albania, Bosnia-Herzegovina, Montenegro, and Serbia (including Kosovo under UNSCR 1244) are potential candidate countries.

The ten new EU members already exhibit considerable convergence to the Maastricht conditions for euro-area membership (ECB, 2006); they all satisfy the fiscal condition of a public debt lower than 60 per cent of GDP; have maintained sufficient stability in their exchange rates (which are supposed to remain, for at least two years before euro adoption, within +/- 15 per cent of a central parity agreed with EU authorities); their inflation and interest rates are below the ceiling fixed by the Maastricht Treaty (respectively 1.5 and 2 per cent over the average of the three least inflationary members of the EU) or well within its reach. The latest challenge for the new EU members is the achievement of the remaining fiscal condition, a public deficit under 3 per cent of GDP, which is hard to achieve in view of the structural nature of the deficit, their low and regressive rate of direct taxation, and the cost of transition. This constraint is also hard to justify, in view of the very low debt/GDP ratio and high GDP growth. There is also, paradoxically, a fiscal shock of accession due to the burden of membership falling on the state budget and transfers from Brussels benefiting the country at large instead of the budget. This might lead to a postponement of the introduction of the euro but will not affect significantly further economic integration within the EU.

Additional challenges for the transition economies are the completion of the reform tasks (with respect to the important but still partial achievements reviewed in Table 15.1); the fight against unemployment, in view of the 'jobless growth' that seems to have accompanied their recovery; the maintenance of their competitiveness in the face of real currency appreciation; the reduction of the inequality and poverty that have risen during the transition; and the consolidation of democracy.

Chapter 16

The Quality of Post-Communist Democracy

Dirk Berg-Schlosser

The preceding chapters have provided detailed accounts of individual countries and major cross cutting features. As they make clear, there has been a high level of political volatility across the region since the regime changes of the late 1980s and early 1990s. At the same time, not only a political transformation but also an economic and social one has taken place as well. Indeed, these multiple transition processes required, in the words of Jon Elster (1993), 'rebuilding the ship at sea'. Together with new freedoms there were considerable hardships and a large majority of the populations had to change their accustomed ways of life.

By now, some more general stocktaking of these developments has become possible and they can be presented here in a more broadly comparative manner. A greater number of countries have become what can be called 'consolidated democracies' (Linz and Stepan, 1996; Diamond, 1999). Others are still struggling in this direction, or have established different kinds of authoritarian regimes. Similarly, over the course of time some positive changes may be observed in the newly established market economies. These developments are still continuing, and have affected these countries in different ways.

In this final chapter, we present a brief overview of these developments and assess the 'qualities' of the new democracies in both a functional and a normative sense. For this purpose, first the respective criteria have to be defined and then linked to currently available databases. In this way, as a second step, different democratic and non-democratic regime types can be identified. This also affects, third, the quality of their respective 'governance'. Finally, an overview of the socio-economic performance of these regimes will also be provided. In doing so, considerable differences between the various countries and sub-regions in Central and Eastern Europe, but also significant changes over time, will become apparent. Any broadly based empirical assessment of this kind must obviously operate within the limitations of the available sources. For this reason, the 'quality' of these sources and their respective strengths and weaknesses must also be kept in mind.

The qualities of democracies as measured by current indicators

Before we operationalize certain measures and attempt to assess their validity, we must have clear definitions of the concepts that underlie them. Here, we must first define the *unit* of analysis, the relevant political system or state and its boundaries. This is often taken for granted and left to the 'shadow theory' of democracy (Dahl, 1989: 4 ff.). As the recent examples of former Yugoslavia and parts of the former Soviet Union demonstrate, however, such an assumption is not warranted even in present day Europe, let alone other parts of the world. An enduring state formation, therefore, has to precede – conceptually and in political practice – any meaningful democratization. This, in the European context, is still painfully evident in Bosnia-Herzegovina and in Kosovo, for example.

If the unit of analysis can be established with relatively undisputed boundaries, and this is an empirical not a conceptual question, then the actual *political system* and its specific 'qualities' come into play. For this purpose we need a sufficiently complex, widely accepted, and empirically operationalizable notion of *democracy* that can adequately capture the differing forms of contemporary appearances of this kind of rule. At the same time, it should be sufficiently distinct to draw meaningful boundaries to other types of political systems and sufficiently open to be linked to existing sub-types and possible future developments.

Such a root concept is Robert Dahl's (1971) notion of 'polyarchy', which has become the most frequently cited referent of empirically oriented democratization studies over recent decades. He explicitly distinguishes two dimensions of this more modest characterization of contemporary democracies: the amount of regular and open *competition* in a political system, and the extent of different forms of *participation* in the process of political decision making by the population of a given society. Implicit in his notion is a third (normative) dimension which concerns basic *civil liberties* such as freedom of information and organization, and a political order that guarantees and maintains the *rule of law* to make regular political contestation and participation possible and meaningful. These three dimensions of the root concept of democracy that emphasize the 'input' side of political systems and the necessary institutional and legal framework have become largely accepted.

To be distinguished from such a definition are the respective historical, economic and cultural bases and *conditions* of democracy, which often have been seen as 'requisites' (Lipset 1960, 1994), and the actual *performance* and *effectiveness* of democratic systems which comprise the 'output' side and various distinct policy areas.

Such criteria may apply, of course, to different types of political system, not just democratic ones. A specific democratic quality, however, concerns the *accountability* of the executive in relation to other democratic institutions and the society at large (Przeworski *et al.*, 1999). Horizontally, this may consist of effective parliamentary and judicial controls, but also some more specialized institutions such as independent auditing offices. Vertically, this refers to the effectiveness of the overall feedback mechanisms between the output and, again, the input side, which is ensured by the perceptions of the political public, an independent pluralist media and, eventually, elections. Furthermore, and increasingly, perceptions and possibly even controls by the outside world, international public opinion, and regional or global organizations such as the EU or the UN also may play a role.

Over and above such functional and (limited) normative criteria, which characterize a 'liberal democracy' in the positive sense of the word, some more demanding *normative* criteria may also be applied. These concern a broader range of *participatory* activities on the part of the citizens in a 'strong democracy' (Barber, 1984); the fuller *inclusion* of women, weaker social strata, cultural minority and other groups (Pateman, 1988); greater *equality* not only of political rights, but also of actual social and economic opportunities and living conditions; and a greater measure of *solidarity* among all members of society involving mutual trust, tolerance and a high level of 'social capital' and cooperation both nationally and, possibly, internationally (Putnam, 1993). The question of the relationship between the economic and the political system of free markets versus public controls, but also the possibility of monopolizing the latter by some dominant actors in the former, also remains a disputed topic (Dahl, 1986). Such questions go beyond the scope of this chapter, but they remain on the political agenda.

Identifying (liberal) democracies and non-democracies

With such dimensions and criteria in mind, we can first of all attempt to identify the existence, or non-existence, of liberal democracy in a minimal sense among the cases to be considered. In a geographical sense, this discussion is limited to the post-communist countries of Central and Eastern Europe including, within the scope of this book, some of the former Soviet republics, but not the present Russian Federation or the Caucasus and Central Asian states. As a West European reference case, data for the United Kingdom are also provided.

Among the large number of studies that have developed indicators of democracy we present only those that are currently available on a longer-term and continuous basis. These are the 'index of democracy' developed by Tatu Vanhanen (1984, 1997), the data set compiled by Ted Gurr (1996, 2002) and his associates, the annual ratings of 'political rights' and 'civil liberties' by Freedom House (1978 ff.), which strictly speaking do not constitute an index of democracy but which often are taken as a proxy in this respect, and, most recently, the data on 'voice and accountability' and the 'rule of law' compiled by the World Bank (Kaufman *et al.*, 2003, 2006). Furthermore, a scale of 'gross human rights violations', which seeks to establish a certain minimum level of basic human rights and the absence of more direct forms of political repression (such as detention without trial for purely political reasons, and so on), has been added (PIOOM, 2001). Another more recent measure is the 'Bertelsmann Transformation Index' (BTI), which attempts to cover both political and economic transformations in terms of increasing democratization and market systems.

Vanhanen takes as his point of departure the two basic dimensions considered by Dahl, competitiveness and political participation, and operationalizes them in a relatively simple, straightforward and more easily measurable form, taking available electoral data as its base. The degree of participation (P) is assessed by voter turnout in consecutive elections, defined as the proportion of persons voting in relation to the total population of a country. The competitiveness of elections (C) is measured by the share of the largest party in national parliamentary elections subtracted from 100. Both measures are then multiplied by each other and divided by 100 to result in a scale ranging from 0 to 100 (P*C/100). A value of 5 on this scale is the minimum threshold for a system to be considered as 'democratic' in his sense.

Gurr *et al.* identify three major dimensions of, as they call it, 'institutionalized democracy', referring to the competitiveness of political participation, the openness of executive recruitment, and constraints on the chief executive. Based on a variety of sources, in particular on the respective constitutions, they code these dimensions and add them up to an 11-point scale ranging from 0 to 10. Cases with scores of 8 and above are considered to be fully democratic.

The third continuous (since 1972) and constantly updated source of information is the annual Freedom House survey, which focuses on political rights and civil liberties. With the help of an elaborate check-list, they score each country on a scale of 1 to 7, with 1 being the highest value and 7 the lowest. A threshold of 2.5 on the political rights dimension is considered to represent the minimum for a liberal democracy.

The World Bank has, since 1996, collated a wealth of data from various sources on 'good governance'. These include some objective economic and social performance data, but also perceptional assessments by public, civil society and business sources such as the Economist Intelligence Unit, Standard and Poor's Country Risk Review, the Gallup Millennium Survey and Transparency International. All these sources with their varying coverage both in depth and scope are aggregated into six dimensions by employing an 'unobserved components model' (Kaufman *et al.*, 1999). In this way, an 'index of indices' is created with a wide coverage and a more or less permanent institutional base. Among these six dimensions are two indices of what they call 'voice and accountability' and the 'rule of law', which can be taken to be essential elements of liberal democracy. These dimensions are scored with a range of –2.5 to +2.5, with 0 being the threshold.

Finally, the 'gross human rights violations' or 'political terror scale' measures such violations on a scale of 1 to 5, 1 being the best value and 5 the worst. No distinct threshold is given here, but certainly values above 2 must be considered to be insufficient for a liberal democratic regime.

The Bertelsmann Transformation Index (only the political transformation index is considered here) assesses elements of stable state formation, levels of political participation, the rule of law, the stability of democratic institutions, and levels of social and political integration on scales ranging from 1 to 10, and aggregates them by taking the arithmetic mean of all of them. The authors do not indicate a specific threshold, but a value of 8 and above can be taken to represent the minimum that is required for a regime to be defined as democratic.

The most recent scores on all these indices are reported in Table 16.1.

When we compare the actual findings on these scales, it becomes apparent that Vanhanen's measure is the least discriminating. In fact, all the countries listed here score above his minimum threshold, even Lukashenka's Belarus. It should also be noted that high values on this index do not represent a *better* democracy in any functional or normative sense, Hungary and Ukraine actually attaining the highest values in 2004. This is because his measure of competitiveness, which is an indication of the degree of fragmentation of the party system, cannot

Table 16.1 *Democratization indices*

Country	(1)	(2)	(3)	(4)	(5)	(6)	(7)	(8)
Albania	20.5	7	3	0.08	-0.84	2	7.25	C
Belarus	16.0	0	7	-1.68	-1.04	3	3.97	D
Bosnia and Herzegovina	21.5	–	4	-0.11	-0.74	2	6.80	D
Bulgaria	27.6	9	1	0.59	-0.19	2	8.45	B
Croatia	28.2	7	2	0.51	0.00	2	9.10	B
Czech Republic	30.1	10	1	1.01	0.70	2	9.45	A
Estonia	24.7	7	1	1.05	0.82	1	9.40	A
Hungary	33.1	10	1	1.10	0.70	2	9.40	A
Latvia	28.3	8	1	0.89	0.43	1	8.30	A-
Lithuania	23.9	10	1	0.90	0.46	1	9.25	A-
Macedonia	21.9	9	3	0.03	-0.38	2	7.55	C
Moldova	10.3	8	3	-0.49	-0.59	3	5.40	C
Poland	20.9	10	1	1.04	0.32	2	9.20	A
Romania	25.3	8	2	0.36	-0.29	2	8.20	B
Slovakia	28.1	9	1	1.04	0.41	2	9.20	A
Slovenia	31.6	10	1	1.08	0.79	1	9.55	A
Ukraine	33.2	7	3	-0.26	-0.60	3	7.10	C
United Kingdom	26.6	10	1	1.30	1.69	2	–	A
Yugoslavia (Serbia and Montenegro)	26.6	6	3	0.12	-0.81	2	7.40	C

Sources: Adapted from (1) Vanhanen's Index of Democracy, 2004 (Vanhanen, 2004); (2) Institutionalized democracy, 2003 (Jaggers/and Gurr – Polity IV); (3) Political Rights Score, 2005 (Freedom House 1978 ff.); (4) Voice and Accountability Score, 2005 (Kaufmann *et al.*, 2006); (5) Rule of Law Score, 2005 (Kaufmann *et al.*, 2006); (6) Gross Human Rights Violations, 2000 (Political Terror Scale, PIOOM, 2001); and (7) the Bertelsmann Transformation Index, 2006 (13TI, 2006). Column (8) shows Political System Type.

be taken as a 'qualitative' standard, but only as a minimum requirement in each case.

The Gurr, Freedom House, World Bank and BTI measures identify between 11 and 15 cases respectively with a relatively high level of agreement among them. On the human rights score, only three cases stand out as insufficient.

Despite the inadequacies of such measures (see Munck and Verkuilen, 2002; Berg-Schlosser, 2004), a meaningful assessment of the existing political systems in post-communist Europe is possible by looking across these scores and combining them into a simple classificatory scheme (see column 8 in Table 16.1). Thus, Belarus and Bosnia clearly can be labelled as non-democratic (category D) where there is a high level of agreement among all of the more discriminating indicators. Cases such as Albania, Macedonia, Moldova, Serbia, and Ukraine can be classified as purely 'electoral democracies' (Diamond, 1999), achieving somewhat better scores on most measures but falling short of the minimum required for a 'liberal democracy' (category C). Among those passing the minimum threshold, certain cases with restrictions on some measures, such as Bulgaria, Croatia, and Romania (category B), can be distinguished from those obtaining fully positive scores (category A).

If, in addition, somewhat higher thresholds are taken for the World Bank data of 'voice and accountability', which are based on the most comprehensive information (values of +1 and above), a further distinction among the fully fledged and consolidated liberal democracies and some states with lower scores (category A-) becomes possible. In addition, the rule of law, as indicated in the World Bank measure, also seems still to be flawed even in a number of the consolidated cases such as Poland or Slovakia.

Some variation over time also becomes apparent when we compare available data for the major indicators for 1996 (the base year of the World Bank data set) with the latest scores on these variables (mostly for 2005). While in most cases there is little significant variation across the period, some show a certain improvement; for instance, Croatia and Romania move from C to B – in effect crossing the minimum threshold – and Estonia, Latvia and Slovakia move from B to A or A-, joining the other more recently consolidated democracies in Central Europe.

Evaluating 'good governance'

Measures indicating the attainment of a certain minimum level of 'liberal democracy' must be distinguished from indices assessing the quality of their actual '*governance*' in a functional sense. The World Bank data are the only ones that cover this aspect more fully. In addition to the 'voice and accountability' and 'rule of law' dimensions already presented, these comprise three other indices: 'government effectiveness' (that is, the quality of the bureaucracy and public services), the 'regulatory burden' (that is, market-unfriendly policies such as price and trade controls), and 'graft' (that is, the exercise of public power for private gain) including various forms of corruption, nepotism or clientelism.

The 'rule of law' dimension (referring to the independence of the judiciary, respect for basic human rights, the enforceability of contracts and so forth), which has been employed already to define the minimum normative requirements of a 'liberal democracy', also overlaps with such characteristics of the central political system. Not all existing democracies, certainly, are 'well governed' in this sense, and there are non-democratic regimes that may be better governed than others with less corruption or at a certain level in respect of the rule of law, such as the Prussian state in former times or, possibly, a country such as present-day Singapore. These data are presented in Table 16.2.

It can be seen that there is a very high level of correspondence between the previous classification of regime type and their quality of governance. All countries classified as D (Belarus and Bosnia) or C (Albania, Macedonia, Moldova, Serbia, and Ukraine) have negative scores on all these indicators. But some that reach the category B threshold, such as Bulgaria and Romania, remain below 0 on some of these measures. If we again raise the threshold to a level of +1 for the remaining cases in order to obtain some differentiation concerning a higher 'quality', practically the same distinctions as before between our A and A- categories become apparent.

Table 16.2   *Indicators of 'good governance'*

Country	(1)	(2)	(3)	(4)	(5)	(6)
Albania	-0.49	-0.37	-0.27	0.08		0.05
Belarus	-1.19	-1.05	-1.53	-0.99	-0.90	-0. 86
Bosnia and Herzegovina	-0.53	–	-0.53	-1.88	-0.32	–
Bulgaria	-0.23	-0.44	0.63	-0.12	-0.05	-0.62
Croatia	0.44	-0.22	0.45	-0.12	0.07	-0.45
Czech Republic	0.94	0.6	1.04	0.98	0.42	0.55
Estonia	1.03	0.45	1.43	1.18	0.88	0.05
Hungary	0.79	0.45	1.11	0.47	0.63	0.59
Latvia	0.68	-0.02	1.03	0.41	0.33	-0.52
Lithuania	0.85	0.05	1.13	0.27	0.26	-0.12
Macedonia	-0.28	-0.22	-0,20	-0.19	-0.50	-0.93
Moldova	-0.75	-0.49	-0.43	0.01	-0.76	-0.19
Poland	0.58	0.47	0.82	0.34	0.19	0.38
Romania	-0.03	-0.53	-0.17	-0.43	-0.23	-0.17
Slovakia	0.95	0.18	1.16	0.18	0.43	0.39
Slovenia	0.99	0.43	0.86	0.38	0.88	0.98
Ukraine	-0.42	-0.59	-0.26	-0.57	-0.63	-0.69
United Kingdom	1.70	1.68	1.53	1.54	1.64	1.78
Yugoslavia (Serbia and Montenegro)	-0.31	-0.57	-0.53	-1.09	-0.55	-0.85

Sources: (1) Government Effectiveness Score 2005 (Kaufmann *et al.*, 2006); (2) Government Effectiveness Score 1996 (Kaufmann *et al.*, 2003); (3) Regulatory Quality Score 2005 (Kaufmann *et al.*, 2006); (4) Regulatory Quality Score 1996 (Kaufmann *et al.*, 2003); (5) Control of Corruption 2005 (Kaufmann *et al.*, 2006); (6) Control of Corruption 1996 (Kaufmann *et al.*, 2003).

Socio-economic performance

These governance characteristics also significantly shape the actual per-formance. If we assess the changes in GDP per capita (measured in purchasing power parities), literacy and life expectancy, which are aggregated by the United Nations Development Programme (1990 ff.) into a composite 'Human Development Index' (HDI) over the period under consideration, similar clear-cut differences can be discerned among the different system types both absolutely and in terms of rela-tive changes. In this way, not only efficiency but also effectiveness and actual outcomes in real terms (increasing life expectancy and so forth) can be measured in some important areas. The detailed results are given in Table 16.3.

The enormous socio-economic diversity in Europe becomes apparent in these figures. Even adjusted for purchasing power parities, the great discrepancy between the United Kingdom (US$ 27,147) and Moldova (with a value of just US$ 1,510) remains striking. Life expectancy at birth is lowest in Ukraine at 66.1 years, by contrast with 78.4 years in the UK. The differences in levels of literacy are less pronounced with the exception of Bosnia (94.6 per cent), literacy rates being close to the maximum in most countries. The overall human development index is lowest for Moldova (0.671), followed by Ukraine (0.766) and Albania (0.780), the U.K. again standing out at 0.939 and Slovenia reaching 0.904.The greatest positive changes overall can be noted in Latvia, Lithuania, and Hungary.

Conclusion

The foregoing has attempted to demonstrate how some of our common tools in empirical political science, such as the currently avail-able and widely used indicators of democratization and good gover-nance, enable some limited but nevertheless meaningful and useful analysis of the 'quality' of the political systems of contemporary post-communist states. As has been shown, the information contained in such indicators and indices can be combined to yield more balanced and meaningful accounts when they are integrated into a more com-prehensive conceptual framework.

As the presented results indicate, first of all, there exists a mean-ingful distinction between liberal democracies and non-democracies, and the identification of certain sub-types becomes possible on this basis. Second, aspects of 'democratic quality' can be distinguished from the criteria of 'good governance' in general. Actual performance in

Table 16.3 *Socio-economic performance*

Country	(1)	(2)	(3)	(4)	(5)	(6)	(7)	(8)	(9)	(10)	(11)	(12)
Albania	4584	2120	0.74	73.8	72.8	1.0	98.7	85.0	13.7	0.780	0.698	0.082
Belarus	6052	4850	0.57	68.1	68.0	0.1	99.0	99.0	0.0	0.786	0.774	0.012
Bosnia and Herzegovina	5967	–	–	74.2	–	–	94.6	–	–	0.786	–	–
Bulgaria	7731	4010	0.72	72.2	71.1	1.1	98.2	98.2	0.3	0.808	0.784	0.024
Croatia	11080	4895	0.87	75.0	72.6	2.4	98.1	97.7	0.4	0.841	0.794	0.047
Czech Republic	16357	10510	0.4	75.6	73.9	1.7	99.0	99.0	0.0	0.874	0.843	0.031
Estonia	13539	5240	0.94	71.3	68.7	2.6	99.0	99.0	0.0	0.853	0.793	0.060
Hungary	14584	7200	0.71	72.7	70.9	1.8	99.0	99.0	0.0	0.862	0.807	0.055
Latvia	10270	3940	0.96	71.6	68.4	3.2	99.0	99.0	0.0	0.836	0.761	0.075
Lithuania	11702	4220	1.01	72.3	69.9	2.4	99.0	99.0	0.0	0.852	0.785	0.067
Macedonia	6794	3210	0.9	73.8	73.1	0.7	96.1	94.0	2.1	0.797	–	–
Moldova	1510	1500	0.43	67.7	67.5	0.2	96.2	98.3	-2.1	0.671	0.704	-0.033
Poland	11379	6520	0.45	74.3	72.5	1.8	99.0	99.0	0.0	0.858	0.810	0.048
Romania	7277	4310	0.35	71.3	69.9	1.4	97.3	97.8	-0.5	0.792	0.765	0.027
Slovakia	13494	7910	0.51	74.0	73.0	1.0	99.0	99.0	0.0	0.849	–	–
Slovenia	19150	11800	0.45	76.4	74.4	2.0	99.0	99.0	0.0	0.904	0.851	0.053
Ukraine	5491	2190	0.99	66.1	68.8	-2.7	99.0	99.0	0.0	0.766	0.748	0.028
United Kingdom	27147	20730	0.17	78.4	77.2	1.2	99.0	99.0	0.0	0.939	0.916	0.023
Yugoslavia (Serbia and Montenegro)	–	–	–	73.3	–	–	96.4	–	–	–	–	–

Note: Indicators shown are (1) Purchasing power parity 2003; (2) Purchasing power parity 1997; (3) Change in PPP (column 1 minus column 2, in percent); (4) Life expectancy at birth 2003; (5) Life expectancy at birth 1997; (6) Change in life expectancy (column 4 minus column 5); (7) Adult literacy rate 2003; (8) Adult literacy rate 1997; (9) Change in adult literacy rate (column 7 minus column 8); (10) Human Development Index 2003; (11) Human Development Index 1995; (12) Change in Human Development Index (column 10 minus column 11).
Source: Derived from UNDP (1990 ff).

these respects points, on the whole, to the better functioning of the 'fully consolidated' liberal democracies, but some of the more recently established, still 'weakly consolidated' democracies seem to be catching up in this regard. A more effective political feedback mechanism thus can bring into line and balance out, to a certain extent, the dual demands of 'representativity' – in terms of high levels of political participation and inclusion – on the input side, and of 'accountability' and political responsiveness – including appropriate checks and balances – on the output side of the political system.

On the whole, it could be shown that in the majority of cases democratic institutions and processes have taken hold and that their new systems, to a great extent, can be considered to be consolidated. Even if, in terms of parties and party systems, the duration of coalitions and governments, and their overall performance, there have been major changes and fluctuations over time, the democratic framework in these cases has been maintained and become accepted by the greater part of the populations. This is particularly evident in the case of the new (and further prospective) EU members. In addition to the favourable international environment in these cases, the centripetal feedback mechanisms of the new democracies have clearly helped to sustain them both in a political and economic sense. These positive developments should not overshadow some of the remaining deficits in some countries; for example, as far as the rule of law, government effectiveness, and control of corruption are concerned. This also could be highlighted by some of the available indicators.

But, even in countries that have remained purely 'electoral democracies' with more form than substance, further changes – as, for example, in Ukraine after the three-round presidential elections of 2004 – cannot be precluded, and the Balkan republics are also making further progress in a democratic direction. The mere holding of regular elections and positive examples in neighbouring countries create new aspirations and demands for more substantive democratic and economic changes.

In socio-economic terms, overall performance as measured by the Human Development Index has been largely positive as well. Only Moldova and Belarus stand out as the worst performers in this respect. But again, some of the distributional aspects that cannot be fully captured by such indicators should not be overlooked either. Some sections of the populations continue to remain poor and suffer considerable hardships. This is especially pronounced in the case of some ethnic or other minorities, such as the Roma in a number of countries. On the whole, however, the patience and endurance shown by many people in these difficult times has been remarkable (Rose *et al.*, 1998).

Nor should we overlook the fact that there is no reason for complacency about the qualities of existing democracies and their performance, either in a functional or a normative sense. These, however, can be better detected by more elaborate qualitative case-by-case analyses, such as the 'democratic audit' (Beetham and Weir, 2000), rather than by the broad overall indicators presented here. It must be hoped that in the future such qualitative studies will be extended more fully across the post-communist countries, allowing broadly based comparisons that go beyond the kinds of quantitative indicators on which this chapter has concentrated.

Guide to Further Reading

An excellent *general history* of the whole region is available in Janos (2000). Crampton and Crampton (1996) provide a useful historical atlas that illustrates the shifting nature of state borders in the twentieth century. Norman Davies' magisterial survey of Europe (1996) redresses the tendency of Western historians of 'Europe' to ignore the whole region, and Mazower (1998) sets out the wider pan-European context in the twentieth century. Mazower's history of the Balkans (2000) challenges Western prejudices about that region, as does Todorova (1997). Kundera's deliberately provocative essay (1984) sparked off a wide-ranging debate about the identity of 'Central Europe', and outstanding responses to this essay are gathered in Schöpflin and Wood (1989). An illuminating perspective on national and ethnic issues by a leading historian of the region is Ingrao (1999). Inter-war history is well covered in Rothschild (1974), as is the communist period by Rothschild and Wingfield (2000).

The meaning of the *1989 revolutions* is discussed in an engaging way by Kumar (2001). Several other works cover the collapse of communism and the early transition years (see, for instance, Kenney 2006, Pittaway 2004, and Swain and Swain, 2003, all of which provide a good introduction to cross-regional trends). Insofar as individual countries are concerned, the literature is uneven; we have excellent studies of the transition and its origins in East Germany (Fulbrook, 1995), Hungary (Tokes, 1996), Romania (Siani-Davies, 2005), and Yugoslavia (Magas, 1993; Woodward, 1995). Other worthwhile studies that focus especially on dissent and political opposition in the 1980s include Kenney (2002) and Ramet (1991).

There are still rather few *single-country monographs* that cover post-communist developments in Poland, Hungary, and the Czech Republic. However, good reviews of historical and institutional development in Hungary may be found in Andor (2000), Korosenyi (1999), and Braun and Barany (1999). For the Czech Republic, see Fawn (2000), Saxonberg (2003) and Rupnik and Zielonka (2003). On Poland, see Castle and Taras (2002) and Sanford (2002). Ost (2005) provides a distinctive interpretation of post-1989 developments. There are excellent surveys of individual countries in Berglund *et al.* (2004). For in-depth coverage of many of the countries in the region, a good place to start is the Postcommunist States and Nations Series. Cox (2005), Dimitrov (2001), Henderson (2002), Roper (2000), and Smith *et al.* (2002) are helpful in placing developments into broader historical perspective. In addition, Gallagher (2005) and Phinnemore (2006b) provide detailed analysis of more recent events in Romania. Moreover, politics in Slovakia, especially during the Meciar era, is well covered in monographs by Deegan-Krause (2006), Fisher (2006), and Haughton (2005).

On the Balkans, a general history is available in Glenny (1999) and, for Yugoslavia in particular, see Lampe (2000). Outstanding accounts of the wars in Yugoslavia by journalists are Little and Silber (1996) and Sudetic (1999). Among the best academic accounts of the crisis of communist Yugoslavia are Cohen (1993) and Pavkovic (2000). Individual country studies include, on Croatia, Tanner (1998); on Serbia, Judah (2000) and Batt (2005); on Kosovo, Judah (2002); on Bosnia-Herzegovina, Bieber (2005) and Bose (2002); on Albania, Vickers and Pettifer (1997); on Macedonia, Poulton (1995). More policy-oriented reports on the state of the region include the International Commission on the Balkans (2005) and Batt (2004). Essential for current political and economic analysis, are the reports on the region of the International Crisis Group (www. crisisgroup.org) and the European Stability Initiative (www.esiweb.org).

The two standard histories of Ukraine are Magocsi (1996) and Subtelny (2000). For an analysis of the drive to independence, see Kuzio and Wilson (1994), and, in more detail, Nahaylo (1999). Wilson (2002) covers both history and the period since independence. On politics since independence, the most up-to-date account is D'Anieri (2006), while on the Orange Revolution there is Wilson (2005a) and McFaul and Aslund (2006). On the Ukrainian economy, there is Havrylyshyn (2006), and on foreign policy Moroney *et al.* (2002) and Wolczuk (2002). Good works on Moldova are harder to find, but the standard work is King (2000). On Belarus, try Garnett and Legvold (1999), Balmaceda (2003), Korosteleva, Lawson and Marsh (2003), and White, Korosteleva and Löwenhardt (2005). On the 2006 election in Belarus, see Marples (2006).

For an overview of how the *EU's enlargement policy* has evolved, see Avery and Cameron (1998) and Mayhew (1998). For an analysis of the EU's decision to enlarge and theoretical approaches to the subject, see Schimmelfennig (2003). The economic implications of the 2004 enlargement are well explained in Boeri *et al.* (2002), and in Grabbe (2001). A number of recent books have appeared that propose new theoretical frameworks to explain the effects of the accession process and discuss particular policy areas in detail: see especially Hughes *et al.* (2004), Vachudova (2005), Schimmelfennig and Sedelmeier (2005), and Jacoby (2004). Dimensions of 'Europeanization' are also considered by Mansfeldova *et al.* (2005) and Pridham (2005).

Political leadership in and after the 1989 revolutions is theoretically addressed in Przeworski (1991), and Colton and Tucker (1995). Higley *et al.* (1996, 1997) consider the formation of post-communist elites while Hanley *et al.* (1997) and Eyal *et al.* (2000) provide data on recruitment and types of elites. Blondel and Müller-Rommel (2001) provide case studies of cabinet government while Baylis (1996 and 2007), Protsyk (2005) and Sedelius (2006) examine intra-executive conflicts. Rose, Mishler and Haerpfer (1998) focus on popular attitudes to leadership. Baylis (1996) and Taras (1998) are comparatively oriented studies of the presidency in post-communist states. Biographies of the three presidents best known in the West include Kurski (1993) on Walesa, Keane (2001) on Havel, and Cohen (2000) on Milosevic. See also Dimitrov, Goetz and Wollman (2006) for a comparative study of political executives.

On *legislatures* see, for instance, Agh (1994), Remington (1994), Longley and Zajc (1998), and Norton and Olson (1996 and 2006). Specific aspects of legislative behaviour and institutional development are considered in Agh and Ilonszki (1996), Olson and Crowther (2002), and Mansfeldova, Linek and Rakusanova (2005). Studies that focus on individual countries include Van der Meer Krok-Paszkowska (2000) and Kopecky (2001).

Electoral institution design in Central and Eastern Europe has received good coverage by scholars. Detailed discussions can be found in Elster (1996) as well as in Elster *et al.* (1998b). Kitschelt *et al.* (1999) provide a slightly different angle on similar material, while Birch *et al.* (2002) include case studies of electoral institution choice in eight states. There are also various studies of electoral system design in individual countries, including those found in Colomer (2004), as well as in Shugart and Wattenberg (2001). Electoral system effects have been examined more fully in journal articles and book chapters, including Ishiyama (1995), Shvetsova (1999), Pettai and Kreuzer (2001), Kostadinova (2002), Bielasiak (2002 and 2005), and several of the chapters in the Colomer and Shugart and Wattenberg volumes. Birch (2003) is a book-length treatment. In addition, the series of volumes on 'founding elections in Eastern Europe', edited by Hans-Dieter Klingemann and Charles Lewis Taylor, provides very useful material on individual countries.

A survey of the first phase of *party development* in the region is contained in Lewis (2000) and more recent details of parties in the eight countries now in the EU can be found in Jungerstam-Mulders (2006). Bugajski (2002) has entries on the major parties, while Millard (2004) offers a broader analysis of parties in selected countries and the context in which they work. Valuable studies of two major party families are found in Bozoki and Ishiyama (2002) and Szczerbiak and Hanley (2006). Comparative studies of particular areas of party development are given in van Biezen (2003), Lewis and Webb (2003), Lewis and Mansfeldova (2006), and Bielasiak (2006). Webb and White (2007) include substantial chapters on the Czech Republic and Slovakia, Hungary, Poland and Ukraine within a more broadly comparative context. See also Grzymala-Busse (2002) and Bozoki and Ishiyama (2002) on the successor parties, Szczerbiak and Hanley (2006) on centre-right parties, and Kopecky and Mudde (2003) and Mudde (2005) on political extremism. Walecki (2005) deals with issues of party finance in Poland, and there are useful chapters on the parliamentary parties in Heidar and Koole (2000).

Several recent monographs have offered comparative analyses of *elections and voting behaviour* in Central and Eastern Europe, often in connection with the development of party systems and/or more general issues of post-communist political development. Among the most successful are Birch *et al.* (2002), Kitschelt *et al.* (1999), Lewis (2001), Kostelecky (2002), Tworzecki (2002), Millard (2004), Bernhard (2005) and Webb and White (2007). See also Linz and Stepan (1996), for a more broadly comparative perspective of new democracies. In addition, there are some fine analyses of elections and related developments in particular countries, such as Tokes (1996), Tworzecki (1996), Szczerbiak (2001) and Jasiewicz (2003). Stimulating discussion of revolutionary upheavals can be found in Dahrendorf (1990), Jowitt (1992), Garton Ash (1993), Cirtautas (1997) and Kenney (2002), among others. And there are comprehensive studies of public attitudes toward democracy in Plasser, Ulram and Waldrauch (1998) and Rose, Mishler and Haerpfer (1998).

The key conceptual studies of *civil society* are Cohen and Arato (1992) and Keane (1988). Among the most convincing and best empirically substantiated accounts on (the weakness of) civil society in the region are Glenn (2001) and Howard (2003). On the specific role of contentious politics, the best theoretical study is Ekiert and Kubik (1999), while Kopecky and Mudde (2003) provide an overview of highly original case studies. See also Crowley and Ost (2001). Studies of civil society include Rose-Ackerman's (2005) comparative assessment of democratic accountability and participation in Poland and Hungary and Kubicek's (2004) study of organized labour in the region. Surdej and Gadowska (2005) examine corruption in Poland.

On *constitution making* in the region, see Elster *et al.* (1998), Howard (1993) and Zielonka (2001a), which deals with 'institutional engineering'. More detailed studies include Brzezinski (1998) on Poland, and Wolczuk (2002) on Ukraine. For a comparative study of semi-presidentialism, see Elgie (1999, 2004). A comparative study of the origins of constitutional systems and of the consequences of semi-presidentialism in the region is available in Sedelius (2006). The texts of the constitutions of the region are conveniently reprinted in Raina (1995) and the International Institute for Democracy (1996, 1997), and may also be found online (see confinder.richmond.edu).

A range of studies of *policy making* includes Simon (2004) on civil-military relations in the Czech Republic and Slovakia. Kirchner (1999) reviews local institutions. Eyal (2003) focuses on the Czechoslovak communist legacy for elite development. Hasselman (2006) deals with economic and social policy in Poland, Hungary, and the Czech Republic, while Seleny (2006) analyzes state-society relations in Poland and Hungary. Myant (2003) deals effectively with the vagaries of Czech economic development. Fodor (2005) assesses the role of women in the labour markets of the Czech Republic, Hungary and Poland. True (2003) deals with issues of gender in the Czech Republic.

The Soviet-type *economic system* and the various attempts to reform it are considered in Nuti (1988). For an overview of post-socialist transition, see Lavigne (1999) and the critical discussion of actual policies and alternatives in Kolodko (2000). On the dynamics of transition processes, see Blanchard (1997). On the transformation recession that accompanied the transition, and the role played in particular by bloc disintegration, see Mundell (1997). An excellent statistical source on economies and societies in transition in 1989–2005 is available at the UNICEF website http://www.unicef-icdc.org/resources/transmonee/. International institutions play an important part in research in this area: see especially the EBRD's annual *Transition Reports*, published since 1994, and *Transition Report Updates*. There are also three useful World Bank Reports: *From Plan to Market* (1996, with an excellent chapter on privatization); *Transition: The First Ten Years* (2002); and *Growth, Poverty and Inequality – Eastern Europe and the FSU* (2005, by Asad Alam *et al.*), all of which may be consulted at www.worldbank.org. On foreign direct investment, see UNCTAD (2006). On the economic aspects of European Union enlargement to the east, see Deutsche Bank Research, *European Monitor*, www.dbresearch.de, and the European Commission and the European Central Bank websites. Recent updates include Kornai (2005) and Svejnar (2006).

Details of the data that are available for the *comparative study of political performance* across the region and beyond it are provided in Chapter 16. The best comprehensive comparative account of the transition period in Eastern Europe is provided by Linz and Stepan (1996). An overview of the findings from the 'New Democracies Barometer' (NDB) is given in Rose *et al.* (1998). The issue of 'quality' is also addressed in a special issue of the *Journal of Communist Studies and Transition Politics*, 20, 1 (March 2004), which has also been issued as a book (Hutcheson and Korosteleva, 2006), and in Diamond and Morlino (2005).

Given the time lags of academic publishing, the best sources on more *recent developments* tend to be journalistic and electronic. *The Financial Times* provides the best daily coverage of the region as a whole; more comprehensive reports on current developments are provided by Radio Free Europe/Radio Liberty, available online at www.rferl.org/newsline. The large and rapidly changing world of internet sources is perhaps best approached through the portals that are maintained by larger academic institutions, such as the British Library (www.bl.uk/collections/easteuropean/slavonicinternet.html), the University of Pittsburgh (www.ucis.pitt.edu/reesweb/), the Bodleian Library at Oxford (www.bodley.ox.ac.uk/dept/slavonic/guide/htm), and the School of Slavonic and East European Studies in London (www.ssees.ac.uk/directory.htm). Many of the countries in the region have their own English-language publications: *The Baltic Times*, for example, is a good source of information. Several academic periodicals deal specifically with the politics of the Central and East European region, including *Communist and Post-Communist Studies* (quarterly), *East European Politics and Societies* (quarterly), *Europe–Asia Studies* (eight issues annually), the *Journal of Communist Studies and Transition Politics* (quarterly), and *Problems of Post-Communism* (six issues annually).

Bibliography

Agh, Attila (ed.) (1994) *The Emergence of East Central European Parliaments: The First Steps*. Budapest: Hungarian Centre of Democracy Studies Foundation.

Agh, Attila (1995) 'Partial Consolidation of the East-Central European Parties: The Case of the Hungarian Socialist Party', *Party Politics*, 1, 4 (October): 491–514.

Agh, Attila (1996) 'Political Culture and System Change in Hungary', in Fritz Plasser and Andreas Pribersky (eds), *Political Culture in East Central Europe*. Aldershot: Avebury: 127–48.

Agh, Attila and Gabriela Ilonszki (eds) (1996) *Parliaments and Organized Interests: The Second Steps*. Budapest: Hungarian Centre of Democracy Studies Foundation.

Alam, Asad, Mamta Murthi, Ruslan Yemtsov, Edmundo Murrugarra, Nora Dudwick, Ellen Hamilton and Erwin Tiongson (2005) *Growth, Poverty and Inequality – Eastern Europe and the FSU*. Washington, DC: World Bank.

Almond, Gabriel and G. Bingham Powell (eds) (1983) *Comparative Politics Today*. Boston, MA: Little, Brown.

Andor, Laszlo (2000) *Hungary on the Road to the European Union: Transition in Blue*. Westport CT: Praeger.

Arato, Andrew (1991) 'Revolution, Civil Society, and Democracy', in Zbigniew Rau (ed.), *The Reemergence of Civil Society in Eastern Europe and the Soviet Union*. Boulder, CO: Westview: 161–81.

Aslund, Anders (2001) *The Myth of Output Collapse after Communism*. Washington, DC: Carnegie Endowment, Working Papers, 18.

Avery, Graham and Fraser Cameron (1998) *The Enlargement of the European Union*. Sheffield: Sheffield Academic Press.

Bakke, Elisabeth and Nick Sitter (2005) 'Patterns of Stability. Party Competition and Strategy in Central Europe since 1989', *Party Politics*, 11, 2 (March): 245–63.

Balmaceda, Margarita (ed.) (2003) *Independent Belarus: Domestic Developments, Regional Dynamics and Implications for the West*. Cambridge, MA: Harvard University Press.

Barber, Benjamin R. (1984) *Strong Democracy: Participatory Politics for a New Age*. Los Angeles, CA: University of California Press.

Bashkirova, Elena (2002) 'Political Participation in Central and Eastern Europe. Results of the 1999 European Values Surveys', in Dieter Fuchs, Edeltraud Roller and Bernhard Wessels (eds), *Burger und Demokratie in Ost und West: Studien zur politischen Kultur und zum politischen Prozess. Festschrift fur Hans-Dieter Klingemann*. Opladen: Westdeutscher: 319–22.

Batt, Judy (ed) (2004) *The Western Balkans: Moving On*. Chaillot Paper no. 70, October. Paris: EU Institute for Security Studies.

Batt, Judy (2006) *The Question of Serbia*. Chaillot Paper no. 81, August. Paris: EU Institute for Security Studies.

Batt, Judy and Kataryna Wolczuk (1998) 'Redefining the State: the Constitutional Process', in Stephen White, Judy Batt and Paul G. Lewis (eds), *Developments in East European Politics 2*. Basingstoke: Macmillan; Durham, NC: Duke University Press: 74–90.

Baun, Michael (2002) 'EU Regional Policy and the Candidate States: Poland and the Czech Republic', *Journal of European Integration*, 24, 3 (September): 261–80.

Baylis, Thomas A. (1996) 'Presidents Versus Prime Ministers: Shaping Executive Authority in Eastern Europe', *World Politics*, 48, 3 (July): 297–323.

Baylis, Thomas A. (2007) 'Embattled Executives: Prime Ministerial Weakness in East Central Europe', *Communist and Post-Communist Studies*, 40, 1 (March): 81–106.

Beetham, David and Stuart Weir (2000) 'Democratic Audit in Comparative Perspective', in H.-J. Lauth *et al.* (eds), *Empirische Demokratiemessung*. Wiesbaden: Westdeutscher Verlag: 73–88.

Berglund, Sten, Joakim Ekman and Frank H. Aarebrot (eds) (2004) *The Handbook of Political Change in Eastern Europe*, 2nd edn. Cheltenham: Edward Elgar.

Berg-Schlosser, Dirk (2004) 'Concepts, Measurement and Sub-Types in Democratization Research', in D. Berg-Schlosser (ed.), *Democratization*. Wiesbaden: VS Verlag: 52–64.

Berliner, Joseph (1957) *Factory and Manager in the USSR*. Cambridge, MA: Harvard University Press.

Berman, Sheri (1997) 'Civil Society and the Collapse of the Weimar Republic', *World Politics*, 49, 3 (July): 401–29.

Berman, Sheri (2003) 'Islamism, Revolution, and Civil Society', *Perspectives on Politics*, 1, 2 (April): 257–72.

Bernhard, Michael (1993) *The Origins of Democratization in Poland*. New York: Columbia University Press.

Bernhard, Michael (2005) *Institutions and the Fate of Democracy: Germany and Poland in the Twentieth Century*. Pittsburgh, PA: University of Pittsburgh Press.

Bertelsmann Transformation Index (2006) *The Bertelsmann Transformation Index 2006*. Consulted at http://www.bertelsmann-transformation-index.de

Bieber, Florian (2005) *Post-war Bosnia: Ethnicity, Inequality and Public Sector Governance*. London: Palgrave.

Bielesiak, Jack (2002) 'The Institutionalisation of Electoral and Party Systems in Post-communist Europe', *Comparative Politics*, 34, 2 (January): 189–210.

Bielasiak, Jack (2005) 'Party Competition in Emerging Democracies: Representation and Effectiveness in Post-communism and Beyond', *Democratization*, 12, 3 (June): 331–56.

Bielasiak, Jack (2006) 'Regime Diversity and Electoral Change in Post-Communism', *Journal of Communist Studies and Transition Politics*, 26, 4 (December): 407–30.

Bilcik, Vladimir (2004) 'Slovakia's Integration to the European Union', in Grigorij Meseznikov and Miroslav Kollar (eds), *Slovakia 2003: A Global Report on the State of Society*. Bratislava: Institute for Public Affairs: 303–20.

Birch, Sarah (2003) *Electoral Systems and Political Transformation in Post-communist Europe*. Basingstoke: Palgrave.

Birch, Sarah (2007) 'Electoral Systems and Electoral Misconduct', *Comparative Political Studies*, 40, 12, forthcoming.

Birch, Sarah, Frances Millard, Marina Popescu and Kieran Williams (2002) *Embodying Democracy: Electoral System Design in Post-communist Europe*. Basingstoke: Palgrave.

Blanchard, Olivier J. (1997) *The Economics of Post-Communist Transition*. Oxford: Clarendon Press.

Blondel, Jean and Ferdinand Müller-Rommel, eds. 2001. *Cabinets in Eastern Europe*. Basingstoke: Palgrave.

Boeri, Tito, Guiseppe Bertola and Herbert Brücker (2002) *Who's Afraid of the Big Enlargement? Economic and Social Implications of the European Union's Prospective Eastern Expansion*. London: Centre for Economic Policy Research.

Borneman, John (1997) *Settling Accounts: Violence, Justice and Accountability in Postsocialist Europe*. Princeton, NJ: Princeton University Press

Bose, Sumantra (2002) *Bosnia After Dayton: Nationalist Partition and International Intervention*. Oxford: Oxford University Press.

Bozoki, Andras (2002) *The Roundtable Talks of 1989: The Genesis of Hungarian Democracy*. Budapest and New York: Central European University Press

Bozoki, Andras and Ishiyama, John (eds) (2002) *The Communist Successor Parties of Central and Eastern Europe*. Armonk, NY: Sharpe.

Braun, A. and Zoltan Barany (eds) (1999) *Dilemmas of Transition. The Hungarian Experience*. Lanham, MD: Rowman & Littlefield.

Brinton, Crane (1965) *The Anatomy of Revolution*. New York: Harper & Row.

Brown, J. F. (1994) *Hopes and Shadows: Eastern Europe after Communism*. Harlow: Longman.

Brubaker, Rogers (1996) *Nationalism Reframed: Nationhood and the National Question in the New Europe*. Cambridge and New York: Cambridge University Press.

Brzezinski, Mark (1998) *The Struggle for Constitutionalism in Poland*. Basingstoke and London: Macmillan.

Bugajski, Janusz (2002) *Political Parties of Eastern Europe: A Guide to Politics in the Post-Communist Era*. Armonk, NY: Sharpe.

Bunce, Valerie (2000) 'The Historical Origins of the East–West Divide: Civil Society, Political Society, and Democracy in Europe', in Nancy Bermeo and Philip Nord (eds), *Civil Society before Democracy: Lessons from Nineteenth-Century Europe*. Lanham, MD: Rowman & Littlefield: 209–36.

Bunce, Valerie J. and Sharon L. Wolchik (2006) 'Favorable Conditions and Electoral Revolutions', *Journal of Democracy*, 17, 4 (October): 5–18.

Castle, Marjorie and Ray Taras (2002) *Democracy in Poland*, 2nd edn. Boulder, CO: Westview.

CBOS (2006) 'Sympatie i antypatie Polakow cztery miesiace po wyborach', Komunikat z badań BS/27/2006, Warsaw. Consulted at http://www.cbos.pl/PL/Raporty/raporty.shtml

Chehabi, H.E., and Juan J. Linz (eds) (1998) *Sultanistic Regimes*. Baltimore, MD: Johns Hopkins University Press.

Cirtautas, Arista Maria (1997) *The Polish Solidarity Movement*. London and New York: Routledge.

Cohen, Jean L. and Andrew Arato (1992) *Civil Society and Political Theory*. Cambridge, MA: MIT Press.

Cohen, Lenard J. (1993) *Broken Bonds: The Disintegration of Yugoslavia*. Boulder CO: Westview.

Cohen, Lenard J. (2000) *Serpent in the Bosom: The Rise and Fall of Slobodan Milosevic*. Boulder, CO: Westview.

Colomer, Josep M. (ed.) (2004) *Handbook of Electoral System Choice*. Basingstoke: Palgrave.

Colton, Timothy J. and Robert C. Tucker (eds) (1995) *Patterns in Post-Soviet Leadership*. Boulder, CO: Westview.

Corrin, Chris (1993) 'People and Politics', in Stephen White, Judy Batt and Paul G. Lewis (eds), *Developments in East European Politics*. Basingstoke: Macmillan; Durham, NC: Duke University Press: 186–204.

Cox, John (2005) *Slovenia: Evolving Loyalties*. London and New York: Routledge.

Crampton, Richard (1994) *Eastern Europe in the Twentieth Century*. London: Routledge.

Crampton, Richard and Ben Crampton (1996) *Atlas of East European History in the Twentieth Century*. London: Routledge.

Crowley, Stephen and David Ost (eds) (2001) *Workers after Workers' States: Labor and Politics in Postcommunist Eastern Europe*. Lanham, MD: Rowman & Littlefield.

Csaba, Laszlo (1990) *Eastern Europe in the World Economy*. Cambridge and New York: Cambridge University Press.

Curry, Jane L. and Irena Pankow (2001) 'Social Movements and Pluralist Theory: The Conundrum of Solidarity in Poland's Democratization', in Dirk Berg-Schlosser and Raivo Vetik (eds), *Perspectives · on Democratic Consolidation in Central and Eastern Europe*. Boulder, CO: East European Monographs: 82–92.

Czesnik, Mikolaj (2006) *Uczestnictwo Wyborcze w III RP w Perspektywie Porownawczej*, unpublished doctoral thesis. Warsaw: ISP PAN.

D'Anieri, Paul (2006) *Understanding Ukrainian Politics: Power, Politics and Institutional Design*. Armonk, NY: Sharpe.

Dahl, Robert A. (1971) *Polyarchy: Participation and Opposition*. New Haven, CT: Yale University Press.

Dahl, Robert A. (1986) *A Preface to Economic Democracy*. Berkeley, CA: University of California Press.

Dahl, Robert A. (1989) *Democracy and its Critics*. New Haven, CT: Yale University Press.

Dahrendorf, Ralf (1990) *Reflections on the Revolution in Europe*. New York: Random House; London: Chatto & Windus.

Dahrendorf, Ralf (1997) *After 1989: Morals, Revolution and Civil Society*. Basingstoke: Macmillan.

Dalton, Russell J. (1988) *Citizen Politics in Western Democracies*. Chatham, NJ: Chatham House.

Dalton, Russell J. and Robert Rohrschneider (2002) 'Political Action and the Political Context: A Multi-Level Model of Environmental Activism', in Dieter Fuchs, Edeltraud Roller and Bernhard Wessels (eds), *Burger und Demokratie in Ost und West: Studien zur politischen Kultur und zum politischen Prozess. Festschfrifft fur Hans-Dieter Klingemann*. Opladen: Westdeutscher: 333–50.

Davies, J. C. (1969) 'The "J" Curve of Rising and Declining Satisfaction as a Cause of Some Great Revolutions and a Contained Rebellion', in H. Gram and T. Gurr (eds), *Violence in America*. New York: Signet, pp. 690–730.

Davies, James C. (1971) *When Men Rebel and Why*. New York: Free Press.

Davies, Norman (1996) *Europe: A History*. Oxford: Oxford University Press.

Deegan-Krause, Kevin (2006) *Elected Affinities: Democracy and Party Competition in Slovakia and the Czech Republic*. Stanford, CA: Stanford University Press.

Deutsche Bank Research, *European Monitor*. Consulted at www.dbresearch. de

Diamond, Larry (1999) *Developing Democracy: Toward Consolidation*. Baltimore, MD: Johns Hopkins University Press.

Diamond, Larry and Leonardo Morlino (eds). (2005) *Assessing the Quality of Democracy*. Baltimore, MD: Johns Hopkins University Press.

Dick, Howard A.E. (ed.) (1993) *Constitution Making in Eastern Europe*. Washington, DC: Woodrow Wilson Centre Press.

Dimitrov, Vesselin (2001) *Bulgaria: The Uneven Transition*. London and New York: Routledge.

Dimitrov, Vesselin, Klaus Goetz and Hellmut Wollmann (2006) *Governing after Communism: Institutions and Policymaking*. Lanham, MD: Rowman & Littlefield.

Dimitrova, Antoaneta (2005) 'Europeanisation and Civil Service Reform in Central and Eastern Europe', in Frank Schimmelfennig and Ulrich Sedelmeier (eds), *The Europeanisation of Central and Eastern Europe*. Ithaca, NY: Cornell University Press: 71–90.

Dryzek, John A. (1996) 'Political Inclusion and the Dynamics of Democratization', *American Political Science Review*, 90, 1 (March): 475–87.

Dvorakova, Vladimira (2003) 'Civil Society in the Czech Republic: "Impulse 99" and "Thank You, Time To Go"', in Petr Kopecky and Cas Mudde (eds), *Uncivil Society? Contentious Politics in Post-Communist Europe*. London: Routledge: 134–56.

Dyczok, Marta (2006) 'Was Kuchma's Censorship Effective? Mass Media in Ukraine before 2004', *Europe–Asia Studies*, 58, 2 (March): 215–38.

EBRD (1994–2006) *Transition Reports* and *Transition Report Updates*, London, annual.

Eisenstadt, S.N. (1978) *Revolution and the Transformation of Societies*. New York: Free Press.

Ekiert, Grzegorz (1996) *The State Against Society*. Princeton, NJ: Princeton University Press.

Ekiert, Grzegorz and Jan Kubik (1998) 'Contentious Politics in New Democracies: East Germany, Hungary, Poland, and Slovakia, 1989–93', *World Politics*, 50, 4 (July): 547–81.

Ekiert, Grzegorz and Jan Kubik (1999) *Rebellious Civil Society: Popular Protest and Democratic Consolidation in Poland, 1989–93*. Ann Arbor, MI: University of Michigan Press.

Elgie, Robert (ed.) (1999) *Semi-Presidentialism in Europe*. Oxford: Oxford University Press.

Elgie, Robert (2004) 'Semi-Presidentialism: Concepts, Consequences and Contesting Explanations', *Political Studies Review*, 2, 3 (September): 314–30.

Elgie, Robert and Jan Zielonka (2001) 'Constitutions and Constitution-Building: a Comparative Perspective', in Jan Zielonka (ed.), *Democratic Consolidation in Eastern Europe, Vol. 1: Institutional Engineering*. Oxford: Oxford University Press: 25–47.

Elster, Jon (1993) 'Constitution-Making in Eastern Europe: Rebuilding the Boat in the Open Sea', *Public Administration*, 71, 1/2 (Spring/Summer): 169–217.

Elster, Jon (1996a) 'The Role of Institutional Interests in Eastern European Constitution-Making: Explaining Legislative Dominance', *East European Constitutional Review,*. 5, 6: 63–5.

Elster, Jon (ed.) (1996b) *The Roundtable Talks and the Breakdown of Communism*. Chicago and London: University of Chicago Press.

Elster, Jon, Claus Offe and Ulrich K. Preuss (1998) *Institutional Design in Post-Communist Societies: Rebuilding the Ship at Sea*. Cambridge and New York: Cambridge University Press.

Enyedi, Zsolt (2006) 'Party Politics in Post-Communist Transition', in Richard S. Katz and William Crotty (eds), *Handbook of Party Politics*. London: Sage.

Enyedi, Zsolt and Gabor Toka (2007) 'The Only Game in Town: Party Politics in Hungary', in Webb and White (2007).

European Central Bank (2006) *Convergence Report 2006*, December. Frankfurt.

European Commission (2006a) *EU Enlargement – 20 Myths and Facts about Enlargement*. Brussels.

European Commission (2006) *Enlargement, Two Years After: An Economic Success*. Communication from the Commission to the Council and the European Parliament, http://ec.europa.eu/economy_finance/publications/enlargement/2006/comm2006en.pdf

Evans, Geoffrey (ed.) (1999) *The End of Class Politics? Class Voting in Comparative Context*. Oxford: Oxford University Press.

Evans, Geoffrey and Stephen Whitefield (1993) 'Identifying the Bases of Party Competition in Eastern Europe', *British Journal of Political Science,*. 23, 4 (October): 521–48.

Eyal, Gil (2003) *The Origins of Postcommunist Elites: From Prague Spring to the Breakup of Czechoslovakia*. Minneapolis, MN: University of Minnesota Press.

Eyal, Gil, Ivan Szelenyi and Eleanor Townsley (2000) *Making Capitalism Without Capitalists: The New Ruling Elites in Eastern Europe*. London: Verso.

Fawn, Rick (2000) *The Czech Republic*. London: Routledge.

Fink-Hafner, Danica (2005) 'Slovenia', *European Journal of Political Research*, 44, issue 7–8 (December): 1180–8.

Fink-Hafner, Danica (2006a) 'Slovenia', *European Journal of Political Research*, 45, issue 7–8 (December): 1260–5.

Fink-Hafner, Danica (2006b) 'Slovenia: Between Bipolarity and Broad Coalition Building', in Susanne Jungerstam-Mulders (ed.), *Post-Communist Member States: Parties and Party Systems*. Aldershot: Ashgate: 203–32.

Fish, M. Steven (1998) 'The Determinants of Economic Reform in the Post-Communist World', *East European Politics and Society*, 12, 1 (Winter): 31–78.

Fish, M. Steven (2000) 'The Executive Deception: Superpresidentialism and the Degradation of Russian Politics', in Valerie Sperling (ed.), *Building the Russian State: Institutional Crisis and the Quest for Democratic Governance*. Boulder, CO: Westview 177–92.

Fisher, Sharon (2006) *Political Change in Post-Communist Slovakia and Croatia: From Nationalist to Europeanist*. New York: Palgrave.

Fodor, Eva (2005) *Women at Work: The Status of Women in the Labour Markets of the Czech Republic, Hungary and Poland*. Geneva: United Nations Research Institute for Social Development.

Fodor, Eva, Eric Hanley and Ivan Szelenyi (1997) 'Left Turn in Postcommunist Politics: Bringing Class Back In?', *East European Politics and Societies*, 11, 1 (Winter): 190–224.

Forbrig, Joerg, David Marples and Pavol Demes (eds) (2006) *Prospects for Democracy in Belarus*. Washington, DC: German Marshall Fund. Available online at www.gmfus.org/doc/Belarus%20book%20final.pdf.

Fowler, Brigid (2001) *Debating Sub-State Reform on Hungary's 'Road to Europe'*, ESRC 'One Europe or Several?', Programme Working Paper 21/01. Brighton: Sussex European Institute.

Fowler, Brigid (2002) *Hungary's 2002 Parliamentary Election*, ESRC 'One Europe or Several?' Programme, Briefing Note 2/02, May. Brighton: Sussex European Institute.

Fowler, Brigid (2004) 'Concentrated Orange: Fidesz and the Remaking of the Hungarian Centre-Right, 1994–2002', *Journal of Communist Studies and Transition Politics*, 20, 3 (September): 80–114.

Freedom House (1978–) *Freedom in the World*. New York: Freedom House, annual.

Frye, Timothy (2002) 'Presidents, Parliaments and Democracy: Insights from the Post-Communist World', in Andrew Reynolds (ed.), *The Architecture of Democracy: Constitutional Design, Conflict Management, and Democracy*. Oxford: Oxford University Press.

Fulbrook, Mary (1995) *Anatomy of a Dictatorship: Inside the GDR 1949–1989*. Oxford: Oxford University Press.

Furtak, Robert K. (ed.) (1990) *Elections in Socialist States*. New York and London: Harvester Wheatsheaf.

Gallagher, Tom (2005) *Theft of a Nation: Romania since Communism*. London: Hurst.

Ganev, Venelin (2001) 'Bulgaria: the (Ir)Relevance of Post-communist Constitutionalism', in Jan Zielonka (ed.), *Democratic Consolidation in Eastern Europe, Vol. 1: Institutional Engineering*. Oxford: Oxford University Press: 186–211.

Garnett, Sherman W. and Robert Legvold, eds. (1999) *Belarus at the Crossroads*. Washington DC: Carnegie Endowment.

Garton Ash, Timothy (1985) *The Polish Revolution: Solidarity*. New York: Vintage Books (a third and expanded edition appeared in 2002: London and New Haven, CT: Yale University Press).

Garton Ash, Timothy (1989) 'Does Central Europe Exist?', in George Schopflin and Nancy Wood (eds), *In Search of Central Europe*. Cambridge: Polity: 191–215.

Garton Ash, Timothy (1993) *The Magic Lantern*. New York: Vintage Books.

George, Stephen (1998) *An Awkward Partner: Britain in the European Community*. Oxford: Oxford University Press.

Gialdino, Carlo Curti (1995) 'Some Reflections on the *Acquis Communautaire*', *Common Market Law Review*, 32: 1089–121.

Gillespie, Richard, Lourdes Lopez Nieto and Michael Waller (eds) (1995) 'Factional Politics and Democratization', special issue of *Democratization*, 2, 1.

Glenn, John K. (2001) *Framing Democracy: Civil Society and Civic Movement in Eastern Europe*. Stanford. CA: Stanford University Press.

Glenny, Misha (1999) *The Balkans: Nationalism, War and the Great Powers*. London: Granta.

Goehring, Jeannette and Amanda Schnetzer (eds) (2005) *Nations in Transit 2005. Democratization from Central Europe to Eurasia*. New York: Freedom House.

Goetz, Klaus H. (2000) 'European Integration and National Executives: A Cause in Search of an Effect?', *West European Politics*, 23, 4 (October): 211–31.

Grabbe, Heather (2001) *Profiting from EU Enlargement*. London: Centre for European Reform.

Grabbe, Heather (2004) *The Constellations of Europe: How Enlargement will Transform the EU*. London: Centre for European Reform.

Grabbe, Heather (2005) 'Regulating the Flow of People across Europe', in Frank Schimmelfennig and Ulrich Sedelmeier (eds), *The Europeanization of Central and Eastern Europe*. Ithaca, NY and London: Cornell University Press: 112–34.

Grabbe, Heather (2006) *The EU's Transformative Power: Europeanisation through Conditionality in Central and Eastern Europe*. Basingstoke: Palgrave.

Gregory, Paul and Robert Stuart (1997) *Comparative Economic Systems*. Boston, MA: Houghton Mifflin.

Greskovits, Bela (1998) *The Political Economy of Protest and Patience. East European and Latin American Transformations Compared*. Budapest: Central European University Press.

Grigorescu, Alexandru (2006) 'The Corruption Eruption in East Central Europe: The Increased Salience of Corruption and the Role of Intergovernmental Organizations', *East European Politics and Societies*, 20, 3 (Summer): 516–49.

Grzymala-Busse, Anna (2002) *Redeeming the Communist Past: The Regeneration of Communist Parties in East Central Europe*. Cambridge: Cambridge University Press.

Gurr, Ted Robert (1971) *Why Men Rebel*. Princeton, NJ: Princeton University Press.

Gurr, Ted R., Keith Jaggers and Monty G. Marshall (2002) *Polity IV: Political Regime Characteristics and Transitions, 1800–2001*. Available online at http://www.cidcm.umd.edu/inscr/polity/index.htm

Gurr, Ted R. and Kenneth Jaggers (1996) *POLITY III: Regime Change and Political Authority, 1800–1994*, 2nd ICPSR version.

Hanley, Sean (2001) 'Towards Breakthrough or Breakdown? The Consolidation of KSCM as a Neo-Communist Successor Party in the Czech Republic', *Journal of Communist Studies and Transition Politics*, 17, 3 (September): 96–116.

Hanley, Sean (2004) 'Blue Velvet: The Rise and Decline of the New Czech Right', *Journal of Communist Studies and Transition Politics*, 20, 3 (September): 28–54.

Harper, Marcus (2003) 'The 2001 Parliamentary and Presidential Elections in Bulgaria', *Electoral Studies*, 22, 2 (June): 335–44.

Harris, Erika (2002) *Nationalism and Democratisation: Politics of Slovakia and Slovenia*. Aldershot and Burlington, VT: Ashgate.

Hasselman, Chris (2006) *Policy Reform and the Development of Democracy in Eastern Europe*. Aldershot and Burlington, VT: Ashgate.

Haughton, Tim (2005) *Constraints and Opportunities of Leadership in Post-Communist Europe*. Aldershot and Burlington, VT: Ashgate.

Haughton, Tim (2006) '"Socialdemokratizacia" strany Smer – socialna demokracia v horizonte volieb 2006', in Martin Muransky (ed.), *Vyvoj a perspektivy socialnej demokracie na Slovensku – pohlad zvnutra a zvonku*. Bratislava: Friedrich Ebert Stiftung: 50–6.

Haughton, Tim (2007a) 'Central and Eastern Europe', in Colin Hay and

Anand Menon (eds), *European Politics*. Oxford: Oxford University Press: 132–47.

Haughton, Tim (2007b) 'When Does the EU Make a Difference? Conditionality and the Accession Process in Central and Eastern Europe', *Political Studies Review*, 5, 2 (May): 233–46.

Havrylyshyn, Oleh (2006) *Divergent Paths in Post-Communist Transitions. Capitalism for All or Capitalism for the Few?* Basingstoke: Palgrave.

Hayes-Renshaw, Fiona and Helen Wallace (2005) *The Council of Ministers*. Basingstoke: Palgrave.

Heidar Knut and Ruud Koole (eds) (2000) *Parliamentary Party Groups in European Democracies: Political Parties Behind Closed Doors*. London: Routledge.

Henderson, Karen (1999) 'Slovakia and the Democratic Criteria for EU Accession', in Henderson (ed.), *Back to Europe: Central and Eastern Europe and the European Union*. London and Philadelphia, PA: UCL Press: 221–40.

Henderson, Karen (2002) *Slovakia: the Escape from Invisibility*. London and New York: Routledge.

Henderson, Karen (2006) *Europe and the Slovak Parliamentary Election of June 2006*, European Parties, Elections and Referendums Network Election Briefing, 26.

Henn, Matt (2001) 'Opinion Polls, Political Elites and Party Competition in Post-Communist Bulgaria', *Journal of Communist Studies and Transition Politics*, 17, 3 (September): 52–70.

Higley, John, and Michael G. Burton (1997) 'Types of Political Elites in Postcommunist Eastern Europe', *International Politics*, 34, 2 (June): 153–68.

Higley, John, Judith Kullberg and Jan Pakulski (1996) 'The Persistence of Postcommunist Elites', *Journal of Democracy*, 7, 2 (April): 133–47.

Howard, Marc Morje (2003) *The Weakness of Civil Society in Post-Communist Europe*. Cambridge and New York: Cambridge University Press.

Holmes, Leslie (1997) *Post-Communism: An Introduction*. Cambridge: Polity.

Howard, A. E. Dick (ed.) (1993) *Constitution Making in Eastern Europe*. Washington DC: Woodrow Wilson Center Press.

Hughes, James, Gwendolyn Sasse and Claire E. Gordon (2004) *Europeanization and Regionalization in the EU's Enlargement to Central and Eastern Europe: The Myth of Conditionality*. Basingstoke: Palgrave.

Huntington, Samuel (1968) *Political Order in Changing Societies*. New Haven, CT: Yale University Press.

Huntington, Samuel (1996) *The Clash of Civilizations and the Remaking of World Order*. New York: Simon & Schuster.

Hutcheson, Derek and Elena A. Korosteleva (eds) (2006) *The Quality of Democracy in Post-Communist Europe*. London: Routledge.

Ilonszki, Gabriella (2000) 'Parties and Parliamentary Party Groups in the Making: Hungary, 1989–1997', in Knut Heidar and Ruud Koole (eds),

Parliamentary Party Groups in European Democracies: Political Parties Behind Closed Doors. London: Routledge: 214–30.

Inglehart, Ronald (1977) *The Silent Revolution: Changing Values and Political Styles among Western Publics*. Princeton, NJ: Princeton University Press.

Ingrao, Charles (1999) 'Understanding Ethnic Conflict in Central Europe: An Historical Perspective', in *Nationalities Papers*, 27, 2 (June): 291–318.

International Commission on the Balkans (2005) *The Balkans in Europe's Future*. Available on line at http://www.balkan-commission.org, April.

International Institute for Democracy (ed.) (1996 *Rebirth of Democracy: 12 Constitutions of Central and Eastern Europe*, 2nd edn. Strasbourg: Council of Europe Press.

International Institute for Democracy (ed.) (1997) *Transition to Democracy: Constitutions of the New Independent States and Mongolia*. Strasbourg: Council of Europe Press.

Ishiyama, John T. (1995) 'Electoral Systems Experimentation in the New Eastern Europe: The Single Transferable Vote and the Additional Member System in Estonia and Hungary', *East European Quarterly*, 29, 4 (Winter): 487–507.

Jacoby, Wade (2004) *The Enlargement of the Europe Union and NATO: Ordering from the Menu in Central Europe*. Cambridge and New York: Cambridge University Press.

Janos, Andrew (2000) *East Central Europe in the Modern World. The Politics of the Borderlands from Pre- to Post-Communism*. Stanford, CA: Stanford University Press.

Jasiewicz, Krzysztof (1998) 'Elections and Voting Behaviour', in Stephen White, Judy Batt and Paul G. Lewis (eds), *Developments in Central and East European Politics 2*. Basingstoke: Macmillan and Durham, NC: Duke University Press.

Jasiewicz, Krzysztof (2003) *Pocketbook or Rosary? Economic and Identity Voting in 2000-2001 Elections in Poland*, Studies in Public Policy, 379. Glasgow: Centre for the Study of Public Policy, University of Strathclyde.

Jasiewicz, Krzysztof (2007) 'Poland: Party System by Default', in Webb and White (2007).

Jaszi, Oscar (1923) 'Dismembered Hungary and Peace in Central Europe', *Foreign Affairs*, 2, 2 (December): 270–81.

Jezermik, Bozidar (2004) *Wild Europe*. London: Saqi Books.

Jowitt, Kenneth (1992) *The New World Disorder*. Berkeley, CA: University of California Press.

Juberias, Carlos Flores (1998) 'Electoral Legislation and Ethnic Minorities in Eastern Europe: For or Against?', in Lawrence D. Longley and Drago Zajc (eds), *The New Democratic Parliaments: The First Years*. Appleton: Research Committee of Legislative Specialists, IPSA: 297–318.

Judah, Tim (2000) *The Serbs*. New Haven, CT and London: Yale University Press.

Judah, Tim (2002) *Kosovo: War and Revenge*, 2nd edn. New Haven, CT and London: Yale University Press.

Jungerstam-Mulders, Susanne (ed.) (2006) *Post-Communist EU Member States: Parties and Party Systems*. Aldershot and Burlington, VT: Ashgate.

Kalecki, Michal (1969) *Introduction to the Theory of Growth in a Socialist Economy*. New York: Kelley.

Karasimeonov, Georgi (1996) 'The Legislature in Post-Communist Bulgaria', *Journal of Legislative Studies*, 2, 1 (Spring): 40–59.

Karatnycky, Adrian, Alexander Motyl and Amanda Schnetzer (eds) (2002) *Nations in Transit 2002. Civil Society, Democracy, and Markets in East Central Europe and the Newly Independent States*. New Brunswick, NJ: Transaction.

Kaser, Michael (1967) *Comecon: Integration Problems of the Planned Economies*, 2nd edn. London: RIIA/Oxford University Press.

Kask, Peet (1996) 'Institutional Development of the Parliament in Estonia', *Journal of Legislative Studies*, 2, 1 (Spring): 193–212.

Katchanovski, Ivan (2006) *Cleft Countries: Regional Political Divisions and Cultures in Post-Soviet Ukraine and Moldova*. Stuttgart: Ibidem.

Katz, Richard S. and Peter Mair (1995) 'Changing Models of Party Organizations and Party Democracy: The Emergence of the Cartel Party', *Party Politics*, 1, 1 (January): 5–28.

Kaufmann, Daniel, Aart Kraay and Massimo Mastruzzi (2003) *Governance Matters III: Governance Indicators for 1996–2002. Draft Paper*. Available online at http://www.worldbank.org/wbi/governance/pubs/govmatters3.html

Kaufmann, Daniel, Aart Kraay and Massimo Mastruzzi (2006) *Governance Matters V: Governance Indicators for 1996–2005*. Available online at http://www.worldbank.org/wbi/governance/govmatters5

Kaufmann, Daniel, Aart Kray and Pablo Zoido-Lobaton (1999) *Aggregating Governance Indicators*, Policy Research Working Paper 2195. Washington, DC: World Bank.

Keane, John (1988) *Democracy and Civil Society*. New York: Verso.

Keane, John (2001) *Vaclav Havel: A Political Tragedy in Six Acts*. New York: Basic Books.

Keane, John (2003) *Global Civil Society?* Cambridge and New York: Cambridge University Press.

Kenney, Padraic (2002) *A Carnival of Revolution: Central Europe 1989*. Princeton, NJ: Princeton University Press.

Kenney, Padraic (2006) *The Burdens of Freedom. Eastern Europe since 1989*. London and New York: Zed Books.

Kimmel, Michael S. (1990) *Revolution*. Philadelphia, PA: Temple University Press.

King, Charles (2000) *The Moldovans: Romania, Russia, and the Politics of Culture*. Stanford, CA: Hoover Institution Press.

Kirchner, Emil (ed.) (1999) *Decentralization and Transition in the Visegrad: Poland, Hungary, the Czech Republic and Slovakia*. Basingstoke: Macmillan.

Kiss, Csilla (2002) 'From Liberalism to Conservatism: The Federation of Young Democrats in Post-Communist Hungary', *East European Politics and Societies*, 16, 3 (Fall): 739–63.

Kitschelt, Herbert (1992) 'The Formation of Party Systems in East Central Europe', *Politics and Society*, 20, 1 (March): 7–50.

Kitschelt, Herbert, Zdenka Mansfeldova, Radoslaw Markowski and Gabor Toka (1999) *Post-Communist Party Systems: Competition, Representation, and Inter-Party Cooperation.* Cambridge and New York: Cambridge University Press.

Kolodko, Grzegorz W. (2000) *From Shock to Therapy. The Political Economy of Postsocialist Transformation.* Oxford and New York: Oxford University Press.

Kolodko, Grzegorz W. and D. M. Nuti (1997) 'The Polish Alternative – Old Myths, Hard Facts and New Strategies in the Successful Polish Economic Transformation', UNU/WIDER Research for Action series 33, Helsinki, May.

Konrad, Gyorgy (1994) *Antipolitics.* London: Quartet.

Kopecky, Petr (2001) *Parliaments in the Czech and Slovak Republics: Party Competition and Parliamentary Institutionalization.* Aldershot and Burlington, VT: Ashgate.

Kopecky, Petr (2004), 'Power to the Executive! The Changing Executive–Legislative Relations in Eastern Europe', *Journal of Legislative Studies*, 10,. 2–3 (Summer/Autumn): 142–53.

Kopecky, Petr (2006a) 'The Rise of the Power Monopoly: Political Parties in the Czech Republic', in Jungerstam-Mulders (2006).

Kopecky, Petr (2006b) 'Political Parties and the State in Post-Communist Europe: The Nature of the Symbiosis', *Journal of Communist Studies and Transition Politics*, 22, 3 (September): 251–73.

Kopecky, Petr (2007) 'Building Party Government: Political Parties in the Czech and Slovak Republics', in Webb and White (2007).

Kopecky, Petr, and Cas Mudde (2000), 'Explaining Different Paths of Democratization: The Czech and Slovak Republics', *Journal of Communist Studies and Transition Politics*, 16, 3 (September): 63–84.

Kopecky, Petr and Cas Mudde (eds) (2002), *Uncivil Society? Contentious Politics in Post-Communist Europe.* London: Routledge.

Kopecky, Petr and Cas Mudde (2003) 'Rethinking Civil Society', *Democratization*, 10, 3 (August): 1–14.

Kornai, Janos (1980) *The Economics of Shortage*, 2 vols. Amsterdam: North Holland.

Kornai, Janos (1986) 'The Soft Budget Constraint', *Kyklos*, 39, 1: 3–30.

Kornai, Janos (2005) 'The Great Transformation of Central Eastern Europe: Success and Disappointment', Presidential Address, International Economic Association, Marrakesh.

Korosenyi, Andras (1999) *Government and Politics in Hungary.* Budapest: CEU Press.

Korosteleva, Elena, Colin W. Lawson and Rosalind J. Marsh (eds) (2003) *Contemporary Belarus: Between Democracy and Dictatorship.* London: Routledge.

Kostadinova, Tatiana (2002) 'Do Mixed Electoral Systems Matter? A Cross-

National Analysis of their Effects in Eastern Europe', *Electoral Studies*, 21, 1 (March): 23 Colin W. Lawson, Rosalind J. Marsh 34.

Kostelecky, Tomas (2002) *Political Parties After Communism*. Washington, DC: Woodrow Wilson Press.

Krastev, Ivan (2003) 'Bringing the state back up'. http://www.suedosteuropa-gesellschaft.com

Krok-Paszkowska, Ania (2003) 'Samoobrona: The Polish Self-Defence Movement', in Kopecky and Mudde (2003): 114–33.

Kubicek, Paul (2004) *Organized Labor in Postcommunist States: From Solidarity to Infirmity*. Pittsburgh, PA: University of Pittsburgh Press.

Kubik, Jan (1994) *The Power of Symbols Against the Symbols of Power*. University Park: Penn State University Press.

Kubik, Jan (2000) 'Between the State and Networks of "Cousins": The Role of Civil Society and Noncivil Associations in the Democratization of Poland', in Nancy Bermeo and Philip Nord (eds), *Civil Society before Democracy: Lessons from Nineteenth-Century Europe*. Lanham, MD: Rowman & Littlefield: 181–207.

Kumar, Krishan (2001) *1989: Revolutionary Ideas and Ideals*. Minneapolis, MN: University of Minnesota Press.

Kundera, Milan (1984) 'The Tragedy of Central Europe', *New York Review of Books*, 26 April: 33–8.

Kurski, Jaroslaw (1993) *Lech Walesa: Democrat or Dictator?* Boulder, CO: Westview.

Kuzio, Taras and Andrew Wilson (1994) *Ukraine: From Perestroika to Independence*. New York: St Martin's.

Laba, Roman (1991) *The Roots of Solidarity: A Political Sociology of Poland's Working-Class Democratization*. Princeton, NJ: Princeton University Press.

Lampe, John R. (1996) *Yugoslavia as History: Twice There Was A Country*. Cambridge, and New York: Cambridge University Press (a second edition appeared in 2000).

Lasswell, Harold D. (1986) 'Democratic Leadership', in Barbara Kellerman (ed.) *Political Leadership*. Pittsburgh, PA: University of Pittsburgh Press.

Lavigne, Marie (1985) *Economie internationale des pays socialistes*. Paris: Armand Colin.

Lavigne, Marie (1999) *The Economics of Transition: From Socialist Economy to Market Economy*, 2nd edn. London: Macmillan.

Letki, Natalia (2003) *Explaining Political Participation in East-Central Europe: Social Capital, Democracy and the Communist Past*. Glasgow: Centre for the Study of Public Policy, University of Strathclyde.

Lewis, Paul G. (2000) *Political Parties in Post-Communist Eastern Europe*. London: Routledge.

Lewis, Paul G. (ed.) (2001) *Party Development and Democratic Change in Post-Communist Europe*. London: Frank Cass.

Lewis, Paul G. (2006) 'Party Systems in Post-Communist Central Europe: Patterns of Stability and Consolidation', *Democratization*, 13, 4 (August): 562–83.

Lewis, Paul G. and Z. Mansfeldova (eds) (2006) *The EU and Party Politics in Central and Eastern Europe*. Basingstoke: Palgrave.

Lewis, Paul G. and Paul Webb (eds) (2003) *Pan-European Perspectives on Party Politics*. Leiden: Brill.

Li, Xiaorong (1999) 'Democracy and Uncivil Societies: A Critique of Civil Society Determinism', in Robert K. Fullinwider (ed.), *Civil Society, Democracy, and Civic Renewal*. Lanham, MD: Rowman & Littlefield: 403–20.

Liebich, Andre (1997) 'The Communists Reincarnated: Their Return in Russia and Eastern Europe', *World Affairs*, 1, 1 (January–March): 66–78.

Lijphart, Arend (1999) *Patterns of Democracy. Government Forms and Performance in Thirty-Six Countries*. New Haven, CT: Yale University Press.

Lijphart, Arend (1991) 'Constitutional Choices for New Democracies', *Journal of Democracy*, 2, 1 (Winter):.73–84.

Lijphart, Arend (ed.) (1992) *Parliamentary versus Presidential Government*. Oxford: Oxford University Press.

Linz, Juan J. (1990a) 'The Perils of Presidentialism', *Journal of Democracy*, 1, 1 (January): 51–69.

Linz, Juan J. (1990b) 'The Virtues of Parliamentarism', *Journal of Democracy*, 1, 4 (Fall): 84–91.

Linz, Juan J. and Alfred Stepan (1996) *Problems of Democratic Transition and Consolidation: Southern Europe, South America, and Post-Communist Europe*. Baltimore, MD: Johns Hopkins University Press.

Lipset, Seymour M. (1960) *Political Man: The Social Bases of Politics*. New York: Doubleday.

Lipset, Seymour M. (1994) 'The Social Requisites of Democracy Revisited', *American Sociological Review*, 59, 1 (February): 1–22.

Little, Alan and Laura Silber (1996) *The Death of Yugoslavia*, revised edn. Harmondsworth: BBC Books/Penguin.

Longley, Lawrence D. and Drago Zajc (eds) (1998) *The New Democratic Parliaments: The First Years*. Appleton: Research Committee of Legislative Specialists, IPSA.

Lynch, Dov (2003) 'Separatist States and Post-Soviet Conflicts', in Andrew Wilson and Wendy Slater (eds), *The Legacy of The Soviet Union*. Basingstoke: Palgrave: 61–82.

Macmillan, Margaret (2001) *Peacemakers: The Paris Conference of 1919 and its Aftermath*. London: John Murray.

Magas, Branka (1993) *The Destruction of Yugoslavia: Tracking the Break-up 1980–92*, London and New York: Verso.

Magocsi, Paul R. (1996) *A History of Ukraine*. Toronto and London: University of Toronto Press.

Mainwaring, Scott (1993) 'Presidentialism, Multipartism, and Democracy', *Comparative Political Studies*, 26, 2 (April): 198–228.

Mair, Peter and Ingrid van Biezen (2001) 'Party Membership in Twenty European Democracies', *Party Politics*, 7, 1 (January): 5–21.

Malova, Darina (1998) 'Nelahka institucionalizacia parlamentnej demokracie na Slovensku', *Politologicka revue*, 1, 43–59.

Malova, Darina and Tim Haughton (2006) 'Challenge from the Pace-Setting Periphery: The Causes and Consequences of Slovakia's Stance on Further European Integration', in W. Sadurski (ed.) *Après Enlargement: Taking Stock of the Immediate Legal and Political Responses to the Accession of Central and Eastern European States to the EU*. Florence: Robert Schuman Centre: 323–38.

Malova, Darina and Danica Sivakova (1996) 'The National Council of the Slovak Republic: Between Democratic Transition and National State-Building', *Journal of Legislative Studies*, 2, 1 (Spring): 108–32.

Malova, Darina and Kevin Krause (2000) 'Parliamentary Party Groups in Slovakia', in Knut Heidar and Ruud Koole (eds), *Parliamentary Party Groups in European Democracies: Political Parties Behind Closed Doors*. London: Routledge: 195–213.

Mansfeldova, Zdenka, Lukas Linek and Petra Rakusanova (eds) (2005) 'Legislatures and Representation in Central and Eastern Europe', special issue of *Czech Sociological Review*, 41, 3.

March, Luke (2005) *The Moldovan Communists: From Leninism to Democracy*. Glasgow: Centre for the Study of Public Policy, University of Strathclyde.

March, Luke and Graeme P. Herd (2006) 'Moldova between Europe and Russia: Inoculating against the Colored Contagion?', *Post-Soviet Affairs*, 22, 4 (October–December): 349–79.

Marples, David (2006) 'Color revolutions: The Belarus case', *Communist and Post-Communist Studies*, 39, 3 (September): 351–64.

Marten Board International (2004). Available at http://www.martenboard.co.yu.

Mason, David S. (1996) *Revolution and Transition in East-Central Europe*, 2nd edn. Boulder CO: Westview.

Mateju, Peter, Branka Rehakova and Geoffrey Evans (1999) 'The Politics of Interests and Class Realignment in the Czech Republic, 1992–96', in Evans (1999).

Mateju, Petr and Blanka Rehakova (1997) 'Turning Left or Class Realignment? Analysis of the Changing Relationship between Class and Party in the Czech Republic 1992–1996', *East European Politics and Societies*, 11, 3 (Fall): 501–42.

Mayhew, Alan (1998) *Recreating Europe: The European Union's Policy towards Central and Eastern Europe*. Cambridge and New York: Cambridge University Press.

Mazower, Mark (1998) *Dark Continent. Europe's Twentieth Century*. London: Penguin.

Mazower, Mark (2000) *The Balkans*. London: Weidenfeld & Nicolson.

McFaul, Michael and Anders Aslund (eds) (2006) *Revolution in Orange: The Origins of Ukraine's Democratic Breakthrough*. Washington, DC: Carnegie Endowment.

Mendelson, Sarah E. (2002) 'Conclusion: The Power and Limits of Transnational Democracy Networks in Postcommunist Societies', in

Mendelson and John K. Glenn (eds), *The Power and Limits of NGOs: A Critical Look at Building Democracy in Eastern Europe and Eurasia*. New York: Columbia University Press: 232–51.

Meyer-Sahling, Jan-Hinrik (2004) 'Civil Service Reform in Postcommunist Europe: The Bumpy Road to Depoliticisation', *West European Politics*, 27, 1 (January): 71–103.

Meyer-Sahling, Jan-Hinrik (2006) 'The Rise of the Partisan State? Parties, Patronage and the Ministerial Bureaucracy in Hungary', *Journal of Communist Studies and Transition Politics*, 22, 3 (September): 274–97.

Milanovic, Branko (1998) *Income, Inequality and Poverty during the Transition from Planned to Market Economy*. Washington, DC: World Bank.

Millard, Frances (2004) *Elections, Parties, and Representation in Post-Communist Europe*. Basingstoke: Palgrave.

Millard, Frances (2006) 'Poland's Politics and the Travails of Transition after 2001: The 2005 Elections', *Europe-Asia Studies*, 58, 7 (November): 1001–31.

Milton, Andrew K. (2005) 'Civil Society and Democratization', in Rachel A. May and Andrew K. Milton (eds), *(Un)Civil Societies: Human Rights and Democratic Transitions in Eastern Europe and Latin America*. Lanham, MD: Lexington: 11–29.

Mircev, Dimitar and Igor Spirovski (1998) 'The Role and Early Experiences of the Macedonia Parliament in the Process of Transition', in Lawrence D. Longley and Drago Zajc (eds), *The New Democratic Parliaments: The First Years*. Appleton: Research Committee of Legislative Specialists, IPSA: 111–24.

Mishler, William and Richard Rose (2001) 'What Are the Origins of Political Trust? Testing Institutional and Cultural Theories in Post-Communist Societies', *Comparative Political Studies*, 34, 1 (February): 30–62.

Miszlevitz, Ferenc (1999) *Illusions and Realities: The Metamorphosis of Civil Society in a New European Space*. Szombatheley: Savaria University Press.

Mokrzycki, Edmund (2000) 'Democracy in a Non-Democratic Society', in Lord Dahrendorf (eds), *The Paradoxes of Unintended Consequences*. Budapest: Central European University Press: 63–72.

Moore, Barrington (1966) *The Social Origins of Dictatorship and Democracy*. New York: Harper & Row.

Moroney, Jennifer D. P., Taras Kuzio and Mikhail Molchanov (eds) (2002) *Ukrainian Foreign and Security Policy: Theoretical and Comparative Perspectives*. Westport, CT: Praeger.

Moser, Robert G. (1999) 'Electoral Systems and the Number of Parties in Post-Communist States', *World Politics*, 51, 3 (April): 359–84.

Mudde, Cas (2001) 'In the Name of the Peasantry, the Proletariat, and the People: Populisms in Eastern Europe', *East European Politics and Societies*, 15, 1 Winter): 33–53.

Mudde, Cas (ed.) (2005) *Racist Extremism in Central and Eastern Europe*. London: Routledge.

Munck, Gerardo L. and Jay Verkuilen (2002) 'Conceptualizing and Measuring Democracy – Evaluating Alternative Indices', *Comparative Political Studies*, 35, 1 (February): 5–34.

Mundell, Robert A. (1997) 'The Great Contractions in Transition Economies', in Mario I. Blejer and Marko Skreb (eds), *Macroeconomic Stabilisation in Transition Economies*. Cambridge: Cambridge University Press: 73–99.

Myant, Martin (2003) *The Rise and Fall of Czech Capitalism: Economic Development in the Czech Republic since 1989*. Cheltenham: Edward Elgar.

Nahaylo, Bohdan (1999) *The Ukrainian Resurgence*. London: Hurst.

Nelson, Daniel and Stephen White (eds) (1982) *Communist Legislatures in Comparative Perspective*. London: Macmillan and Albany, NY: SUNY Press.

North, Douglass C. (1992) *Institutions, Institutional Change, and Economic Performance*. Cambridge and New York: Cambridge University Press.

Norton, Philip (1990) 'General Introduction', in Philip Norton (ed.) *Legislatures*. Oxford: Oxford University Press: 1–16.

Norton, Philip and David M. Olson (eds) (1996) *The New Parliaments of Central and Eastern Europe*. London: Frank Cass.

Norton, Philip and David M. Olson (eds) (2006) *Post Communist Parliaments*. London: Routledge.

Nuti, D. Mario (1986) 'Hidden and Repressed Inflation in Soviet-type Economies: Definitions, Measurements and Stabilisation', *Contributions to Political Economy*, 5, 37–82.

Nuti, D. Mario (1988) 'Perestroika: Transition from Central Planning to Market Socialism', *Economic Policy*, 7 (October): 353–90.

Nuti, D. Mario (1997) 'Employeeism: Corporate Governance and Employee Share Ownership in Transition Economies', in Mario I. Blejer and Marko Skreb (eds), *Macroeconomic Stabilisation in Transition Economies*. Cambridge: Cambridge University Press: 126–54.

O'Dwyer, Connor (2006) *Runaway State-Building: Patronage Politics and Democratic Development*. Baltimore, MD: Johns Hopkins University Press.

O'Dwyer, Conor and Branislav Kovalcik (2005) 'Party System Institutionalization and Second-Generation Economic Reform in the New EU Member States: The Advantages of Underdevelopment', Paper presented to the European Union Studies Association Ninth Biennial International Conference, Austin, Texas, 31 March–2 April.

Olson, David M. (1993) 'Compartmentalized Competition: The Managed Transitional Election System of Poland', *Journal of Politics*, 55, 2 (May): 415–41.

Olson, David M. (1997) 'Paradoxes of Institutional Development: The New Democratic Parliaments of Central Europe', *International Political Science Review*, 18, 4 (October): 401–16.

Olson, David M. (1998) 'The Parliaments of New Democracies and the Politics of Representation', in Stephen White, Judy Batt and Paul G. Lewis (eds), *Developments in Central and East European Politics 2*. Basingstoke: Macmillan; Durham NC: Duke University Press: 126–46.

Olson, David M. and William Crowther (eds) (2002) *Committees in Post-Communist Democratic Parliaments: Comparative Institutionalization.* Columbus, OH: Ohio State University Press.

Ost, David (1990) *Solidarity and the Politics of Anti-Politics: Opposition and Reform in Poland since 1968.* Philadelphia, PA: Temple University Press.

Ost, David (2005) *The Defeat of Solidarity.* Ithaca, NY: Cornell University Press.

Ost, David and Stephen Crowley (2001) 'Introduction: The Surprise of Labor Weakness in Postcommunist Society', in Crowley and Ost (eds), *Workers after Workers' States: Labor and Politics in Postcommunist Eastern Europe.* Lanham, MD: Rowman & Littlefield: 1–12.

Pakovic, Aleksandr (2000) *The Fragmentation of Yugoslavia: Nationalism and War in the Balkans,* 2nd edn. Basingstoke: Macmillan.

Parrott, Bruce (1997) 'Perspectives on Postcommunist Democratization', in Karen Dawisha and Parrott (eds), *The Consolidation of Democracy in East-Central Europe.* Cambridge and New York: Cambridge University Press: 1–39.

Pateman, Carole (1988) *The Sexual Contract.* Cambridge: Polity.

Peeva, Ralitsa (2001) 'Electing a Czar: The 2001 Elections and Bulgarian Democracy', *East European Constitutional Review,* 10, 4 (web edition posted at www.law.nyu.edu/eecr).

Pettai, Vello and Marcus Kreuzer (2001) 'Institutions and Party Development in the Baltic States', in Paul Lewis (ed.), *Party Development and Democratic Change in Post-Communist Europe: The First Decade.* London and Portland, OR: Frank Cass: 107–25.

Phinnemore, David (2006a) 'Beyond 25: The Changing Face of EU Enlargement: Commitment, Conditionality and the Constitutional Treaty', *Journal of Southern Europe and the Balkans,* 8, 1 (April): 7–26.

Phinnemore, David (ed.) (2006b) *The EU and Romania: Accession and Beyond.* London: Tauris.

Piano, Aili, Arch Puddington and Mark Y. Rosenberg (eds) (2006) *Freedom in the World 2006: The Annual Survey of Political Rights and Civil Liberties.* New York and Lanham, MD: Freedom House/Rowman & Littlefield.

Pintor, Rafael Lopez and Maria Gratschew (2002) *Voter Turnout Since 1945. A Global Report.* Stockholm: International Institute for Democracy and Electoral Assistance.

PIOOM (2001) *World Conflict and Human Rights Map 2001/2002.* Consulted at http://www.goalsforamericans.org/publications/pioom/atf_world_conf_map.pdf

Pittaway, Mark (2004) *Eastern Europe, 1939–2000.* London: Hodder Arnold.

Plasser, Fritz, Peter A. Ulram and Harald Waldrauch (1998) *Democratic Consolidation in East-Central Europe.* Basingstoke and New York: Macmillan.

Plecita-Vlachova, Klara and Stegmaier, Mary (2007) 'Parliamentary Elections in the Czech Republic: June 2–3, 2006', *Electoral Studies,* forthcoming.

Poulton, Hugh (1995) *Who are the Macedonians?* London: Hurst.

Pravda, Alex (2001) 'Introduction', in Jan Zielonka and Pravda (eds), *Democratic Consolidation in Eastern Europe.* Volume 2: *International and Transnational Factors.* Oxford: Oxford University Press: 1–27.

Pridham, G. (2005) *Designing Democracy: EU Enlargement and Regime Change in Post-Communist Europe*. Basingstoke: Palgrave.

Protsyk, Oleh (2005) 'Politics of Intra-Executive Conflict in Semi-Presidential Regimes in Eastern Europe', *East European Politics and Society*, 19, 2 (Spring): 1–20.

Przeworski, Adam (1991) *Democracy and the Market: Political and Economic Reforms in Eastern Europe and Latin America*. Cambridge and New York: Cambridge University Press.

Przeworski, Adam (1992) *Democracy and the Market*. Cambridge: Cambridge University Press.

Przeworski, Adam, Susan C. Stokes and Bernard Manin (eds) (1999). *Democracy, Accountability, and Representation*. Cambridge: Cambridge University Press.

Putnam, Robert (2000) *Bowling Alone. The Collapse and Revival of American Community*. New York: Simon & Schuster.

Putnam, Robert D., Robert Leonardi and Raffaella Nanetti (1993) *Making Democracy Work: Civic Traditions in Modern Italy*. Princeton, NJ: Princeton University Press.

Raik, Kristi (2006) *Promoting Democracy through Civil Society: How to Step Up the EU's Policy towards the Eastern Neighbourhood*. Brussels: Centre for European Policy Studies, CEPS Working Document 237.

Raina, Peter (ed.) (1995) *The Constitutions of New Democracies in Europe*. Cambridge: Merlin Books.

Ramet, Sabrina P. (1991) *Social Currents in Eastern Europe: the Sources and Meaning of the Great Transformation*. Durham, NC: Duke University Press.

Rechel, Bernd (2005) *Minority Rights in Post-Communist Bulgaria*, unpublished PhD thesis, University of Birmingham.

Remington, Thomas F. (ed.) (1994) *Parliaments in Transition*. Boulder, CO: Westview.

Reynolds, Andrew, Ben Reilly and Andrew Ellis (2005) *Electoral System Design: The New International IDEA Handbook*. Stockholm: International IDEA.

Rigby, T.H. and Ferenc Feher (eds) (1982) *Political Legitimation in Communist States*. New York: St Martin's.

Roper, Stephen (2000) *Romania: The Unfinished Revolution*. London and New York: Routledge.

Rose, Richard (2004) 'Europe Expands, Turnout Falls: The Significance of the 2004 European Parliamentary Election', Stockholm: International Institute for Democracy and Electoral Assistance. Available online at www.idea.int/publications/voter_turnout_weurope/upload/Annex_Euro_Gap.pdf.

Rose, Richard (2005) *Insiders and Outsiders: New Europe Barometer 2004*. Glasgow: Centre for the Study of Public Policy, University of Strathclyde.

Rose, Richard and William Mishler (1996) 'Representation and Leadership in Post-Communist Political Systems', *Journal of Communist Studies and Transition Politics*, 12, 2 (June): 224–46.

Rose, Richard, William Mishler and Christian Haerpfer (1998) *Democracy and its Alternatives: Understanding Post-Communist Societies.* Cambridge: Polity; Baltimore, MD: Johns Hopkins Press.

Rose-Ackerman, Susan (2005) *From Elections to Democracy: Building Accountable Government in Hungary and Poland.* Cambridge and New York: Cambridge University Press.

Rossteutscher, Sigrid (2002) 'Advocate or Reflection? Associations and Political Culture', *Political Studies*, 50, 3 (October): 514–28.

Rothschild, Joseph (1974) *East Central Europe between the Two World Wars.* Seattle, WA: University of Washington Press.

Rothschild, Joseph and Nancy M. Wingfield (2000) *Return to Diversity*, 3rd edn. New York: Oxford University Press.

Rupnik, Jacques (1990) 'Central Europe or Mitteleuropa?', *Daedalus*, 119, 1 (Winter) : 249–78.

Rupnik, Jacques and Jan Zielonka (eds) (2003) *The Road to the European Union. Vol. 1: The Czech and Slovak Republics.* Manchester: Manchester University Press.

Rychard, Andrzej (1992) 'Politics and Society after the Breakthrough: the Sources and Threats to Political Legitimacy in Post-Communist Poland', in George Sanford (ed.), *Democratization in Poland, 1988–90.* London: Macmillan; New York: St Martin's: 136–61.

Sachs, Jeffrey (1993) *Poland's Jump to the Market Economy.* Cambridge MA: MIT Press.

Sanford, George (2002) *Democratic Government in Poland: Constitutional Politics since 1989.* Basingstoke: Palgrave.

Savkova, Lyubka (2005) 'Europe and the Parliamentary Election in Bulgaria 25 June 2005', *European Parties, Elections and Referendums Network Election Briefing*, 21.

Saxonberg, Steven (2003) *The Czech Republic Before the New Millennium.* Boulder, CO: East European Monographs.

Schimmelfennig, Frank (2003) *The EU, NATO and the Integration of Europe: Rules and Rhetoric.* Cambridge and New York: Cambridge University Press.

Schimmelfennig, Frank and Ulrich Sedelmeier (eds). (2005) *The Europeanization of Central and Eastern Europe.* Ithaca, NY: Cornell University Press.

Schopflin, George and Nancy Wood (eds) (1989) *In Search of Central Europe.* Cambridge: Polity.

Schopflin, Gyorgy (2006) 'After the Elections: Left and Right in Hungary', *Budapest Analyses*, 25 May. Available online at www.budapestanalyses.hu/docs/En/Analyses_Archive/analysys_90_en.html.

Schumpeter, Joseph A. (1976) *Capitalism, Socialism and Democracy*, 5th edn. London: Allen & Unwin.

Sedelius, Thomas (2006) *The Tug-of-War between Presidents and Prime Ministers: Semi-Presidentialism in Central and Eastern Europe.* Orbero: Orbero Studies in Political Science.

Seleny, Anna (2006) *The Political Economy of State-Society Relations in*

Hungary and Poland: From Communism to the European Union. Cambridge and New York: Cambridge University Press.

Shepherd, Robin (2000) *Czechoslovakia. The Velvet Revolution and Beyond.* Basingstoke: Palgrave.

Shugart, Matthew S. and John M. Carey (1992) *Presidents and Assemblies: Constitutional Design and Electoral Dynamics.* Cambridge and New York: Cambridge University Press.

Shugart, Matthew Soberg and Martin P. Wattenberg (eds) (2001) *Mixed-Member Electoral Systems: The Best of Both Worlds?* Oxford: Oxford University Press.

Shvetsova, Olga (1999) 'A Survey of Post-Communist Electoral Institutions, 1990–1998', *Electoral Studies*, 18, 3 (September): 397–409.

Siani-Davies, Peter (2005) *The Romanian Revolution of 1989.* Ithaca NY and London: Cornell University Press.

Sikk, Allan (2004) 'Successful New Parties in the Baltic States: Similar or Different?', Paper prepared for the conference 'The Baltic States: New Europe or Old?', Glasgow University, 22–23 January.

Sikk, Allan (2005a) 'How Unstable? Volatility and the Genuinely New Parties in Eastern Europe', *European Journal of Political Research*, 44, 3 (May): 391–412.

Sikk, Allan (2005b) 'Newness as a Project: Successful New Parties in the Baltic States', Paper prepared for the ECPR General Conference, Budapest, 8–10 September.

Silitski, Vitali (2005) 'Preempting Democracy: The Case of Belarus', *Journal of Democracy*, 16, 4 (October): 83–97.

Simecka, Milan (1984) *The Restoration of Order: The Normalization of Czechoslovakia 1969-1979*, trans. A.G. Brain. London and New York: Verso.

Simon, Jeffrey (2004) *NATO and the Czech and Slovak Republics: A Comparative Study in Civil-Military Relations.* Lanham, MD: Rowman & Littlefield.

Skocpol, Theda (1979) *States and Social Revolutions.* Cambridge and New York: Cambridge University Press.

Smelser, Neil (1962) *A Theory of Collective Behavior.* New York: Free Press.

Smith, David (2003) 'Minority Rights, Multiculturalism and EU Enlargement: The Case of Estonia', *Journal on Ethnopolitics and Minority Issues in Europe*, 1, posted at http://www.ecmi.de/jemie/download/Focus1-2003_Smith.pdf

Smith, David, Artis Pabriks, Aldis Purs, and Thomas Lane (2002) *The Baltic States: Estonia, Latvia and Lithuania.* London and New York: Routledge.

Smith, Karen E. (2001) 'Western Actors and the Promotion of Democracy', in Jan Zielonka and Alex Pravda (eds), *Democratic Consolidation in Eastern Europe.* Vol. 2: *International and Transnational Factors.* Oxford: Oxford University Press: 31–57.

Sobell, Vlad (2006) *Central Europe Unhinged.* London and Hong Kong: Daiwa Institute of Research.

Spirova, Maria (2005) 'Political Parties in Bulgaria: Organizational Trends in Comparative Perspective', *Party Politics*, 11, 5 (October): 601–22.

Stark, David, Balazs Vedres and Laszlo Bruszt (2005) *Global Links, Local Roots? Varieties of Transnationalization and Forms of Civic Integration*. Working Papers Series, Center on Organizational Innovation, Columbia University.

Subtelny, Orest (2000) *Ukraine: A History*, 3rd edn. Toronto and London: University of Toronto Press.

Sudetic, Chuck (1999) *Blood and Vengeance: One Family's Story of the War in Bosnia*. New York: Putnam's.

Surdej, A. and K. Gadowska (2005) *Political Corruption in Poland*. Bremen: Forschungstelle Osteuropa der Universitat Bremen.

Svejnar, Jan (2006) 'Strategies for Growth: Central and Eastern Europe', Conference Paper, University of Michigan.

Swain, Nigel and Geoffrey Swain (2003) *Eastern Europe since 1945*, 3rd edn. London, Longman.

Szabo, Mate (1995) 'Politischer Protest in den postkommunistischen Staaten Ost-Mitteleuropas: Slowakei, Slowenien, Ungarn 1993', *Osterreichische Zeitschrift fur Politikwissenschaft*, 24, 4: 491–504.

Szacki, Jerzy (1995) *Liberalism after Communism*. Budapest: Central European University Press.

Szalai, Julia (1998) 'Women and Democratization: Some Notes on Recent Changes in Hungary', in Jane S. Jaquette and Sharon L. Wolchik (eds), *Women and Democracy: Latin America and Central and Eastern Europe*. Baltimore, MD: Johns Hopkins University Press: 185–202.

Szczerbiak, Aleksander (2001) *Poles Together? The Emergence and Development of Political Parties in Postcommunist Poland*. Budapest: Central European University Press.

Szczerbiak, Aleks (2006) 'Power Without Love: Patterns of Party Politics in Post-1989 Poland', in Jungerstam-Mulders (2006).

Szczerbiak, Aleks and Sean Hanley (eds) (2006) *Centre-Right Parties in Post-Communist East-Central Europe*. London: Routledge.

Szelenyi, Ivan, Eva Fodor and Eric Hanley (1997) 'Left Turn in Postcommunist Politics: Bringing Class Back In?', *East European Politics and Societies*, 11, 1 (Winter), pp. 190–224.

Taagepera, Rein (2006) 'Meteoric Trajectory: The Res Publica Party in Estonia', *Democratization*, 13, 1 (February): 78–94.

Tanner, Marcus (1998) *Croatia: A Nation Forged in War*. London and New Haven, CT: Yale University Press.

Taras, Ray (1998) *Postcommunist Presidents*. Cambridge and New York: Cambridge University Press.

Tenfelde, Klaus (2000) 'Civil Society and the Middle Classes in Nineteenth-Century Germany', in Nancy Bermeo and Philip Nord (eds), *Civil Society before Democracy: Lessons from Nineteenth-Century Europe*. Lanham, MD: Rowman & Littlefield: 83–108.

Tilly, Charles (1978) *From Mobilization to Revolution*. Reading, MA: Addison-Wesley.

Tocqueville, Alexis de (1955) *The Old Regime and the French Revolution.* New York: Anchor.

Tocqueville, Alexis de (1966) *The Ancien Regime and the French Revolution,* trans. Stuart Gilbert. London: Fontana.

Todorova, Maria (1997) *Imagining the Balkans.* New York and Oxford: Oxford University Press.

Tokes, Rudolf L. (1996) *Hungary's Negotiated Revolution: Economic Reform, Social Change and Political Succession, 1957–1990.* Cambridge and New York: Cambridge University Press.

Toole, James (2003) 'Straddling the East-West Divide: Party Organisation and Communist Legacies in East Central Europe', *Europe–Asia Studies,* 55, 1 (January): 101–18.

Touraine, Alan (1983) *Solidarity: Poland 1980-81.* Cambridge and New York: Cambridge University Press.

True, Jacqui (2003) *Gender, Globalization, and Postsocialism: The Czech Republic after Communism.* New York: Columbia University Press.

Tucker, Robert C. (1981) *Politics as Leadership.* Columbia, MO: University of Missouri Press.

Tworzecki, Hubert (1996) *Parties and Politics in Post-1989 Poland.* Boulder, CO: Westview.

Tworzecki, Hubert (2002) *Learning to Choose: Electoral Politics in East-Central Europe.* Stanford, CA: Stanford University Press.

UNCTAD (United Nations Conference for Trade and Development) (2006) *World Investment Report – FDI from Developing and Transition Economies.* New York and Geneva, October.

UNICEF (2006) TransMONEE data bank, http://www.unicef-icdc.org /resources/transmonee/.

United Nations Development Programme (UNDP) (1990ff) *Human Development Report.* Geneva: UNDP, annual.

USAID (2006) *The 2005 NGO Sustainability Index for Central and Eastern Europe and Eurasia.* 9th edn. Washington, DC: USAID.

Uslaner, Eric M. and Gabriel Badescu (2003) 'Legacies and Conflicts: The Challenge to Social Capital in the Democratic Transition', in Gabriel Badescu and Eric M. Uslaner (eds), *Social Capital and the Transition to Democracy.* London: Routledge: 219–32.

Uvalic, Milica (1992) *Investment and Property Rights: The Long Transition to a Market Economy.* Cambridge and New York: Cambridge University Press.

Vachudova, Milada Anna (2005) *Europe Undivided: Democracy, Leverage and Integration after Communism.* Oxford: Oxford University Press.

van Biezen, Ingrid (2003) *Political Parties in New Democracies.* Basingstoke: Palgrave.

van der Meer Krok-Paszkowska, Ania (2000) *Shaping the Democratic Order. The Institutionalisation of Parliament in Poland.* Leuven: Garant.

Van Zon, Hans (2001) 'Neo-Patrimonialism as an Impediment to Economic Development: the Case of Ukraine', *Journal of Communist Studies and Transition Politics,* 17, 3 (September): 71–95.

Vanhanen, Tatu (1984) *The Emergence of Democracy: A Comparative Study of 119 States*. Helsinki: Societas Scientiarum Fennica.

Vanhanen, Tatu (1997) *Prospects of Democracy: A Study of 172 Countries*. London: Routledge.

Vanhanen, Tatu (2004) *Measures of Democracy 1810-2004*. Available online at http://www.fsd.uta.fi/english/data/catalogue/FSD1289.

Verheijen, Tony (1999) 'The Civil Service System of Bulgaria: Hope on the Horizon', in Verheijen and Alexander Kotchegura (eds), *Civil Service Systems in Central and Eastern Europe*. Cheltenham: Edward Elgar: 92–130.

Verheijen, Tony, with the cooperation of Alexander Kotchegura (1999) *Civil Service Systems in Central and Eastern Europe*. Cheltenham: Edward Elgar.

Vermeersch, Peter (2002) 'Ethnic Mobilization and the Political Conditionality of European Union Accession: The Case of the Roma in Slovakia', *Journal of Ethnic and Migration Studies*, 28, 1 (January): 83–101.

Vickers, Miranda and James Pettifer (1997) *Albania: from Anarchy to a Balkan Identity*. London: Hurst.

Vlachova, Klara (2001) 'Party Identification in the Czech Republic: Inter-Party Hostility and Party Preference', *Communist and Post-Communist Studies*, 34, 4 (December): 479–99.

von Beyme, Klaus (2001) 'Institutional Engineering and Transition to Democracy' in Jan Zielonka (ed.), *Democratic Consolidation in Eastern Europe, Vol. 1: Institutional Engineering*. Oxford: Oxford University Press: 3–24.

Walecki, Marcin (2005) *Money and Politics in Poland*. Warsaw: Institute of Public Affairs.

Wallace, Helen, William Wallace and Mark A. Pollack (eds) (2005), *Policy-Making in the European Union*, 5th edn. Oxford: Oxford University Press.

Waterbury, Myra (2006), 'Internal Exclusion, External Inclusion: Diaspora Politics and Party-Building Strategies in Post-Communist Hungary', *East European Politics and Societies*, 20, 3 (Summer): 483–515.

Way, Lucan (2003) 'Weak States and Pluralism: The Case of Moldova', *East European Politics and Societies*, 17, 3 (Summer): 454–82.

Way, Lucan (2005) 'Authoritarian State-Building and the Sources of Regime Competitiveness in the Fourth Wave: The Cases of Belarus, Moldova, Russia, and Ukraine,' *World Politics*, 57, 2 (January): 231–61.

Way, Lucan (2006) 'Sources and Dynamics of Competitive Authoritarianism in Ukraine', in Derek Hutcheson and Elena Korosteleva (eds), *The Quality of Democracy in Post-Communist Europe*. New York: Routledge.

Webb, Paul and Stephen White (eds) (2007) *Party Politics in New Democracies*. Oxford: Oxford University Press.

Weldon, Steven (2006) 'Downsize My Polity? The Impact of Size on Party Membership and Member Activism', *Party Politics*, 12, 4 (July): 467–81.

Welz, Christian and Timo Kauppinen (2005) 'Industrial Action and Conflict Resolution in the New Member States', *European Journal of Industrial Relations*, 11, 1 (March): 91–105.

Wheaton, Bernard and Zdenek Kavan (1992) *The Velvet Revolution: Czechoslovakia, 1988–1991*. Boulder, CO: Westview.

White, Stephen (1990) 'Democratizing Eastern Europe: The Elections of 1990', *Electoral Studies*, 9, 4 (December): 27787.

White, Stephen, Elena Korosteleva and John Lowenhardt (eds) (2005) *Postcommunist Belarus*. Lanham, MD: Rowman & Littlefield.

White, Stephen and Elena Korosteleva-Polglase (2006) 'The Parliamentary Election and Referendum in Belarus, October 2004', *Electoral Studies*, 25, 1 (March): 155–60.

Williams, Kieran (1997) *The Prague Spring and its Aftermath: Czechoslovak Politics 1968–1970*. Cambridge and New York: Cambridge University Press

Williams, Kieran (2003) 'Proportional Representation in Post-Communist Eastern Europe: The First Decade', *Representation*, 40, 1: 44–54.

Wilson, Andrew (2002) *The Ukrainians: Unexpected Nation*, 2nd edn. London and New Haven, CT: Yale University Press.

Wilson, Andrew (2005a) *Ukraine's Orange Revolution*. London and New Haven, CT: Yale University Press.

Wilson, Andrew (2005b) *Virtual Politics: Faking Democracy in the Post-Soviet World*. London and New Haven, CT: Yale University Press.

Wolchik, Sharon L. (1998) 'Women and the Politics of Transition in the Czech and Slovak Republics', in Marilyn Rueschemeyer (ed.), *Women in the Politics of Postcommunist Eastern Europe*, revised edn. Armonk, NY: Sharpe: 116–41.

Wolczuk, Kataryna (2002) *The Moulding of Ukraine: The Constitutional Politics of State Formation*. Budapest: Central European University Press.

Woldendorp, Jaap, Hans Keman and Ian Budge (2000) *Party Government in 48 Democracies (1945–1998). Composition-Duration-Personnel*. Dordrecht: Kluwer.

Woodward, Susan L. (1995) *Balkan Tragedy: Chaos and Disillusion after the Cold War*. Washington, DC: Brookings Institution.

World Bank (1996) *From Plan to Market*. Washington, DC: World Bank.

World Bank (2002) *Transition: The First Ten Years, Analysis and Lessons for Eastern Europe and the Former Soviet Union*. Washington, DC: World Bank.

Zakaria, Fareed (2003) *The Future of Freedom: Illiberal Democracy at Home and Abroad*. New York: Norton.

Zielonka, Jan (ed.) (2001a) *Democratic Consolidation in Eastern Europe, Vol. 1: Institutional Engineering*. Oxford: Oxford University Press.

Zielonka, Jan (2001b) 'Conclusions: Foreign Made Democracy', in Zielonka and Alex Pravda (eds), *Democratic Consolidation in Eastern Europe. Vol. 2: International and Transnational Factors*. Oxford: Oxford University Press: 511–32.

Index